D0956116

English Grammar and Composition

FRANKLIN EDITION

Fourth Course

English Grammar and Composition

Fourth Course

John E. Warriner

FRANKLIN EDITION

Harcourt Brace Jovanovich, Publishers

New York Chicago San Francisco Atlanta Dallas *and* London

THE SERIES:

English Grammar and Composition: First Course
English Grammar and Composition: Second Course
English Grammar and Composition: Third Course
English Grammar and Composition: Fourth Course
English Grammar and Composition: Fifth Course
English Grammar and Composition: Complete Course

Test booklet and teacher's manual for each above title.

CORRELATED SERIES:

English Workshop: First Course
English Workshop: Second Course
English Workshop: Third Course
English Workshop: Fourth Course
English Workshop: Fifth Course
English Workshop: Review Course

Composition: Models and Exercises, First Course
Composition: Models and Exercises, Second Course
Composition: Models and Exercises, Third Course
Composition: Models and Exercises, Fourth Course
Composition: Models and Exercises, Fifth Course
Advanced Composition: A Book of Models for Writing, Complete
   Course

Vocabulary Workshop: First Course
Vocabulary Workshop: Second Course
Vocabulary Workshop: Third Course
Vocabulary Workshop: Fourth Course
Vocabulary Workshop: Fifth Course
Vocabulary Workshop: Complete Course

John E. Warriner taught English for thirty-two years in junior and senior high schools and in college. He is chief author of the *English Grammar and Composition* series, coauthor of the *English Workshop* series, general editor of the *Composition: Models and Exercises* series, and editor of *Short Stories: Characters in Conflict*. His co-authors have all been active in English education.

To the Student

The reason English is a required subject in almost all schools is that nothing in your education is more important than learning how to express yourself well. You may know a vast amount about a subject, but if you are unable to communicate what you know, you are severely handicapped. No matter how valuable your ideas may be, they will not be very useful if you cannot express them clearly and convincingly. Language is the means by which people communicate. In your part of the world, it is English, a remarkably rich and flexible language. By learning how your language functions and by practicing language skills, you can acquire the competence necessary to express adequately what you know and what you think.

You have two guides to help you in your study of English. One is your teacher; the other is your textbook. This textbook is designed to help you improve your ability to use English. It will show you how the English sentence works, how words are combined in sentences, and how the parts of sentences may best be arranged for clear communication. You will learn the difference between sentences which are strong and clear and smooth, and sentences which are weak and confusing and awkward. You will learn to plan and organize units of writing much larger than the sentence. You will learn to use standard English, the kind of English that is most widely considered acceptable. The more you put to use the things you learn from this book—in other words, the more you practice the skills explained here—the greater will be your command of English.

Do not limit your use of this book to the times when you are given an assignment in the book. Learn to use the book as a reference book in which you can look up answers to questions that arise when you are writing something for an assignment in any of your courses. As you become familiar with the contents and arrangement of the book, you will know where to look for specific kinds of information. By using the index, you can quickly find answers to questions about grammar and standard usage, punctuation, capital letters, sentence structure, spelling, outlining, letter writing, and many other matters. By using the book in this way, you are actually teaching yourself, which is a very good way to learn.

J. W.

Contents

Preface   **v**

PART ONE: Grammar

1. The Parts of Speech   **3**
Their Identification and Function

    The Noun   3
    The Pronoun   5
    The Adjective   7
    Articles   8
    Pronoun or Adjective?   9
    Nouns Used as Adjectives   11
    The Verb   11
    Action Verbs   11
    Linking Verbs   13
    The Verb Phrase   14
    The Adverb   16
    Adverbs Modifying Verbs   17
    Adverbs Modifying Adjectives   17
    Adverbs Modifying Other Adverbs   18
    The Preposition   21
    The Conjunction   22
    The Interjection   24
    Determining Parts of Speech   24
    Summary of Parts of Speech   27

2. The Sentence 28
Subjects, Predicates, and Complements

Subject and Predicate 28
The Simple Predicate and the
  Complete Predicate 29
The Verb Phrase 30
The Simple Subject and the Complete
  Subject 31
How to Find the Subject of a Sentence 32
The Subject in an Unusual Position 34
Sentences in Which the Subject Is
  Understood 35
Compound Subjects and Verbs 35
Fragments 37
The Sentence Base 38
Complements 39
The Subject Complement 41
Distinguishing Between Subject and
  Complement 42
Direct and Indirect Objects 43
Compound Complements 45
Sentences Classified by Purpose 46
Diagraming Sentences 48
Diagraming the Subject and Verb 48
Diagraming Modifiers 49
Diagraming Compound Subjects and
  Compound Verbs 49
Diagraming *Here, There,* and *Where* as
  Modifiers 50
Diagraming *There* When It Does Not
  Modify Anything 51
Diagraming a Modifier of a Modifier 51
Diagraming the Predicate Nominative and
  the Predicate Adjective 53
Diagraming the Direct and Indirect
  Object 54

3. The Phrase 58

Prepositional, Verbal, and Appositive
Phrases

Prepositional Phrases 59
Adjective Phrases 60
Adverb Phrases 61
Diagraming Prepositional Phrases 62
Verbals and Verbal Phrases 64
The Participle 64
The Participial Phrase 68
The Gerund 70
The Gerund Phrase 71
The Infinitive 72
The Infinitive Phrase 73
The Infinitive With 'to' Omitted 74
Diagraming Verbals and Verbal
  Phrases 74
Appositives and Appositive Phrases 77

4. The Clause 81

Independent and Subordinate
Clauses

Kinds of Clauses 81
Independent Clauses 81
Subordinate Clauses 82
The Uses of Subordinate Clauses 84
The Adjective Clause 84
The Adverb Clause 88
The Noun Clause 90
Sentences Classified by Structure 93

PART TWO: Usage

5. Kinds of Usage   101
What Is Usage?

Standard and Nonstandard English   102
Two Kinds of Standard English   102

6. Correct Agreement   107
Subject and Verb, Pronoun and Antecedent

Singular and Plural Number   107
Agreement of Subject and Verb   108
The Compound Subject   115
Other Problems in Agreement   117
Agreement of Pronoun and
    Antecedent   124

7. Using Pronouns Correctly   131
Nominative and Objective Case

Case Forms of Personal Pronouns   131
The Nominative Case   133
The Objective Case   137
Special Problems in Pronoun Usage   143
Who and *Whom*   143
The Pronoun in Incomplete
    Constructions   150

8. Using Verbs Correctly   153
Principal Parts, Tense, Voice

Kinds of Verbs 153
Principal Parts 154
Regular Verbs 154
Irregular Verbs 155
Common Irregular Verbs 155
Tense 159
Active and Passive Voice 166
Six Troublesome Verbs 168
Lie and *Lay* 169
Sit and *Set* 172
Rise and *Raise* 174

9. Using Modifiers Correctly   179
Comparison, Placement of Modifiers

Adjective and Adverb Forms 179
Bad and *Badly* 180
Well and *Good* 181
Slow and *Slowly* 182
Comparison of Modifiers 184
Regular Comparison 185
Irregular Comparison 186
Use of Comparative and Superlative Forms 186
Dangling Modifiers 189
Misplaced Modifiers 191
Misplaced Phrase Modifers 191
Misplaced Clause Modifiers 196

10. Glossary of Usage   196

PART THREE: Composition: Sentence Structure

11. Writing Complete Sentences 219
Sentence Fragments and Run-on Sentences

Sentence Fragments 219
The Phrase Fragment 221
The Appositive Fragment 223
The Subordinate Clause Fragment 224
The Run-on Sentence 227

12. Sentence Combining and Revising 230
Emphasis and Variety in Sentences

Sentence Combining 231
Varying Sentence Beginnings 244
Varying Sentence Structure 250

PART FOUR: Composition

13. The Paragraph 259
Structure, Unity, and Coherence in Paragraphs

The Structure of a Paragraph 260
The Topic Sentence 260

The Concluding, or Clincher,
Sentence 262
Development of a Paragraph   265
Planning a Paragraph   266
The Paragraph Outline   267
Unity in the Paragraph   267
Coherence in the Paragraph   271
Four Types of Paragraphs   271
The Expository Paragraph   272
Order of Details in an Expository
Paragraph   273
The Descriptive Paragraph   279
Order of Details in a Descriptive
Paragraph   280
The Narrative Paragraph   282
The Persuasive Paragraph   283
Order of Details in a Persuasive
Paragraph   284
Transitional Expressions   285
Checklist for Paragraph Revision   288

14. Exposition   290

Planning and Writing the Longer
Composition

Choosing and Limiting a Subject   290
Planning the Composition   295
Writing the Composition   302
The Introduction   303
The Body   303
The Conclusion   304
Transitions Between Paragraphs   304
Revising the Composition   306
Composition Checklist   306
A Model Expository Composition   308
List of Suggested Composition
Topics   310

15. Specific Writing Assignments 315

Explaining a Process 315
Hints for Writing the Explanation of a
  Process 315
Checklist for Explanations 318
Writing the Essay Answer 319
Hints for Writing the Essay Answer 319
Checklist for Essay Answers 322
Description of a Character 323
Hints for Writing the Character
  Description 323
Checklist for Character Descriptions 327
The Critical Review 327
Hints for Writing the Critical Review 328
Checklist for Critical Reviews 331
The Essay of Opinion 331
Hints for Writing the Essay of
  Opinion 332
Checklist for Essays of Opinion 335
The Definition 336
Limited Definition 336
Extended Definition 337
Checklist for Definitions 339

16. Creative Writing 341

**Develop the Habit of Close
  Observation 341**
**In Descriptive Writing, Select Words That
  Appeal to the Senses 345**
Describing the Sense of Sound 346
Describing the Senses of Smell and
  Taste 347
Describing the Sense of Touch, or
  Feeling 348
Fill Your Writing With Vivid Details 350

Similes and Metaphors 352
A Model Narrative 355

17. The Business Letter 357

**Appearance and Form of a Business
  Letter** 357
Appearance and Stationery 358
Form 358
The Letter Picture 358
Content of the Business Letter 365
Types of Business Letters 365
The Request Letter 365
The Order Letter 368
The Letter of Application 369

PART FIVE: Mechanics

18. Capitalization 375

Standard Uses of Capitalization

Diagnostic Test 376
Summary Style Sheet 391

19. Punctuation 393

End Marks and Commas

**Periods, Question Marks, and
  Exclamation Points** 394

Commas 397
Items in a Series 397
Comma Between Independent
  Clauses 400
Introductory Elements 406
Summary of the Uses of the Comma 416

20. Punctuation   420

Semicolons and Colons

The Semicolon 420
The Colon 423

21. Punctuation   426

Underlining (Italics) and Quotation
Marks

Underlining (Italics) 426
Quotation Marks 428

22. Punctuation   434

Apostrophes, Hyphens, Dashes,
Parentheses

Apostrophes 434
Pronouns in the Possessive Case 436
Compounds in the Possessive Case 437
Contractions 439
Hyphens 442

Grammar

PART ONE

Chapter **1**

The Parts of Speech

Their Identification and Function

Words are classified according to the jobs they perform in sentences. Some name or otherwise identify people and objects; others express action, connect other words, or do still other kinds of work. There are eight main ways that words are used in sentences; the eight kinds of words that perform these jobs are called parts of speech. They are *noun, pronoun, adjective, verb, adverb, preposition, conjunction,* and *interjection.* Even though you may have studied the parts of speech before, you will review them and learn more about them in this chapter.

THE NOUN

1a. A *noun* is a word used to name a person, place, thing, or idea.

A noun names something. Your own name is a noun. The name of your school is a noun. *House* is a noun. The names of things which you cannot see or touch are nouns: for instance, *compassion, freedom, length, kindness, justice, equality.* These words do not name tangible things, but they do name qualities or ideas. The name of a quality or an idea is just as truly a noun as the name of anything which has size or shape. A noun names the thing we are talking about.

EXERCISE 1. There are twenty-five nouns in the following paragraph. List them in order, and place before each the number of the sentence. If a noun is used more than once, list it each time it appears.

1. Women now compete in sports that were once limited to men. 2. Many teen-age girls in this country play soccer. 3. For years, the game had been played almost exclusively by males. 4. Girls now also play baseball on teams in organized leagues. 5. For the first time in history, female crews participate in international rowing events. 6. Female runners are a familiar sight to spectators at marathons. 7. Driving cars at high speeds, women race for the checkered flag.

EXERCISE 2. How many nouns can you spot in the following paragraph? List them on your paper. Place before each noun the number of the sentence in which it appears. Treat as single nouns all capitalized names of more than one word.

1. Susan B. Anthony, a leader in the American movement for suffrage for women, was born on a farm in Massachusetts in 1820. 2. As a child she was taught the religious tenets of the Quakers. 3. They included the belief in the equality of women. 4. At meetings both men and women spoke and held seats of honor. 5. She became a teacher and at one time managed the family farm. 6. In 1848 her parents and younger sister attended the first convention for the rights of women in Seneca Falls, New York. 7. Later she met Elizabeth Cady Stanton, who had proposed a resolution demanding the vote for women. 8. Susan B. Anthony was also a tireless supporter of the abolition of slavery. 9. Her exceptional organizational ability and her keen political insight were invaluable to her colleagues in the movement for suffrage. 10. She worked behind the scenes securing speakers and raising money to stage a series of local and national conventions. 11. As a reformer she was influential in securing improvement in the Married Woman's Property Law by the New York State Legislature in 1860.

The Proper Noun and the Common Noun

Nouns may be divided into two classes: *proper nouns* and *common nouns*. A proper noun names a *particular* person, place, or thing; a common noun names a *class* of things.

PROPER NOUNS	COMMON NOUNS
Atlanta, Asia, Lake Michigan	city, continent, lake
Emily Dickinson, Admiral Nelson	poet, admiral
Bronx Zoo, Golden Gate Bridge	zoo, bridge
The Spirit of Seventy-six	painting

► NOTE Compound nouns are composed of two or more words put together to form a single noun. Some of them are written as one word (*volleyball*), some as two or more words (*high school, Pen and Pencil Club*), and some with hyphens (*brother-in-law*). The compound nouns are in bold-faced type in the following example.

EXAMPLE My **sister-in-law** is a member of the **Bowling Club,** which meets weekly at the **Hollywood Lanes.**

EXERCISE 3. For each of the following common nouns, write a proper noun after the corresponding number.

EXAMPLE 1. river
1. *Mississippi River*

1. novel	6. ship	11. general
2. mountain	7. church	12. writer
3. car	8. singer	13. building
4. war	9. magazine	14. poem
5. lake	10. state	15. ocean

THE PRONOUN

1b. A *pronoun* **is a word used in place of a noun or of more than one noun.**

EXAMPLE Janet went to the game with her father and mother. **She** enjoyed **it** more than **they** did. [*She* is used in place of "Janet," *it* in place of "game," *they* in place of "father and mother."]

Personal Pronouns

The pronouns that have appeared in the preceding example are called *personal* pronouns. In this use, *personal* refers to one of the three possible ways of making statements: The person speaking can talk about himself or herself (first person) or about the person being spoken to (second person) or about anyone or anything else (third person). The few pronouns in English that have different forms to show person are called *personal pronouns*.

	Singular	*Plural*
FIRST PERSON	I, my, mine, me	we, our, ours, us
SECOND PERSON	you, your, yours	you, your, yours
THIRD PERSON	he, his, him	they, their, theirs, them
	she, her, hers	
	it, its	

Here are some other kinds of pronouns that you will encounter as you study this textbook:

RELATIVE PRONOUNS (used to introduce adjective and noun clauses; see pages 85–86)

who   whom   whose   which   that

INTERROGATIVE PRONOUNS (used in questions)

Who...?   Whose...?   What...?
Whom...?   Which...?

DEMONSTRATIVE PRONOUNS (used to point out a specific person or thing)

this   that   these   those

INDEFINITE PRONOUNS (not referring to a definite person or thing)

all	each	more	one
another	either	most	other
any	everybody	much	several
anybody	everyone	neither	some
anyone	everything	nobody	somebody
anything	few	none	someone
both	many	no one	such

REFLEXIVE PRONOUNS (the *-self, -selves* forms of the personal pronouns)

myself	ourselves
yourself	yourselves
himself, herself, itself	themselves

▶ **NOTE**   Never write or say *hisself* or *theirselves*.

EXERCISE 4.   Number your paper 1–6. Referring if necessary to the preceding lists of pronouns, write after each number the pronouns in the correspondingly numbered sentence. You should find twenty-five pronouns.[1]

1. Everybody enjoys going to the amusement park, and some of us really love it. 2. Our group decided to try the roller coaster, although a few of the timid raised objections to this. 3. One of the ticket sellers called out, "Hurry! Hurry! Step up, all of you, for the most thrilling ride in the park. 4. Many will find it exciting; others will find it the experience of their lives." 5. Some of us were a little scared, but we soon decided to buy our tickets and try it. 6. When we ended the ride, everyone who could still talk said, "That was the ride of my life."

THE ADJECTIVE

1c. An *adjective* is a word used to modify a noun or a pronoun.

Adjectives are words used to make the meaning of a noun or a pronoun more definite. Words used in this way are called *modifiers*.

An adjective may modify a noun or pronoun by telling *what kind* it is:

blue ink   **new** ideas   **warm** weather

An adjective may indicate *which one:*

this hat   **those** books   **that** car

---

[1] When words in the first list on page 6 immediately precede a noun (*my* friend, *his* brother, etc.), they are considered possessive *pronouns* in this book, rather than *adjectives*.

An adjective may tell *how many:*

> **twenty-five** kilometers   **two** men   **many** people

An adjective is not always placed next to the word it modifies. It may be separated from the word it modifies by other words.

> The coat was very **expensive.** [expensive coat]

> The report sounds **dull.** [dull report]

► **NOTE** An adjective modifying a pronoun is almost always separated from the pronoun.

> She looked **old.**

> They seemed **heavy.**

Articles

The most frequently used adjectives are *a, an,* and *the.* These little words are usually called *articles.*

A and *an* are indefinite articles; they refer to one of a general group.

EXAMPLES   **A** woman greeted us.
I did not have **an** answer ready.
We waited **an** hour.

A is used before words beginning with a consonant sound; *an* is used before words beginning with a vowel sound. Notice in the third example above that *an* is used before a noun beginning with the consonant *h,* because the *h* in *hour* is not pronounced. *Hour* is pronounced as if it began with a vowel (like *our*). Remember that the *sound* of the noun, not the spelling, determines which indefinite article will be used.

The is the definite article. It indicates that a noun refers to someone or something in particular.

EXAMPLES   **The** woman greeted us.
I did not know **the** answer.
The hour for our departure finally arrived.

EXERCISE 5. In the following paragraphs the adjectives (except *a, an,* and *the*) are printed in italics. List the adjectives after the appropriate number, and after each one, write the word it modifies.

1. The beauty of Psyche was *extraordinary*. 2. Her *honest* neighbors thought she was a *new* birth of the *divine* Venus. 3. Venus was *jealous* of *every* honor paid to Psyche. 4. The *angry* goddess summoned her *mischievous* son Cupid. 5. Venus asked him to lure Psyche into falling in love with an *ugly* creature. 6. Meanwhile Psyche's *great* beauty discouraged *all* suitors from approaching her. 7. She was *lonely* and her *anxious* family did not know what to do. 8. Finally Psyche's father was instructed by the gods to give her to an *immortal* husband. 9. Psyche found herself in a *gorgeous* palace in a *green* wood. 10. At night she was attended by a *mysterious* but *kind* husband. 11. One night Psyche disobediently shone a *bright* lamp on her *gentle* husband. 12. It was *fair* Cupid himself. 13. A *small* drop of *hot* oil fell on his *bare* shoulder and awakened him. 14. Without a word he rose on his *white* wings.

EXERCISE 6. Copy the following sentences, supplying adjectives in the blank spaces. Try to supply meaningful, interesting adjectives. Read the paragraph through before you start to write.

Horseshoe Lake, one of the —— lakes in our part of the state, is not easily accessible by car. The road is a —— trail, but the —— scenery makes up for this. Once you reach the lake, you obtain a —— view of the —— country. Small —— streams feed the —— lake, and the —— water is always —— and ——. Those who stay overnight will be lulled into a —— sleep by the —— waters and the —— sighing of pine trees. The —— riser will witness a —— sunrise as the sun's —— rays gleam across —— mountains. What a —— sight this is to a —— city dweller in search of a —— retreat!

Pronoun or Adjective?

Some words may be used either as adjectives or as pro-

---

[1] Pronouns used before nouns, like *our* in the sixth sentence, are sometimes called adjectives because they modify a noun. In this book such pronouns are called *possessive pronouns.* Follow your teacher's wishes in referring to such words.

nouns (*this, which, each,* etc.). To tell them apart, you must keep in mind what they do.

Adjectives *modify* nouns, while pronouns *take the place of* nouns. In the first sentence in each pair below, the bold-faced word is used as a pronoun. In the second sentence of each pair, the word is used as an adjective.

PRONOUN **That** is a delicious cookie.
ADJECTIVE **That** cookie is delicious.

PRONOUN **Some** have raisins in them.
ADJECTIVE **Some** cookies have raisins in them.

PRONOUN Do you want **this**?
ADJECTIVE Do you want **this** cookie?

Notice that a noun must follow immediately if the word is used as an adjective.

EXERCISE 7. List the numbered, italicized words in a column on your paper. After each word, tell whether it is used as a pronoun or an adjective, using the abbreviations *pron.* or *adj.* For each adjective, write the word it modifies.

a. Brown trout, (1) *which* were imported into (2) *this* country in the nineteenth century, are unlike the brook trout (3) *that* we find in the ice-cold streams of Maine.
b. (4) *These* native trout are brilliantly colored.
c. The rainbow trout, (5) *another* native American species, is found in the Far West.
d. (6) *Many* streams are now so impure that the native brook trout cannot live in (7) *them.*
e. Consequently, (8) *many* have been stocked with brown trout, (9) *which* do not seem to mind warm water.
f. (10) *Both* kinds of trout are splendid game fish, and (11) *both* will readily take a dry fly if (12) *it* looks to (13) *them* like a natural insect.
g. (14) *Many* experts tie flies so small that two dozen of (15) *them* may easily be put into a thimble.
h. (16) *Many* tie these tiny flies to the ends of nylon leaders (17) *which* are fifteen feet long.
i. (18) *Some* prefer even longer leaders, (19) *which* are tapered like a bullwhip, from very thick at the butt, or beginning, to very thin at the tippet, or end.

j. (20) *One* angler, using (21) *these* flies, may catch dozens of fine trout while (22) *another*, using worms, may simply muddy the water and catch (23) *none*.

k. At (24) *other* times, however, the trout may prefer worms and not be tempted by (25) *any* type of fly.

EXERCISE 8. The following words may be used as either pronouns or adjectives. Write a pair of sentences for each word. In the first sentence of each pair, use the word as a pronoun; in the second, use it as an adjective.

1. more	6. all
2. both	7. neither
3. each	8. many
4. another	9. few
5. these	10. which

Nouns Used as Adjectives

Sometimes nouns are used as adjectives.

salad fork   **turkey** dinner
book cover   **gold** ring

When you are identifying parts of speech and find a noun used as an adjective, call it an adjective.

THE VERB

1d. A *verb* is a word that expresses action or otherwise helps to make a statement.

All verbs help to make statements. Some do it by expressing action; others, by telling something about the subject.

Action Verbs

Words such as *come, tell, go,* and *dance* are action verbs. Some action verbs express an action that cannot be seen; examples are *think, believe, estimate,* and *consider*.

EXERCISE 9. Make a list of twenty action verbs not including those listed above. Include and underline at least five verbs that express an action that cannot be seen.

There are two general classes of action verbs — *transitive* and *intransitive*. A verb is *transitive* when the action it expresses is directed toward a person or thing named in the sentence.

EXAMPLES   She **designed** the flag. [The action of the verb *designed* is directed toward *flag*. The verb is transitive.]
Zora Neal Hurston **wrote** novels.

In these examples the action passes from the doer — the subject — to the receiver of the action. Words that receive the action of a transitive verb are called *objects*.

A verb is *intransitive* when it expresses action (or helps to make a statement) without reference to an object. The following sentences contain intransitive verbs.

EXAMPLES   The eagle **soars.**
The steamboat **passed.**

The same verb may be transitive in one sentence and intransitive in another. A verb that can take an object is often used intransitively when the emphasis is on the action rather than on the person or thing affected by it.

EXAMPLES   Miss Montez **painted** the room. [transitive]
Miss Montez **painted** every day. [intransitive]
Mallory **climbs** the mountain. [transitive]
Mallory **climbs** higher. [intransitive]

EXERCISE 10. Some of the action verbs in the following sentences are transitive and some are intransitive. Write the verb of each sentence after the proper number on your paper, and label it as a dictionary would — *v.t.* for transitive, *v.i.* for intransitive.

1. The winter lasted too long.
2. Eventually the snow disappeared.
3. We packed lunches for our annual spring hike and nature study.

4. The winds blew across the open fields.
5. Carmelita examined the sulphur-yellow buds of the bitternut hickory.
6. She tasted the blue berries of the hackberry trees.
7. The old berries had a terrible taste.
8. She chewed the twigs of the black birch.
9. The aromatic sap identified the twigs as black birch, not black cherry.
10. On the hilltop stood a grove of chestnut oaks.

Linking Verbs

Some verbs help to make a statement, not by expressing an action, but by serving as a link between two words. These verbs are called *linking verbs*.

The most commonly used linking verbs are forms of the verb *be*. You should become thoroughly familiar with these.

be	shall be	should be
being	will be	would be
am	has been	can be
is	have been	could be
are	had been	should have been
was	shall have been	would have been
were	will have been	could have been

Any verb ending in *be* or *been* is a form of the verb *be*. In addition to *be*, the following verbs are often used as linking verbs.

Other Common Linking Verbs

appear	grow	seem	stay
become	look	smell	taste
feel	remain	sound	

Notice in the following sentences how each verb is a link between the words on either side of it. The word that follows the linking verb fills out or completes the meaning of the verb and refers to the subject of the verb.

The hop hornbean and the blue beech are members of the birch family.   [hop hornbean and blue beech = members]
The heartwood of the red cedar smells good.   [good heart-wood]
The leaves of the red maple become scarlet in the fall.   [scarlet leaves]
Rosa might be a botanist.   [Rosa = botanist]

► NOTE   Many of the linking verbs listed above can be used as action (nonlinking) verbs as well.

Rosa feels happy out-of-doors.   [linking verb: happy Rosa]
Rosa feels the rough, deeply creviced bark of the chestnut oak.   [action verb]
Black oaks grow tall.   [linking verb: tall oaks]
Black oaks grow acorns every two years.   [action verb]

Even *be* is not always a linking verb. It may be followed by only an adverb: *She was there.* To be a linking verb, the verb must be followed by a word that refers to (names or describes) the subject.

EXERCISE 11. For each of the following verbs, write two sentences. In the first sentence, use the verb as a linking verb; in the second sentence, use it as an action verb.

1. appear
2. sound
3. smell
4. grow
5. look

The Verb Phrase

A verb frequently has one or more *helping verbs*. The verb and the helping verbs make up a unit that is called the *verb phrase*.

Commonly used helping verbs are *will, shall, have, has, had, can, may, might, do, does, did, must, ought, should, would,* and the forms of the verb *be* (see page 13).

EXAMPLES   This year's budget **has been approved.**
We **are leaving** tomorrow.
Ann **will ride** the moped.

Did she **clean** the carburetor?
You **should have changed** the oil.
You **can tune** the motor.

EXERCISE 12. Study each italicized verb in this paragraph. Tell whether it is an action verb or a linking verb.

1. Situated on the banks of the Nile in Egypt, the ruins at Karnak *are* some of the most impressive sights in the world. 2. The largest ruin *is* the Great Temple of Ammon. 3. Its immense size is astonishing to people who *know* little about the scale of Egyptian architecture. 4. If you *should follow* the avenue of sphinxes which leads to the main entrance, you *would be amazed* at the 42-meter-high gateway. 5. The ceiling of the temple *is* extremely high — more than 23 meters above the floor. 6. The central columns that *support* the stone roof *are* enormous. 7. The surfaces of the columns *are decorated* with low relief carvings, and despite the passage of time, which *has erased* some of the rich coloring, many of the columns still *retain* their bright shades. 8. Even an amateur engineer *can appreciate* the tremendous effort which *must have gone* into the completion of this temple. 9. We now *know* that inclined planes, combined with levers and blocking, *enabled* the ancient Egyptians to raise the large stones. 10. Nevertheless, the temple *seems* an incredible undertaking.

EXERCISE 13. Write the verbs in the following sentences after the proper numbers on your paper. Be sure to include all the helping verbs, especially when the parts of the verb are separated by other words. The word *not* in a phrase such as *could not go* is not a verb. *Not* is an adverb.

1. Tonight was opening night, and Flo was frantically mumbling her lines as she headed backstage. 2. She clutched a script in her hands, shouted a greeting to some friends, and almost bumped into some scenery from the prop room. 3. The stage crew had finished their jobs yesterday, but Flo noticed that the lighting squad was making a last-minute adjustment to the footlights. 4. Flo knew the saying that a poor dress rehearsal means a good first performance, but nothing as bad as yesterday's fiasco could be reassuring. 5. She had not remembered all her lines, and she had stumbled over a footstool. 6. In addition to that, somebody had put so much brown greasepaint under her eyes that she looked

like a raccoon. 7. "Well," thought Flo, "tonight will be the test." 8. She summoned her courage and walked into the dressing room. 9. "Hi, gang. Is everybody ready for the first round? The crowd is just coming in, and the photographers will be here shortly." 10. As she said this, Flo thought to herself, "I should have gone over my lines at least one more time."

EXERCISE 14. After the proper number, list all twenty-five verbs in the following sentences. Include all the parts of every verb.

1. After the United States purchased the Louisiana Territory from the French government, President Jefferson chose Meriwether Lewis as leader of a scouting expedition. 2. Lewis selected William Clark, an experienced guide and soldier, as his partner. 3. Lewis and Clark hoped that they would discover an overland route to the Pacific Ocean. 4. In the spring of 1804, the forty-five member expedition started up the Missouri River from St. Louis. 5. By fall they had traveled 1600 miles. 6. In what is now the state of North Dakota, a Shoshoni Indian woman, Sacajawea, joined the party as an interpreter. 7. The expedition proceeded northwest by boat until the rivers became too shallow. 8. They outfitted horses and rode north through Lolo Pass. 9. With the help of local residents, they constructed canoes and paddled down the Snake River to the Columbia River, which they followed until it flowed into the Pacific. 10. The next year they returned to St. Louis by approximately the same route. 11. Because of the great care with which plans had been made, the expedition was remarkably successful. 12. Lewis and Clark had lost only one man, who had probably been a victim of appendicitis. 13. They had found a land route to the Pacific and improved the nation's access to the Oregon Territory, which was rich in resources.

THE ADVERB

1e. An *adverb* is a word used to modify a verb, an adjective, or another adverb.

Adverbs qualify the meaning of the words they modify by telling *how, when, where,* or *to what extent.*

Adverbs Modifying Verbs

Just as there are words (adjectives) that modify nouns and pronouns, there are words that modify verbs. For example, the verb *dance* may be modified by such words as *gracefully, awkwardly, slowly,* etc. The word *run* may be modified by *quickly, fast, far, rapidly,* etc. A word which modifies a verb is an *adverb.* It qualifies the meaning of the verb.

EXAMPLES   The cat is purring **upstairs.** [*where*]
The cat purred **yesterday.** [*when*]
The cat purred **quietly.** [*how*]
The cat purrs **often.** [*to what extent*]

EXERCISE 15. Supply two adverb modifiers for each of the following verbs. Do not use the same modifier twice.

1. jump
2. gave
3. read
4. arrived
5. began
6. talked
7. sing
8. draw
9. fell
10. learn

EXERCISE 16. There are ten adverbs in the following sentences. List them, and after each, write the verb that it modifies.

1. The Hungarian Crown of Saint Stephen is fascinating because the crown has again and again disappeared and reappeared throughout the last nine hundred years. 2. In its turbulent history, it has been secretly hidden in a cushion, carefully disguised as a baby's bowl, and abruptly seized by the Russians before it landed safely in the United States. 3. The crown, which is beautifully decorated with rough-cut stones and enamel inlays, has a tilted cross on the top, but no one knows positively whether this was an accident or part of the original design. 4. What we do know definitely is that, in order to become king of Hungary, one had to gain possession of the crown. 5. This fact readily accounts for the many intrigues connected with the crown.

Adverbs Modifying Adjectives

Sometimes an adverb modifies an adjective.

EXAMPLES It was a **bitterly** cold day. [The adverb *bitterly*, telling *how cold*, modifies the adjective *cold*.]

The teacher was a **deeply** thoughtful person. [The adverb *deeply* modifies the adjective *thoughtful*.]

► NOTE Probably the most frequently used adverb is *very*. It is so overworked that you should avoid it whenever you can find a more exact word to take its place.

EXERCISE 17. In each of the following sentences, there is an adverb modifying an adjective. List these adverbs on your paper, and after each one, write the adjective which it modifies.

1. An immensely long wagon train started out from Denver.
2. Both oxen and mules were used to pull unusually large wagons.
3. The trail through the mountains was fairly hazardous.
4. A moderately hard rain could turn the trail into a swamp.
5. When the trail was too muddy, the heavier wagons became mired.
6. Wagons that were extremely heavy then had to be unloaded before they could be moved.
7. Stopping for the night along the trail was a consistently welcome experience.
8. It offered relief to thoroughly tired bones and muscles.
9. Nights in the mountains could be quite cold.
10. On terribly cold nights, the travelers would roll themselves in blankets and sleep close to their campfires.

Adverbs Modifying Other Adverbs

You have learned that an adverb may modify a verb or an adjective. An adverb may also modify another adverb.

EXAMPLE The scientist worked **somewhat** cautiously.

You can recognize *cautiously* as an adverb modifying the verb *worked*. It tells *how* the scientist worked. You can also see that *somewhat* modifies the adverb *cautiously*. It tells *how* cautiously.

► NOTE Many adverbs end in –*ly*. Do not make the mistake, however, of thinking that all words ending in –*ly* are adverbs. For instance, the following words are adjectives: *costly, lovely, friendly, deadly.* Moreover, some common adverbs do not have the –*ly* ending: for example, *always, never, very, soon, not.*

EXAMPLE The U.S. hockey team did **not** win an Olympic gold medal between 1960 and 1980. [The adverb *not* comes between the parts of the verb phrase *did win.*]

EXERCISE 18. Use each of the following adverbs in a sentence. Draw an arrow from the adverb to the word it modifies.

1. politely
2. too
3. utterly
4. seldom
5. rapidly
6. more
7. back
8. tomorrow
9. soon
10. somewhat

EXERCISE 19. There are twenty-five adverbs in the following paragraphs. List them after the appropriate numbers on your paper. After each, write the word that the adverb modifies, and tell whether this word is a verb, an adjective, or another adverb.

1. Yesterday my sister June and I shopped for houseplants. 2. The large ones were too expensive for us. 3. Also, we knew that large plants are nearly always raised in hothouses. 4. They do not adjust easily to homes in extremely cold climates.

5. Suddenly June got a brainstorm. 6. "Let's buy some seeds and grow them indoors. 7. That way we can choose a rather scarce species, and the seedlings will automatically adapt themselves to the climate in our house."

8. At the seed store the owner, Mrs. Miller, greeted us cheerfully. 9. We told her we wanted seeds for a plant seldom sold in local shops. 10. We mentioned that our room almost never gets bright sunlight and that during the winter it is especially dark. 11. "I know exactly what you need," Mrs. Miller replied. 12. "These are seeds of the bo tree, a member of the fig family native to India. 13. There it is sacred to Buddhists, for it is said that Buddha received enlightenment under a bo tree."

14. At home we carefully planted the seeds in a container filled with moist dirt and a layer of damp peat moss. 15. Then we covered the container with a sheet of transparent plastic film. 16. Eventually the seeds sprouted and our trees grew. 17. To our surprise, we discovered that each leaf of the bo tree ends in a delicately tapered tip. 18. The leaves were the most unusual ones we had ever seen!

EXERCISE 20. The following words may be used as either adjectives or adverbs. Write a pair of sentences for each word. In the first sentence, use the word as an adjective; in the second, use it as an adverb.

EXAMPLE 1. kindly
1. *John had a kindly manner.* [adjective]
   John spoke kindly. [adverb]

1. daily 4. more
2. fast 5. far
3. late

REVIEW EXERCISE A. List on your paper the italicized words in the following paragraph. After each word, tell what part of speech it is. In a third column, write the word modified by each italicized adjective and adverb.

In the nineteenth century large sections of (1) *our* (2) *western* (3) *plains* were (4) *black* with the herds of American buffalo. (5) *They* fed on the (6) *lush* grass of the prairies and roamed (7) *far* and wide over the land. (8) *These* animals were (9) *generally* (10) *placid* and would not attack unless sufficiently provoked. Great numbers of buffalo were killed by buffalo hunters, (11) *who* (12) *highly* (13) *prized* their juicy and savory flesh, which (14) *closely* (15) *resembles* beef. The (16) *mature* buffalo often weighed as much as two thousand pounds and stood six feet high at the shoulder. The animals were swift and had (17) *so* keen a sense of (18) *smell* that hunters (19) *often* (20) *had* (21) *difficulty* in approaching them. Hunters often set fire to the prairie grass to drive (22) *them* in a (23) *particular* (24) *direction*. Frequently the herd was driven over a cliff. The chase of the buffalo was attended with (25) *some* (26) *danger* because (27) *occasionally* the animals (28) *trampled* the hunters under their hooves. Pemmican, a favorite food, was made from the flesh and fat, and the skins were used for blankets and clothing. The great (29) *herds* of the plains have disappeared, but (30) *small* (31) *numbers* of buffalo (32) *still* (33) *exist.*

THE PREPOSITION

1f. A *preposition* **is a word that shows the relationship of a noun or a pronoun to some other word in the sentence.**

Prepositions are important because they point out different relationships. Notice in the examples below how the prepositions in bold-faced type show three different relationships between *road* and *strolled* and between *corner* and *house.*

I strolled **across** the road.   The house **at** the corner is mine.
I strolled **down** the road.   The house **near** the corner is mine.
I strolled **up** the road.   The house **around** the corner is mine.

A preposition always introduces a phrase (see page 59). The noun or pronoun that ends a prepositional phrase is the *object* of the preposition which introduces the phrase. In the preceding examples the objects of the prepositions are *road* and *corner.*

Commonly Used Prepositions

aboard	below	for	past
about	beneath	from	since
above	beside	in	through
across	besides	inside	to
after	between	into	toward
against	beyond	like	under
along	but (meaning	near	underneath
amid	*except*)	of	until
among	by	off	up
around	concerning	on	upon
at	down	onto	with
before	during	outside	within
behind	except	over	without

Compound prepositions consist of more than one word.

according to	in addition to	instead of
because of	in front of	on account of
by means of	in spite of	prior to

► **NOTE** The same word may be either an adverb or a preposition, depending on its use in a sentence.

EXAMPLES   Marge climbed **down.** [adverb]
Marge climbed **down** the ladder. [preposition]

EXERCISE 21. Use the following words as prepositions in sentences. Underline the phrase which each preposition introduces. Be able to tell between which words the preposition shows a relationship.

1. during	3. through	5. beyond	7. into	9. aboard
2. beneath	4. with	6. between	8. toward	10. among

EXERCISE 22. Use the following words as adverbs in sentences.

1. up	5. besides	8. around
2. near	6. past	9. by
3. on	7. along	10. over
4. across		

THE CONJUNCTION

1g. A *conjunction* **joins words or groups of words.**

Conjunctions are used to join parts of a sentence that function in the same way or in a closely related way. The parts joined may be words, phrases, or clauses. In the following examples the conjunctions are in bold-faced type, and the words they join are underscored.

EXAMPLES   They had three <u>hamburgers</u> **and** a <u>quart</u> of milk for lunch.
You may <u>buy your lunch here</u> **or** <u>bring it from home.</u>
I saw <u>George,</u> **but** <u>he didn't see me.</u>

There are three kinds of conjunctions: *coordinating, correlative,* and *subordinating.*

Coordinating conjunctions. Conjunctions that join equal parts of a sentence are called coordinating conjunctions. They are *and, but, or, nor, for,* and *yet.*[1]

Correlative conjunctions. Some conjunctions are used in pairs. Examples of these are *either . . . or; neither . . . nor; both . . . and; not only . . . but also.* Study the pairs of conjunctions in the following sentences. Conjunctions of this kind, which are used in pairs, are *correlative conjunctions.*

> **Either** the editor of the yearbook **or** the assistant editor will call the photographer.
> **Neither** the business manager **nor** her staff will attend the conference.
> **Both** the seniors **and** the faculty had their pictures taken for the yearbook.
> The yearbook is sold **not only** to students **but also** to teachers, parents, and alumni.

Subordinating conjunctions will be discussed later in connection with subordinate clauses (page 88).

EXERCISE 23. List the coordinating and correlative conjunctions in the following paragraphs.

1. Once Nantucket and New Bedford were home ports of great whaling fleets. 2. Nantucket was the first whaling port in New England, but New Bedford soon became larger and more important. 3. Whaling channeled tremendous profits into these ports, but the golden days of whaling ended about the time of the War Between the States. 4. The crew on a whaling ship could not count on receiving regular wages or a paycheck. 5. Both the captain and the crew worked on a profit-sharing basis. 6. All the whalers received shares in the profits of a trip, and the size of a share depended upon the importance of the job. 7. Naturally the captain's portion was the largest and was usually about one tenth of the total.

8. A whaling trip was no pleasure cruise for either the captain

---

[1] The conjunctions *and, but, or,* and *nor* can join words, phrases, or clauses. However, *for* and *yet* can join only clauses, and for this reason some grammarians consider these two words subordinating conjunctions, not true coordinating conjunctions. Follow your teacher's wishes in classifying these two conjunctions.

or the crew, for they worked long hours during a day on the sea. 9. Maintaining order was no easy task on a long voyage because the food and living conditions gave rise to discontent. 10. Inevitably the sailors had time on their hands, for they didn't encounter a whale every day. 11. To relieve the dullness and boredom on long voyages, whaling ships often would exchange visits. 12. Not only the captain but also the whole crew looked forward to such visits. 13. All enjoyed the chance to chat and exchange news.

14. The decline of whaling and of the whaling industry began about 1860. 15. Our country no longer needed large quantities of whale oil; for kerosene, a cheaper and better fuel, had replaced it.

THE INTERJECTION

1h. An *interjection* **is a word that expresses emotion and has no grammatical relation to other words in the sentence.**

There are a few words which can be used to show sudden or strong feeling, such as fright, anger, excitement, joy, etc.

EXAMPLES **Help!**   **Wow!**   **Whew!**   **Gosh!**   **Good grief!**

These words are usually followed by an exclamation mark. An interjection that shows only mild emotion is followed by a comma:

Oh, she will win the race.

EXERCISE 24. Make a list of ten interjections other than those given above. Be sure to include an exclamation point after each interjection.

DETERMINING PARTS OF SPEECH

1i. What part of speech a word is depends on how the word is used.

In the following sentences you will see that one word is used as three different parts of speech.

What part of speech is *iron* in each sentence?

Hal plugged in the electric **iron**.
An **iron** deer adorned her lawn.
Thanks to permanent-press fabrics, people do not **iron** their clothing as often as they did in the past.

EXERCISE 25. Number your paper 1–20. Study the use of each of the italicized words in the following sentences. On your paper, write the part of speech of the word after the proper number. Be prepared to explain to the class why the word is that part of speech.

1. We went to the greenhouse for *cut* flowers and plants.
2. The florist and her assistants *cut* five hundred roses each day.
3. One of them has a *cut* on his thumb.
4. Many customers *long* for red roses.
5. Roses with *long* stems are very expensive.
6. How *long* do you think roses last?
7. Each day the *plants* are thoroughly watered.
8. The gardener *plants* many new seedlings each day.
9. On a large *stand* in the greenhouse are pots of geraniums.
10. They *stand* in a bright corner of the room.
11. The manager told the driver, "*Back* your car up."
12. The truck was at the *back* door.
13. The driver went *back* to see the manager.
14. The florist *bills* her customers at the end of the month.
15. Some of the *bills* are paid by check.
16. We were blinded by the *light*.
17. Please *light* the fire.
18. The box looked heavy, but it was really very *light*.
19. This year we are studying *plane* geometry.
20. One of the boys will *plane* these boards for you.

REVIEW EXERCISE B. Write three sentences for each of the following words, using the word as a different part of speech in each sentence. At the end of the sentence, write the part of speech.

1. right   4. still
2. out   5. wrong
3. trim

REVIEW EXERCISE C. Now that you have reviewed the eight parts of speech, you should be able to classify each italicized word. Number your paper 1–10. After the appropriate number, list the italicized words, and after each, write what part of speech it is.

1. *Some* of the strangest living creatures *are* freshwater tropical fish.
2. The pacú, for example, *lives* in streams overhung with grape-vines.
3. *Often,* overripe grapes fall *into* the water, *and* hungry pacús eat them.
4. The pacú is *probably* the only grape-eating fish in the world.
5. The leaf fish is also very *strange*.
6. *It* is thin, with a jagged *outline*.
7. It *remains* motionless *near* the *surface* of the water.
8. *Its* blotchy gold and brown coloring makes it look like *either* a *dead* leaf *or* a piece of bark.
9. Another *oddity* that amazes *anyone* who sees it is the archer-fish.
10. This *small* striped fish *can shoot* a stream of water *at* an insect a few feet away and bring it *down*.

REVIEW EXERCISE D. List the thirty-three italicized words and expressions on your paper. After each word or expression, write what part of speech it is.

In early colonial days the (1) *most* (2) *reliable* means of transportation was the (3) *saddle horse,* since the condition of the roads prevented any (4) *very* (5) *extensive* use of wheeled vehicles. (6) *Some* well-to-do families in the towns did keep family carriages. Usually (7) *these* were heavy, lumbering vehicles (8) *that* were drawn by two (9) *or* more horses. The carriages were satisfactory for short trips within the town, (10) *but* they were not very (11) *practical* for long journeys.

Stagecoaches (12) *were introduced* in (13) *America* about 1750. By this (14) *time* there were roads running between such major cities as New York (15) *and* Boston. Although the roads (16) *were* little more than rough, (17) *muddy* tracks, (18) *they* were wide enough for a four-wheeled coach. (19) *Three* or four (20) *pairs* of horses were harnessed to a coach. The coaches were so heavy, however, that the horses (21) *tired* (22) *rapidly* and had to be changed frequently at post houses (23) *along* the route.

In the (24) *western* parts of the colonies, where there were no roads at all, the (25) *Conestoga wagon* was developed for use on long trips. It (26) *had* huge wheels that were (27) *sometimes* six feet in diameter, and (28) *its* body was built like a barge, (29) *with* raised sides and a curved bottom. When a Conestoga wagon (30) *came* (31) *to* a river that was (32) *too* deep to be forded, the wagon was floated (33) *across*.

SUMMARY OF PARTS OF SPEECH

Rule	Part of Speech	Use	Examples
1a	noun	names	**Jim** raises **dogs.**
1b	pronoun	takes the place of a noun	**She** and **I** go. Speak to **nobody.**
1c	adjective	modifies a noun or a pronoun	It's a **fine** day. The sun is **warm.**
1d	verb	shows action or helps to make a statement	He **runs** and **leaps.** She **could be** the winner.
1e	adverb	modifies a verb, an adjective, or another adverb	He runs **fast.** She is **very** smart. It runs **quite** fast.
1f	preposition	relates a noun or a pronoun to another word	The birds are **in** the tree **in** the yard **behind** the house.
1g	conjunction	joins words	Sue **or** Mary won.
1h	interjection	expresses strong emotion	**Good grief!** **Oh,** no you don't!

Chapter 2

The Sentence

Subjects, Predicates, and Complements

In speech, we often leave out parts of our sentences. For example, we often answer a certain kind of question in a few words, not bothering to speak in sentences.

"Why was Angela late?"
"Car trouble."
"Really?"
"Yes."

When we write, however, our words have to convey the whole message. Our readers cannot hear us, and if they do not understand, they cannot ask for a repetition. Therefore, when we put our thoughts on paper, we are expected to express them in complete sentences. Before we discuss all that can go into a complete sentence, we must review the definition of a sentence.

2a. A *sentence* **is a group of words containing a subject and verb and expressing a complete thought.**

The two parts of this definition are closely related. To express a complete thought, a sentence must refer to someone or something (the subject), and it must tell us something about that person or thing. This job of telling about something is done by the predicate, which always contains a verb.

SUBJECT AND PREDICATE

2b. A sentence consists of two parts: the *subject* and the *predicate*. The *subject* of the sentence is that part

about which something is being said. The *predicate* is
that part which says something about the subject.

subject   predicate

The most dangerous saltwater fish | is probably the great
barracuda.

predicate   subject

Sleek and sharp-eyed are | the members of this species.

subject   predicate

All West Indian divers | fear the attack of the barracuda.

EXERCISE 1. Find the subject and predicate of each of
the following sentences. If your teacher directs you to copy
the sentences onto your paper, draw *one* line under the
complete subject and *two* lines under the complete predicate. Keep in mind that the subject may come after the
predicate.

1. The fabric known as batik has an interesting history.
2. The dyeing of batik became an art in Java more than a thousand years ago.
3. The sarong of a Javanese girl frequently represents many
   hours of labor.
4. Javanese can read in its intricate design volumes of information about the wearer.
5. One design might tell them of her family, her village, and her
   tribe.
6. They might learn from another her family connections and the
   respect due her.
7. The finest batiks have a soft, creamy tone unknown in Western fabrics.
8. The design is painted on the cloth with wax.
9. The waxed part of the fabric resists the dye in the vat.
10. Boiling removes the wax and leaves the design.

The Simple Predicate and the Complete Predicate

The predicate of a sentence is that part which says something about the subject. This part is properly called the

complete predicate. Within the complete predicate, there is always a word or word group that is the "heart" of the predicate. It is essential because it is the key word in completing the statement about the subject. This word or word group is called the *simple predicate,* or *verb.*

2c. The principal word or group of words in the complete predicate is called the *simple predicate,* or the *verb.*

EXAMPLES Dolphins **communicate** with each other by high-pitched whistles and grunts. [complete predicate: *communicate with each other by high-pitched whistles and grunts;* verb: *communicate*]

A couple of flashlights **blinked** in the distance. [complete predicate: *blinked in the distance;* verb: *blinked*]

The Verb Phrase

Often the simple predicate, or verb, will consist of more than one word. It will be a verb phrase like the following: *are walking, will walk, has walked, might have walked,* etc. When this is so, do not forget to include all parts of a verb phrase when you are asked to pick out the simple predicate of any sentence.

EXAMPLES Has Jane arrived yet? [simple predicate: *has arrived*]

The new stadium will certainly contain many more seats. [simple predicate: *will contain*]

In the following sentences, the verb is underscored; the complete predicate is in bold-faced type. Study the sentences carefully so that you will be able to pick out the verb in the sentences in the next exercise.

The coach <u>posted</u> **the names of the basketball players on the bulletin board.**

He <u>had selected</u> **the players very carefully.**

Everybody <u>rushed</u> **to read the notice.**

Peter <u>was biting</u> **his nails from nervousness.**

Some of the players <u>were disappointed</u> by the news.

Throughout the rest of this book, the simple predicate is referred to as the verb.

EXERCISE 2. Number from 1–10 in a column on your paper. Find the verb in each of the following sentences, and write it after the proper number on your paper. If you find a verb phrase, be sure to include all the helping verbs.

1. In 1608 a Dutch maker of spectacles held two ordinary lenses in his fingers.
2. Idly, he stared through one of them at a nearby church steeple.
3. The steeple, of course, appeared smaller.
4. The man sighed with boredom.
5. The long hot summer afternoon was drowsy with sun and quiet.
6. Listlessly, he lifted both lenses to the steeple.
7. Within seconds, he gasped with astonishment.
8. In the nearer lens of the telescope, the steeple had miraculously grown in size.
9. This little incident may never have occurred.
10. Nevertheless, legend gives this account of the discovery of the telescope.

The Simple Subject and the Complete Subject

The subject of a sentence is that part about which something is being said. This part is properly called the *complete subject.* Within the complete subject there is always a word (or group of words) which is the "heart" of the subject, and this principal word within the complete subject is called the *simple subject.*

2d. The *simple subject* is the main word or group of words in the complete subject.

EXAMPLE   The **cost** of paper has increased. [complete subject: *the cost of paper;* simple subject: *cost*]

In naming the simple subject, consider compound nouns as one word.

EXAMPLE   The **Taj Mahal** in India is one of the most beautiful buildings in the world.   [complete subject: *The Taj Mahal in India;* simple subject: *Taj Mahal*]

Throughout the rest of this book unless otherwise indicated, the word *subject* will mean "the simple subject."

Caution: Remember that *noun* and *subject* do not mean the same thing. A *noun* is the name of a person, place, thing, or idea. A *subject* is the name of a part of a sentence; it is usually a noun or pronoun.

How to Find the Subject of a Sentence

Because the subject may appear at almost any point in the sentence, you will find it easier to locate the subject if you pick out the verb first. For instance:

The leaders of the troops were carefully chosen.

The verb is *were chosen.* Now ask yourself, "Who or what were chosen?" Your answer is *leaders;* hence *leaders* is the subject. In the sentence *Into the house rushed the dog* the verb is *rushed.* Ask yourself, "Who or what rushed?" Your answer is *dog;* therefore *dog* is the subject.

EXERCISE 3.   Number your paper 1–10. Find the subject and verb of each sentence, and write them down, subject first, then verb, after the proper number on your paper. Underline the subject once and the verb twice.

1. A year later in Venice, Galileo heard of the curious story of the Dutchman's experience with the lenses.
2. Soon afterward Galileo hurried home to Padua.
3. He set a convex lens in one end of a lead tube and a concave lens in the other end.
4. The primitive telescope focused clearly only on objects a certain distance away.

5. Those nearer or farther away would blur.
6. The distance between the lenses had to be changed for different distances.
7. Galileo quickly taught himself the art of lens-grinding.
8. He soon scanned the skies with an efficient telescope.
9. With Padua beneath him, he turned the telescope on Jupiter.
10. For the first time, the four large moons around the planet appeared to human eyes.

EXERCISE 4. Follow the directions for Exercise 3.

1. A book about the Chinese experience in America has been written by Victor G. Nee and Brett de Bary Nee.
2. The title of the book is *Longtime Californ': A Documentary Study of an American Chinatown.*
3. The book traces the history of Chinese immigration and the development of the Chinese-American community.
4. The first immigrants came for jobs in the gold mines and on the railroads in the 1850's.
5. In the beginning only men could immigrate.
6. In time the early immigrants sent to China for their wives.
7. During the 1920's the cohesive family society of Chinatown developed.
8. Interviews of old and young residents of today's Chinatown give the book its immediate and authentic character.
9. A good example of this technique is the interview with Lisa Mah about her return to Chinatown after her family's departure.
10. The spirit of the Chinatown community is subtly captured.

EXERCISE 5. Add predicates to the subjects listed below. After you have done so, underline the simple subject once and the verb twice.

1. These days
2. A single red rose
3. My best friend
4. Most athletes with ability
5. The students in my class
6. The ocean
7. Life in the city
8. The strange monster
9. The climate in our region
10. The best possible time

The Subject in an Unusual Position

There are two kinds of sentences which may at first confuse you when you wish to find the verb and its subject. These are (1) sentences that begin with the words *there* or *here*, and (2) sentences that ask a question.

Sentences Beginning with *There* or *Here*

When the word *there* or *here* comes at the beginning of a sentence, it may appear to be the subject, but it is not. Use the "*who* or *what*" formula to find the subject. This will prevent you from mistaking *here* and *there* for the subject.

EXAMPLE There are many trees in the yard. [What are? *Trees.*]

Sentences That Ask Questions

Questions usually begin with a verb or a verb helper. Also they frequently begin with words like *what, when, where, how, why,* etc. Either way, the subject usually follows the verb or verb helper.

EXAMPLES Why are **you** leaving?
Will **she** visit soon?

In questions that begin with a helping verb, the subject always comes between the helping verb and the main verb. Another way to find the subject is to turn the question into a statement, find the verb, and ask "Who?" or "What?" in front of it.

EXAMPLES *Question:* Were your friends early?
Statement: Your friends were early.
[Who were early? *Friends*]
Subject: **Friends**

Question: Has the dog been fed?
Statement: The dog has been fed.
[What has been fed? *Dog*]
Subject: **Dog**

EXERCISE 6. Number 1–10 in a column. Select the verb and the simple subject in each of the following sentences, and write them after the proper number on your paper. Select the verb first. Be sure to write down all parts of a verb phrase.

1. There were three questions on the final exam.
2. Here is my topic for the term paper.
3. What did you choose for a topic?
4. Will everyone be ready on time?
5. There will be no excuse for lateness.
6. When should we go to the library?
7. There were very few books on the subject.
8. Are there any magazine articles about the bald eagle?
9. Where will our conference be held?
10. Have you begun the next chapter?

Sentences in Which the Subject Is Understood

In requests and commands the subject is usually left out of the sentence. The subject of a command or request is *you* (understood but not expressed).

EXAMPLES   Close the door.
Take this to the office.

In these sentences the verbs are *close* and *take*. In both sentences the subject is the same. Who must *close* and *take?* The subject is *you,* even though the word does not appear in either of the sentences. A subject of this kind is said to be *understood.*

Compound Subjects and Verbs

2e. Two or more subjects connected by *and* or *or* and having the same verb are called a *compound subject.*

EXAMPLE   **Mr. Holmes** and his **friends** went on a fishing trip. [verb: *went;* compound subject: *Mr. Holmes* (and) *friends*]

2f. Two or more verbs joined by a connecting word and having the same subject are called a *compound verb.*

EXAMPLES   On our last trip to Europe, we **sailed** on a freighter and **saved** a great deal of money. [compound verb: *sailed* (and) *saved;* subject: *we*]

I **have cut** the grass and **clipped** the hedges. [The subject is *I;* the compound verb is *have cut* (and) *have clipped.* Notice that the helping verb *have* goes with both *cut* and *clipped.*]

2g. The subject is never in a prepositional phrase.

A prepositional phrase is a group of words which begins with a preposition and ends with a noun or pronoun: *around the house, of us.* Finding the subject when it is followed by a phrase may be difficult.

EXAMPLE   One of my relatives has taken a trip to Europe.

You see at once that the verb is *has taken.* When you ask "Who has taken?" you may be tempted to answer *relatives.* However, that is not what the sentence says. The sentence says, "*One* of my relatives has taken a trip to Europe. The subject is *One.* Notice that *relatives* is part of the phrase *of my relatives.* In many sentences you can easily isolate the subject and verb simply by crossing out all prepositional phrases.

EXAMPLE   The bus ~~with the skiers~~ will leave ~~for the lodge in three minutes.~~ [verb: *will leave;* subject: *bus*]

EXERCISE 7. Write two sentences containing an understood subject, two containing a compound subject, two containing a compound verb, two in which the subject follows the verb, and two in which the subject is followed by a prepositional phrase.

EXERCISE 8. Number your paper 1–10. Write the subject and the verb of each sentence. If the subject of the sentence is understood, write *you* as the subject, placing parentheses around it.

EXAMPLES   1. Fortunately, there are two gallons of ice cream in the freezer.

1. *gallons   are*
2. My niece and nephew will arrive early in August and stay for three weeks.
2. *niece, nephew   will arrive, will stay*
3. Lend me your notebook.
3. *(you)   lend*

1. Jackets and ties are required in the dining room.
2. Are there bears living in these woods?
3. There are five new students in our class this semester.
4. Bring both a pencil and a pen to the exam on Thursday.
5. Frank neither sings nor plays an instrument.
6. Where do you and Liz buy your cassettes?
7. Both of the math problems were difficult.
8. Play ball!
9. There is much wisdom in folk sayings and proverbs.
10. Is one of the kittens sick?

FRAGMENTS

You have learned that a sentence contains a verb and its subject. However, not all groups of words containing a subject and verb are sentences. Some do not express a complete thought. For example, *When she was sixteen* contains a verb and its subject—the verb is *was;* the subject is *she.* Yet the group of words is not a sentence because it does not express a complete thought. It suggests that more is to be said. It is a fragment, a part of a longer sentence.

She passed her driving test when she was sixteen.

Now you have a sentence. The thought has been completed.

EXERCISE 9.   Number your paper 1–20. If a word group is a sentence, put an *S* beside the proper number on your paper. If it is not a sentence, write an *F* for fragment. Ask yourself whether the group of words has a verb and a subject and whether it expresses a complete thought.

1. Jessamyn West was born in Indiana of Quaker parents
2. Educated in California
3. Her writing and career interest me
4. Because I have gone to school in California and have lived most of my life there
5. After graduating from Whittier College
6. And after continuing her studies in England
7. She attended the University of California
8. I know that she has been a teacher and a lecturer
9. Her writing has appeared in many periodicals
10. Including the *New Yorker* and the *Atlantic Monthly*
11. If you are a short story fan
12. You should get one of her exciting collections and read it
13. In the story which I have just read
14. The main character is a young girl
15. She sits and sews and listens to the story of a stranger
16. With whom she silently falls in love
17. He tells a story of his own lost love
18. Filled with mystery, romance, realistic detail, and a pervasive shadow of tragedy and unfulfillment
19. Of all the stories so far this is my favorite
20. Jessamyn West's short stories range broadly from past to present, and her characters represent a sweep of personalities

THE SENTENCE BASE

Every sentence has a base. The base may be compared to the foundation of a building. It is the part upon which all other parts rest. The sentence base is composed usually of two parts: the subject and the verb.

EXAMPLES   A cloud of smoke appeared.   [base: *cloud appeared*]
Our plans for the trip were discussed.   [base: *plans were discussed*]

In these examples, the sentence base consists of only a subject and verb. In many sentences, however, something else is required in the predicate to complete the meaning of the subject and verb. This third element is a *complement* (a completer).

COMPLEMENTS

2h. A *complement* is a word or group of words which completes the meaning begun by the subject and verb.

The following example will show you how the complement does this.

$$\text{The drought ruined the crops.}$$
$$\qquad\quad \text{S} \qquad \text{V} \qquad \text{C}$$

"The drought ruined" would not be a complete statement by itself, even though it contains a subject and a verb. "The drought ruined *what?*" a reader would ask. The word *crops* completes the meaning of the sentence by telling *what* the drought ruined. Study the following sentences, in which subjects, verbs, and complements are labeled. Name the part of speech of each complement.

$$\text{Mrs. Hill is our new senator.}$$
$$\text{She is very tall.}$$
$$\text{Our science teacher performed an experiment.}$$
$$\text{The moon is a satellite of the earth.}$$
$$\text{The ground feels dry.}$$
$$\text{Both Jim and George appeared quite confident.}$$

EXERCISE 10. Construct sentences from the following sentence bases. Do not be satisfied with adding only one or two words. Make interesting sentences.

SUBJECT	VERB	COMPLEMENT
1. student	left	room
2. remarks	were	clever

SUBJECT	VERB	COMPLEMENT
3. center	passed	ball
4. chemical	was identified	
5. child	looked	unhappy
6. report	was	short
7. shirts	were	warm
8. bells	rang	
9. teacher	helped	student
10. library	furnishes	information

► **NOTE** Like the subject of a sentence, a complement is never in a prepositional phrase.

I intercepted **one** of the passes. [The complement is *one*, not *passes; passes* is in a prepositional phrase.]

An adverb modifying a verb is not a complement. Complements may be nouns, pronouns, or adjectives.

Bess studies hard. [*Hard*, an adverb, is not a complement.]
That noise is **mysterious**. [*Mysterious*, an adjective, is a complement.]

EXERCISE 11. Number your paper 1–20 in a column. For each of the following sentences, list the subject and verb. If there is a complement, list it after the verb.

1. Every year the Arctic Ocean contains more open water.
2. Melting ice will raise the level of the oceans.
3. The sea could invade coastlands and could submerge islands.
4. Millions of people in the Temperate Zone would fear the approach of winter.
5. Outside, the wind would moan ceaselessly throughout the short days.
6. Great quantities of moisture would evaporate from the ice-free waters of the Arctic Ocean.
7. This moisture would condense and would fall on the continents as snow.
8. The warmth of the short, cool summers would not melt the huge drifts of winter.
9. Autumn would bring new and more terrible blizzards.
10. A thousand years of storms would create mountains of ice.

11. Their own weight would set the glaciers in motion southward.
12. These masses of ice would create vast lakes.
13. Along the forefront of these glaciers, blizzards would rage continually.
14. Farther southward, heavy rains would change the deserts.
15. The Sahara and Gobi deserts would become vast, rich grasslands.
16. Enormous herds of antelope would darken the grasslands.
17. Sheets of ice might cover most of North America.
18. The refreezing of the Arctic Ocean would probably bring the cycle to a halt.
19. Once again, the seas would grow warmer.
20. At last the great storms would slacken and would then stop altogether.

The Subject Complement

2i. A *subject complement* is a noun, pronoun, or adjective that follows a linking verb. It identifies, describes, or explains the subject.

EXAMPLES   Michael is an eagle **scout.**
Susan grew **weary.**

In the first example, *scout* identifies the subject *Michael*. In the second, *weary* describes the subject *Susan*.

There are two kinds of subject complements. If the subject complement is a noun or a pronoun, it is a *predicate nominative*. If it is an adjective, it is a *predicate adjective.*

Predicate nominatives (nouns and pronouns) explain the subject or give another name for the subject. Predicate adjectives describe the subject. Both predicate nominatives and predicate adjectives are linked to the subject by linking verbs. The common linking verbs are *be, become, feel, smell, taste, look, grow, seem, appear, remain, sound, stay.*[1]

EXAMPLES   The acorn becomes an **oak.** [predicate nominative]

---

[1] The forms of *be* are *am, is, are, was, were,* and verb phrases ending in *be* or *been: can be, has been,* etc.

The flower appears **red** but is actually **purple**. [predicate adjectives]

EXERCISE 12. Number your paper 1–10. Select the subject complement from each of the following sentences, and write it after the corresponding number on your paper. (First find the verb and its subject, then the complement.) After each complement, write what kind it is: predicate nominative or predicate adjective.

1. The last scene of the play is very tense.
2. The two small birds are finches.
3. The music sounded lively.
4. This costume looks elegant.
5. My goldfish is growing larger every day.
6. Andrea's report on digital recording is a detailed one.
7. The setting of the story is an old castle.
8. Your solution to this algebra problem is clever.
9. We felt full after our huge dinner.
10. His entire story seems almost unbelievable.

Distinguishing Between Subject and Complement

When the subject is not in the normal position before the verb, it is sometimes hard to tell which is the subject and which is the complement. When the word order is normal, there is no problem—the subject comes before the verb and the subject complement comes after:

$$\overset{\text{S}}{\text{Matthew Henson}} \overset{\text{V}}{\text{was}} \text{ a famous } \overset{\text{C}}{\text{explorer}}.$$

When the word order is reversed, as in questions, the subject still comes before the subject complement in most cases:

$$\overset{\text{V}}{\text{Was}} \overset{\text{S}}{\text{he}} \text{ the } \overset{\text{C}}{\text{leader}} \text{ of the expedition?}$$

Sometimes, however, a writer or speaker may put the subject complement first for emphasis:

$$\text{How } \overset{\text{C}}{\text{sweet}} \overset{\text{V}}{\text{is}} \overset{\text{S}}{\text{freedom}}!$$

$$\text{What a fine } \overset{\text{C}}{\text{athlete}} \overset{\text{S}}{\text{Ray}} \overset{\text{V}}{\text{is}}!$$

When this happens, you must consider which word is more likely to be the subject of the sentence. Usually the subject will be the word that specifically identifies the person or thing that the sentence is about. The first example above presents little difficulty because *sweet* is an adjective and cannot be the subject. In the second example, however, both the subject complement (*athlete*) and the subject (*Ray*) are nouns. In this case you must ask yourself which noun more specifically identifies the subject. *Ray* has a more specific meaning than *athlete*, and consequently it is a more likely subject for the sentence.

EXERCISE 13. Copy the following sentences, and pick out the subject, the verb, and the subject complement. Label the subject of the sentence *S*, the verb *V*, and the subject complement *C*.

1. Were my directions clear?
2. How soft the night air seems.
3. Harriet Tubman was a woman of magnificent courage.
4. "Tiger of the Snows" is a wonderful story.
5. Does he appear sad?
6. What a fine dancer Sally is!
7. What a giant Joe has become!
8. How happy they look!
9. When does a child become an adult?
10. Sleep is a gentle thing.

Direct Objects and Indirect Objects

There is another kind of complement that does not refer to the subject. Instead, it receives the action of the verb or shows the result of the action.

EXAMPLE The secretary typed the **report**. [base: *secretary typed report*]

In sentences of this kind, the complement is called the *direct object*.

2j. The *direct object* is a word or group of words that directly receives the action expressed by the verb or

shows the result of the action. It answers the question "What?" or "Whom?" after an action verb.

EXAMPLES
$$\overset{\text{S}}{\text{The dentist}} \overset{\text{V}}{\text{cleaned}} \overset{\text{DO}}{\text{my teeth.}}$$

$$\overset{\text{S}}{\text{She}} \overset{\text{V}}{\text{filled}} \overset{\text{DO}}{\text{a small cavity.}}$$

In the first sentence, *teeth* is the direct object. It directly receives the action expressed by the verb. It answers the question "What?" after the verb. Cleaned what? Cleaned *teeth.* In the second sentence, *cavity* is the direct object, telling *what* the dentist filled.

Objects are used after action verbs only. Verbs like *think, believe, imagine,* which express mental action, are action verbs just as truly as are verbs like *jump, hit,* or *knock,* which express physical action.

EXERCISE 14. List the direct objects on your paper. Be able to name the verb whose action the object receives. *Caution:* Like all complements, the object of a verb is never part of a prepositional phrase.

1. I borrowed my parents' new camera recently.
2. First I loaded the film into the camera.
3. Then I set the opening of the shutter.
4. I focused the camera on a distant object.
5. I could read the shutter speed in the viewfinder.
6. A flashing red light means an incorrect setting.
7. Slowly and carefully I pressed the button.
8. I then moved the film forward for the next shot.
9. By the end of the day, I had snapped thirty-six pictures.
10. Unfortunately the film processor lost my roll of film.

2k. An *indirect object* is a noun or pronoun in the predicate that precedes the direct object. It tells "to whom" or "for whom" the action of the verb is done.

EXAMPLES   The instructor gave some lessons.
The instructor gave **me** some lessons.

You recognize *lessons* as the direct object in both sentences. It tells what the instructor gave. In the second sentence you have another word which also receives the action of the verb. That word is *me. Me,* which comes before the direct object, tells *to whom* the lessons were given. It is an *indirect object.*

What is the indirect object in this sentence?

Experience taught the campers many things.

Things is the direct object. *Campers* is the indirect object. It is the campers *to whom* things were taught.

If the words *to* and *for* are used in the sentence itself, the word following them is part of a prepositional phrase and not an indirect object. Compare the following pairs.

Robert baked me a cake. [*Me* is the indirect object.]
Robert baked a cake for me. [no indirect object]
The teacher told the class a story. [*Class* is the indirect object.]
The teacher told a story to the class. [no indirect object]

Caution: When identifying complements, do not be confused by adverbs in the predicate.

We went **home.** [noun used as adverb telling *where*]
We built a new **home.** [direct object]

Compound Complements

Complements may be compound.

EXAMPLES The names of the dogs are **Gypsy** and **Boots.** [compound predicate nominative]

She is **tall** and **slim.** [compound predicate adjective]

The next group includes the **collies** and the **terriers.** [compound direct object]

The noise had given my **brother** and **me** a scare. [compound indirect object]

EXERCISE 15. Number your paper 1–10. After the proper number, write the objects in each sentence. Write *i.o.* after an indirect object and *d.o.* after a direct object. Not all sentences contain both kinds of objects.

1. Last fall George told us his plans for the summer.
2. He wanted a job at a camp.
3. We gave him the name of a camp near Tupper Lake.
4. We also gave him all kinds of advice.
5. George wrote the manager a letter.
6. The letter of application cost him a great deal of effort.
7. Usually camps need many counselors for the summer.
8. Most camps do not pay their counselors much money.
9. A job as counselor does provide a free home for two months.
10. The manager offered George a position.

EXERCISE 16. Write one sentence containing a compound subject, one containing a compound verb, two containing a compound predicate nominative, two containing a compound predicate adjective, two containing a compound direct object, and two containing a compound indirect object.

SENTENCES CLASSIFIED BY PURPOSE

2l. Sentences may be classified according to their purpose.

There are four kinds of sentences: (1) declarative, (2) imperative, (3) interrogative, and (4) exclamatory.

(1) A sentence which makes a statement is a *declarative* sentence.

Its purpose is to declare something. Most of the sentences you use are declarative.

EXAMPLES   As far as I'm concerned, a house can't be built with with too many closets.
In the summer I am constantly fighting crabgrass and cutworms.

(2) A sentence which gives a command or makes a request is an *imperative* sentence.

EXAMPLES   Tell the truth.
           Please, keep off the grass.

(3) A sentence which asks a question is an *interrogative* sentence.

An interrogative sentence is followed by a question mark.

EXAMPLES   Can you speak Spanish?
           Where are you going?

(4) A sentence which expresses strong feeling is an *exclamatory* sentence.

An exclamatory sentence is followed by an exclamation mark.

EXAMPLES   What a beautiful day this is!
           How we love cool, sunny weather!

Caution: A declarative, an imperative, or an interrogative sentence may be spoken in such a way that it will be exclamatory. Then it should be followed by an exclamation mark.

EXAMPLES   That noise must stop! [Declarative becomes exclamatory.]
           Use the brakes! [Imperative becomes exclamatory.]
           What do you want! [Interrogative becomes exclamatory.]

EXERCISE 17. Classify the sentences below according to whether they are declarative, imperative, interrogative, or exclamatory. Write the proper classification after the number of each sentence.

1. The loudspeakers in our living room are small yet powerful.
2. Turn down the sound!
3. Is that music or static, Joyce?
4. Listening to loud music every day can damage one's hearing.

5. How many watts does your amplifier produce?
6. Sound levels are measured in units called decibels.
7. Do you know that an increase of ten decibels represents a tenfold increase in the sound level?
8. Do not blast your sound system.
9. Keep it quiet!
10. Music played softly is relaxing.

DIAGRAMING SENTENCES

Many students find that they can understand sentence structure better when they draw a diagram. A diagram is a way of arranging a sentence in picture form. The picture shows clearly how the various parts of the sentence fit together and how they are related.

The first thing to do in making a diagram is to draw a horizontal line on your paper. On this horizontal line you will write the sentence base. In approximately the center of the line you will draw a short vertical line cutting the horizontal one. This vertical line is the dividing point between the complete subject and the complete predicate. The subject and all words relating to it (complete subject) go to the *left* of this vertical line; the verb and all words relating to it (the complete predicate) go to the *right*.

Diagraming the Subject and Verb

The subject of the sentence is written first on the horizontal line. The verb is written on the second half of this line.

For an understood subject, use the word *you* in parentheses as the subject in your diagram.

EXAMPLE   Ring the bell.

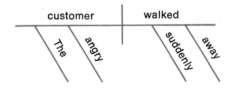

Diagraming Modifiers

Modifiers of the subject and verb (adjectives and adverbs) are written on slanting lines beneath the subject or the verb.

EXAMPLE   **The angry** customer **suddenly** walked **away**.

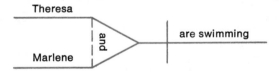

Diagraming Compound Subjects and Compound Verbs

If the subject is compound, diagram it as in the following example. Notice the position of the coordinating conjunction on the broken line.

EXAMPLE   **Theresa** and **Marlene** are swimming.

If the verb is compound, diagram it in this way:

EXAMPLE   Bill **runs** and **hides**.

If the sentence has both a compound subject and a compound predicate, diagram it in this way:

EXAMPLE **He** and **I** **live** and **learn.**

Notice how a compound verb is diagramed when the helping verb is not repeated:

EXAMPLE Sue **was reading** and **studying.**

Since *was* is the helping verb for both *reading* and *studying,*
it is placed on the horizontal line, and the conjunction *and*
joins the main verbs *reading* and *studying.*

When the parts of a compound subject or a compound
predicate are joined by correlative conjunctions, diagram
the sentence in this way:

EXAMPLE **Either** Mary **or** Sue will **not only** compete **but also** win.

Diagraming *Here, There,* and *Where* as Modifiers

When the words *here, there,* and *where* are modifiers of
the verb, diagram them as in the following illustrations.

Where are you going?

There they are.

Here come the alligators!

Diagraming *There* When It Does Not Modify Anything

When *there* begins a sentence but does not modify either the verb or the subject, it is diagramed on a line by itself, as in the following example. When used in this way, *there* is called an *expletive.*

EXAMPLE   There were two candidates.

Diagraming a Modifier of a Modifier

A word which modifies another modifier is diagramed like *very* in the following example.

They played very well.

EXERCISE 18. Diagram the following sentences. Diagrams of the first five are provided for you to copy and fill in.

1. Sound travels very rapidly.

2. A plane circled low.

3. The plane rose quickly and flew silently away.

4. There was a loud scream.

5. Never eat too fast.

6. The team practices daily.
7. Our new members play quite professionally.
8. The small white dog ran away yesterday.

9. Where is my new hat?
10. An unusually heavy rain fell today.
11. Alan often comes here.
12. The cadets marched along smartly.
13. The heavy jacket was torn apart.
14. There are no amateurs here.
15. I stepped back and fell down.
16. Where does she usually go?
17. Does the express train still stop here?
18. Forward march!
19. Margaret sings very well and dances beautifully.
20. The old man and his daughter were born and raised here.

Diagraming the Predicate Nominative and the Predicate Adjective

A subject complement (predicate nominative or predicate adjective) should be placed on the same horizontal line with the simple subject and the verb. It comes after the verb, and a line slanting toward the subject and drawn upward from the horizontal line separates it from the verb. The line slants toward the subject to show that the subject complement is closely related to the subject.

PREDICATE NOMINATIVE   Our dog is a fat **bulldog.**

PREDICATE ADJECTIVE   Our dog is **fat.**

EXERCISE 19.   Diagram the following sentences.

1. Some old books are very valuable.
2. Does the recording sound scratchy?
3. That might have been her fastest race.
4. Hockey is my favorite sport.
5. Some people are always cheerful.
6. Are you our new teacher?
7. Drivers should be more careful.
8. Charles has grown careless lately.
9. This sweater is too large.
10. Beggars can not be choosers.

Diagraming the Direct and Indirect Object

The direct object is diagramed in almost the same way as the predicate nominative. The only difference is that the line separating the object from the verb is vertical (not slanting) as in the following examples:

May joined the **team**.

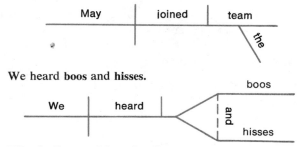

We heard **boos** and **hisses**.

The indirect object is diagramed on a horizontal line beneath the verb. A slanting line connects the horizontal line and the verb. Notice how the slanting line extends slightly below the horizontal line.

Everybody promised **her** a surprise.

EXERCISE 20. Diagram the following sentences.

1. The nights were long and cold.
2. The stars looked exceptionally bright.
3. The cold weather froze the pond.
4. My friends and I usually enjoy winter sports.
5. My parents recently gave me some figure skates.

REVIEW EXERCISE A. Before you continue your study of the parts of a sentence, you should review what you have learned so far. Be sure that you understand everything you have covered because you will be building constantly upon what you have just learned. Can you give in your own words a definition of each of the following and make up an example to illustrate it?

1. A sentence
2. A complete subject
3. A complete predicate
4. A subject (simple)
5. A subject complement
6. A verb (simple predicate)
7. A verb phrase
8. A direct object
9. An understood subject
10. An indirect object

REVIEW EXERCISE B. Number 1–15 in a column on your paper. Select from each of the following sentences the subject and the verb, and write them after the proper number on your paper. Be especially careful to include all parts of a verb phrase.

1. How would you like a ticket to the dog show?
2. There will be a number of fine dogs there.
3. All of the dogs have been washed and brushed by their owners.
4. Are there many of these shows each year?
5. There must have been hundreds of champion dogs at Madison Square Garden.
6. A young handler in a blue apron stopped work and answered a few of our questions.
7. All training and teaching should be done by word and by the tone of your voice.
8. Never smack a dog or hurt it in any way.

9. The tone of your voice will convey your feelings.
10. A few hours of training may well be worthwhile.
11. Where will Larry and I find the collies?
12. Do you see them over there?
13. Look at these short little dogs.
14. What do you call them?
15. Tell me the Chinese legend about the origin of the Pekingese.

REVIEW EXERCISE C. Copy the numbered underlined words in a column on your paper. After each, write the correct one of the following identifications, using these abbreviations: subject, *s.;* verb, *v.;* predicate adjective, *p.a.;* predicate nominative, *p.n.;* direct object, *d.o.;* indirect object, *i.o.;* object of a preposition, *o.p.*

Did you ever wonder about the (1) pyramids of Egypt? How could an ancient (2) race, even with 100,000 workers, build such enormous (3) monuments? Almost every visitor (4) makes a trip out into the desert to see the massive tombs. They appear (5) majestic from a distance. The Great Pyramid of Khufu is (6) one of the wonders of the ancient world. (7) It was once encased with blocks of polished (8) limestone. However, weather and thievery (9) have combined to destroy its original casing. The pyramids (10) look (11) weather-beaten. Still, they are impressive (12) sights.

Invading Arabs about A.D. 650 needed (13) stone for the palaces and mosques in Cairo. Naturally it was (14) easier for them to obtain blocks of stone from the pyramids than to cut new ones from the (15) quarries. They removed the outer limestone blocks, but the two-ton (16) blocks at the bases of the pyramids were too (17) heavy. The task became (18) impossible. There was no (19) way of leveling the pyramids to the ground.

One Arab ruler decided to rob the tomb of Khufu. This ruler was (20) one of many people who believed there were vast treasures hidden in the Great Pyramid. With hundreds of workers at his disposal, he gave the (21) men his (22) instructions. The workers (23) hacked through the solid blocks of granite. The stone was (24) hard; their chisels were (25) poor. By accident, they suddenly (26) broke into a tunnel. Imagine the (27) excitement! All too soon they (28) discovered an enormous (29) plug of granite blocking their way. They cut a passage around the plug and soon reached the inner (30) <u>chamber.</u>

Strangely enough, there was no (31) <u>gold.</u> No vast treasures (32) <u>sparkled</u> under the light of the torches. Probably the tomb had been robbed many centuries earlier by (33) <u>Egyptians</u> familiar with its secret entranceways.

Chapter 3

The Phrase

Prepositional, Verbal, and Appositive Phrases

You already know that a group of words used as a verb is a verb phrase. Two or more words may serve together as one verb. *Have been sleeping, is sleeping,* and *will be sleeping* are examples of verb phrases. Similarly, other groups of words sometimes serve together to perform the function of a single part of speech. Some word groups, or *phrases,* may serve as adjectives or as adverbs or as nouns.

3a. A *phrase* **is a group of related words that is used as a single part of speech and does not contain a verb and its subject.**

In the first of each of the following pairs of examples, a single word is bold-faced. In the second part of each pair, a group of words which performs exactly the same function in the sentence appears in bold-faced type. These word groups are *phrases.*

Air is a **colorless** substance.   [adjective]
Air is a substance **without color.**   [adjective phrase]
The **morning** is the best time to study.   [noun]
In the morning is the best time to study.   [noun phrase]
He parked his car **there.**   [adverb]
He parked his car **in the driveway.**   [adverb phrase]

Phrases can be classified in two ways: according to the job they do in sentences (adjective, adverb, noun, verb) or according to the way in which they are formed. We use the latter method in distinguishing prepositional, participial, gerund, and infinitive phrases.

PREPOSITIONAL PHRASES

3b. A *prepositional phrase* **is a group of words beginning with a preposition and usually ending with a noun or pronoun.**

The prepositional phrases are bold-faced in the following examples:

They were standing **near the door.**
The woman **with the helmet** is a motorcyclist.
The cashier gave the change **to me.**

The preposition in the last example is *to*. Do not confuse this common preposition with the *to* that is the sign of the infinitive form of a verb: *to play, to see, to run.*

3c. **The noun or pronoun that ends the prepositional phrase is the** *object* **of the preposition that begins the phrase.**

PHRASE	PREPOSITION	OBJECT
during the long winter	during	winter
in the last inning	in	inning
along the highway	along	highway
after her next birthday	after	birthday
for him	for	him

A preposition may, of course, have a compound object:

in **schools** and **colleges**
by **bus, train,** or **plane**

Prepositional phrases usually do the work of adjectives and adverbs in sentences.

Adjective Phrases

Prepositional phrases may be used to modify nouns or pronouns in much the same way as single-word adjectives:

EXAMPLES a **heroic** act   an act **of heroism**
the **blue** one   the one **in blue**

3d. A prepositional phrase that modifies a noun or pronoun is an *adjective phrase*.

The rooms **of the house** smelled damp and musty.

Few **of the villagers** had ever been there before.

Several adjective phrases often modify the same noun:

The girl **with the trumpet in the next house** keeps us awake.

An adjective phrase may also modify the object of another prepositional phrase:

The book on the table **in the hallway** is mine. [*In the hallway* modifies *table*, the object of the preposition *on*.]

EXERCISE 1. Each of the following sentences contains two adjective phrases. List them in order on your paper. After each phrase, write the noun it modifies.

EXAMPLE 1. The veterans of the war in Gaul remained loyal.
       1. *of the war — veterans*
         in Gaul — war

1. The roads of ancient Rome linked the far corners of the empire.
2. Large blocks of the hardest stone paved the surface of the major routes.
3. Close communication between provinces strengthened the position of the Roman rulers.
4. Caesar's interest in military roads showed his concern with communication.
5. Roman roads were one reason for the success of Caesar's military operations.

Adverb Phrases

3e. A prepositional phrase that modifies a verb, an adjective, or another adverb is an *adverb phrase.*

EXAMPLES   The fox escaped **into its hole.** [The phrase modifies the verb *escaped.*]

Althea Gibson was graceful **on the tennis court.** [The phrase modifies the adjective *graceful.*]

The sun rises earlier **in the morning** now. [The phrase modifies the adverb *earlier.*]

Adverb phrases tell *when, where, why, how,* or *to what extent.*

EXAMPLES   The wind came up **during the night.** [when]
We spent the day **at the beach.** [where]
The children combed the shore **for shells.** [why]
I usually travel **by bus.** [how]
She missed the train **by a few seconds.** [to what extent]

Unlike adjective phrases, which always follow the words they modify, adverb phrases can appear at various places in the sentence. More than one adverb phrase can modify the same word.

EXAMPLE   **In the first inning** she pitched **with great control.** [The adverb phrases *In the first inning* and *with great control* both modify the verb *pitched.* The first adverb phrase tells *when* and the second adverb phrase tells *how.*]

EXERCISE 2.   Number 1–10, and list the adverb phrases in the following sentences. After each phrase, list the word it modifies and the part of speech of that word.

1. Eerie sounds came from the abandoned house.
2. Are some old houses haunted by ghosts?
3. On a moonlit night, my parents and I searched throughout the unused house.

4. We weren't afraid of any ghosts.
5. In the cellar we found two alley cats.
6. The strange noises were made by these animals.
7. We carefully placed the cats in a box.
8. They both seemed happy with their temporary home.
9. We walked up the steps, out the door, and across the lawn.
10. At a leisurely pace, we returned to our own house.

Diagraming Prepositional Phrases

Prepositional phrases are diagramed in much the same way as adjectives and adverbs. The preposition that begins the phrase is placed on a slanting line leading down from the word the phrase modifies. The object of the preposition is placed on a horizontal line drawn from the slanting line. As with the indirect object, the slanting line extends slightly below the horizontal line.

EXAMPLE The steep slopes **of the mountains** are covered **with forests.**

EXAMPLE They sailed late **in the fall.**   [adverb phrase modifying an adverb]

EXAMPLE They were imprisoned **without food and water.**

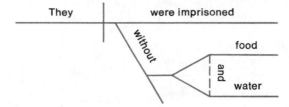

EXAMPLE **Down the valley and over the plain** wanders the river.

EXAMPLE The princess lived in a castle **on the mountain.**

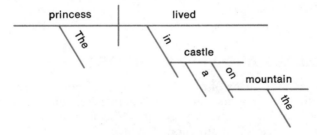

EXERCISE 3. Diagram the following sentences.

1. She sells seashells at the seashore.
2. The tourist wandered across the street and into the store.
3. They gave help to every person in need.
4. In Texas in the early spring the bluebells cover the fields.

EXERCISE 4. Complete each sentence by inserting an appropriate prepositional phrase in each blank. Be able to tell whether it is an adjective or an adverb phrase.

EXAMPLE 1. —— Mrs. Wagner wrote a letter.
    1. *After lunch Mrs. Wagner wrote a letter.*

1. —— the boys watched the sun rise.
2. I heard the noise ——.
3. My friend suggested a hike ——.
4. Their mascot ran ——.
5. The hikers climbed slowly ——.
6. Thousands —— appeared.
7. The steep path wound ——.
8. —— they reached the top.
9. There —— stood a tall pine.
10. The class lasts ——.

EXERCISE 5. Complete the following four sentences, adding adverb phrases according to the directions.

1. The sound engineer repaired the microphone ——. (Tell how.)
2. The microphone was needed ——. (Tell why.)
3. The job was finally done ——. (Tell when.)
4. The repaired microphone was placed ——. (Tell where.)

VERBALS AND VERBAL PHRASES[1]

Verbals are forms of a verb that are used not as verbs but as other parts of speech. Verbals act very much like verbs: they may be modified by adverbs and may have complements. Their chief function, however, is to act as other parts of speech: adjective, noun, adverb.

There are three kinds of verbals: *participles, gerunds,* and *infinitives.*

The Participle

3f. A *participle* **is a verb form used as an adjective.**

Since the participle is part verb and part adjective, it might be called a "verbal adjective."

---

[1] For work on verbal phrases as sentence fragments, see page 221. For verbals as dangling modifiers, see page 189.

EXAMPLES   The **burning** leaves smelled good.
A **cracked** record can ruin a stylus.

In the first example, *burning* is part verb because it carries the action of the verb *burn,* and part adjective because it modifies the noun *leaves — burning leaves.* In the second, *cracked,* formed from the verb *crack,* modifies the noun *record.* Because they are formed from verbs and used as adjectives, *burning* and *cracked* are participles.

There are two kinds of participles: *present* and *past.*

(1) *Present participles* consist of the plain form of the verb plus –*ing.*

EXAMPLES   The **sleeping** dog groaned.
Glancing at the clouds, the farmer shook his head.

In the first example, *sleeping* (formed by adding –*ing* to the verb *sleep*) is a present participle modifying the noun *dog.* In the second, the present participle *glancing* (consisting of the plain form of the verb *glance* plus –*ing*) modifies the noun *farmer — glancing farmer.* Verb forms used as adjectives, like these, are participles.

In addition to its use as a verbal, the present participle can be part of a verb phrase:

EXAMPLES   The dog **was sleeping.**
The farmer **is glancing** at the clouds.

A present participle alone cannot be a verb. It can, however, be part of a verb phrase if it is preceded by a helping verb: *was sleeping.* A participle in a verb phrase is part of the verb; it is not considered a separate adjective.

(2) *Past participles* consist of the plain form of the verb plus –*d* or –*ed.* A few are irregularly formed.[1]

EXAMPLES   **Bruised** by the fall, the **defeated** runner limped to the sidelines. [The past participles *bruised* and *defeated* modify the noun *runner.*]
Discouraged by the mishap, the boy hung his head. [The past participle *discouraged* modifies the noun *boy — discouraged boy.*]

---

[1] See the discussion of irregular verbs, on pages 155–56.

Like a present participle, a past participle can also be part of a verb phrase.

EXAMPLES   I was not **alarmed.**

               I had been informed that Ms. Garcia would not be there.

EXERCISE 6. Number your paper 1–10. List the participles used as adjectives in the following sentences. After each participle, write the noun or pronoun modified.

1. *Pigeon,* a word derived from the Old Norse, is the name of certain species of dove.
2. A pigeon is any bird of the family *Columbidae,* having a compact body and short legs, with a square or round tail.
3. Traced back through the centuries, the lineage of all pigeons leads to a common ancestor.
4. This ancestor, the Blue Rock pigeon, once domesticated, was bred into several different varieties.
5. Carrier pigeons, for example, bred in the fourth century B.C. in Egypt, have been used until very recent times for swift communication.
6. Passenger pigeons, migrating in vast numbers every spring and fall, were considered a nuisance by many farmers in the last century.
7. The roosting birds would often so overburden the trees that all but the largest branches would break off and fall.
8. John Audubon, wandering through such a roosting site after the birds had left, compared the damage to the effects of a hurricane.
9. Once numbered in the billions, passenger pigeons have now become extinct.
10. A severe hailstorm, killing many of the birds and destroying their eggs, wiped out one enormous flock of birds at a single stroke.

EXERCISE 7. Each of the following sentences is followed by a participle inside parentheses. Rewrite each sentence by inserting the participle next to the noun it modifies.

EXAMPLES
  1. The candidate thanked each one of her supporters. (*winning*)
  1. *The winning candidate thanked each one of her supporters.*
  2. We collected funds for the restoration of the building. (*damaged*)
  2. *We collected funds for the restoration of the damaged building.*

1. The train was greeted loudly this afternoon. (*arriving*)
2. The committee selected three television shows for their educational value. (*nominating*)
3. My sister in the living room did not hear the doorbell. (*ringing*)
4. The carpenter was supposed to teach us how to fix this chair. (*broken*)
5. The Tasmanian wolf is a species seen only rarely since 1930. (*endangered*)
6. The stream crosses the farmer's land at three places. (*winding*)
7. A message on the back of an envelope was handed to me. (*crumpled*)
8. The book included three interesting facts about dinosaurs. (*illustrated*)
9. A Douglas fir had become the haven for several small creatures. (*fallen*)
10. The plane narrowly missed a tall radio antenna. (*circling*)

EXERCISE 8. Pick out from the following sentences all the participles, both present and past. List them on your paper, and after each one, write the word which the participle modifies. Be careful not to confuse participles with the main verbs of the sentences.

1. The dogs, excited and yelping, looked very eager.
2. Brought from the stables, the horses arrived at the starting point ready for the hunt.
3. Dressed in their traditional costumes, the members of the hunting party mounted their horses.

4. Sensing danger, a nearby fox ran off across the fields.

5. Released from their leashes and following each other in close formation, the dogs set off after the fox.

6. Stumbling upon the uneven ground and treacherous soft spots, some of the horses threw their riders.

7. Sniffing at the trail and baying loudly, the dogs raced energetically along the path.

8. Snarling in fury, the desperate fox doubled back from the tree line at the edge of the fields and snapped at the dogs.

9. The lead dog of the pack, taken by surprise, halted and yelped as the fox escaped into the forbidding, dense forest.

10. Disappointed by their failure, the hunters regrouped to make a fresh start.

The Participial Phrase

A participle may be modified by an adverb or by a prepositional phrase used as an adverb, and it may have a complement. These related words combine with the participle to make a participial phrase.

3g. A *participial phrase* consists of a participle and its related words, such as modifiers and complements, all of which act together as an adjective.

The participial phrase in each of the following sentences is in bold-faced type. An arrow points to the noun or pronoun which the phrase modifies.

▶ NOTE Some participial phrases contain one or more prepositional phrases.

EXAMPLES **Approaching the curve,** the truck slowed down.

I could see Frank **sitting three seats away.**

I heard him **whispering to his friend.**

Acquitted by the jury, the defendant shook hands with her lawyer.

The ship, **buffeted by the** storm, struggled to safety.

EXERCISE 9. Each of the following sentences contains one or more participial phrases. Copy each participial phrase, and write after it the noun or pronoun it modifies.

EXAMPLE   1. Hindered by bad weather, the British expedition lost the race to the South Pole, arriving a month after the Norwegians.

       1. *Hindered by bad weather — expedition*
          arriving a month after the Norwegians — expedition

1. Hoping to be the first to reach the South Pole, the British explorer Robert Scott, taking four men with him, began his final dash to the pole on January 4, 1912.

2. Leading Scott by sixty miles, however, a Norwegian expedition, commanded by Roald Amundsen, was moving swiftly.

3. Having learned about Amundsen, Scott realized a race was on.

4. Plagued by bad weather and bad luck, Scott fell farther behind.

5. Reaching the pole on January 17, the British found the Norwegians had already been there.

6. Weakened by scurvy, frostbite, and exhaustion, the five explorers, knowing they had little hope of survival, set out on the eight-hundred-mile journey back to their base ship.

7. One member of the party, overcome by exhaustion and injuries, died before half the journey had been completed.

8. On March 15, another member, leaving the camp at night, walked deliberately to his death in a violent blizzard.

9. Eight months later, a rescue mission, sent to find out what had happened, found the bodies of Scott and his companions.

10. Today the ill-fated Scott expedition, acclaimed for its heroism, is better known than the successful Amundsen expedition.

EXERCISE 10. Participles can add variety to your writing. Use the following participial phrases in sentences of your own.

1. torn from its mooring	6. broadcast last night
2. taken by surprise	7. clutched in her hand
3. jumping to her feet	8. winning the prize
4. viewed from the bridge	9. adding sugar
5. recorded last week	10. blocking the path

The Gerund

Gerunds and present participles are formed exactly alike. Both are formed by adding –*ing* to the plain form of the verb. The difference between them is in their use. Present participles are used as *adjectives;* gerunds are used as *nouns.*

3h. A *gerund* is a verb form ending in –*ing* that is used as a noun.

Study the bold-faced words in the following sentences. They are gerunds. Note that each word is part verb and part noun. For instance, *walking* in the first sentence is formed from the verb *walk;* yet it names an action. It is the name of something; therefore it is used as a noun. Further proof that *walking* is used as a noun is its use as the subject of a sentence.

EXAMPLES **Walking** is good exercise.
Pointing is impolite.
I enjoy **playing** the flute.
Watering the lawn produced good results.
We avoided the rush by **mailing** the cards early.

You can see that each of the bold-faced words is used as a noun. In some sentences it is used as the subject; in one it is used as the object of the verb; in the last sentence it is used as the object of a preposition. Note that gerunds always end in –*ing.*

EXERCISE 11. Number your paper 1–10. In each of the following ten sentences, you will find verbals ending in –*ing.* Some will be gerunds and some will be present participles. Copy them, and label them either *G* for gerund or *P* for participle. If the verbal is a gerund, tell how it is used (subject, object, predicate nominative, object of a preposition). If the verbal is a participle, tell what word it modifies.

EXAMPLES 1. Thinking clearly is essential.
           1. *thinking — G — subject*
           2. A thinking person will avoid excess.
           2. *thinking — P — person*

1. Their whispering caught the attention of the teacher.
2. Shirley enjoys hiking.
3. Besides eating, what else do you like to do?
4. A discriminating viewer occasionally shuts off the TV and reads a good book.
5. Telling the difference between the twins is hard even for their parents.
6. An unforgettable experience was visiting the zoo for the first time.
7. Climbing to the top of the mountain, Carl could see for miles.
8. Jenny occupied herself by writing song lyrics.
9. My new puppy does not like staying by itself in an empty house.
10. Sensing the danger nearby, he began to shout for help.

EXERCISE 12. From the following verbs make gerunds, and use each one in a sentence. Tell how each is used. It may be one of the following in the sentence: subject of verb, object of verb, predicate nominative, object of a preposition.

1. leave   6. dream
2. grow   7. go
3. work   8. row
4. plant   9. hike
5. talk   10. draw

The Gerund Phrase

3i. A *gerund phrase* **consists of a gerund together with its complements and modifiers, all of which act together as a noun.**

EXAMPLES **Looking at the clock** is a bad habit. [The gerund phrase is used as the subject of the sentence. The gerund *looking* is modified by the prepositional phrase *at the clock.*]

She dislikes **gossiping about one's friends.** [The gerund phrase is the direct object of the verb *dislikes*. It consists of the gerund itself and the adverb phrase *about one's friends* that modifies it.]

He improved his appearance by **losing weight.** [The gerund phrase is the object of the preposition *by*. The gerund *losing* has a direct object: *weight.*]

EXERCISE 13. Write five sentences, each containing one or more gerund phrases. Underline each phrase, and write above it how it is used. Use the following abbreviations — *subj.,* subject; *obj.,* object; *p.n.,* predicate nominative; *o.p.,* object of a preposition. Include an example of each use.

The Infinitive

3j. An *infinitive* is a verb form, usually preceded by *to,* that is used as a noun, adjective, or adverb.

An infinitive consists of the plain form of the verb, usually preceded by *to*. It can be used as a noun, an adjective, or an adverb. Study the following examples carefully.

Infinitives used as nouns

To err is human. [The infinitive *to err* is the subject.]

Lorna attempted **to flee.** [The infinitive *to flee* is the direct object of the verb *attempted.*]

Infinitives used as adjectives

She is a candidate **to watch.** [The infinitive *to watch* modifies the noun *candidate.*]

The doctor **to call** is Inada. [The infinitive *to call* modifies the noun *doctor.*]

Infinitives used as adverbs

The plane was ready **to go.** [The infinitive *to go* modifies the adjective *ready.*]

The tiger tensed its muscles **to spring.** [*To spring* modifies the verb *tensed.*]

► **NOTE** *To* plus a noun or pronoun (*to the store, to school, to her*) constitutes a prepositional phrase. *To* is only the sign of the infinitive when it is followed by the plain form of a verb (*to be, to discuss, to see*).

EXERCISE 14. List on your paper the infinitives in the following sentences. After each infinitive, tell how it is used —as subject, object, predicate nominative, adjective, or adverb. You may use abbreviations.

1. Do you want to meet at the corner?
2. We are eager to go.
3. One way to relax is to listen to classical music.
4. I am easy to please.
5. We are waiting to talk with the principal.
6. The soup is still too hot to eat.
7. To learn, you must listen.
8. This summer she hopes to travel in the West.
9. To hike through the woods is fun.
10. To forgive is sometimes difficult.

The Infinitive Phrase

3k. An *infinitive phrase* **consists of an infinitive together with its complements and modifiers.**[1]

Like infinitives alone, infinitive phrases can be used as adjectives, adverbs, and nouns.

EXAMPLES **To hit a curve ball solidly** is very difficult. [The infinitive phrase is used as a noun, as the subject of the sentence. The infinitive has an object, *ball,* and is modified by the adverb *solidly.*]

This kind of book is hard **to read rapidly.** [The

[1] Unlike the other verbals, an infinitive may have a subject: *I asked him to come to my party.* (*Him* is the subject of the infinitive *to come.*) An infinitive phrase that includes a subject may sometimes be called an *infinitive clause.*

infinitive *to read* is used as an adverb to modify the adjective *hard*. The infinitive is itself modified by the adverb *rapidly*.]

She wants to be the captain. [The infinitive *to be* is the direct object of the verb *wants* and is followed by the predicate nominative *captain*.]

The Infinitive with "to" Omitted

Occasionally, the *to* that is usually the sign of the infinitive will be omitted in a sentence. This happens frequently after such verbs as *see, hear, feel, watch, help, know, dare, need, make, let,* and *please.*

EXAMPLES Did you watch her [to] **run the race?**
He doesn't dare [to] **tell the teacher.**
She would not let the dog [to] **go.**

EXERCISE 15. List on your paper the infinitive phrases in the following sentences. After each phrase, tell how it is used—as subject, object, predicate nominative, adjective, or adverb.

1. My assignment was to read *I Know Why the Caged Bird Sings.*
2. In the story of her life, Maya Angelou tries to present a true picture of her childhood.
3. To tell the truth of her experience was her aim.
4. She desired to communicate her true feelings to her readers.
5. To write a successful book meant a new career.
6. Angelou had many ways to use her talents.
7. To dance successfully in Europe and Africa was another one of her accomplishments.
8. Maya Angelou attempted to express herself and her culture in every possible medium.
9. To write a television series on African traditions in American life was an outstanding achievement.
10. In all her work she was able to express great emotion.

Diagraming Verbals and Verbal Phrases

Participles and participial phrases are diagramed as follows:

EXAMPLE **Walking to school,** Ted saw the first spring robin.

EXAMPLE **Waving her hat,** Sara flagged the train **speeding down
the track.**

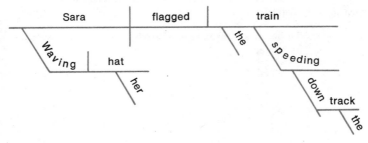

Gerunds and gerund phrases are diagramed differently.

EXAMPLE **Waiting patiently for hours** is usually a sure means of
observing wild animals. [The gerund phrase *waiting
patiently for hours* is used as the subject of the verb
is; the gerund phrase *observing wild animals* is used
as the object of the preposition *of.* The first gerund
phrase is modified by the adverb *patiently* and the
prepositional phrase *for hours.* The second gerund
phrase has a direct object, *animals.*]

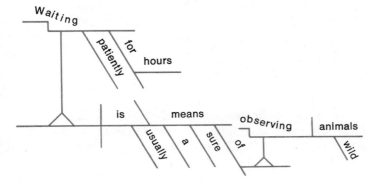

Infinitives and infinitive phrases used as modifiers are diagramed like prepositional phrases.

EXAMPLE   He plays **to win.**

Infinitives and infinitive phrases used as nouns are diagramed as follows.

EXAMPLE   **To be always on time** is often difficult.   [infinitive used as subject]

EXAMPLE   She is hoping **to see him again.**   [infinitive used as object]

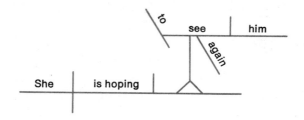

In the following sentence notice how the subject of an infinitive is diagramed, and how the infinitive itself is diagramed when the *to* is omitted.

EXAMPLE   My brother watched **me climb the tree.**

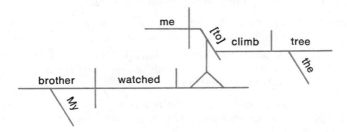

EXERCISE 16.   Diagram the following sentences.

1. Slowing down, the driver changed gears.
2. I have never liked waiting in line.
3. Carol gets good marks by concentrating on her work.
4. To pay cash is surely the best way to buy.
5. Ed saw me run away.

APPOSITIVES AND APPOSITIVE PHRASES

Nouns and pronouns, as you know, are modified by adjectives and adjective phrases. Occasionally a noun or pronoun will be followed immediately by another noun or
pronoun that identifies or explains it.

EXAMPLE   My older brother **Thomas** is twenty-one.

In this sentence the noun *Thomas* tells which brother.
The noun *Thomas* is said to be in apposition with the noun
brother. *Thomas* in this sentence is called an *appositive*.

3l. An *appositive* **is a noun or pronoun that follows
another noun or pronoun to identify or explain it.**

Like any noun or pronoun, an appositive may have adjective or adjective phrase modifiers. If it does, it is called
an *appositive phrase*.

3m. An *appositive phrase* **is made up of an appositive
and its modifiers.**

Examine the appositives and the appositive phrases in the examples below. They are in bold-face type.

EXAMPLES My aunt and uncle, **the Giovannis,** own a store, **the Empire Shoe Shop on Main Street.**

A **good all-around athlete,** Roland is a promising candidate for the decathlon, **the Olympic event that tests ten different skills.**

▶ **NOTE** Occasionally (as in the first appositive in the second example above) an appositive phrase precedes the noun or pronoun explained.

Appositives and appositive phrases are set off by commas, unless the appositive is a single word closely related to the preceding word. The comma is always used when the word to which the appositive refers is a proper noun.

EXAMPLES Dr. Blumenthal, our family doctor, is a fine woman.
Her son Bill is my best friend.
Natalie, her daughter, is another good friend.

In diagraming, place the appositive in parentheses after the word with which it is in apposition.

EXAMPLE Ed Robbins, **our newest classmate,** comes from Goshen, **a town near Middletown.**

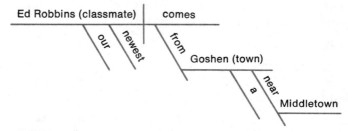

EXERCISE 17. List on your paper the appositive phrases in each of the following sentences. Underline the appositive in each phrase, and be sure you know the word to which each appositive refers.

1. My hobby, amateur botany, is lots of fun.
2. My laboratory, the patch of meadow and woods along the river, contains dozens of interesting species.

3. Mr. Jeffers, an old friend of the President's, will be our new ambassador to India.
4. Hausa, a language of the Sudan, is widely used as a trade language throughout western Africa.
5. The new sponsor, the Acme Razor Company, objected to the parts of the series in which the hero always seemed to need a shave.

REVIEW EXERCISE A. Number your paper 1–10. Identify the following words and phrases in italics by writing *p.* for participle, *g.* for gerund, *i.* for infinitive, and *ap.* for appositive.

1. Jeanne liked *to listen to music.*
2. She listened at the nearest library, *a resource center with an extensive jazz collection.*
3. The librarian, *a clarinetist,* surprised Jeanne with a generous gift.
4. *Handing a clarinet to Jeanne* took only an instant.
5. *Having located an instructor close to her home,* Jeanne soon began lessons.
6. *To learn proper phrasing,* she listened to jazz records.
7. She learned *to play her clarinet rather well.*
8. *Practicing daily,* she improved her tone.
9. *Practicing her music* eliminated minor flaws.
10. Jeanne later won a *paying* position with a local orchestra and performed in many concerts.

REVIEW EXERCISE B. The following sentences contain verbal and appositive phrases. List the phrases on your paper; there are fifteen of them. After each, tell what kind it is: participial, gerund, infinitive, or appositive. Modifiers and complements of a verbal are considered part of the phrase. You may use abbreviations.

EXAMPLE 1. To perform well, all musicians devoted to their art must study the playing of experts.
     1. *to perform well — i.*
      devoted to their art — p.
      the playing of experts — g.

1. The United States Marine Band, a group of one hundred musicians, has participated in our nation's history by playing at official functions since the early 1800's.
2. Dressed in their scarlet uniforms, the band members seem to add a special touch to any program.
3. Marching in parades or playing at the White House, the band strives to uphold its tradition of faultless performance.
4. Arriving for tea with the President, guests may find the band ready to entertain them by playing popular tunes.
5. The members of the band, all expert musicians, rehearse daily throughout the concert season.
6. Listening to the concerts is a pleasant way to relax.
7. In the early days of the Marines, the band spent much time playing in the streets to encourage enlistments.

REVIEW EXERCISE C. Copy the verbal phrases from the following sentences in order. After each, tell what kind it is: participial, gerund, or infinitive.

Driving a car is a skill learned only by much experience. Some beginners think they have learned to drive when they can start a car, steer it around the block, and stop it. Anyone above the age of five can start a car by turning a key and by pressing the accelerator. Steering a car through deserted streets is child's play. Handling an automobile, however, requires quick judgment and carefully attuned responses based on experience. Taking the car out, you face a series of emergency situations demanding quick action. You may run into a traffic jam; you will almost certainly have to make a left turn when you are facing traffic. A driver must always anticipate the actions of other drivers. Perhaps most difficult of all is estimating distance and speed when you are passing a car going in the same direction.

Chapter **4**

The Clause

Independent and Subordinate Clauses

A clause, like a phrase, is a group of related words used together as part of a sentence. Clauses, however, contain a subject and verb, whereas phrases do not.

PHRASE   We had our midterms **before spring.** [The prepositional phrase *before spring* contains neither a subject nor a verb.]

CLAUSE   We had our midterms **before spring began.** [*Spring* is the subject of the clause and *began* is the verb.]

4a. A *clause* **is a group of words that contains a verb and its subject and is used as part of a sentence.**

KINDS OF CLAUSES

All clauses have a subject and verb, but not all of them express a complete thought. Those that do are called *independent clauses*. Such clauses could be written as separate sentences. We think of them as clauses when they are joined with one or more additional clauses in a single larger sentence. Clauses that do not make complete sense by themselves are called *subordinate clauses*. Subordinate clauses function as nouns, adjectives, or adverbs just as phrases do.

Independent Clauses

4b. **An** *independent* **(or** *main***)** *clause* **expresses a complete thought and can stand by itself.**

Each of the following sentences is the same as an independent clause:

> The outfielders were missing easy fly balls.
> The infielders were throwing wildly.

To show the relationship between these two ideas, we can combine them as independent clauses in a single sentence:

> The outfielders were missing easy fly balls, **and** the infielders were throwing wildly.

Independent clauses may also be joined by the conjunctions *but, or, nor, for,* and *yet.*

> Should we go for a walk, **or** is it too hot outside?
> Gladys was not tired, **but** her tennis partner was.

Subordinate Clauses

4c. A *subordinate* (or *dependent*) *clause* **does not express a complete thought and cannot stand by itself.**

Subordinate means "lesser in rank or importance." Subordinate clauses are so called because they need an independent clause to complete their meaning.

SUBORDINATE CLAUSES
> who spoke to our class yesterday
> that many students are eligible for scholarships
> because no students have applied for them

Notice that each of these subordinate clauses has an incomplete sound when read by itself. Each one leaves you expecting more to be said. Words like *if, when, although, since,* and *because* always make the clause they introduce sound unfinished. These words signal that what follows is only part of a sentence: **if** *you are late;* **when** *I was a child.* The subordinate clauses given as examples above fit into sentences as follows:

> The woman **who spoke to our class yesterday** informed us of financial aid for college applicants.
> She said **that many students are eligible for scholarships.**

Some scholarships are still available **because no students have applied for them.**

EXERCISE 1. Number your paper 1–10. After the corresponding number, identify each italicized clause as *independent* or *subordinate*.

1. Joan, *who was an experienced baby-sitter,* was never short of cash.
2. *The king did not express his suspicions about his brother;* instead, he sent him to almost certain death in battle.
3. Mr. Dillon likes to have plenty of room *when he parks his car.*
4. *As soon as the program is over,* refreshments will be served.
5. *The children behaved perfectly* while we were watching them.
6. The people *that live there* have a pet skunk.
7. If the burglars had realized that the door was open, *they would not have broken in through the window.*
8. *Donna sang ten songs,* but the audience wanted more.
9. We guessed *that we were not very welcome.*
10. People *who belong to tenants' organizations* usually get better service from their landlords.

Complements and Modifiers in Subordinate Clauses

A subordinate clause, like an independent clause or a simple sentence, may contain complements and modifiers.

EXAMPLES   This is the book **which** the critics attacked.   [*Which* is the direct object of *attacked.*]

I did not know **who** he was.   [*Who* is a predicate nominative: He was *who.*]

Because she gave **me the letter** . . .   [*Me* is the indirect object of *gave; letter* is the direct object of *gave.*]

If you are so **sure** . . .   [*Sure* is a predicate adjective.]

While she was dancing **with me** . . .   [*With me* is an adverb phrase modifying *was dancing.*]

EXERCISE 2. Copy on your paper the italicized subordinate clauses in the following sentences. In each clause, underline the subject once and the verb twice, and identify any complements, using these abbreviations:

> *d.o.* — direct object   *p.n.* — predicate nominative
> *i.o.* — indirect object   *p.a.* — predicate adjective

If the verb has more than one word, underline each word.

EXAMPLE   1. *When she has finally given us her permission,* I will thank her.

>   *i.o.   d.o.*
> 1. *When she has finally given us her permission*

1. I'd like to know *who did this.*
2. I know *who the captain was,* but I don't know *which team won the game.*
3. He is the player *whom you were watching.*
4. Is this the suit *that you wore to church?*
5. We saw a woman *who was very tall.*
6. *When you see Gary,* please give him my message.
7. She left *before I could give her the message.*
8. *Although he had called me,* I missed him.
9. Do you know *when she sent us the order?*
10. *If you can possibly spare a dollar,* give it to him.

EXERCISE 3.   Write ten sentences containing subordinate clauses. Underline the clauses and, using the abbreviations in Exercise 2, name the complements in each.

THE USES OF SUBORDINATE CLAUSES

Subordinate clauses fulfill the same function in sentences as adjectives, adverbs, and nouns. Subordinate clauses are named according to the job they do in sentences.

The Adjective Clause

4d.   An *adjective clause* is a subordinate clause used as an adjective to modify a noun or pronoun.

EXAMPLES   The novel **that I borrowed from the library** is about the Irish revolt of 1798.

Our town's civic center, **which was renovated last year,** has just been declared a landmark.

An adjective clause always follows the noun or pronoun it modifies. It is sometimes set off by commas and sometimes not. If the clause is *needed* to identify the word modified, no commas are used. Thus in the first example, the adjective clause is not set off because it is needed to identify *which* novel the sentence is about. If the clause merely adds information that is *not essential,* as in the second example, commas are used. (See pages 403–05.)

Relative Pronouns

Adjective clauses are usually introduced by the pronouns *who, whom, whose, which,* and *that.* These pronouns are called *relative pronouns* because they relate the adjective clause to the word the clause modifies (the antecedent of the relative pronoun). In addition to referring to the word the clause modifies, the relative pronoun has a job to do within the adjective clause.

EXAMPLES   Sarah Boone was the woman **who invented the iron-
ing board.** [The relative pronoun *who* relates the adjective clause to *woman.* It also functions as the subject of the adjective clause.]

Ellen is one of the people **whom I invited.** [*Whom* relates the adjective clause to *people;* it also functions as the direct object of the clause: *I invited whom.*]

The answer **for which you have been searching** is obvious. [*Which* relates the clause to *answer;* it functions as the object of the preposition *for* within the adjective clause.]

The boys apologized to the man **whose window they had broken.** [*Whose* relates the clause to *man.* Within the adjective clause it functions as a modifier of *window.*]

In some cases the relative pronoun is omitted. The pronoun is understood and still is thought of as having a function in the clause.

EXAMPLES   Mrs. Sato is the senator [**that**] **I meant.**   [The relative pronoun — *that* or *whom* — is understood. The pronoun relates the adjective clause to *senator* and functions as the direct object of the adjective clause.]

Is this the coat [**that**] **you talked about?**   [The relative pronoun *that* or *which* is understood.]

In addition to relative pronouns, adverbs are sometimes used to introduce adjective clauses.

EXAMPLES   There are times **when Mrs. Willard loses her temper.**

This is the place **where I found it.**

EXERCISE 4. Each of the following sentences contains at least one adjective clause. Copy the adjective clauses. Underline the subject of each clause once and the verb twice, and circle the relative pronoun that introduces the clause. After the clause, write the word it modifies.

EXAMPLE   1. The topic that Melissa chose for her paper was a difficult one.

1. (*that*) *Melissa chose for her paper* — *topic*

1. A speech community is a group of people who speak the same language.

2. There are speech communities that consist of millions of people and some that contain only a few hundred.

3. The language that we use during our childhood is called our native language.

4. A person who has mastered a second language is bilingual.

5. People who conduct business internationally should know more than one language.

6. English, French, and Spanish, which many diplomats can speak, are among the five official languages of the United Nations in New York.

7. Russian and Chinese are the other two languages that are used officially at the UN.

8. People for whom language study is important include telephone operators, hotel managers, and police officers.

9. Tourists who travel to other countries need to know a language that is understood in different parts of the world.

10. French, for example, is a language which is spoken in Europe, Africa, and Southeast Asia.

Diagraming Adjective Clauses

An adjective clause beginning with a relative pronoun is joined to the noun it modifies by a broken line. This line runs from the modified word to the relative pronoun.

EXAMPLE   The coat **that I wanted** was too expensive.

EXAMPLE   The box **that contained the treasure** was missing.

EXAMPLE   She is the woman **from whom we bought the used car.**

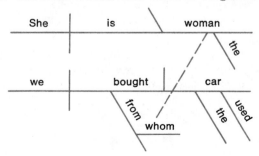

The Adverb Clause

4e. An *adverb clause* **is a subordinate clause that modifies a verb, an adjective, or an adverb.**

Like adverbs, adverbial clauses modify words by telling *how, when, where,* or *under what conditions.*

EXAMPLES   **Kim** looks **as if she had heard the good news.** [*As if she had heard the good news* tells *how* she looks.]
Before we left, we turned off the lights. [*Before we left* tells *when* we turned off the lights.]
Wherever you go, you will find other tourists. [*Wherever you go* tells *where* you will find other tourists.]
If we win, we will be in first place. [*If we win* tells *under what condition* we will be in first place.]

The Subordinating Conjunction

Adverb clauses are introduced by subordinating conjunctions. As its name suggests, a subordinating conjunction makes its clause a subordinate part of the sentence — a part that cannot stand alone. Unlike relative pronouns, which introduce adjective clauses, subordinating conjunctions do not serve a function within the clause they introduce.

Common Subordinating Conjunctions

after	before	unless
although	if	until
as	in order that	when
as if	since	whenever
as long as	so that	where
as soon as	than	wherever
because	though	while

► **NOTE** Many of the words in this list can be used as other parts of speech. For instance *after, as, before, since,* and *until* can also be used as prepositions.

Diagraming Adverb Clauses

An adverb clause is written on a horizontal line below the

independent clause and is joined to it by a broken line connecting the verb of the adverb clause to that word in the independent clause (usually the verb) which the clause modifies. On the broken line, write the subordinating conjunction which introduces the subordinate clause.

EXAMPLE **Before a hurricane strikes,** ample warning is given.

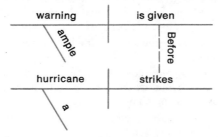

EXERCISE 5. Copy the adverb clause from each of the following sentences. Circle the subordinating conjunction in each clause.

1. Naomi worked on the car while I painted the garage.
2. The car looked as if it really needed polish.
3. Wherever you looked, you saw rust on the chrome.
4. Naomi brought some rags so that she could wash the windows.
5. Naomi put the polish down where she could reach it easily.
6. When you want to do a good job, you should take your time.
7. After she had polished the car, it sparkled in the sun.
8. She vacuumed the upholstery because it was dusty.
9. As soon as the job was finished, Dad gave her some money.
10. Naomi acted as though she were reluctant to accept it.

EXERCISE 6. Write ten sentences, using in each a different one of the subordinating conjunctions in the list already given on page 88. After each, state whether the clause tells *how, when, where, why,* or *under what conditions.*

REVIEW EXERCISE A. List on your paper the subordinate clauses in the following sentences. After each clause, state whether it is an adjective clause or an adverb clause.

1. In 1978, aeronauts Ben Abruzzo, Max Anderson, and Larry Newman, whose home was Albuquerque, New Mexico, became the first to pilot a balloon across the Atlantic Ocean.
2. Although Abruzzo and Anderson had been forced to land in the ocean near Iceland on their 1977 attempt in *Double Eagle,* they had not been discouraged by this failure.
3. They acquired a new balloon, which they named *Double Eagle II,* and since experience had shown the need for another crew member, they took Newman with them.
4. A balloon rises because it is filled with helium, which is a lightweight gas.
5. If a balloon loses altitude, the crew moves it upward by discarding ballast, and when it gains too much altitude, they lower it by releasing some of the gas.
6. Aeronauts must know meteorology so that they can take advantage of favorable winds.
7. As the pilots were eager to point out, *Double Eagle II* was flown across the Atlantic; it did not just drift across.
8. The gondola, which was shaped like a boat, had an open cockpit that measured only six by eight feet.
9. On its journey from Maine to France, *Double Eagle II* was airborne for 137 hours, which is a little less than six days.
10. As the balloon landed in France, the crew was cheered.

The Noun Clause

4f. A *noun clause* is a subordinate clause used as a noun.

Compare the two sentences in each pair below. Notice that in the second sentence in each pair, a *subordinate clause takes the place of a noun in the first sentence.* Tell whether the clause in each of these sentences is used as the subject, object, or predicate nominative.

She believes **the saying.**
She believes **that hard work means success.**

His illness was Todd's excuse.
That he was ill was Todd's excuse.

Books have been written about **Callas' singing.**
Books have been written about **how Callas sang.**

I do not remember **the assignment.**
I do not remember **what the assignment was.**
We knew **the author** of the book.
We knew **who the author was.**

Noun clauses are usually introduced by such connectives as *that, whether, what, who, whoever, whose, where, why,* etc. Sometimes the introductory word does not have any function in the clause.

EXAMPLE   I know that $\overset{\text{S}}{\text{he}}$ $\overset{\text{V}}{\text{will}}$ $\overset{\text{DO}}{\text{find them.}}$ [The connecting word *that* plays no part in the clause.]

At other times, the introductory word does function in the clause.

EXAMPLE   I know $\overset{\text{DO}}{\text{what}}$ $\overset{\text{S}}{\text{they}}$ $\overset{\text{V}}{\text{want.}}$

Like adjective clauses, noun clauses are sometimes used without the usual introductory word. Compare the noun clauses in the following paired sentences.

The teacher said **that the class could leave.**
The teacher said **the class could leave.**   [The conjunction *that* is understood.]

EXERCISE 7.   There are ten noun clauses in the following sentences. Copy them on your paper. Label the subject and the verb of each noun clause. After each clause, tell whether it is the subject of the sentence, the direct object, the indirect object, the predicate nominative, or the object of a preposition. You may abbreviate.

1. Bob knows who broke the window.
2. No one can say whether he will tell.
3. That is what the teacher wants.
4. The teacher told Bob she had asked the rest of us.
5. How the window was broken is a mystery to us.
6. We told the teacher we did not know anything.
7. Whoever broke it should admit the fact.
8. The reason is that its repair will cost money.
9. The bill should be paid by whoever broke the window.

10. The teacher will not give whoever confesses any further punishment.

Diagraming Noun Clauses

A clause used as subject, object, predicate nominative, or object of a preposition is supported by an upright line resting on the line of the subject, object, predicate nominative, or object of a preposition.

NOUN CLAUSE AS SUBJECT **What she said** convinced me.

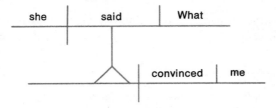

NOUN CLAUSE AS OBJECT We know **that you won the prize.** [*That* introduces the clause but plays no part in it.]

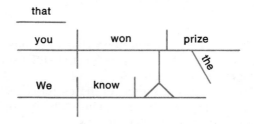

EXERCISE 8. Diagram the sentences in Exercise 7.

REVIEW EXERCISE B. Here are ten sentences containing all three kinds of subordinate clauses: adjective, adverb, and noun. Copy each clause on your paper. Label the verb and the subject in the clause, and name the kind of clause.

1. When the West was young, travelers often had difficulty finding accommodations for the night.

2. Experienced travelers, who realized they would frequently have to camp out, brought tents along on their journeys.

3. After stagecoach routes were opened, crude inns were built along the trails.

4. These early inns were what we would call a combination store, tavern, and farmhouse.

5. Spending the night in a sod-house inn was an irritating experience for those who were used to more comfortable surroundings.

6. When the wind blew, the dirt from the sod would fall on the sleepers.

7. Another complaint about the inns was that the food was poor.

8. The presence of fleas, mice, and other vermin was another discomfort that annoyed the early travelers.

9. Because the partition walls of some early Western hotels were made of calico, fire was a great danger.

10. On the ground floors of many railroad hotels were found dance palaces that resounded with the noisy revelry of cowhands.

SENTENCES CLASSIFIED BY STRUCTURE

4g. When classified according to structure, there are four kinds of sentences *— simple, compound, complex, compound-complex.*

(1) A *simple sentence* **is a sentence with one independent clause and no subordinate clause.**

EXAMPLE   Cats are independent animals.

Although we often think of simple sentences as short, this is not necessarily so.

EXAMPLE   On his way home from the game, Jake stopped for a
$\overset{\text{s}}{}\quad\overset{\text{v}}{}$
hamburger at the diner with the rest of the team. [Notice that there are plenty of phrases but only one subject and one verb.]

(2) A *compound sentence* **is a sentence composed of two or more independent clauses but no subordinate clauses.**

EXAMPLES
$\overset{\text{S}}{\text{I}} \overset{\text{V}}{\text{bought}}$ the blouse, but the $\overset{\text{S}}{\text{brooch}}$ $\overset{\text{V}}{\text{was given}}$ to me. [two independent clauses]

The $\overset{\text{S}}{\text{plants}}$ $\overset{\text{V}}{\text{are}}$ not large, but $\overset{\text{S}}{\text{they}}$ $\overset{\text{V}}{\text{are}}$ healthy, and $\overset{\text{S}}{\text{they}}$ $\overset{\text{V}}{\text{bloom}}$ regularly.   [three independent clauses]

Other words used to join the clauses of a compound sentence are *consequently, therefore, nevertheless, however, moreover, otherwise,* etc. These are called conjunctive adverbs. When a word of this kind is used between two independent clauses, it is preceded by a semicolon.

Each independent clause in a compound sentence is diagramed like a separate sentence. A broken line joins the clauses. The line is drawn between the verbs of the two clauses, and the conjunction is written on a solid horizontal line connecting the two parts of the broken line.

EXAMPLE   I bought the blouse, but the brooch was given to me.

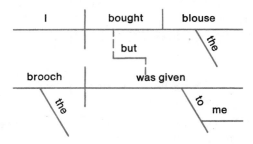

Caution: Do not confuse the compound predicate of a simple sentence with the two subjects and two predicates of a compound sentence.

EXAMPLES
$\overset{\text{S}}{\text{She}}$ $\overset{\text{V}}{\text{turned}}$ on the television and $\overset{\text{V}}{\text{watched}}$ a baseball game.   [simple sentence with a compound predicate]

$\overset{\text{S}}{\text{She}}$ $\overset{\text{V}}{\text{turned}}$ on the television, and $\overset{\text{S}}{\text{she}}$ $\overset{\text{V}}{\text{watched}}$ a baseball game.   [compound sentence with two independent clauses]

(3) A *complex sentence* is a sentence containing one independent clause and at least one subordinate clause.

EXAMPLE When we reached the pier, the boat had docked.

Since you have already learned how to diagram a sentence containing a subordinate clause (adjective, adverb, and noun clause), you know how to diagram a complex sentence.

(4) A *compound-complex sentence* contains two or more independent clauses and at least one subordinate clause.

EXAMPLE The room that Carrie painted had been white, but she changed the color. [two independent clauses and one subordinate clause]

In diagraming a compound-complex sentence, first diagram the independent clauses. Then attach the subordinate clauses to the words they modify. Give yourself plenty of room.

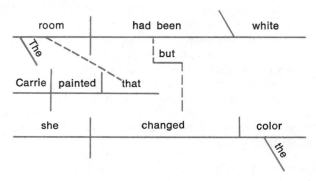

EXERCISE 9. Write and label two simple sentences, two compound sentences, two complex sentences, and two compound-complex sentences.

EXERCISE 10. Number your paper 1–10. After the proper number, write what kind of sentence each of the following is: simple, compound, complex, compound-complex.

1. Americans, who are familiar with natural disasters like hurricanes, tornadoes, and floods, learned about a less common kind when a volcano in southwest Washington erupted.

2. On May 18, 1980, Mount St. Helens, a volcanic mountain in the Cascade Range, literally blew its top.

3. When the volcano could no longer contain the enormous pressure of molten rock, steam, and gas that had been building inside it, the top blew off in a great explosion.

4. The explosion was equivalent to the force of five hundred atom bombs of the type that was dropped on Hiroshima.

5. The explosion removed fifteen hundred feet of rock from the top of the ten-thousand-foot mountain, and it left a crater two and one-half miles in diameter and one mile deep.

6. The outflow of superheated mud melted two glaciers and produced a wall of debris that roared down the mountain at thirty miles an hour.

7. The temperature of water in nearby rivers rose from fifty to nearly ninety degrees.

8. The most costly damage occurred in the region around the mountain, but cities in three states to the east were crippled by a fallout of gray ash.

9. For two months before exploding, the mountain had been rumbling ominously, and scientists, who had placed instruments on its slopes to monitor the activity inside, knew the eruption was coming.

10. The area around the volcano, which had been popular for fishing and recreation, was officially closed to the public weeks before the eruption, and many of its permanent residents were evacuated.

EXERCISE 11. What kind of sentence is each of the following? Be prepared to explain your answer.

1. After the supplies are delivered, we will decorate the gym.
2. We know that the art department has worked very hard, and we appreciate their efforts.
3. Place the chairs wherever you wish.
4. If we start early, we can finish before noon.
5. Arrange the flowers artistically.
6. Have you made the arrangements for the tickets?
7. Somebody must stand at the door and collect the tickets.
8. This dance should be a success, because we have already sold several hundred tickets.

9. We have elected a king and queen for the dance, and they will lead the Grand March.

10. The clean-up committee will report tomorrow at noon.

EXERCISE 12. Diagram the sentences in Exercise 11.

REVIEW EXERCISE C. Number your paper 1–25. After the proper number, identify each of the italicized word groups by means of the following abbreviations: *prep. ph.* (prepositional phrase); *part. ph.* (participial phrase); *inf. ph.* (infinitive phrase); *adj. cl.* (adjective clause); *adv. cl.* (adverb clause); *n. cl.* (noun clause).

Today few people doubt (1) *that women are as capable as men.* One of the few fields (2) *in which women have not been equally represented* is space travel. Dr. W. Randolph Lovelace began screening candidates (3) *for the space program.* He wanted (4) *to test the suitability* of women. He selected twenty-four (5) *of America's most prestigious women pilots.* Fourteen agreed (6) *that they would undergo the tests.*

The first candidate (7) *reporting for the rigorous exams* was Jerrie Cobb. Cobb began flying (8) *when she was twelve years old.* (9) *By the time she began the Lovelace tests,* she had logged 10,000 hours in the air in all types of aircraft. (10) *Having achieved one world record for distance flying,* eventually Cobb would gain two others for speed and altitude.

One test (11) *that she underwent* was called "Isolation Run." It tested (12) *how long a person could stand being alone.* (13) *To achieve profound sensory deprivation,* Cobb was lowered into an eight-foot tank of water. The water was heated to exact body temperature (14) *so that she could feel absolutely no sensation.* The tank, (15) *which was both soundproof and lightproof,* further guarded against sensory stimulation. Cotton wads (16) *smeared with petroleum jelly* were placed in her ears. She was pulled (17) *from the tank* after ten hours. Her tolerance was judged (18) *to be astounding.*

Cobb's ability (19) *to make a crash landing* also was tested. She was strapped into a mock-up of an airplane cockpit (20) *which was mounted above a pool.* (21) *Released from the restraining chute,* the mock-up drove into the water and turned over. Cobb had to escape from the mock-up (22) *while she was upside down* under sixteen feet of water. She was judged physically and psychologically fit (23) *for space travel.*

(24) *What the results showed* about women's durability convinced Lovelace of their suitability as astronauts. Although she did not make the trip into outer space, Jerrie Cobb continued her career as a pilot, flying doctors, anthropologists, missionaries, and medical supplies to South American Indian tribes (25) *who otherwise would be isolated.*

Usage

PART TWO

Chapter 5

Kinds of Usage

What Is Usage?

You have had enough experience in using English and in hearing others use English to know that there are differences in the way people use the language. There are differences in pronunciation, in word choice, in grammar. Your own usage, your own particular way of using English, has been determined by the usage of the people among whom you have lived. You pronounce words as your parents and friends pronounce them. Your vocabulary reflects to some extent the vocabularies of those around you. Your grammar is their grammar. The language habits you have acquired, while they may be different from the habits acquired by others, are perfectly natural habits, acceptable to those from whom you learned them.

Nevertheless, you probably weren't very old when you discovered that for some reason your parents began to object to some of the language habits you were forming, and your teachers began to "correct" your English. Even now you may be wondering why you should have to break old language habits and adopt new ones taught in school. What difference does it make, for example, whether you say, "Kim and me was lucky" or "Kim and I were lucky"? Anyone can understand the first sentence as well as the second. The meaning is clear. Yet you know that in most situations, "Kim and me was" would be considered incorrect usage.

STANDARD AND NONSTANDARD ENGLISH

The truth is that there does exist a kind of English, perhaps somewhat different from your own, that you should learn for your own good. This kind of English is called *standard English*. Standard English is a term used to describe conventions of usage most widely recognized as acceptable. Radio and television announcers and newscasters, newspaper and magazine writers, business and professional people use standard English. No matter how unfair or snobbish it may seem, people sometimes judge a person's competence by the kind of English the person uses. Your school teaches you standard English to prevent your ever being misjudged by your English usage.

The English of those who do not make the same choices as do the speakers of standard English is called *nonstandard English*. Choosing "Kim and me was" instead of "Kim and I were" is using nonstandard usage; other examples are choosing "ain't" for "isn't" and "have went" for "have gone." The rules and exercises in the usage chapters of this book are concerned with teaching standard English. It is well to remember, however, that nonstandard English is the language of millions of Americans. You can learn standard usage without setting yourself off from those who do not use it.

Two Kinds of Standard English

We often speak of English as though it has always been the same. The English of 1100, however, was very different from the English of the 1980's. The language spoken in the British Isles is different from the English spoken in your community. Just as time and geography make for differences in language, so does the situation in which language is used. We use one kind of language on the athletic field and another in our place or worship; one kind in a friendly letter, another in a formal report.

There are many other situations, each of which calls for

an appropriate kind of language. We can't name all of the different kinds, but we can distinguish two general types of standard English: *formal* and *informal.*

Formal English is the language of serious and solemn occasions. A President's inaugural address, a court decision, a scholarly book or article, and the kind of formal report that has footnotes and a bibliography are situations in which formal English is likely to be used. In these situations an audience will naturally expect the speaker or writer to avoid slang or other informal aspects of language.

Informal English, on the other hand, is the everyday language most of us use. Because it is used in a wide variety of situations, informal English has many gradations. When it appears in books and magazines, it is often close to formal English; when it appears in friendly conversations and letters, it may contain some slang. The examples below will give you a better idea of the differences between formal and informal English and between different levels of informal English.

In the example of formal writing that follows, the scholar and philosopher Susan Sontag discusses photography as an art form.

> Like other steadily aggrandizing enterprises, photography has inspired its leading practitioners with a need to explain, again and again, what they are doing and why it is valuable. The era in which photography was widely attacked (as parricidal with respect to painting, predatory with respect to people) was a brief one. Painting of course did not expire in 1839, as one French painter hastily predicted; the finicky soon ceased to dismiss photography as menial copying; and by 1854 a great painter, Delacroix, graciously declared how much he regretted that such an admirable invention came so late. Nothing is more acceptable today than the photographic recycling of reality, acceptable as an everyday activity and as a branch of high art. Yet something about photography still keeps the first-rate professionals defensive and hortatory: virtually every important photographer right up to the present has written manifestoes and credos expounding photography's moral and aesthetic mission. And photographers give the most contradictory ac-

counts of what kind of knowledge they possess and what kind of art they practice.[1]

If you read part of this passage aloud, you will notice that the sentences have a formal sound that is quite different from ordinary conversation. More than anything else, it is the structure of the sentences that gives us this impression. Such carefully organized sentences as the first one in the passage are usually born on paper, even though they may be spoken later from a platform or pulpit. Formal English is chiefly written English. Its sentences are likely to be longer than those of informal English, and one idea is often balanced against another. The vocabulary is formal, too; words like *aggrandizing, parricidal, menial,* and *hortatory* may appear in speech, but they appear much more often in writing. Formal English rarely admits slang and makes little use of contractions. Like the structure of the sentences, all these features suggest a calm and unhurried comment on a subject.

The following is an example of informal writing:

> Don't call an exterminator if your home is plagued with termites. Call Carol Miller; then put on the frying pan.
>
> Mrs. Miller, a home economics major at California State Polytechnic University in San Luis Obispo, says termites top the list, at least from the standpoint of taste, of all the bugs she eats.
>
> "I have a great termite pilaf recipe," she said. "And if you use wild rice, you can't tell the termites from the shafts of rice."
>
> Mrs. Miller and her husband, Dennis, a soil scientist, regularly eat insects. She lunches on grasshoppers, termites, bees, crickets, and beetles almost daily.
>
> She believes eating insects may be at least a partial answer to the problems of malnutrition and starvation throughout the world. She plans to do graduate work in entomophagy — insect eating — a virtually unknown field.

---

[1] Selection from page 119 in *On Photography* by Susan Sontag. Copyright © 1973, 1974, 1977 by Susan Sontag. Reprinted by permission of Farrar, Straus and Giroux, Inc., and Penguin Books Ltd. Published in Great Britain by Allen Lane, 1978.

"The fact is, bugs are good eating and rich in protein. Whereas beef has 15 percent to 20 percent protein and chicken has 20 percent, termites, for example, have 40 percent protein and grasshoppers have 60 percent."

In addition to her termite pilaf, Mrs. Miller also makes bee won ton and uses bees as croutons in salads. Another favorite is Jiminy—as in cricket—bread, made with grasshoppers. She uses insects in soups and stews and bakes grasshopper and termite cookies.[1]

There are almost no words in this piece of writing that suggest the formal vocabulary. The word *entomophagy* may be an exception, but it is used for humorous effect. Salted throughout the selection are informal, conversational expressions such as *plagued with, put on the frying pan,* and *top the list.* To make the writing chatty and informal, the author addresses the reader directly in the first paragraph and later quotes Mrs. Miller.

Good formal writing always sounds as though it has been carefully written and edited; good informal prose usually has been carefully written and edited, but it tries not to sound like it. In its attempt to sound like good conversation, it sticks much closer to the vocabulary and rhythms of speech, making use of contractions, slang, and everyday expressions.

EXERCISE. Decide whether each of the following passages is standard or nonstandard English, and label it accordingly on your paper. If the passage is standard, indicate whether it is formal or informal standard English. If it is nonstandard English, be able to show what words or expressions make it so.

1. About the time we was getting set to start filming, that old lion let out a roar you could a heard the other side of the mountain. Seems he was trying to tell us something. Everybody stopped what they was doing and just stared at him.
2. For the life of me, I will never understand people. Sheila and I

---

[1] "There's a Termite in My Soup!" (May 25, 1976). Reprinted by permission of the Associated Press.

are canvassing the neighborhood for votes, but incredible as it seems, most people don't even have an opinion. You would think people would be eager to make choices that will affect their own futures. The issues are important and worthy of interest. But instead of interest, we're finding apathy. How can a democracy work if people don't care enough to make it work?

3. To have that sense of one's intrinsic worth which constitutes self-respect is potentially to have everything: the ability to discriminate, to love, and to remain indifferent. To lack it is to be locked within oneself, paradoxically incapable of either love or indifference. If we do not respect ourselves, we are on the one hand forced to despise those who have so few resources as to consort with us, so little perception as to remain blind to our fatal weaknesses. On the other, we are peculiarly in thrall to everyone we see, curiously determined to live out—since our self-image is so untenable—their false notions of us.[1]

4. When the courthouse burned, me and Percy got invited to ride over with our neighbors and wait for the roof to fall in. And guess who come in sight with the fellows bringing things out, the water cooler and such as that. My own Daddy! I hadn't seen him in five years, and then he was too busy to wave back.[2]

Despite the differences within standard English, formal and informal English usually make certain choices that distinguish them from nonstandard English. These choices are the ones that are discussed in the next five chapters. Occasionally, in an exercise, you will be asked to make a choice between forms that are different in formal and informal English. When this occurs, you are to select the formal way. This is done to give you needed practice in using formal English, not because you are expected always to be formal.

---

[1] Extract from "On Self-Respect" from *Slouching Towards Bethlehem* by Joan Didion. Copyright © 1961, 1968 by Joan Didion. Reprinted by permission of Farrar, Straus and Giroux, Inc., and William Morris Agency, Inc. on behalf of Joan Didion.

[2] Excerpt from *Losing Battles* by Eudora Welty. Copyright © 1970 by Eudora Welty. Reprinted by permission of Random House, Inc.

Chapter 6

Correct Agreement

Subject and Verb, Pronoun and Antecedent

Agreement, as it is used here, refers to the fact that certain closely related words in sentences have matching forms. Subjects are closely related to their verbs, and a careful speaker makes them agree with each other by matching verb forms to subject forms. In the same way pronouns and their antecedents are closely related and must be made to agree with each other by matching forms. When such words are correctly matched, we say that they *agree.* When they fail to match, we say there is an error in *agreement.*

SINGULAR AND PLURAL NUMBER

6a. When a word refers to one person or thing, it is *singular* **in number. When a word refers to more than one, it is** *plural* **in number.**

The bold-faced words below agree in number.

EXAMPLES   **One** of the boys **has** not cast **his** vote.   [singular]
Many of the boys **have** not cast **their** votes.   [plural]

Nouns and pronouns have number. The following nouns and pronouns are singular because they name only one person or thing: *building, woman, it, poem.* The following are plural because they name more than one person or thing: *buildings, women, they, poems.*[1]

EXERCISE 1. List the following words on your paper. After each plural word, write *P* for plural; after each singular word, write *S* for singular.

1. books	6. mouse	11. measles
2. one	7. many	12. love
3. several	8. civics	13. both
4. lights	9. ability	14. alumni
5. people	10. area	15. woman

AGREEMENT OF SUBJECT AND VERB

Verbs, too, have number; certain forms are used when a verb's subject is singular and others when the subject is plural. In standard English, verbs agree with their subjects.

6b. A verb agrees with its subject in number.

(1) Singular subjects take singular verbs.

EXAMPLE   Pia **sells** insurance, but Wendy **does** not. [The singular verb *sells* agrees with the singular subject *Pia;* the singular verb *does* agrees with the singular subject *Wendy.*]

(2) Plural subjects take plural verbs.

EXAMPLE   Pia and Wendy **sell** insurance, but the other women **do** not. [The plural verb *sell* agrees with the plural subject *Pia and Wendy,* and the plural verb *do* agrees with the plural subject *women.*]

In general, nouns ending in *s* are plural (*boys, girls, friends, stores*) but verbs ending in *s* are singular (*plays, eats, is, was, has*). Singular *I* and *you,* however, generally take verbs which do not end in *s* (*I go, you go, I am, you are*).

---

[1] For rules regarding the formulation of plurals of nouns, see pages 533–36.

► NOTE   The form *were* is normally plural except when used with the singular *you* and in sentences like the following:

> If I **were** in charge, I would make some changes.
> **Were** Johnny here now, he would protest.

EXERCISE 2. Decide which one of the verbs in parentheses should be used to agree with the subject given.

1. student (walks, walk)
2. one (is, are)
3. several (runs, run)
4. it (works, work)
5. Joan (was, were)
6. Carol (sings, sing)
7. many (looks, look)
8. two (was, were)
9. people (plays, play)
10. Ed and Rita (writes, write)
11. dogs (barks, bark)
12. the result (is, are)
13. both (believes, believe)
14. crews (sails, sail)
15. women (seems, seem)
16. a person (thinks, think)
17. oxen (drags, drag)
18. Fran and Tom (goes, go)
19. the books (lies, lie)
20. all men (buys, buy)

6c. The number of the subject is not changed by a phrase following the subject.

Do not be confused when a phrase comes between the subject and the verb. Since the subject is never a part of a phrase, a word in a phrase cannot influence the verb.

EXAMPLES   **One** of the girls **is going.** [The phrase *of the girls* does not affect the number of the subject *one: one is,* not *girls are.*]

One	is going

Both **girls** in the family **are** in the chorus. [The phrase *in the family* does not affect the number of the subject *girls: girls are,* not *family is.*]

girls	are

Even prepositional phrases beginning with expressions

like *with, together with, in addition to, as well as,* and *along with* do not affect the number of the verb.

EXAMPLES Miss Walsh, with her two sisters, **has** gone to visit friends. [Miss Walsh . . . has]

The star, as well as the producer and the director, **was** a little nervous on opening night. [The star . . . was]

Lou's backhand, in addition to his strong serve, **makes** him an excellent tennis player. [Lou's backhand . . . makes]

The logic of this will be clearer to you if you rearrange the first sentence about Miss Walsh:

EXAMPLE Miss Walsh **has** gone with her two sisters to visit friends.

Another source of trouble is the negative construction. When such a construction comes between the subject and its verb, it is often mistakenly allowed to affect the number of the verb and so to throw it out of agreement with its proper subject. Treat negative constructions exactly like phrases following the subject.

EXAMPLE Jim, not José and his friend, **is** coming with me.

EXERCISE 3. In each of the following sentences, you have a choice of verbs. Write the subject of each verb on your paper. Select the one of the two verbs in parentheses which agrees in number with the subject. Remember that the verb and subject must agree in number.

1. Two of these cassettes (is, are) mine.
2. A large pile of broken bricks and stones (was, were) left outside of town.
3. Carelessness in the use of simple tools (causes, cause) many household accidents.
4. An exhibit of student drawings and photographs (is, are) on display in the main hall.
5. The buildings along the waterfront (seems, seem) to be unoccupied.

6. Judy, along with Steve, Ricardo, and Natalie, (has, have) decided to become a teacher.
7. The sound of the violins (was, were) pleasing.
8. The fancy basket of apples (was, were) a gift.
9. The plans of the troop (was, were) kept secret.
10. Deputies from the sheriff's office (was, were) rerouting all traffic.
11. A letter from Ned's relatives (explains, explain) the easiest route to take.
12. The coach's remarks concerning Gina (was, were) most flattering.
13. The price of the albums (was, were) too high.
14. This picture of us (was, were) taken many years ago.
15. The opinions of the critics, not the acclaim of the audience, often (determines, determine) the success of a play.
16. The players on our team (looks, look) tired.
17. The fire lit by the shipwrecked sailors (was, were) seen by one of the search vessels.
18. The loss of the last two track meets (leaves, leave) us in last place.
19. In bobsledding, perfect rhythm on the turns, in addition to a certain disregard of danger, (is, are) necessary to win.
20. Participation in class discussions, not just high test scores, (counts, count) toward one's final grade.

6d. The following pronouns are singular: *each, either, neither, one, everyone, everybody, no one, nobody, anyone, anybody, someone, somebody.*

These words are called indefinite pronouns because they refer only generally, indefinitely, to some thing or person. Very often they are followed by a prepositional phrase containing a plural word. When this situation occurs, be sure to make the verb agree with the indefinite pronoun, not with a word in the prepositional phrase.

NONSTANDARD	One of the uniforms were green. [The verb *were* does not agree with the singular subject, *one*.]
STANDARD	One of the uniforms **was** green. [The verb agrees with the subject.]

Read the following pairs of sentences aloud, stressing the subjects and verbs in bold-faced type.

EXAMPLES **Neither is** running.
Neither of the trains **is** running.
Each was working on a project.
Each of the students **was** working on a project.
One was silver.
One of the rings **was** silver.
Everybody takes English.
Everybody in both classes **takes** English.
Everyone plans to attend the game.
Every one of the girls **plans** to attend the game.

6e. The following pronouns are plural: *several, few, both, many.*

EXAMPLES **Several** of the girls **are** discouraged.
Few in the audience **were** aware of the danger.
Both have tried harder.
Many of the tourists **stop** here and **rest.**

6f. The pronouns *some, all, any, most,* **and** *none,* **may be either singular or plural, depending on the meaning of the sentence.**

A writer may use either a singular or a plural verb to agree with the words *some, all, any, most,* and *none,* depending upon the meaning of the sentence. These words are plural if they refer to a plural word; they are singular if they refer to a singular word.

SINGULAR **Some** of the cargo **was** lost.   [*Some* refers to *cargo,* which is a singular word.]
PLURAL **Some** of the books **were** damaged.   [*Some* refers to *books,* which is a plural word.]
SINGULAR **Has any** of the paint been delivered?   [*Any* refers to *paint,* which is a singular word.]
PLURAL **Have any** of the guests arrived?   [*Any* refers to *guests,* which is a plural word.]
SINGULAR **All** of the cake **has** been eaten.   [*All* refers to *cake,* which is singular.]

PLURAL   **All** of the bicycles **have** been rented. [*All* refers to *bicycles,* which is plural.]

In each of the examples above, the prepositional phrase following the subject provides a clue to the number of the subject. You may think of this as an exception to rule **6c.** These pronouns can also be used without a prepositional phrase after them:

EXAMPLES   Some was lost.   [an amount of money, time, cargo, etc.]
Some were damaged.   [a number of books, cars, houses, etc.]

EXERCISE 4. *Oral Drill.* Repeat each of the following sentences aloud three times, stressing the italicized words.

1. *One* of these pens *is* mine.
2. Every *one* of them *writes* well.
3. *Neither* of the girls *has* a new calculator.
4. *Some* of the tomatoes *are* green.
5. Not *one* of the stories *appeals* to me.
6. *One* of us *is* sure to win.
7. *Neither* of the topics *was* interesting.
8. *Either* of the books *is* acceptable.
9. *Several* of the trees *were* affected by a blight.
10. *Every* player on the team *trains* diligently.

EXERCISE 5. Rewrite each of the following twenty sentences according to the directions in parentheses. If necessary, change the number of the verb to agree with the new subject or to accord with the altered sense of the sentence.

1. Each of the flowers is beautiful. (Change *each* to *some.*)
2. Some of the grain was shipped. (Change *grain* to *tractors.*)
3. Both of the girls were fifteen. (Change *both* to *neither.*)
4. All of the money was marked. (Change *money* to *dollar bills.*)
5. Have any of the apples been harvested? (Change *apples* to *wheat.*)
6. Somebody was here before. (Change *somebody* to *few.*)

7. Everyone is going to be there. (Change *everyone* to *most of us*.)
8. Each of the tires needs air. (Change *each* to *several*.)
9. The size of the insects was astonishing. (Change *insects* to *insect*.)
10. Have all of the tickets been punched? (Change *all* to *each*.)
11. None of the glasses were imported. (Change *glasses* to *iron ore*.)
12. Everyone eats in the cafeteria. (Change *everyone* to *nobody*.)
13. Is there enough paper to go around? (Change *paper* to *books*.)
14. Few of the elms are healthy. (Change *few* to *not one*.)
15. Both of the movies were good. (Change *both* to *one*.)
16. One of your answers is incorrect. (Change *one* to *neither*.)
17. Most of the days were sunny. (Change *days* to *day*.)
18. Either of them is able to play first base. (Change *either* to *both*.)
19. Have any of the students arrived? (Change *any* to *either*.)
20. A wagonload of hay was blocking the lane. (Change *hay* to *pine logs*.)

EXERCISE 6. Number 1–20 in a column on your paper. Read each of the sentences carefully. If the verb and subject agree, write a + after the proper number on your paper. If the verb and subject do not agree, write a 0 after the proper number.

1. Every one of the screens needs paint.
2. One of the submarines was powered by atomic energy.
3. Neither of my two brothers have been elected to the Student Council.
4. Some of the dogs in this neighborhood are poorly trained.
5. Every one of them have to report to the principal.
6. Both of the tables is lopsided.
7. Neither of them is capable of repairing the faucet.
8. Each of the cheerleaders practice after school every day.
9. One of us has to help out on Saturday.
10. Several of the missing works of art has been found in Italy.
11. All of the seats were too near the movie screen.

12. Neither of my friends bowl very well.
13. Are one of the boxes large enough?
14. Either of the assistants goes for the mail.
15. Each of the ingredients is carefully measured.
16. Some of the machines were in good condition.
17. Some of the play was rather boring.
18. Many of the termites were destroyed.
19. Not one of us were going to tell you.
20. One of Helen's letters was delivered to Henry by mistake.

The Compound Subject

6g. Most compound subjects joined by *and* take a plural verb.

EXAMPLES   Oscar and she **do** the gardening.
            Her right arm and his left leg **were** broken.

A few compound subjects joined by *and* name a single person or thing and therefore take a singular verb.

EXAMPLES   Ham and eggs **is** my favorite dish.   [one dish]
            Law and order **was** maintained by the police.   [one civil responsibility]

6h. Singular subjects joined by *or* or *nor* take a singular verb.

EXAMPLES   Neither rain nor snow **stops** the delivery of mail.
            Has either Grandmother or Grandfather arrived yet?
            Neither the record player nor the tape recorder **works** very well.

Note that the word *either* may be omitted, but the number of the subject is not changed so long as the parts are joined by *or*.

EXAMPLE   Marcia or Bill **was** going to do the cooking for their family.

Note also that this use of *either . . . or, neither . . . nor* should not be confused with that of the correlative conjunction *both . . . and,* which takes a plural verb.

EXAMPLES   Both the American Legion and the Kiwanis Club **are** planning a parade.

Neither the American Legion nor the Kiwanis Club **is** planning a parade.

6i. When a singular subject and a plural subject are joined by *or* or *nor*, the verb agrees with the nearer subject.

EXAMPLES   Neither Alan nor his sisters want to go to the pool. [sisters want]

Either the waiters or the cook is at fault. [cook . . . is]

In the first sentence *sisters* is nearer to the verb *want* than *Alan,* the other part of the compound subject. The verb must be plural to agree with the nearer subject, *sisters.* Likewise, in the second sentence the verb *is* must agree with *cook,* since this singular part of the compound subject is nearer to it. This kind of construction is often awkward, however, and it is usually best to avoid it.

EXAMPLES   Alan **doesn't** want to go to the pool, and neither **do** his sisters.

Either the waiters **are** at fault, or the cook **is.**

EXERCISE 7. *Oral Drill.* Repeat each of the following sentences aloud three times, stressing the italicized words.

1. *Each* of the boys *has* gone.
2. *Neither* Joe *nor* Ramón *is* interested.
3. A *few* of our plans *were* made.
4. *Either* Julia *or* Helen *has* your pen.
5. *One* of the books *was* lost.
6. Every *one* of his teeth *was* extracted.
7. *Both* Florence *and* Joan *are* hockey players.
8. *Several* of them *were* here yesterday.
9. *Each was* welcome.
10. Not *one* of the trucks *was* working.

EXERCISE 8. From the parentheses in the following sentences, choose the correct verb. Write the verbs in a column on your paper.

1. Neither Bob nor they (believes, believe) that story.
2. Both Stan and she (hopes, hope) to attend the game.
3. Neither the geranium nor the lilies (was, were) blooming.
4. Either the principal or the class adviser (is, are) going with us.
5. Neither the carnations nor the dahlias (has, have) been weeded.
6. Either the captains or the umpire (calls, call) time out.
7. Larry and she (was, were) editors of the yearbook.
8. My parents and yours (pays, pay) state and local taxes.
9. My club or yours (is, are) going to build a float for the parade.
10. Either a transistor or a capacitor (has, have) burned out in this receiver.
11. Both New York and San Francisco (has, have) world-famous bridges.
12. Cake or pie (is, are) a good dessert.
13. The director and the producer of the play (is, are) awaiting the verdict of the critics.
14. Either my horse or hers almost always (wins, win).
15. The news story and the feature article (differs, differ) from the editorial.
16. Neither the refrigerator nor the stove (has, have) been installed.
17. Both the mayor and her advisers (was, were) opposed to the village ordinance.
18. The worst feature of such storms (was, were) the blowing sand.
19. Marie or Eileen (has, have) been elected to the Student Council.
20. Neither fishing nor hunting (appeals, appeal) to his son.

Other Problems in Agreement

6j. Collective nouns may be either singular or plural.

You may be in doubt at times about the number of a word which names a group of persons or objects. This kind of word is known as a *collective noun.*

A collective noun is singular and takes a singular verb when the group is thought of *as a unit or whole.*

A collective noun is plural and takes a plural verb when members of the group are thought of *as individuals acting separately.* Study the following pairs of sentences.

The faculty **has** a meeting this afternoon. [*Faculty* is thought of as a unit.]

The faculty **were** giving **their** ideas on the new marking procedure. [*Faculty* is thought of as a number of individuals.]

Jo's family **has** gone to Myrtle Beach for the summer. [*Family* is a unit.]

Jo's family **have** been dividing the chores among **themselves.** [Family members are acting as individuals.]

The class **is** a very large one. [one unit]

The class **are** writing **their** compositions. [The class is thought of as individuals.]

The following is a list of some collective nouns:

jury	crowd	flock	team
herd	class	choir	committee
club	troop	group	audience
army	family	swarm	faculty

EXERCISE 9. Select five collective nouns, and write five pairs of sentences like those given above, showing clearly how the words you choose may be either singular or plural.

EXERCISE 10. Rewrite the following ten sentences according to the instructions in parentheses, changing the number of the verb if necessary.

1. Either Jill or her brothers were expected momentarily. (Reverse the order of the subjects.)
2. The choir has been arguing with the conductor. (Change *with the conductor* to *among themselves.*)
3. Neither of the contestants has left. (Change *neither* to *both.*)

4. Both Kay and Sylvia enjoy deep-sea fishing. (Change *both* ... *and* to *neither* . . . *nor*.)
5. None of the teachers were available. (Change *teachers* to *money*.)
6. Bill and Rick expect to be chosen. (Change *and* to *or*.)
7. The troop of scouts was observed marching in good order. (Change *marching in good order* to *going their separate ways*.)
8. All of his poems are here. (Change *all* to *both*.)
9. Each sophomore girl has been asked to serve on a committee. (Change *each* to *every*.)
10. Ham and eggs is a good midnight snack. (Change *and* to *or*.)

6k. A verb agrees with its subject, not with its predicate nominative.

In the examples below the subject is marked s and the predicate nominative PN.

EXAMPLES
            s   PN
The biggest **problem** in gardening **is** the **weeds.**

     s   PN
Weeds are the biggest **problem** in gardening.

     s   PN
A **requirement** for safe driving **is** good **tires.**

     s   PN
Good **tires are** a **requirement** for safe driving.

Often this kind of agreement problem can be avoided by changing the sentence so as to avoid using a predicate nominative:

EXAMPLE   Safe **driving requires** good **tires.**

6l. When the subject follows the verb, as in sentences beginning with *there* and *here,* be careful to anticipate the subject and make sure that the verb agrees with it.

NONSTANDARD   There is fourteen thousand people in my town. [not *people . . . is*]

STANDARD   There are fourteen thousand people in my town. [*people . . . are*]

EXERCISE 11. Number 1–20 in a column on your paper. Read each sentence aloud. If the verb agrees with the subject, put a + on your paper after the proper number. If the verb does not agree with the subject, write a 0. Be ready to explain the reasons for your choice.

1. Soap and water is the best cleanser for my face.
2. Here's the items you ordered, Mrs. Jones.
3. Neither the station wagon nor the jeep are in the garage.
4. Where was the fullback and the halfbacks at that moment?
5. Both my grandfather and my uncle live in Colorado.
6. Either my dog or yours are going to be picked as the winner.
7. Macaroni and cheese are my favorite dish.
8. There's several cars in the driveway.
9. Every one of these socks have a hole in the toe.
10. There's some strawberries in the freezer.
11. Each of the women has been to the art show.
12. There's more than enough booklets to go around.
13. Here is several widely varying interpretations of the same poem.
14. Rhonda, as well as Agnes and Millie, were at home.
15. Neither of the candidates has run for office before.
16. Do every one of your relatives live in Seattle?
17. Both Mary Ann and Jean are officers in the Press Club.
18. The dog and cat, together with the white mice and the hamsters, are creating difficulties in the family.
19. Have any of the students turned in their compositions?
20. Mrs. Hofman, not her children, are painting the house and garage.

6m. Words stating amount are usually singular.

EXAMPLES   Fifteen dollars was too much to pay for the sweater.
Three weeks is the usual incubation period.
Ninety percent of the student body is present.

When the sense of the sentence indicates that the subject designates a collection of individual parts rather than a single unit or quantity, the verb must be plural in number.

EXAMPLES   Two nickels **are** on the table.
Three long weeks **pass** before the eggs hatch.
Ninety percent of the students **are** present today.

Two such amount-stating expressions deserve special mention — *the number of* and *a number of.* They should not be confused. *The number of* takes a singular verb, and *a number of* takes a plural verb.

EXAMPLES   **The number of** women in the professions **is** increasing.
A number of women **are** attracted to the professions.

6n. *Every* or *many a* **before a word or a series of words is followed by a singular verb.**

EXAMPLES   **Every** man, woman, and child **is** proud of the city's record.
Many a philosopher **has** wondered about that question.

6o. The title of a work of art, literature, or music, even when plural in form, takes a singular verb.

EXAMPLES   Paul Laurence Dunbar's *Majors and Minors* **is** a collection of his poetry.
Millet's *The Gleaners* **is** a famous nineteenth-century French painting.
Gertrude Stein's *Three Lives* **has** influenced many writers.

6p. *Don't* **and** *doesn't* **must agree with their subjects.**

With the subjects *I* and *you,* use *don't* (*do not*); with other singular subjects use *doesn't* (*does not*); with plural subjects use *don't* (*do not*).

EXAMPLES   I **don't** want to go.
You **don't** know the answer.
It (he, she) **doesn't** answer the question.
They **don't** feel nervous.

Do not use *don't* after *he, she,* or *it.*

NONSTANDARD	It don't seem possible.
STANDARD	It **doesn't** seem possible.
NONSTANDARD	He don't want the ticket.
STANDARD	He **doesn't** want the ticket.

EXERCISE 12. Write in a column on your paper the correct form (*don't* or *doesn't*) for the following sentences.

1. Your answer —— sound right.
2. It —— look at all like you.
3. He —— want to attend the rally.
4. She —— believe that she won the prize.
5. It —— happen very often.
6. You —— have to watch the program.
7. —— he ever get tired?
8. —— it make sense?
9. Simone —— like to dance.
10. Some of the girls —— like the color.

EXERCISE 13. Choose the correct one of the two verbs given in parentheses in the sentences below, and list them in a column on your paper.

1. The President, as well as two aides, (was, were) in the reviewing stand.
2. Phil, and not Joyce or Sally, (is, are) making the decorations for the party.
3. They (wasn't, weren't) interested in learning the accordion.
4. Welty, of all the writers, (appeals, appeal) most to me.
5. Some of us (learns, learn) faster than others.
6. *Popular Sport Stories* (has, have) been read by every member of the class.
7. The boat to the islands (leaves, leave) the dock at noon.
8. Rex, one of the best fox terriers in his class, (is, are) sure to win first prize.
9. Several of the older girls, including my sister Joan, (is, are) taking the college entrance examination.

10. (Doesn't, Don't) Bryan want to do the weeding?
11. Lynn, as well as several other girls, (was, were) called on to read her report.
12. I am sure that nobody in the resort business (welcomes, welcome) rainy days during the busy season.
13. A new box of artist's crayons (was, were) left on the table by mistake.
14. My mother, like many baseball fans, (plans, plan) to attend the opening game of the series.
15. Neither of his parents (wants, want) him to take up scuba diving.
16. There (is, are) too many books in my bookcase now.
17. It (doesn't, don't) matter how you go, as long as you get there.
18. The museum, which has several of Bridget Riley's paintings, (has, have) made plans to acquire one more.
19. (Doesn't, Don't) all of you remember your very first swimming lesson?
20. Both of the skaters (is, are) hoping to become members of the Olympic team.

REVIEW EXERCISE A. In some of the following sentences, the verbs agree with their subjects; in others, the verbs do not agree. Number 1–33 in a column. If the verb and subject agree in a sentence, write *C* after the proper number. If the verb does not agree with its subject, supply the correct form of the verb after the proper number.

1. The jury has returned its verdict.
2. Apple pie and cheese is his favorite dessert.
3. Either Judy or Joan are supposed to be there.
4. Neither of them leaves until five o'clock.
5. Several of the girls in the chorus are absent today.
6. He don't do very well in the track meets.
7. Neither Lois nor her sisters was going to the dance.
8. There's one pair of candlesticks on the table.
9. Do every one of the committee members think that Russ will win the election?
10. Several of the boys appear to have colds.

11. Trudy, as well as her two sisters, seems to have a knack for writing.

12. Neither of us care to go.

13. Each of the basketball fans were excited by the game.

14. A few other things, in addition to his speaking voice, has contributed to the candidate's success.

15. There is few that can equal her ability.

16. Not one of those snakes is dangerous.

17. *The Three Musketeers* deals with the period in French history from 1625 to 1665.

18. Neither Dave nor Helen have any intention of going to the meeting.

19. Where was the jewels hidden?

20. Some of these lobsters are rather small.

21. Only a few of my friends like to play backgammon.

22. One of the players have ignored training rules.

23. In the trunk there's some nails and a hammer.

24. The audience was divided in their opinions about the school play.

25. Each of us has a long way to go.

26. Every one of the new automatic washers come with a free box of nonpolluting soap.

27. The herd of sheep were pressing against one another for warmth.

28. Three quarters of the supplies were piled in the warehouse.

29. The various clubs in this community perform many charitable deeds.

30. Where have the club decided to hold its rally?

31. It don't really matter to me.

32. There, in a pile of old clothes, was both of the missing kittens.

33. Doesn't these questions bother you?

AGREEMENT OF PRONOUN AND ANTECEDENT

Personal pronouns (*I, you, he,* etc.) have matching forms that must agree with their antecedents. The antecedent is the word to which a pronoun refers.

6q. A pronoun agrees with its antecedent in gender and number.

A small number of nouns in English name persons or things that are clearly masculine: *boy, bull, rooster.* About the same number name persons or things that are feminine: *girl, cow, hen.* Most nouns name things that may be either masculine or feminine (*student, child*) or to which the idea of sex does not apply (*house, opinion*). Nouns which apply to both masculine and feminine, or which do not carry any idea of either masculine or feminine, are said to be *neuter* or to have *common gender.*

Personal pronouns usually match the gender of their antecedents.

EXAMPLES   Did **Alice** remember **her** appointment? [The pronoun *her* is feminine to agree with *Alice.*]

If you find my **book,** please bring **it** with you. [The pronoun *it* agrees with *book* in gender.]

Personal pronouns also have forms that reflect the number of their antecedents.

EXAMPLES   The **soldiers** wanted **their** pay. [The pronoun is plural to agree with *soldiers.*]

The **soldier** left **his** post. [This time the antecedent is singular and the singular pronoun is used.]

(1) The words *each, either, neither, one, everyone, everybody, no one, nobody, anyone, anybody, someone, somebody* **are referred to by a singular pronoun —** *he, him, his, she, her, hers, it, its.*

The use of a phrase after the antecedent does not change the number of the antecedent.

EXAMPLES   **Each** of the planes kept **its** place in the formation.
Everyone in the club cast **his** [not *their*] vote against the motion.
Look, **somebody** left **his** [not *their*] notebook here.

When the antecedent may be either masculine or feminine, as in the last two examples above, it is standard formal usage to use only the masculine pronoun.

► USAGE NOTE On certain occasions when the *idea* of the sentence (the meaning of the antecedent) is clearly plural, one must use the plural pronoun even though the singular form of the pronoun is called for grammatically. For example, to use a singular pronoun in the following sentence would be absurd:

> If everyone comes to the party, it will be impossible to accommodate them [not *him*].

It is usually possible to avoid such constructions.

BETTER   If all of the guests come to the party, it will be impossible to accommodate them.

(2) Two or more singular antecedents joined by *or* or *nor* should be referred to by a singular pronoun.

EXAMPLE   Neither Judy nor Corinne has brought her hiking boots with her.

(3) Two or more antecedents joined by *and* should be referred to by a plural pronoun.

EXAMPLE   The captain and the sergeant have their wits about them.

(4) The number of a relative pronoun (*who, which, that*) is determined by the number of the word to which it refers — its antecedent.

EXAMPLES   Rhea is one of those people who are continually amazed by their own success. [*Who* is plural because it refers to *people*. Therefore the plural forms *are* and *their* are used to agree with *who*.]
Anyone who wants to volunteer should raise his hand. [*Who* is singular because *anyone* is singular. Therefore the singular forms *wants* and *his* are used to agree with *who* in this sentence.]

EXERCISE 14. Number 1–15 in a column on your paper. For each blank in the following sentences, select a pronoun which will agree with its antecedent, and write it after the proper number on your paper.

1. After the hike, all of the scouts complained that ―― feet hurt.
2. Either Susan or Roxie will give ―― speech first.
3. Everybody in the band is responsible for having ―― own uniform cleaned and pressed.
4. Every police officer did ―― duty.
5. Each of the girls in the troop has to make ―― own bed.
6. Several of the girls brought ―― repair manuals.
7. Every chef has ―― favorite recipe.
8. Nobody in the class has turned in ―― book report yet.
9. Sam and his brother were so thirsty ―― tongues were hanging out.
10. Both applicants brought ―― credentials with them.
11. If anyone calls, get ―― name and telephone number.
12. Everyone has ―― own opinion about the coach.
13. Few of the campers put ―― tents in good locations.
14. Neither girl did ―― best.
15. Sheila and her brother received ―― tetanus shots at the clinic.

EXERCISE 15. List on your paper the singular or the plural form of the verb *be* for the sentences that require verbs. List a singular or plural pronoun for the sentences that require pronouns.

1. Both of the bats ―― cracked.
2. Neither of them ―― usable.
3. One of the boys sprained ―― ankle.
4. Each actress spoke ―― own lines.
5. Where ―― your books?
6. If one of the boys ―― still there, ask him to wait.
7. Neither Dad nor Mother ―― likely to agree with you.
8. Each of the students has received ―― report card.
9. One of them did not sign ―― name.
10. If anyone asks, tell ―― your name.

REVIEW EXERCISE B. In some of the following sentences,

either a verb does not agree with its subject, or a pronoun does not agree with its antecedent. Number your paper 1–20. If a sentence is correct, place a + after the corresponding number; if it is incorrect, place a 0.

1. Neither of the tractors were in good condition.
2. One of the women is always making more sales than anyone else.
3. Giorgio, along with several other seniors, have won many awards.
4. Neither Ted nor Herb has finished their test.
5. Both of the boys clean up their rooms in the morning.
6. There was three members absent from the last meeting.
7. A few of the club members handed in their resignations.
8. Either Joan or Karen will bring her microphone.
9. Each of the girls was supposed to bring their own flashlight.
10. Neither of the dogs want to eat their food.
11. Every one of the trees needs pruning.
12. Either of them could get an A if he worked at it.
13. Is there any volunteers for the job?
14. Another rule everyone learns is to leave the camping area neater than they found it.
15. Some of the campers had their first-aid kits with them.
16. Each choir member had their own robe.
17. If anyone doesn't like my cooking, they can starve.
18. One soon learns to keep his mouth closed.
19. Where's the six dollars you owe me?
20. Both Leo and Elena tie their own trout flies.

REVIEW EXERCISE C. Number your paper 1–20. In each sentence, select the correct one of the two forms given in parentheses, and write it after the corresponding number on your paper.

1. Everyone insisted on having (his, their) own way.
2. Neither Muriel nor her two brothers (was, were) ever seen again in our town.
3. If anybody wants to buy a ticket, (he, they) had better hurry.

4. Neither of the tires (needs, need) air.
5. Each of the candidates (seems, seem) well qualified.
6. Either Felicia or her brother (is, are) in charge of refreshments.
7. Mrs. Jong, as well as her two partners, (attends, attend) every town meeting.
8. There (is, are) not enough pencils to go around.
9. A few of our classmates (was, were) invited.
10. Where (is, are) the groceries we ordered?
11. If anyone wishes to see the principal, (he, they) must make an appointment.
12. Nobody likes to find (himself, themselves) left out of school activities.
13. Muriel, as well as her two brothers, (was, were) missed by everyone.
14. Several of the buses (was, were) late.
15. Neither of the sick dogs could raise (its, their) head.
16. Where (is, are) the girls?
17. *The Reivers* (is, are) a book by William Faulkner.
18. Every one of the clarinet players (was, were) on time for the rehearsal.
19. Anyone who desires the companionship of a pet must also make it (his, their) business to be responsible for its care.
20. Occasionally someone is smart enough to find (himself, themselves) a seat in the front row.

REVIEW EXERCISE D. Rewrite each of the following sentences, (1) following the directions in parentheses, (2) changing the number of the verb to agree with the subject if necessary, and (3) changing the number of the pronoun to agree with its new antecedent.

EXAMPLE 1. The girls have finished their biology assignments. (Change *the girls* to *each of the girls*.)
1. *Each of the girls has finished her biology assignment.*

1. All club members have until next Friday to pay their dues. (Change *all club members* to *each club member*.)

2. Elizabeth, together with her sister, has not arrived yet. (Change *her sister* to *her sisters*.)

3. Neither Ann nor the Riley twins have ever been out of California. (Change *neither Ann nor the Riley twins* to *neither the Riley twins nor Ann*.)

4. The swarm of hornets has abandoned its nest. (Change *the swarm of* to *many of the*.)

5. Have William and Nan ever been to Salt Lake City? (Change *and* to *or*.)

6. Some of the girls have brought their own lunch. (Change *some* to *not one*.)

7. The number of failures has been announced. (Change *the number of* to *a number of*.)

8. Three books were ordered. (Change *three* to *a set of three*.)

9. Nobody in the group has brought his money. (Change *nobody* to *many*.)

10. Few of my friends get along very well with their brothers or sisters. (Change *few* to *neither*.)

Chapter 7

Using Pronouns Correctly

Nominative and Objective Case

A small number of pronouns have three forms: a *nominative* form that is used when the pronoun is a subject or predicate nominative; an *objective* form that is used when it is a direct or indirect object or the object of a preposition; and a *possessive* form that is used to show ownership or relationship. These three forms, called *cases,* are illustrated below.

NOMINATIVE CASE   **I** voted for Betty.
                        She voted for someone else.

OBJECTIVE CASE   I voted for **her.**
                        Betty voted for **him.**

POSSESSIVE CASE   It was **my** vote.
                        She wasted **her** vote.

CASE FORMS OF PERSONAL PRONOUNS

Personal pronouns are those pronouns which change form in the different persons.

First person is the person speaking: *I* (*We*) go.
Second person is the person spoken to: *You* are going.
Third person is a person or thing other than the speaker or the one spoken to: *He* (*She, It, They*) will go.

Study the following list of personal pronouns, noticing the changes in person and case form.

Personal Pronouns

Singular

	NOMINATIVE CASE	OBJECTIVE CASE	POSSESSIVE CASE
FIRST PERSON	I	me	my, mine
SECOND PERSON	you	you	your, yours
THIRD PERSON	he, she, it	him, her, it	his, her, hers, its

Plural

	NOMINATIVE CASE	OBJECTIVE CASE	POSSESSIVE CASE
FIRST PERSON	we	us	our, ours
SECOND PERSON	you	you	your, yours
THIRD PERSON	they	them	their, theirs

Two of the pronouns in the list above — *you* and *it* — have the same form in the nominative and objective case; therefore they present no special problems. Ignore these two and concentrate on the following forms:

NOMINATIVE CASE	OBJECTIVE CASE
I	me
he	him
she	her
we	us
they	them

EXERCISE 1. On your paper, write the case of each pronoun below. If you find that you need to consult the list of pronouns above, you should review the nominative and objective forms until you know them thoroughly.

1. me
2. him
3. she
4. I
5. them
6. her
7. we
8. they
9. he
10. us

EXERCISE 2. Write from memory the following personal pronouns.

1. First person plural, objective case
2. Third person singular, nominative case, feminine
3. Third person plural, nominative case
4. First person plural, nominative case
5. Third person singular, possessive case, masculine
6. First person singular, objective case
7. Third person singular, objective case, feminine
8. Third person plural, objective case
9. First person singular, nominative case
10. Third person singular, possessive case, neuter

THE NOMINATIVE CASE

7a. The subject of a verb is in the nominative case.

EXAMPLES   Both **he** and **I** noticed the mistake.   [*He* and *I* are subjects of the verb *noticed.*]

My parents and **she** arrived on time.   [*She* is the subject of *arrived.*]

We expected **they** would drive.   [*We* is the subject of *expected,* and *they* is the subject of *would drive.*]

Most errors involving pronouns as subjects arise when the subject is compound. People who would never say, "Me went to the movies," often do make the mistake of saying, "George and me went to the movies." The best way of avoiding this error is to try each subject separately with the verb, adapting the verb form as necessary. Your ear will tell you which form is correct.

NONSTANDARD   Her and me are cocaptains.   [*Her* is a cocaptain? *Me* is a cocaptain?]

STANDARD   **She** and **I** are cocaptains.   [*She* is a cocaptain. *I* am a cocaptain.]

The pronouns *we* and *they* frequently sound awkward as part of a compound subject. In such cases, it is usually easy enough to revise the sentence.

AWKWARD   We and they plan to go to camp together.
  BETTER   We plan to go to camp with them.

Pronouns are sometimes used with a noun appositive:

We road racers run every day.

To determine the right case form to use in such a situation, try reading the sentence without the appositive.

We run every day.

EXERCISE 3. *Oral Drill.* Read each of the following sentences aloud several times, stressing the italicized words.

1. *She* and *I* are good friends.
2. Irving and *he* plan to try out for the soccer team.
3. Either Nancy or *she* will illustrate the book.
4. *We* judges have made up our minds.
5. Neither *we* nor *they* are at fault.
6. When are *you* and *she* coming to see me?
7. The team and *we* cheerleaders have to leave early.
8. At the end of the movie, *he* and *she* are reunited.
9. Are *she* and *I* partners again?
10. Our family and *they* have known each other for years.

EXERCISE 4. Number your paper 1–15. Choose correct pronouns for the blanks in the following sentences. Vary your pronouns. Do not use *you* or *it*.

1. The others and —— saw the movie.
2. Luci and —— went to the game last week.
3. My friend Walt and —— solved the equation.
4. Finally —— fellows found the subway.
5. —— and —— didn't have the right change.
6. The usher said that —— and —— were in the wrong seats.
7. Neither Betsy nor —— has ever been to Seattle.
8. Yesterday —— and —— mailed our applications for the job.
9. Mother explained why —— and —— would not be able to attend.

10. —— girls are having a basketball game this afternoon.

11. Mrs. Hanifan suggested that —— and —— serve the refreshments.

12. —— and —— were the proofreaders for the yearbook.

13. Erica and —— delivered the newspapers.

14. —— boys had been given some tough assignments.

15. Seymour and —— sauntered down the hall.

EXERCISE 5. Use the following subjects in sentences of your own.

1. My best friend and I
2. We experts
3. They and their parents
4. Betty, Alice, and she
5. He and I

EXERCISE 6. Number 1–20 in a column on your paper. Read each of the following sentences *aloud*. Decide whether the italicized pronouns are in the correct case. If all of them in a sentence are correct, put a + after the proper number on your paper; if any of them is not, put a 0 and write the correct form of any incorrect pronoun.

1. Frank and *he* are taller than Bob and *I* are.
2. You know that Sally and *me* are leaving.
3. You and *I* were selected to represent our school in the finals.
4. *Him* and *me* went to see the guidance counselor.
5. Louise and *her* decided to join the Glee Club.
6. *He* and the principal have been talking for a long time.
7. *We* sophomores are going to play the juniors next week.
8. Everybody believed that you and *her* were good friends.
9. *They* and *she* will meet the five o'clock train.
10. What did *he* and your friend want?
11. You and *him* must have known each other a long time.
12. Can Lydia and *she* borrow the record player?
13. My kid brother and *her* always embarrassed Helen.
14. Abe and *him* will be pleased with the results.

15. Did you know that Ann and *me* were planning a party?
16. Your mother and *he* look very happy.
17. Will you and *she* hand out the papers?
18. *Us* band members got new uniforms.
19. I hope that Fred and *me* don't get lost.
20. Sara and *I* will supply the cake for the party.

7b. A predicate nominative is in the nominative case.

A predicate nominative is a noun or pronoun in the predicate that refers to the same thing as the subject of the sentence. It follows a linking verb. The exercises and examples in this chapter concentrate on pronouns as predicate nominatives, since nouns in this position present no problem.

COMMON FORMS OF *be*		PREDICATE NOMINATIVE
am		I
is, are		he
was, were	*are*	she
may be, can be, will be, etc.	*followed*	we
may have been, etc.	*by*	you
want to be, like to be, etc.		they

EXAMPLES   It was **they** who suggested the picnic.
Are you sure it was **she?**
It might have been **he.**

► USAGE NOTE   It is now perfectly acceptable to use *me* as a predicate nominative in informal usage: *It's me.* (The construction rarely comes up in formal situations.) The plural form (*It's us*) is also generally accepted. However, using the objective case for the third person form of the pronoun (*It's him, It's them*) is still often regarded as unacceptable. When you encounter any of these expressions in the exercises in this book or in the various tests you take, you will be wise to take a conservative attitude and use the nominative forms in all instances.

EXERCISE 7.   Remembering that a predicate nominative is in the nominative case, supply the pronouns specified for the following:

1. It might have been ———.   (Third person singular, feminine)

2. It could be ———. (Third person plural)
3. That was ———. (Third person singular, masculine)
4. It certainly wasn't ———. (Third person plural)

REVIEW EXERCISE A. Number your paper 1–20. After the proper number, write a pronoun that will correctly fill each space in the following sentences. Try to use as many different pronouns as you can. Do not use *you* or *it*. Be ready to explain the reasons for your choice.

1. Dad and ——— put the screens up.
2. I didn't know it was ———.
3. I hope Juanita and ——— will attend the reception.
4. ——— clarinet players were told to report to the band room.
5. Everyone applauded when Pat and ——— took a bow.
6. What do John and ——— think?
7. Did you know that ——— and ——— were there?
8. The best writers for the paper are ——— and ———.
9. Efram and ——— were going to typing class.
10. It was ——— who delivered the message.
11. Sue and ——— will arrange the posters in the display case.
12. Was it ——— or Jean who wanted a special meeting of the Student Council?
13. Jerry believed that it was Toni and ——— who had made the arrangements.
14. They said that ——— girls should go to the end of the line.
15. Neither Richard nor ——— can attend practice today.
16. My aunt and ——— come from Richmond, Virginia.
17. ——— fellows can't make up our minds.
18. ——— and ——— are never satisfied with their work.
19. I am sure that the winner could not have been ———.
20. Did ——— and ——— object to your leaving so early?

THE OBJECTIVE CASE

The pronouns *me, him, her, us,* and *them* are in the objective case. These pronouns are used as direct and indirect objects and as objects of prepositions.

7c. The object of a verb is in the objective case.

EXAMPLES   Our coach has been training **us.** [direct object]
I paid **him** a compliment.   [indirect object]

As with the nominative forms, the objective forms are mainly troublesome in compound constructions. It is unnatural to say, "The explosion frightened *I*," but you might carelessly say, "The explosion frightened Jim and I." Once again, the solution is to try the parts of the compound object separately.

Pronouns in the objective case may also have noun appositives. Whenever a pronoun is used with a noun in this way, you can always determine the case by omitting the noun.

Everyone knows **us** pranksters.   [They know *us,* not *we.*]

EXERCISE 8.   Remembering that the pronoun objects are always in the objective case, supply appropriate pronouns for the blanks in the following sentences. Avoid using the same pronoun throughout. Do not use *you* or *it.*

1. The City Council invited —— to their next meeting.
2. The jury acquitted —— after a long trial.
3. The private saluted —— in an odd way.
4. Did you see Muriel and ——?
5. I thanked —— for her help.
6. The neighbors left —— their dog.
7. Where did you meet ——?
8. We asked his brother and —— about their trip.
9. He accused Roger and —— of not helping with the cooking.
10. Did you really invite Peggy and ——?
11. She helped Joan and —— with our assignment.
12. I invited Agnes and —— to the barbecue.
13. The new rule affects neither —— nor ——.
14. Did you choose Inez and —— for your committee?
15. The coach criticized Paul and —— for sloppy blocking.
16. Has the artist sketched either Hope or —— yet?

17. He told —— boys what we wanted to know.

18. The mayor decided to force the governor and —— into declaring their views on the new taxes.

19. The hot sun affected Linda and —— more than it affected me.

20. Mother sent —— girls several gifts from Sweden.

EXERCISE 9. Write ten sentences using personal pronouns (except *you* and *it*). Divide the ten in the following way:

> three using pronouns in compound subjects of verbs;
> three using pronouns in compound predicate nominatives;
> four using pronouns in compound objects of verbs or prepositions.

EXERCISE 10. Write ten sentences, each using a different one of the verbs below. After each verb use a pronoun in a compound direct or indirect object. Do not use *you* or *it*.

1. tell	4. baffle	7. select	10. convince
2. met	5. ask	8. recommend	11. promise
3. encourage	6. give	9. expect	12. guarantee

REVIEW EXERCISE B. Number your paper 1–10. After the proper number, write the personal pronoun that can be substituted for each italicized expression. In those sentences calling for [1st person pron.], use the appropriate one of the following pronouns: *I, we, me, us.*

EXAMPLES   1. Did you call Rose and *Sheila?*
                    1. *her*
                    2. Only [1st person pron.] was to blame.
                    2. *I*

1. The singers were Andy and *Larry.*

2. Mr. Pence showed *Julia* and her mother his new house.

3. She bought Pete and [1st person pron.] some food.

4. The lieutenant and *the sergeant* were in a dangerous position.

5. Did my father give you and *Janet* his usual greeting?

6. Please tell Dan and [1st person pron.] what you want us to do.

7. Was it *Charlie* that you were discussing?
8. The best swimmers in camp are Robert and *Eric*.
9. When were you expecting Jane and [1st person pron.]?
10. Everyone was astonished to learn that the nominees were *Jeff and Stanley*.

REVIEW EXERCISE C. Number your paper 1–15. Select the correct one of the two pronouns in parentheses, and write it after the corresponding number on your paper. Be ready to explain your answers.

1. Jan called Sally and (I, me) last week.
2. Several others and (she, her) were planning a fishing trip.
3. (We, Us) girls would charter a boat.
4. The only inexperienced anglers would be two other girls and (I, me).
5. Jan gave the teacher and (I, me) directions on how to get to the dock in Freeport.
6. When we arrived at the dock, the captain told Sally and (we, us) where to park our cars.
7. After I had parked the car, the others and (I, me) climbed aboard the boat.
8. I looked for Jan and noticed that (she, her) and the captain were discussing something.
9. The captain warned (we, us) novices that the ocean was rough.
10. (He, Him) and the crew thought it would be perfectly safe.
11. Sally distributed the gear while (I, me) set out the bait for (she, her).
12. After fifteen minutes, Jan and (she, her) and several of (we, us) girls were reeling in fish.
13. Sally gave the girls and (I, me) some instructions which helped (we, us).
14. (She, Her) and (I, me) caught the most fish.
15. By four o'clock, some of (we, us) had had enough fishing for the day, but (we, us) decided to go again.

REVIEW EXERCISE D. Using the pronouns below, write ten correct sentences of your own. Include sentences with pronouns used as subjects, predicate nominatives, and objects of verbs. After each sentence, tell how the pronouns are used.

1. he and Al	6. she and I
2. he and I	7. Vera and they
3. you and me	8. Fred and him
4. my aunt and them	9. you and he
5. us girls	10. we students

7d. The object of a preposition is in the objective case.

A prepositional phrase begins with a preposition and ends with a noun or pronoun that is the *object of the preposition*. When the object of a preposition is a pronoun, it must be in the *objective* case.

EXAMPLES for **us**   between **you** and **me**   to **him**

Errors in usage occur most often when the object of a preposition is compound. You can usually tell the correct pronoun by trying the parts of the compound object separately.

EXAMPLE I wrote to Martha and (she, her).
I wrote to she. [nonstandard]
I wrote to her. [standard]
I wrote to Martha and her.

Try this test on the following correct examples:

Jobs were available for my *brother* and *me*.
My mother gave the jewelry to *Gail* and *me*.
Did a letter come from *Bess* and *her*?

EXERCISE 11. In the following sentences, pick out the prepositions which take pronoun objects and list them on your paper. After each, write the correct one of the two pronouns given in parentheses.

1. The coach gave instructions to Chuck and (I, me).
2. The costumes were exactly right for Abby and (she, her).
3. He yelled at Beth and (I, me).

4. All of us can play except Cindy and (she, her).
5. The feelings against Don and (he, him) became worse.
6. Everybody except Paula and (I, me) had taken the test.
7. The performance was directed by Todd and (he, him).
8. The dog ran after Elmer and (she, her).
9. Will you go with Ann and (I, me)?
10. The editor assigned the story to Greg and (I, me).

EXERCISE 12. Select the correct one of the two pronouns in parentheses, and write it on your paper.

1. The complaints were presented to the Student Council by (he, him) and (I, me).
2. When Father said that they had shown good sense, he paid a high compliment to Madge and (he, him).
3. The President had to choose between the colonel and (he, him).
4. They were talking about you and (she, her) for a long time.
5. The distribution of the posters was assigned to (they, them) and (we, us).
6. We took a bus tour yesterday with Terry and (he, him).
7. The guide stood behind Marc and (I, me).
8. The mayor lives near you and (she, her).
9. Mr. Lindsay had nothing to say to Ken and (I, me).
10. The dog growled at (she, her) and (I, me) all during the visit.

EXERCISE 13. Write sentences of your own, using each of the following prepositions with a compound object, at least one part of which is a pronoun.

EXAMPLE 1. to
    1. *Please hand this message to John and her.*

1. beside   6. between
2. toward   7. for
3. from   8. by
4. against   9. over
5. without   10. except

EXERCISE 14. *Oral Drill.* Read *aloud* five times each of the following sentences, putting the stress on the italicized words.

1. Nan finished the test *after* Lisa and *me*.
2. They sent gifts *to him* and *me*.
3. Nothing was done *by* either Mr. Arnold or *him*.
4. I left *before* Jan and *her*.
5. Divide the papers *between* Howard and *him*.
6. Allegra was walking *toward* Rosalie and *me*.
7. I went to the movies *with* Don and *them*.
8. The pictures look exactly *like* Maria and *her*.
9. Get the tickets *for* Steve and *us*.
10. The joke was *on* Linda and *me*.

SPECIAL PROBLEMS IN PRONOUN USAGE

Who and Whom

The use of *who* and *whom* in questions can no longer be reduced to a strict law. In modern spoken English the distinction between *who* and *whom* is gradually disappearing altogether, and *whom* is going out of use. *Who do you mean?* and *Who do you know?* are standard, even though, according to the rule you have learned about the case of the object of a verb, the speaker should say *whom* in these sentences. For the exercises in this book, follow the rules of standard formal usage. However, the rules are applied strictly only in formal writing.

Using *who* and *whom* in subordinate clauses, however, is a different matter. In subordinate clauses the distinction between *who* and *whom* is generally observed in both formal and informal writing.

7e. The use of *who* and *whom* in a subordinate clause is determined by the pronoun's function in the clause.

EXAMPLE Mae was the reporter **who wrote the stories.** [*Who* is in the nominative case because it is the subject of the verb *wrote* in the subordinate clause.]

EXAMPLE Mae was the reporter **whom the critics praised.** [*Whom* is in the objective case because it is the object of the verb *praised*, the verb in the subordinate clause.]

EXAMPLES She is the one **about whom we were talking.**

or

She is the one **whom we were talking about.** [*Whom* is in the objective case because it is the object of the preposition *about* in the subordinate clause.]

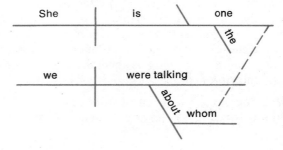

Follow these steps in deciding whether to use *who* or *whom* in a subordinate clause:
1. Pick out the subordinate clause.
2. Decide how the relative pronoun is used in that clause.
3. Determine the case of the pronoun according to the usual rules.
4. Select the correct form of the pronoun.

PROBLEM   Peter is the student (who, whom) got a perfect score.

Step 1   The subordinate clause is *(who, whom) got a perfect score.*

Step 2   The relative pronoun is the subject of the clause.

Step 3   Since it functions as a subject, the pronoun must be in the nominative case.

Step 4   The nominative form is *who*.

SOLUTION   Peter is the student **who** got a perfect score.

PROBLEM   That is my friend Carol, (who, whom) I met at camp.

Step 1   The subordinate clause is *(who, whom) I met at camp.*

Step 2   The relative pronoun is the object of the verb *met: I met (who, whom).*

Step 3   The object of a verb is in the objective case.

Step 4   The objective form of *who* is *whom*.

SOLUTION   That is my friend Carol, **whom** I met at camp.

PROBLEM   Do you know (who, whom) he is?

Step 1   The subordinate clause is *(who, whom) he is.*

Step 2   The relative pronoun is the predicate nominative: *he is (who, whom).*

Step 3   A predicate nominative is in the nominative case.

Step 4   The nominative form is *who*.

SOLUTION   Do you know **who** he is?

It is important to remember that no words outside the clause affect the case of the pronoun. In the third problem, the whole clause *who he is* is the object of the verb *know* in the independent clause. Within the subordinate clause, however, *who* is used as a predicate nominative and takes the nominative case.

► USAGE NOTE *Whom* is often omitted (understood) in subordinate clauses.

EXAMPLE The person [whom] I vote for must have experience.

EXERCISE 15. Number your paper 1–10. For each sentence below, copy the subordinate clause containing *who* or *whom*. Then tell how the relative pronoun (*who* or *whom*) is used in its own clause—as a subject, predicate nominative, object of a verb, or object of a preposition.

EXAMPLE 1. She is someone whom we all admire.
      1. *whom we all admire, object of verb*

1. Fabiola Cabeza de Baca, about whom you may have studied, grew up in New Mexico.
2. She was a writer who recorded the history of her state.
3. The *curanderas,* whom she described, were women familiar with the healing power of plants.
4. Women who understood plant medicine played an important role in the life of the community.
5. It was the *curandera* to whom the ranchers brought the sick.
6. Do you know who it was that halted the spread of smallpox in the village of La Liendre?
7. Doña Estefana Delgado de Baca persuaded the villagers who were very fearful of modern ways to have their children vaccinated.
8. Because she was a person whom they greatly admired, she had many, many godchildren in the village.
9. She personally vaccinated her children, grandchildren, and godchildren, whom she greatly loved.
10. You can read about this woman and others who influenced the history of New Mexico in *We Fed Them Cactus.*

EXERCISE 16. Number your paper 1–10. After the proper number, give the use of the pronoun in parentheses. After the use, write the correct form of the pronoun.

EXAMPLE   1. Do you know after (who, whom) the moon crater Mitchell is named?

   1. *object of preposition, whom*

1. Maria Mitchell grew up in Nantucket among people to (who, whom) a knowledge of the stars was important.
2. The islanders were people (who, whom) early in life developed the habit of watching the skies.
3. When she was twelve years old, she began assisting her father, (who, whom) observed stars.
4. As an adult she continued her observations, and many of the people with (who, whom) she was acquainted had great expectations for her.
5. We know (who, whom) the influential people in her life were.
6. On October 1, 1847, she became the first person (who, whom) discovered a comet through a telescope.
7. Mitchell also became the first woman (who, whom) the American Academy of Arts and Science elected to membership.
8. She was the person on (who, whom) the King of Denmark conferred the gold medal for achievement.
9. When Vassar opened in 1865, Maria Mitchell was one of the women (who, whom) were invited to join the faculty.
10. Leading scientists, including Ellen Swallow Richards and Christine Ladd-Franklin, were among those (who, whom) Maria Mitchell taught.

REVIEW EXERCISE E. Number your paper 1–20. After the proper number, write how the pronoun in parentheses is used — subject, predicate nominative, object of a verb, object of a preposition. Use the usual abbreviations for these terms.

On the basis of its use, select the correct pronoun and write it on your paper.

1. The instructions were given to Tina and (I, me).
2. We all knew (who, whom) the winner would be.

3. The teacher wants to see you and (I, me) after school.
4. Are Marie and (she, her) in charge of the election?
5. Have the packages arrived for Doris and (I, me)?
6. You may ask (whoever, whomever) you want.
7. My mother was seated near Dad and (I, me).
8. (He, Him) and (I, me) run the school store.
9. The people selected as ushers were Lupe and (he, him).
10. Was it you or (she, her) who borrowed my tennis racket?
11. The director inteviewed (whoever, whomever) was recommended for the part.
12. I believe you know (who, whom) we are referring to.
13. Is there anyone (who, whom) she likes?
14. There are some letters for Don and (he, him) on the table.
15. My aunt and (he, him) always shop at that store.
16. They introduced Jay and (I, me) to the new girls.
17. After the dance we took Eve and (she, her) out to dinner.
18. She sounds like somebody (who, whom) knows what she is talking about.
19. Do you suppose it might have been (they, them)?
20. My sister and (I, me) argue constantly.

REVIEW EXERCISE F. Number your paper 1–20. Write the correct pronoun next to the proper number.

1. This book appeals to Joe and (he, him).
2. I just told you (who, whom) they are.
3. We don't know (who, whom) we should send.
4. Claire will meet (whoever, whomever) arrives by train.
5. Between you and (I, me), he won't play in the first game.
6. Were you and (he, him) here when they arrived?
7. (We, Us) students are learning computer programming.
8. Give the book to (whoever, whomever) wants it.
9. Judy passed the ball to Gwen and (I, me).
10. Think of all the people (who, whom) she has helped.
11. The boss hired Ellen and (I, me).
12. Lou and (we, us) rented tuxedos for the dance.
13. Don't you know (who, whom) he invited?

14. The officer gave a warning to him and (I, me).
15. They thanked Paul and (I, me) for our help.
16. (Whoever, Whomever) sits in the last seat will distribute the dictionaries.
17. Tell Helen and (I, me) all the details.
18. (We, Us) girls enjoyed talking to you.
19. We sat so far away that we could not tell (who, whom) the player was.
20. Consider how Frank and (he, him) must be sweltering under the hot sun.

REVIEW EXERCISE G. Number your paper 1–20. For each sentence in which the pronouns are all in the proper case, place a + after the corresponding number on your paper; for each incorrect sentence, place a 0.

1. Should Candace and I bring our guitars?
2. Tell Dad and me what you need.
3. I do not know who you mean.
4. My family goes to the dentist who Ms. Calhoun recommended.
5. Your statements are incorrect according to Jean and she.
6. Althea explained the procedure to Tim and I.
7. The usher showed Stella and me to our seats.
8. We laughed at Irene and him.
9. They handed Carl and him the banners.
10. Under the tree were sitting Louise and he.
11. The announcer introduced we girls to the audience.
12. Peggy and me had practiced for days.
13. Everybody but Ken and him crossed the finish line.
14. You and I know the value of good marks.
15. The book was written for people like Ella and he.
16. Faye and me fixed the broken latch.
17. We saw your brother and them at the bus station.
18. Harriet showed Gwen and me her new album.
19. The rains came before he and I had a chance to close the windows.
20. It was us girls who were caught in the storm.

The Pronoun in Incomplete Constructions

7f. After *than* and *as* in an incomplete construction, use the form of the pronoun you would use if the construction were completed.

The following are examples of incomplete constructions. In each one, part of the sentence is omitted and is included in the brackets.

My sister is older than **I.**   [than *I* am old]
They like her more than **me.**   [than they like *me*]

From these two examples of an incomplete construction, you will notice that you should use the form of the pronoun which you would use if you completed the sentence. Thus in the first sentence, *I* is correct because it is the subject of the clause *I am old.* In the second sentence, *me* is correct because it is the object of the verb *like* in the clause *they like me.*

Now examine this pair of sentences:

I know Jerry better than **he.**   [than *he* knows Jerry]
I know Jerry better than **him.**   [than I know *him*]

As you can see, the case of the pronoun depends on how the sentence is completed. Both the sentences above are correct, but the sentences are quite different in meaning; they are completed in different ways.

EXERCISE 17. Write out each of the following sentences, supplying the omitted part and using the correct form of the pronoun. After the sentence, write the use of the pronoun in its clause. Some of the sentences may be completed in two different ways.

1. Few get better grades than (she, her).
2. We ate more than (they, them).
3. Hazel left just as early as (I, me).
4. I am a little shorter than (he, him).
5. Mrs. Jones likes Melinda more than (she, her).

6. Owen complained that he needed more practice than (we, us).
7. Did you do as well in the test as (I, me)?
8. Isabel started later than (we, us).
9. She did more for Marge than (I, me).
10. I'm sure I can't run as fast as (she, her).

REVIEW EXERCISE H. Number your paper 1–20. Select the correct one of the two pronouns given in parentheses, and write it after the proper number on your paper. Be prepared to give reasons for your answer.

1. Betty and (he, him) sang a duet.
2. The teacher gave the assignment to (whoever, whomever) was absent yesterday.
3. Can you speak French as well as (he, him)?
4. The scholarship winners were Linda, Janet, and (she, her).
5. I met Kathy and (she, her) at the corner.
6. He planned to sit across from Ted and (I, me).
7. Somebody must know (who, whom) caused the delay.
8. I would rather ask you than (he, him).
9. No one else can draw as well as (she, her).
10. You and (I, me) should get together soon.
11. The check was cashed by either Perry or (he, him).
12. Marie saw both Sandy and (I, me) at the game.
13. Mom taught Ronnie and (I, me) how to drive.
14. The man praised (he, him) and (I, me).
15. It is necessary for (he, him) and (I, me) to reduce our expenses.
16. Did they arrive earlier than (we, us)?
17. Did you receive a card from Al and (he, him)?
18. We are just as excited as (they, them).
19. The author (who, whom) the critics had praised autographed a copy of his novel for me.
20. The dog frisked around Kevin and (I, me).

REVIEW EXERCISE I. Number your paper 1–25. If a sentence contains an incorrect pronoun, write the correct form after the proper number on your paper. For each correct sentence, write *C* after the corresponding number on your paper.

1. I don't know whom it was.
2. You should do better than her.
3. Don and him play in the backfield.
4. Can you tell the difference between his brother and him?
5. No one knew to whom the article referred.
6. Mrs. Osaka gave Toni and I a ride home.
7. Ask Sam and he when they are leaving.
8. Jessie and me will take turns.
9. Dolores is better prepared than I.
10. I will take whomever wants to come.
11. I do not know who I should believe.
12. Karen and her can make up their work.
13. If it was them, you will soon know it.
14. The amplifier was assembled by Ricki and she.
15. There are some students whom no teacher can interest.
16. Kurt and I decided not to bother you and them.
17. Consuelo and he asked whom the guest speaker was.
18. Is there any mail for Dorothy or I?
19. I am sure that us students will be criticized.
20. He is a person whom everyone likes.
21. I met Mona and she at the bus station.
22. Jim and he are not so successful as them.
23. Is Phil expecting you or I?
24. Please tell Keith and I what she said.
25. If you expect we band members at the rally, you will have to provide a bus.

Chapter 8

Using Verbs Correctly

Principal Parts, Tense, Voice

People frequently use verbs in a nonstandard way when they speak. You may hear someone say, "He has brung," "She had drunk," or "The tree is laying in the middle of the road." Fiction writers sometimes use nonstandard speech to add lifelike detail to dialogue. Although nonstandard verb usage may occur in everyday speech, it is not always appropriate, especially on occasions, such as job interviews, when formal standard English is expected. This chapter will help you learn the standard usage of verbs in speaking and writing.

KINDS OF VERBS

All verbs help to make a statement about their subjects. *Action* verbs do so by expressing an action performed by the subject:

ACTION VERBS Ruth **swims** every day.
Macbeth **remembered** the witches' prediction.

As the second example indicates, the action expressed may be mental as well as physical: *dream, think,* and *ignore* are action verbs, just as *run, jump,* and *strike* are.

Some verbs help to make a statement by linking with the subject a word in the predicate that explains, describes, or in some other way makes the subject more definite. Such verbs are called *linking* verbs.

LINKING VERBS   Our team **was** victorious. [The adjective *victorious* describes the subject *team*.]

Catfish **are** scavengers. [The noun *scavengers* gives information about the subject *catfish*.]

    Some verbs can be either action or linking verbs, depending upon the way they are used.

ACTION VERB   We **felt** the cold wind on our faces.
LINKING VERB   We **felt** chilly.

    There are not many linking verbs in English; you will find a list of the commonly used ones on page 13. If you can recognize the difference between linking verbs and action verbs, you will then be able to choose the appropriate form of a pronoun that follows the verb. (See pages 136–38.)

PRINCIPAL PARTS

Verbs have four basic forms from which all other forms are made. These are called the principal parts of the verb.

8a. The principal parts of a verb are the *infinitive,* the *present participle,* the *past,* and the *past participle.*

INFINITIVE	PRESENT PARTICIPLE	PAST	PAST PARTICIPLE
play	(is) playing	played	(have) played
go	(is) going	went	(have) gone

The words *is* and *have* are included to remind you that the present participle is used with some form of the helping verb *be* and the past participle mainly with a form of the helping verb *have*.

Regular Verbs

8b. A *regular verb* is one that forms its past and past participle by adding *-ed* or *-d* to the infinitive form.[1]

---

[1] A few regular verbs have an alternative past form ending in *–t*; for example, it *burns* (present), it *burned* or *burnt* (past), and it has *burned* or *burnt* (past participle).

INFINITIVE	PAST	PAST PARTICIPLE
work	worked	(have) worked
receive	received	(have) received
saddle	saddled	(have) saddled

Irregular Verbs

8c. An *irregular verb* is one that forms its past and past participle in some way other than a regular verb.

Some irregular verbs form the past and past participle forms by changing the vowels, some by changing the consonants, and others by making no change at all.

INFINITIVE	PAST	PAST PARTICIPLE
bring	brought	(have) brought
begin	began	(have) begun
fly	flew	(have) flown
burst	burst	(have) burst
sit	sat	(have) sat
tear	tore	(have) torn

Since irregular verbs form their past and past participles in unpredictable ways, there is nothing to do but memorize the forms of at least the most common ones. You doubtless already know most of the irregular verbs in the list which follows. Nevertheless, you should study all of them carefully, concentrating on the ones that give you trouble.

Common Irregular Verbs

INFINITIVE	PRESENT PARTICIPLE	PAST	PAST PARTICIPLE
begin	beginning	began	(have) begun
blow	blowing	blew	(have) blown
break	breaking	broke	(have) broken
bring	bringing	brought	(have) brought
burst	bursting	burst	(have) burst
choose	choosing	chose	(have) chosen
come	coming	came	(have) come
do	doing	did	(have) done

drink	drinking	drank	(have) drunk
drive	driving	drove	(have) driven
fall	falling	fell	(have) fallen
freeze	freezing	froze	(have) frozen
give	giving	gave	(have) given
go	going	went	(have) gone
ride	riding	rode	(have) ridden
ring	ringing	rang	(have) rung
run	running	ran	(have) run
see	seeing	saw	(have) seen
shrink	shrinking	shrank	(have) shrunk
speak	speaking	spoke	(have) spoken
steal	stealing	stole	(have) stolen
swim	swimming	swam	(have) swum
take	taking	took	(have) taken
throw	throwing	threw	(have) thrown
write	writing	wrote	(have) written

EXERCISE 1. Your teacher will dictate to you the first principal part of the twenty-five irregular verbs listed above. Write from memory the past and the past participle. Placing *have* before the past participle will help you to learn that this is the form used with *have, has,* and *had.*

EXERCISE 2. After the appropriate number on your paper, write the correct form (past or past participle) of the verb given at the beginning of the sentence. If necessary, refer to the list above.

1. *do* Yesterday the girls —— their assignments in the study hall.

2. *come* Nobody —— to take away our rubbish last week.

3. *begin* I had already —— my homework.

4. *run* Because Adam had —— the projector before, he didn't need any help.

5. *see* In the newspaper last Saturday, Barry —— an advertisement for smoke detectors.

6. *write* She has —— to them for information.

7. *ring*   The late bell has not —— yet.

8. *go*   The family has —— to Glacier Park in Montana for a vacation.

9. *give*   Clyde has —— the garage two coats of paint.

10. *drink*   Mike —— a whole quart of milk with his lunch.

11. *break*   She has —— her watch again.

12. *speak*   The guidance counselor had —— to the seniors about the new college requirements.

13. *swim*   Last week he —— the entire length of Long Lake.

14. *throw*   My mother has —— all the old shoes out.

15. *take*   They had —— ten dollars with them.

16. *ride*   We have —— on this bus once too often.

17. *blow*   The fence had been —— down by the storm.

18. *burst*   The small child —— into the room and began looking for the presents.

19. *choose* The candidates have been —— by the student body.

20. *bring*   Had anybody —— the can opener?

21. *fall*   A few shingles had —— off the roof the year before we moved.

22. *drive*   Haven't you ever —— a car before?

23. *shrink* My shirt has —— in the wash.

24. *steal*   Somebody has —— his gym shoes.

25. *freeze* The pond has —— over twice this year.

EXERCISE 3. Choose the correct one of the two verbs in parentheses, and write it after the proper number on your paper. When your paper has been corrected, read each sentence to yourself several times, using the correct word.

1. The robot glided into the control room and (began, begun) blinking its lights.
2. She had (wrote, written) her ideas on scraps of paper.
3. Someone actually (threw, throwed) a chocolate cream pie at the actor.
4. We (did, done) everything we could to help him.
5. Who has (drunk, drank) the rest of the orange juice?

6. My sister (came, come) barging into my room to remind me to clean up the mess in the kitchen.
7. Last night, I (saw, seen) a TV show about whales.
8. Someone has already (tore, torn) the coupon out.
9. Who's (took, taken) the phone off the hook?
10. Once again the cat has (broke, broken) the lamp.
11. What (give, gave) you the right to mark up my book?
12. She (ran, run) the ditto machine last week.
13. I wish you had (spoke, spoken) to me about it sooner.
14. I dived off the high board and (swam, swum) the length of the pool.
15. You must have (rang, rung) the doorbell when I was out.
16. They just (came, come) back from the rink.
17. They could have (went, gone) to the movies.
18. Nancy had never (ate, eaten) a tamale before.
19. Lois (blowed, blew) the balloon up.
20. Suddenly the balloon (burst, bursted).
21. Ice cream that has (froze, frozen) is like a rock.
22. Joyce was (chose, chosen) to represent our school.
23. Marc's puppy was (brought, brung) back by a neighbor.
24. We were (drove, driven) to the train station in a taxi.
25. My suitcase had (fell, fallen) off the luggage rack.

EXERCISE 4. Number your paper 1–20. If the first principal part is given, change it to the past form. If the past form is given, change it to the past participle. Write *have* before the past participle form.

EXAMPLES   1. see
           1. *saw*
           2. ran
           2. *have run*

1. break	6. rode	11. drank	16. throw
2. climbed	7. steal	12. fall	17. write
3. swam	8. rang	13. shrink	18. brought
4. drive	9. blew	14. do	19. go
5. chose	10. froze	15. spoke	20. took

TENSE

Verbs change form to show the time of the action or the idea they express. The time indicated by the form of a verb is called its *tense*. There are six tenses, each of which is formed in one way or another from the principal parts of the verb. A systematic listing of all the verb forms used in the six tenses is called a *conjugation*.

The conjugations that follow for the verbs *walk* and *grow* illustrate the tense forms of two common verbs, one regular and the other irregular.

8d. Learn the names of the six tenses and how the tenses are formed.

Conjugation of the Verb Walk

Present infinitive: *to walk*   Perfect infinitive: *to have walked*

Principal Parts

INFINITIVE	PRESENT PARTICIPLE	PAST	PAST PARTICIPLE
walk	walking	walked	walked

Present Tense

Singular	Plural
I walk	we walk
you walk	you walk
he, she, it walks	they walk

Present progressive: *I am walking,* etc.[1]

Past Tense

Singular	Plural
I walked	we walked
you walked	you walked
he, she, it walked	they walked

Past progressive: *I was walking,* etc.

---

[1] The present progressive is not a separate tense but a form of the present tense since it shows present time. There is a progressive form for each of the six tenses.

Future Tense

(*will* or *shall* + the infinitive[1])

Singular	*Plural*
I will (shall) walk	we will (shall) walk
you will walk	you will walk
he, she, it will walk	they will walk

Future progressive: *I will (shall) be walking,* etc.

Present Perfect Tense

(*have* or *has* + the past participle)

Singular	*Plural*
I have walked	we have walked
you have walked	you have walked
he, she, it has walked	they have walked

Present perfect progressive: *I have been walking,* etc.

Past Perfect Tense

(*had* + the past participle)

Singular	*Plural*
I had walked	we had walked
you had walked	you had walked
he, she, it had walked	they had walked

Past perfect progressive: *I had been walking,* etc.

Future Perfect Tense

(*will have* or *shall have* + the past participle)

Singular	*Plural*
I will (shall) have walked	we will (shall) have walked
you will have walked	you will have walked
he, she, it will have walked	they will have walked

Future perfect progressive: *I will (shall) have been walking,* etc.

Conjugation of the Verb Grow

Present infinitive: *to grow*   Perfect infinitive: *to have grown*

Principal Parts

INFINITIVE	PRESENT PARTICIPLE	PAST	PAST PARTICIPLE
grow	growing	grew	grown

[1] For a discussion of the use of *shall* and *will,* see page 206.

Present Tense

Singular	Plural
I grow	we grow
you grow	you grow
he, she, it grows	they grow

Present progressive: *I am growing*, etc.

Past Tense

Singular	Plural
I grew	we grew
you grew	you grew
he, she, it grew	they grew

Past progressive: *I was growing*, etc.

Future Tense

(*will* or *shall* + the infinitive)

Singular	Plural
I will (shall) grow	we will (shall) grow
you will grow	you will grow
he, she, it will grow	they will grow

Future progressive: *I will (shall) be growing*, etc.

Present Perfect Tense

(*has* or *have* + the past participle)

Singular	Plural
I have grown	we have grown
you have grown	you have grown
he, she, it has grown	they have grown

Present perfect progressive: *I have been growing*, etc.

Past Perfect Tense

(*had* + the past participle)

Singular	Plural
I had grown	we had grown
you had grown	you had grown
he, she, it had grown	they had grown

Past perfect progressive: *I had been growing*, etc.

Future Perfect Tense
(*will have* or *shall have* + the past participle)

Singular	*Plural*
I will (shall) have grown	we will (shall) have grown
you will have grown	you will have grown
he, she, it will have grown	they will have grown

Future perfect progressive: *I will (shall) have been growing,* etc.

8e. Learn the uses of the six tenses.

Each of the six tenses has its own uses. Sometimes the tense of a verb expresses time only; at other times tense may tell whether or not the action is still going on. Study the following explanations and examples carefully, and then refer to these pages frequently as you work to complete the exercises.

(1) The *present tense* is used to express action (or to help make a statement about something) occurring now, at the present time.

EXAMPLES   Sonja **owns** a calculator.
Elmer **is** our new president.
They **are planning** a party.

► NOTE   The third example illustrates the present progressive tense. Each tense has a progressive form, which is used to indicate that the action expressed by the verb is continuing.

In addition to indicating present time, the present tense has some special uses. It is used to indicate habitual action:

He **practices** the piano an hour every day.

The present tense is also used to express a general truth — something that is true at all times.

Gus found it hard to believe that the earth **is** [not *was*] round.

(2) The *past tense* is used to express action (or to help make a statement about something) that occurred in the past but did not continue into the present. The past is regularly formed by adding *–d* or *–ed*.

EXAMPLES   I **grabbed** for the railing.
I **was grabbing** for the railing.
We **discussed** the poem in class.

(3) The *future tense* **is used to express action (or to help make a statement about something) which will occur at some time in the future. The future tense is formed with** *will* **or** *shall.*

EXAMPLES   I **will study** harder from now on.
I **will be studying** harder from now on.

There are several other ways of indicating future time.

EXAMPLES   I **am going to study** harder from now on.
I **start tomorrow.**   [present tense with another word clearly indicating future time]

(4) The *present perfect tense* **is used to express action (or to help make a statement about something) which occurred at no definite time in the past. It is formed with** *have* **or** *has.*

EXAMPLE   She **has spoken** often before.

The present perfect tense is also used to express action (or to help make a statement about something) which occurred in the past and continues into the present.

EXAMPLES   She **has lived** here for two years. [She is still living here.]
I **have been doing** my homework for hours.   [I am still doing it.]

(5) The *past perfect tense* **is used to express action (or to help make a statement about something) completed in the past before some other past action or event. It is formed with** *had.*

EXAMPLES   After she **had revised** her essay, she handed it in. [The action of revising preceded the action of handing it in.]
When he **had worked** for an hour, he suddenly quit the task.

(6) The *future perfect tense* **is used to express action (or to help make a statement about something) which will be**

completed in the future before some other future action or event. It is formed with *shall have* or *will have*.

EXAMPLES By the time I leave, I **will have packed** all my clothes. [The packing will precede the leaving.]
By the time I finish, I **shall have been working** steadily for three hours.

EXERCISE 5. Explain the difference in meaning between the sentences in the following pairs. Both sentences in each pair are correct. Name the tense used in each sentence.

1. She took ballet lessons for two years.
   She has taken ballet lessons for two years.
2. How long have you been a pilot?
   How long were you a pilot?
3. When I am nineteen, I will join the Marines.
   When I am nineteen, I will have joined the Marines.
4. What went on at the dance?
   What has been going on at the dance?
5. Have you waited long?
   Had you waited long?
6. Nina was told that her mother was well known.
   Nina was told that her mother had been well known.
7. When you come back, I will finish.
   When you come back, I will have finished.
8. I believed the car was running well.
   I had believed the car was running well.
9. The coach said Hal had poison ivy.
   The coach said Hal had had poison ivy.
10. Georgette was a volunteer for two years.
    Georgette has been a volunteer for two years.

EXERCISE 6. Copy the following sentences on your paper, changing the tenses of the verbs as indicated in parentheses.

1. When the bell rings, I will finish. (Change *will finish* to future perfect.)
2. Ivan worked there for a year. (Change to past perfect.)
3. Is she sleeping? (Change to present perfect progressive.)

4. Were you sick? (Change to past perfect.)
5. When I leave, will you wash the dishes? (Change *will wash* to future perfect.)
6. Olivia enjoys bowling. (Change to future tense.)
7. The soloist sings well. (Change to present perfect.)
8. The truck had broken down. (Change to past.)
9. At four, Joel will have finished. (Change to future.)
10. I was in Paris for two weeks. (Change to present perfect.)

Consistency of Tense

Young writers, especially when writing essays or narratives, sometimes begin their compositions in one tense and then lapse into another tense. Such lapses are due largely to carelessness, for students usually understand the error when it is pointed out to them.

8f. Do not change needlessly from one tense to another.

CARELESS Luke lunged at the basketball and grabs it before the
past   *present*
past
Meadville player could reach him.   [mixture of past and present tenses]

CORRECT Luke lunged at the basketball and grabbed it before
past   *past*
past
the Meadville player could reach him.   [past tense throughout]

CORRECT Luke lunges at the basketball and grabs it before the
present   *present*
present
Meadville player can reach him.   [present tense throughout]

EXERCISE 7. Number your paper 1–20. After each number, list the verbs that are in the wrong tense. After each, write the appropriate tense form. If there are no incorrectly used verbs in a particular sentence, write *C* after the proper number on your paper.

1. One of the most important battles of the Revolutionary War occurred in September and October, 1777, at Saratoga, New York. 2. The leader of the British troops, General John Burgoyne, had set up camp near Saratoga and is planning to march south to the city of Albany. 3. Burgoyne's army has been recently weakened by an attack from an American militia, which had ambushed some of his troops at Bennington, Vermont. 4. Although the march to Albany is dangerous, Burgoyne decided to take the risk because he feels bound by orders from the War Office in London. 5. Meanwhile, also near Saratoga, the American troops under General Horatio Gates and General Philip Schuyler gather reinforcements and supplies. 6. The American forces outnumbered their British enemies by a margin of two to one. 7. The Americans are much better equipped than the British, whose provisions are badly depleted.

8. In spite of these disadvantages, the British open an attack on the Americans on September 19, 1777. 9. After four hours of fierce fighting, the Americans, led by Benedict Arnold (who later became an infamous traitor to the American cause), withdraw. 10. The British, however, have suffered serious losses, including many officers. 11. Burgoyne quickly sends a message to the British command in New York and asked for new orders. 12. He never received a response from his superiors, possibly because the message is intercepted. 13. Burgoyne's tactics became desperate. 14. He boldly leads a fresh attack against the Americans on October 7. 15. This time, however, his troops endure even worse casualties, and the next day Burgoyne prepares to retreat. 16. The Americans surround Burgoyne's army before it leaves Saratoga. 17. Trapped and helpless, Burgoyne begins negotiating his surrender. 18. The Convention of Saratoga, by which Burgoyne gave up his entire force of six thousand troops, is signed on October 17. 19. Saratoga becomes a turning point in the Revolutionary War. 20. Six years later, in 1783, the British signed a peace treaty with the Americans and the Revolutionary War ended.

ACTIVE AND PASSIVE VOICE

In most English sentences, the subject performs the action of the verb. If there is a receiver of the action, it is expressed by the object of the verb, as in this example:

EXAMPLE The raging flood waters **destroyed** the bridge. [The subject, *waters,* performs the action; the object, *bridge,* tells what was destroyed.]

A verb that expresses action performed by the subject is said to be in the *active voice.*

For reasons of emphasis, however, such sentences are often switched around so that the object becomes the subject:

EXAMPLE The bridge **was destroyed** by the raging flood waters.

Notice that the object has been moved forward to the subject position and that the original subject is now expressed in a prepositional phrase. In addition, the verb has been changed from *destroyed* to *was destroyed.* Verbs that express action performed *upon* their subjects are said to be in the *passive voice.* The passive verb is always a verb phrase consisting of some form of *be* (*is, was,* etc.) plus the past participle.

ACTIVE She **grows** tomatoes and corn on her farm.
PASSIVE Tomatoes and corn **are grown** on her farm.
ACTIVE She **will plant** the corn in two weeks.
PASSIVE The corn **will be planted** in two weeks.
ACTIVE No one **had plowed** the field yet.
PASSIVE The field **had** not **been plowed** yet.

Notice that the passive sentences above do not give the performer of the action. When it is important to know who or what performed the action in a passive sentence, the performer is named in a prepositional phrase.

Although the passive construction is useful in situations in which the performer of the action is unknown or unimportant, it can easily be overused. A succession of passive sentences has a weak and awkward sound and should be avoided.

WEAK PASSIVE The party was enjoyed by all of the guests.
BETTER All of the guests enjoyed the party.

AWKWARD PASSIVE   When she needed new shoes, another pair of sneakers was bought by her.

BETTER   When she needed new shoes, she bought another pair of sneakers.

EXERCISE 8. After the appropriate number, indicate whether each of the following sentences is active or passive.

1. The art of Lucia Wilcox was admired by artists around the world.
2. Her blindness during her last years made her final works particularly interesting.
3. Dufy, Leger, Motherwell, and Pollock were among her teachers and friends.
4. Exhibits of her paintings were shown all over the art world.
5. Her blindness was sudden, though not wholly surprising.
6. It was caused by a tumor near the optic nerve.
7. After she became blind, she claimed she had better sight than anyone else.
8. Her vision and her mind were "free of static and distractions."
9. Her style was altered from energetic silhouettes to larger canvases in lush spreading colors.
10. These visions during her period of blindness were imitated by many well-known artists.

EXERCISE 9. There are five passive sentences in Exercise 8. Rewrite each one as an active sentence.

SIX TROUBLESOME VERBS

There are three pairs of verbs in English that account for many usage errors: *lie, lay; sit, set;* and *rise, raise.* Because the meanings of each pair are related and their forms are similar, it is easy to get them mixed up. The exercises in this section will help you to keep these common verbs straight.

Lie and *Lay*

The verb *lie* means "to recline" and does not take an object. Its principal parts are *lie, lying, lay, (have) lain.*

The verb *lay* means "to put or place" and takes an object. The principal parts of lay are *lay, laying, laid, (have) laid.*

INFINITIVE	PRESENT PARTICIPLE	PAST	PAST PARTICIPLE
lie (to recline)	lying	lay	(have) lain
lay (to put or place)	laying	laid	(have) laid

EXAMPLES   The rug **lies** on the floor.
The tree **lay** across the path.
It **has lain** there for months.

Lay the book on the table.
Workers **laid** the foundation.
He **has laid** the package on the desk.

When faced with a *lie-lay* problem, ask yourself two questions:

1. What is the meaning I intend? (Is it "to be in a lying position," or is it "to put something down"?)

2. What is the time expressed by the verb? (Only one of the principal parts which you have memorized will express this time accurately.)

PROBLEM   After school I (lay, laid) on the grass too long.
Question 1:   The meaning is "to remain in a lying position." Therefore the proper verb is *lie.*
Question 2:   The time is past. Therefore the proper principal part is *lay* (lie, *lay,* lain).
SOLUTION   After school I **lay** on the grass too long.

PROBLEM   The dog (lay, laid) the stick at my feet.
Question 1:   The meaning is "to put." Therefore the proper verb is *lay.*
Question 2:   The time is past. Therefore the proper principal part is *laid* (lay, *laid,* laid).
SOLUTION   The dog **laid** the stick at my feet.

EXERCISE 10. *Oral Drill.* Read each of the following sen-

tences aloud three times, stressing the italicized verbs.
Be able to explain, in the light of the information given,
why each verb is correct.

1. The ketchup bottle should *lie* on its side.
2. The smog *lay* over the city like a blanket.
3. She *laid* the letter down unopened.
4. The letter was *lying* there a long time.
5. The mayor *laid* the cornerstone yesterday.
6. *Lay* the hammer over there.
7. Please *lie* still.
8. The patient had just *lain* down.
9. He *laid* his hand over his heart and made a vow.
10. The package is *lying* around somewhere.

EXERCISE 11. Number your paper 1–10, and write the
correct form of *lie* or *lay* for each of the following blanks.

1. The glasses —— on your bureau all day yesterday.
2. Who —— them there?
3. The rake has —— outside for at least a week.
4. Yesterday we —— our plans before the Student Council.
5. —— there helplessly, the old dog seemed to be pleading for water.
6. I —— my keys on the hall table.
7. I was so tired I had to —— down and rest.
8. You must have been —— in the sun for hours.
9. Have you —— the new floor covering yet?
10. The President will —— great emphasis on tax reform.

EXERCISE 12. Select from each sentence the correct one
of the two words in parentheses, and write the word after
the proper number on your paper.

1. The town (lies, lays) in the heart of the mountains.
2. A mist (lay, laid) over the valley.
3. He (lay, laid) the plates on the table.
4. Don't (lie, lay) those records there.

5. The snow has (lain, laid) on the ground for six weeks without melting.

6. Your hat is (lying, laying) on the chair.

7. Kay (lay, laid) the tape recorder on the bench.

8. The theories developed by Albert Einstein (lay, laid) the groundwork for many later scientific discoveries.

9. That material must have (lain, laid) in the stockroom for years.

10. Mitch was (lying, laying) under the tree.

11. How long has he (lain, laid) there?

12. The truce hasn't (lain, laid) our fears to rest.

13. (Lie, Lay) the plants around the borders of the garden.

14. You must (lie, lay) awake nights dreaming up those schemes.

15. Tupper Lake (lies, lays) between Saranac Lake and Long Lake.

16. (Lying, Laying) the jewelry on the counter, the clerk began to show us the rings.

17. Our furniture has (lain, laid) in storage since we sold our old house.

18. She (lay, laid) most of the flagstones for the path.

19. Were you (lying, laying) down?

20. Marita (lay, laid) her receipt on the counter.

EXERCISE 13. Number 1–20 in a column on your paper. Read each of the following sentences, and determine whether the verb is correctly used. If it is correct, place a + after the corresponding number on your paper; if it is incorrect, place a 0. Think of the *meaning* of the verb.

1. Don't lay too long in the sun and get sunburned.

2. She must have lain in the sun for hours.

3. The clothes lying in the basket have just been washed.

4. When the doctor arrived, the patient lay in a coma.

5. After lunch he will lay down and take a nap.

6. Was she lying there long?

7. Look at all the papers laying on the floor.

8. The painter laid the brushes on the ladder.

9. During a storm, you can find the dog lying under the bed.

10. Lay the dishes in the sink, and we'll do them later.
11. He lay his book down and looked out the window.
12. All you can do in the summer is lay around and try to keep cool.
13. The soldier was laying in wait for the enemy.
14. Looking around the room, she found the pen laying just where she had been working.
15. It was lying under some papers.
16. Last week he lay great emphasis on footnote form.
17. Don't you think you have laid around long enough?
18. The principal glanced up and lay the phone down.
19. The child was lying peacefully in her crib.
20. When I went out, the book laid on the table.

Sit and Set

The verb *sit* means "to be in a sitting position." The principal parts of *sit* are *sit, sitting, sat, (have) sat.*

The verb *set* means "to put," "to place (something)." The principal parts of *set* are *set, setting, set, (have) set.*

INFINITIVE	PRESENT PARTICIPLE	PAST	PAST PARTICIPLE
sit (to rest)	sitting	sat	(have) sat
set (to put)	setting	set	(have) set

Study the following examples:

Please **sit** here.	Books **sit** on the shelves.
Set the case down.	He **sets** them on the shelf.

You will have little difficulty using these verbs correctly if you will remember two facts about them: (1) Like *lie,* the verb *sit* means "to be in a certain position." It almost never has an object. (2) Like *lay,* the verb *set* means "to put (something)." It may take an object. *Set* does not change form in the past or the past participle. Whenever you mean "to place" or "to put," use *set.*[1]

[1] Several uses of the verb *set* do not mean "to put" or "to place"; for example: "the sun sets," "setting hens," "set your watch," "set a record," "set out to accomplish something."

EXERCISE 14. *Oral Drill.* Read each of the following sentences aloud three times, stressing the italicized verb.

1. *Sit* down and rest for a few minutes.
2. *Set* the silverware on the table.
3. Last week we *set* out the plants in the garden.
4. I have *sat* here long enough.
5. How long have you been *sitting* there?
6. Rosa *set* the time of the tremor at 5 P.M.
7. She spoke and then *sat* down.
8. Do you intend to *sit* there all day?
9. Did you *set* a good example for Betty?
10. We *sat* under the trees.

EXERCISE 15. Select from each sentence the correct one of the two words in parentheses, and write the words in a column on your paper.

1. He (sat, set) back and pretended to be asleep.
2. Several of them were (sitting, setting) around the campfire.
3. Mary (sat, set) the flowers on the mantel.
4. Where did he (sit, set) the bag of groceries?
5. Let's (sit, set) outside on the lawn.
6. He likes to (sit, set) on the porch and rock.
7. She (sat, set) the plant on the table.
8. I often (sit, set) here in the sun.
9. Melodie (sat, set) the glass on the floor.
10. (Sitting, Setting) by the window, Nick can see the activities on the athletic field.

REVIEW EXERCISE A. Number your paper 1–20. Choose the correct verb in parentheses, and write it after the proper number on your paper.

1. (Sitting, setting) on the table was a pair of scissors.
2. Please (sit, set) the carton down carefully.
3. She (lay, laid) awake for hours.
4. (Sit, set) all the way back in your seat.

5. The dirty dishes had (lain, laid) in the sink for hours.
6. Yesterday Tom (lay, laid) the blame on his alarm clock.
7. The cat always (sits, sets) on the couch.
8. If only we could have (lain, laid) our hands on that buried treasure!
9. My eyeglasses were (sitting, setting) right where I left them.
10. King Tut's tomb (lay, laid) undisturbed for centuries.
11. Have you ever (sat, set) around with nothing to do?
12. She (sat, set) down at her desk with her checkbook and calculator in front of her.
13. The two children were (sitting, setting) in the playpen.
14. The beached rowboat (lay, laid) on its side.
15. She (sat, set) looking toward the horizon.
16. Laura had just (sat, set) down when the phone rang.
17. Julie (lay, laid) her handbag on the counter.
18. Pieces of the jigsaw puzzle were (laying, lying) on the floor.
19. Jack was (sitting, setting) outside on the top step.
20. Were you (laying, lying) down for a while before dinner?

Rise and Raise

The verb *rise* means "to go in an upward direction." Its principal parts are *rise, rising, rose, (have) risen.*

The verb *raise* means "to move something in an upward direction." Its principal parts are *raise, raising, raised, (have) raised.*

Study the following:

PRESENT	PRESENT PARTICIPLE	PAST	PAST PARTICIPLE
rise (go up)	rising	rose	(have) risen
raise (force upward)	raising	raised	(have) raised

Just like *lie, rise* never has an object. Like *lay* and *set, raise* may have an object.

EXERCISE 16. Fill in the blanks in the following sentences with a correct form of *rise* or *raise*, whichever is required by the meaning.

1. If you know the answer, —— your hand.
2. The curtain always —— a few minutes late on opening night.
3. —— the windows, and let some fresh air in.
4. Higher and higher —— the eagle.
5. Gerri —— her grade in math this term.
6. Slowly the old woman —— out of her chair.
7. Prices have —— in the last few years.
8. They said that the sun would —— in an hour.
9. Your question —— a new problem for us to solve.
10. The farmer —— at dawn to do his chores.

EXERCISE 17. Number 1–10 in a column on your paper. Select from each sentence the correct one of the two words in parentheses, and write it after the corresponding number on your paper.

1. As our plane (rose, raised) from the runway, I held my breath.
2. We couldn't take off until the fog had (risen, raised).
3. If the price has (risen, raised), I can't afford it.
4. A column of smoke was (rising, raising) over Bear Lake.
5. The tide (rises, raises) at 4 P.M. today.
6. How high will the balloon (rise, raise)?
7. Stock prices (rose, raised) during the afternoon.
8. Has anyone —— that question before?
9. The sun had just (risen, raised) when we started on the fishing trip.
10. Heated air (rises, raises).

REVIEW EXERCISE B. Number 1–40 in a column on your paper. Read each of the following sentences, and determine whether it is correct. If it is correct, place a + after the corresponding number; if it is incorrect, place a 0.

1. The detective lay the file on her desk and began reading.
2. Set the candlesticks down.
3. Your clothes are laying in a heap on the floor.

4. The dog has been sitting by the gate waiting for the children to return.
5. Why don't you lay back and relax?
6. What makes a plane rise?
7. Stewart set the dial for his favorite program.
8. Instead of laying down, you should be getting some exercise.
9. Interest has risen in our new project.
10. Set your chair in the shade.
11. The dishes have laid in the sink since breakfast.
12. Shall we sit in the orchestra or the balcony?
13. Gasping for air, the diver raised to the surface.
14. Everyone rose when the judge entered the crowded courtroom.
15. We laid out the maps and began to plot our route.
16. All of the press corps raised from their seats when the President entered.
17. Out at sea the submarine raised from the depths.
18. Isn't it too cold to lie on the beach today?
19. Just set anywhere you want, Mrs. Wright.
20. As the runner reached the finish line, the excitement of the crowd rose higher and higher.
21. Haven't you laid the boundary lines yet?
22. The boy was thrilled when he set in the governor's chair.
23. The electric fan lay unused during the cold weather.
24. We were sitting in the station waiting for the train to come in.
25. A howl of despair raised from the throats of the fans.
26. Set up straight in your chair.
27. There the dog laid with its head on its paws.
28. Engineers expect the river to rise another foot.
29. The humidity hasn't risen in three days.
30. The ambassador lay her proposal before the committee.
31. You may have one of the pictures laying on the table.
32. Everyone was fascinated by the little puffs of steam that were raising from the pool.
33. The pipe was so hot it must have lain out in the sun for hours.
34. I set there in his office, growing nervous.
35. We set the boxes in the trunk.
36. She was setting there smiling at me.

37. There the boat laid in only a few feet of water.
38. She skillfully lay the mortar on.
39. Because the bank stock raised in value, he felt elated.
40. The dog always lies on my favorite chair.

REVIEW EXERCISE C. Number your paper 1–40. After the corresponding number on your paper, write the correct one of the two words in parentheses.

1. Have you (wrote, written) the address down?
2. Little Billy was (lying, laying) in wait for us.
3. You might have (thrown, throwed) your arm out of joint.
4. We had (took, taken) our visitors to the World Trade Center.
5. He was instructed to (lie, lay) the nets in the sun.
6. I haven't (swam, swum) in the pool this year.
7. Who has (stole, stolen) my stapler?
8. The frightened animal (shrank, shrunk) back into the corner.
9. The child (burst, bursted) the balloon.
10. Nobody enjoys (sitting, setting) in a cold room.
11. There it (lay, laid), covered with mold.
12. They certainly have (ran, run) a successful campaign.
13. Wanda (rose, raised) to her feet and protested the umpire's decision.
14. After I (saw, seen) it, I couldn't believe it.
15. She has (rode, ridden) this horse in all the local parades.
16. I (brought, brung) you a sample of my writing.
17. What could have (went, gone) wrong with the engine?
18. The dog has (broke, broken) its leash.
19. It was so cold I was almost (froze, frozen).
20. The bad weather has (began, begun) to clear up.
21. When the bell (rang, rung), the wrestlers came out of their corners.
22. The tree was (lying, laying) across the road.
23. It had (fell, fallen) during the storm.
24. They (did, done) all the math problems in class.
25. We (sat, set) for an hour in the waiting room.

26. He (drank, drunk) the medicine without any protests.
27. The wind has (blown, blowed) the leaves all over the yard.
28. He hasn't (gave, given) us any trouble so far.
29. I looked out of the plane and saw the mountains (lying, laying) below.
30. Have you ever (drove, driven) a car with four-wheel drive?
31. When you (come, came) back, was the door locked?
32. She (lay, laid) great emphasis on correct spelling.
33. The cheers (rose, raised) from all parts of the room.
34. Tony had (chose, chosen) the wrong number.
35. Why don't you (sit, set) in a more comfortable chair?
36. I could have (ran, run) the machine better.
37. That tape recorder hasn't (gave, given) us any trouble.
38. Janet (lay, laid) the record down carefully.
39. Last night they (came, come) in at one o'clock.
40. Nobody could have (run, ran) the race as fast as Alicia.

Chapter **9**

Using Modifiers Correctly

Comparison, Placement of Modifiers

Knowing when to use an adverb and when to use an adjective is not just a matter of form, but of meaning. Notice the difference in meaning in the following two sentences:

Pearl made **careful** plans. [adjective]
Pearl made the plans **carefully.** [adverb]

A modifier is a word or a group of words that makes the meaning of another word more definite. Two parts of speech are used as modifiers: the adjective, which modifies a noun or pronoun; and the adverb, which modifies a verb, an adjective, or another adverb.

ADJECTIVE AND ADVERB FORMS

You will have little difficulty using most adjectives and adverbs correctly. Almost the only common problem in distinguishing an adverb from an adjective concerns the following three pairs: *bad–badly, good–well, slow–slowly.* Your problem is to learn when to use the adverb form and when to use the adjective form.

Apply the following rule to the three troublesome pairs.

9a. If a word in the predicate modifies the subject of

the verb, choose the adjective form. If it modifies the verb, choose the adverb form.[1]

EXAMPLES The driver is **cautious.** [The adjective *cautious* modifies the noun *driver—cautious driver.*]

He drives **cautiously.** [The adverb *cautiously* modifies the verb *drives—drives cautiously.*]

Linking verbs are usually followed by a predicate adjective. The following are the most commonly used linking verbs: *be, become, seem, grow, appear, look, feel, smell, taste, remain, stay, sound.*

In general, a verb is a linking verb if you can substitute for it some form of the verb *seem.*

She **looked** tired. [She seemed tired.]
The crowd **remained** calm. [The crowd seemed calm.]

Because many verbs may be used as either linking verbs or action verbs, you must be able to tell which way a verb is used in a particular sentence.

LINKING The corn **grows** tall. [verb followed by an adjective modifying the subject: The corn *seems* tall.]

ACTION The corn **grows** slowly. [verb modified by an adverb]

LINKING The actor **appeared** nervous. [verb followed by an adjective modifying the subject: The actor *seemed* nervous.]

ACTION The actor **appeared** briefly in the skit. [verb modified by an adverb]

LINKING The teacher **looked** calm. [verb followed by an adjective modifying the subject: The teacher *seemed* calm.]

ACTION The teacher **looked** calmly around the room. [verb modified by an adverb]

Bad and Badly

Bad is an adjective; in most uses *badly* is an adverb.

[1] Most adjectives become adverbs by adding *–ly: nice–nicely, vague–vaguely, incidental–incidentally.* A few adjectives, however, also end in *–ly* (*lively, lonely, friendly*), so you cannot always be sure that an *–ly* word is an adverb.

EXAMPLES The play was **bad.** [bad play]

The play was written **badly.** [adverb modifying the verb *was written*]

The weather looked **bad.** [After the linking verb *looked,* the adjective *bad* modifies the subject *weather.*]

Our team performed **badly.** [The adverb *badly* modifies the verb *performed.*]

With linking verbs the adjective form is used.

NONSTANDARD The fish smell badly.

STANDARD The fish smell **bad.** [The adjective *bad* modifies the subject *fish.*]

NONSTANDARD These look badly.

STANDARD These look **bad.** [The verb *look* is a linking verb. *Bad* modifies the subject *these.*]

▶ **USAGE NOTE** One prominent exception to this rule is the use of *badly* after the sense verb *feel.* In informal English either *bad* or *badly* is acceptable after *feel.*

He feels **bad** about his remarks.
He feels **badly** about his remarks. [informal]

However, formal English calls for *bad* after *feel.*

He feels **bad** [not *badly*] about his remarks.

Follow the rules for formal written English in doing the exercises in this book.

Well and Good

Well may be used as either an adjective or an adverb. As an adjective, *well* has three meanings:

1. To be in good health

Alice is well.
She feels well.

2. To appear well dressed or well groomed

She looks well in her gray suit.

3. To be satisfactory

> It is well.
> All is well.

As an adverb, *well* means *capably*.

> The work was done well.

Good is always an adjective. It should not be used to modify a verb.

NONSTANDARD   She skates good.
 STANDARD   She skates **well.**
NONSTANDARD   The band played good.
 STANDARD   The band played **well.**
 STANDARD   That suit looks **good** on you.   [adjective following linking verb]

▶ USAGE NOTE   *Well* is also acceptable in sentences like the last example above: That suit looks *well* on you.

Slow and Slowly

Slow is used as both an adjective and an adverb. *Slowly* is always an adverb.

EXAMPLES   Drive **slow.**   [*Slow* is an adverb modifying *drive.*]
 Drive **slowly.**   [*Slowly* is an adverb modifying *drive.*]

In most adverb uses (other than *Go slow* or *Drive slow*), it is better to use the form *slowly* as an adverb instead of *slow.*

EXAMPLES   He trudged home **slowly.**
 Very **slowly** the tiger crept forward.

▶ USAGE NOTE   Certain words like *loud, hard, deep, fast* may be used as adverbs without changing their forms.

EXAMPLES   The horse ran **fast.**
 He reached **deep** into his pocket.
 Mae hit the nail **hard.**

EXERCISE 1. Number your paper 1–20. Select the cor-

rect one of the two words in parentheses, and write it after
the corresponding number on your paper.

1. I can't hear you (well, good) when the water is running.
2. The opening paragraph is written (well, good).
3. The situation looks (bad, badly).
4. Why does ketchup come out of the bottle so (slow, slowly)?
5. She certainly plays the marimba (well, good).
6. Can you dance as (well, good) as you sing?
7. These shoes don't fit (bad, badly) at all.
8. Our gym teacher told us to do the exercise (slow, slowly).
9. Did you do (well, good) on the last algebra test?
10. The chef at the corner café cooks very (bad, badly).
11. Your orange shirt goes (well, good) with those pants.
12. The bus moved (slow, slowly) in the rush-hour traffic.
13. This furniture polish smells (bad, badly).
14. I can ice-skate really (well, good).
15. Those boots don't look too (bad, badly) to me.
16. We felt (bad, badly) that you missed the class trip.
17. He can't draw as (well, good) as his brother.
18. The line was moving so (slow, slowly) that we thought we
    would miss our train.
19. Our dress rehearsal didn't go (well, good) at all.
20. For emphasis, the police officer spoke (slow, slowly).

EXERCISE 2. Number your paper 1–20. If the sentence
is correct, place a + after the corresponding number; if it
is incorrect, place a 0. Be able to explain your answers.

1. All went well at the interview.
2. He talks too slow to suit me.
3. We walked back to camp slow.
4. If you can't see good, get glasses.
5. Brenda felt bad about losing the match.
6. I didn't think that he played so bad.
7. Chris writes very slow.
8. That color looks well on you.
9. By turning the lens very slow, you can focus the projector.

10. She arranged the flowers good.
11. That horse may look slow, but it isn't.
12. Joe did bad on the midterm test, but he improved his grade on the final.
13. I didn't do as well as I had hoped.
14. I did as good on the test as Shirley.
15. You certainly play the piano good.
16. Don't feel bad about not being able to take typing this year.
17. All of his repair work was done good.
18. The train went very slow before it came to the underpass.
19. The car ran good all winter.
20. Speak slow, so we can take notes.

COMPARISON OF MODIFIERS

Adjectives state qualities of nouns or pronouns:

> a **bright** light   **happy** people   **rough** cloth

You can show the degree or extent to which one noun has a quality by comparing it with another noun which has the same quality. For instance:

> This light is **brighter** than that one.

Similarly, you can show degree or extent by using adverbs to make comparisons:

> We play well, but they play even **better**.

9b. The forms of modifiers change as they are used in comparison.

There are three degrees of comparison: *positive, comparative*, and *superlative*. Notice below how the forms of modifiers change to show comparison.

POSITIVE	COMPARATIVE	SUPERLATIVE
low	lower	lowest
fearful	more fearful	most fearful
promptly	more promptly	most promptly
bad	worse	worst
good	better	best

Regular Comparison

(1) A modifier of one syllable regularly forms its comparative and superlative by adding *–er* **and** *–est.*

POSITIVE	COMPARATIVE	SUPERLATIVE
cold	colder	coldest
late	later	latest

(2) Some modifiers of two syllables form their comparative and superlative degrees by adding *–er* **and** *–est;* **other modifiers of two syllables form their comparative and superlative degrees by means of** *more* **and** *most.*

In general, the *–er* and *–est* forms are used with two-syllable modifiers unless they make the word sound awkward. The *more, most* forms are used with adverbs ending in *–ly.*

POSITIVE	COMPARATIVE	SUPERLATIVE
humble	humbler	humblest
pretty	prettier	prettiest
famous	more famous	most famous
slowly	more slowly	most slowly

▶ USAGE NOTE Some two-syllable modifiers may use either *–er, –est* or *more, most* correctly: *handsome, handsomer, handsomest* or *handsome, more handsome, most handsome.*

(3) Modifiers having more than two syllables form their comparative and superlative degrees by means of *more* **and** *most.*

POSITIVE	COMPARATIVE	SUPERLATIVE
industrious	more industrious	most industrious
favorably	more favorably	most favorably
fortunate	more fortunate	most fortunate

(4) Comparison to indicate less or least of a quality is accomplished by using the words *less* **and** *least* **before the modifier.**

POSITIVE	COMPARATIVE	SUPERLATIVE
useful	less useful	least useful
often	less often	least often

Irregular Comparison

Adjectives and adverbs that do not follow the regular methods of forming their comparative and superlative degrees are said to be compared irregularly.

POSITIVE	COMPARATIVE	SUPERLATIVE
bad	worse	worst
good well }	better	best
little	less	least
many much }	more	most

Caution: Do not add *-er, -est* or *more, most* to irregular forms: *worse*, not *worser* or *more worse*.

EXERCISE 3. Write the comparative and superlative forms of the following modifiers.

1. beautiful
2. curious
3. old
4. cloudy
5. rich
6. agreeable
7. simple
8. well
9. stern
10. substantial
11. friendly
12. much
13. smoky
14. wily
15. good

Use of Comparative and Superlative Forms

9c. Use the comparative degree when comparing two things; use the superlative degree when comparing more than two.

The comparative form of a modifier is used for comparing two things, as these examples indicate.

EXAMPLES One twin seems **brighter** than the other.
Texas is **larger** than Rhode Island.
Miguel can write **better** than Charlie.

The superlative form of a modifier is used for comparing three or more things.

EXAMPLES Alaska is the **largest** state in the Union.
Maxine is the **best** batter on the team.
Which of the three did you like **best?**

In informal speech it is common to use the superlative for emphasis, even though only two things are being compared.

> May the **best** person [of two] win.
> Put your **best** foot forward.

In writing, however, you will do well to observe the distinction stated in 9c.

EXERCISE 4. Write five sentences correctly using adjectives or adverbs to compare two things, and five sentences using the same adjectives and adverbs to compare three or more things.

9d. Do not omit the word *other* or *else* when comparing one thing with a group of which it is a part.

It is absurd to say "Stan is taller than anyone in his class." Stan must obviously be a member of the class himself, and he can hardly be taller than himself. The word *else* should be supplied: "Stan is taller than anyone else in his class."

ABSURD	Our school is smaller than any in the county. [This would mean that the school is smaller than itself.]
ACCURATE	Our school is smaller than any **other** in the county.
ABSURD	Ellen is smarter than anybody in her class. [This means that Ellen, a member of her class, is smarter than herself.]
ACCURATE	Ellen is smarter than anybody **else** in her class.
ABSURD	New York is larger than any city in America.
ACCURATE	New York is larger than any **other** city in America.

9e. Avoid double comparisons.

A double comparison is one in which the comparative or superlative is incorrectly formed by adding *-er* and *-est* in addition to using *more* or *most*.

NONSTANDARD	Today is even more colder than yesterday.
STANDARD	Today is even colder than yesterday.
NONSTANDARD	She is the most liveliest person I know.
STANDARD	She is the most lively [or *liveliest*] person I know.

9f. Be sure your comparisons are clear.

In making comparisons, you should always state clearly what things are being compared. For example, in the sentence "The population of New York is greater than Chicago," the comparison is not clear. *The population of New York* is not being compared to Chicago, but rather to the *population* of Chicago. The sentence should read: "The population of New York is greater than the population of Chicago."

AWKWARD The Martin family prefers camping in the wilderness to big hotels.

CLEAR The Martin family prefers camping in the wilderness to staying at big hotels.

Often an incomplete clause is used in making comparisons. Both parts of the comparison should be fully stated if there is danger of misunderstanding.

NOT CLEAR I like her better than Tina.

BETTER I like her better than I like Tina.
I like her better than Tina does.

EXERCISE 5. If the sentence is correct, write a + after the corresponding number on your paper; if it is incorrect, write a 0. Be prepared to explain your answers.

1. He peered out of the nearer of the two windows.
2. Your story is good, but mine is even more better.
3. Doris is the most happiest girl I've ever seen.
4. Which is the better of the two books?
5. Who is the youngest, Harvey or Tim?
6. Of the two scientists, Marie Curie is perhaps the best known.
7. This is the shortest route I know to Spirit Lake.
8. Of all the mountain lakes, this is the most beautiful.
9. Which of the two jackets do you like best?
10. The flowers look more lovelier than ever this year.
11. Traveling in airplanes is supposed to be safer than automobiles.

12. Our dog is more friendlier than yours.
13. Denver has a higher elevation than any major city in the United States.
14. It is difficult to say which problem was the most hardest.
15. The weather couldn't have been much worser.
16. He was considered the most reliable student in school.
17. Our class sold more subscriptions in the magazine drive than any class in the school.
18. She says that if she could train every day, she could run even more speedier than you.
19. Which is biggest, Lake Superior or Lake Huron?
20. Earth is closer to the sun than Mars is.

DANGLING MODIFIERS

9g. A phrase or clause that does not clearly and sensibly modify a word in the sentence is a *dangling modifier*.

A modifier consisting of a phrase or a clause may be momentarily confusing to a reader if it appears to modify a word that it cannot sensibly modify. Verbal phrases are particularly likely to dangle, since they have only a loose grammatical relationship with the rest of the sentence.

CONFUSING   Sitting in the back row of the theater, the actors could hardly be heard. [The participial phrase seems illogically to modify *actors*.]

Convinced of my sincerity, I was given one more chance. [The participial phrase seems to modify *I*.]

In both examples the participial phrase appears to modify a word that it cannot logically modify. The word that each phrase is supposed to modify has been omitted from the sentence. Compare the following correct examples.

CLEAR   Sitting in the back row of the theater, we could hardly hear the actors.

Convinced of my sincerity, the principal gave me another chance.

Dangling modifiers can be corrected by rearranging the words in the faulty sentence or by adding words that make the meaning clear and logical.

CONFUSING   Watching the auto races, an accident occurred.

CLEAR   Watching the auto races, I saw an accident occur.

CONFUSING   While stirring the batter, the spices were added.

CLEAR   While stirring the batter, Vicky added the spices.

CLEAR   While Vicky was stirring the batter, Lauren added the spices.

CONFUSING   To qualify for the Olympics, many trial heats must be won.

CLEAR   To qualify for the Olympics, a runner must win many trial heats.

CLEAR   Before a runner may qualify for the Olympics, he must win many trial heats.

EXERCISE 6. Rewrite each sentence so that the modifier *clearly* and *sensibly* modifies a word in the sentence. You may have to supply some words to fill out the sentence properly.

1. After reading the assignment again, it still was not clear.
2. Finishing her performance, the audience applauded the acrobat.
3. To learn to dance, a few lessons should be taken.
4. Going around the bend, the ocean came into view.
5. While typing my report, the keys jammed.
6. Having saved part of her allowance, the transistor radio was soon hers.
7. To grow plants successfully, light, temperature, and humidity must be carefully controlled.
8. Peering over the cliffs, the canyon seemed gigantic.
9. While shaving, his lip started to bleed.
10. Hanging in the closet, he found the jacket.

EXERCISE 7. Follow the instructions for Exercise 6.

1. After finishing our dinner, coffee and cake were served.

2. Having rung the bell at Jud's house, a voice shouted that I should go in.
3. While playing the violin, my dog started to howl.
4. While eating lunch, the phone rang.
5. After correcting a few mistakes, the editorial was ready for the printer.
6. To drive safely, the brakes should be checked regularly.
7. To learn the rules of the game, a book was bought.
8. Cleaning up the cabin, pine needles were found in the corner.
9. To repair miniaturized circuits in home appliances, patience is required.
10. When confined to bed, a get-well card can cheer up a patient.
11. After launching the boat, a celebration was suggested.
12. When on vacation, the dog is sent to Dr. Stevenson's kennel.
13. Before viewing the exhibit, your umbrella must be left with the attendant.
14. Having walked a few blocks, my watch suddenly stopped.
15. Drinking the juice in gulps, the glass was soon emptied.

MISPLACED MODIFIERS

9h. Modifying words, phrases, and clauses should be placed as near as possible to the words they modify.

Most of the errors in modification in the preceding examples resulted from the omission of the word that was supposed to be modified. Unclear sentences can also result from placing modifiers too far away from the words they modify.

Misplaced Phrase Modifiers

(1) Modifying phrases should be placed as near as possible to the words they modify.

The sentences below will indicate the importance of observing this rule.

CONFUSING   Did you see a person in the bus with a brown cap?

CLEAR   Did you see a person with a brown cap in the bus? [The phrase *with a brown cap* obviously modifies *person*. It should be placed next to *person*. Otherwise it appears to modify *bus* and gives the impression that it was a bus with a brown cap.]

CONFUSING   We learned that Pearl Buck wrote *The Good Earth* in our English class.

CLEAR   In our English class we learned that Pearl Buck wrote *The Good Earth*.

CONFUSING   We borrowed an extension ladder from a neighbor thirty-five feet long.

CLEAR   We borrowed an extension ladder thirty-five feet long from a neighbor.

CLEAR   From a neighbor we borrowed an extension ladder thirty-five feet long.

EXERCISE 8. Read each of the following sentences. Pick out the misplaced phrase, decide what word the phrase should modify, and rewrite the sentence, placing the phrase near this word.

1. Cheryl slammed the door in a bad frame of mind.
2. We found the injured sparrow on the way to school.
3. He spoke of the need for building new tennis courts in the strongest possible terms.
4. He bought the shirt at the shop with the brown collar.
5. Mrs. Stevens went to Florida after her husband had joined the army to live with relatives.
6. Janet was stung by a bee hoeing weeds in her yard.
7. I came upon an interesting old bookshop wandering about the narrow streets.
8. Mr. Beatty saw many Japanese beetles looking over his garden.
9. We saw a woman with her elkhound in high-heeled shoes.
10. A package was delivered by a messenger wrapped in red paper.
11. We noticed several signs riding down the highway.
12. We could see corn growing from our car window.

13. The children were offered a piece of chocolate layer cake by a baker with white frosting.
14. A collision occurred in the middle of the block between a delivery car and a fire truck.
15. I had been talking to a woman on the train with three children.
16. Careening down the street out of control, fortunately no pedestrians stood in the path of the runaway car.
17. A strange-looking dog was led onto the stage by one of the actors with shaggy hair and a stubby tail.
18. We watched plane after plane land and take off sitting in the observation tower at the airport.
19. I saw them leave before the sun came up in a long red car.
20. He described the part of the story about killing the lion in English class.

Misplaced Clause Modifiers

In using modifying clauses, you should follow the rule which applies to phrases.

(2) Place the clause as near as possible to the word it modifies.

The following sentences will show you how a misplaced clause may make a sentence ridiculous.

AWKWARD A ship sailed into the harbor that carried a cargo of wheat.

CLEAR A ship that carried a cargo of wheat sailed into the harbor.

The modifying clause *that carried a cargo of wheat* modifies *ship*, not *harbor*. In the second sentence the clause has been put next to the word it modifies.

AWKWARD There are books on the shelves that must be distributed.

CLEAR On the shelves there are books that must be distributed.

AWKWARD Sue mailed a letter from one of the cities she visited that lacked sufficient postage.

CLEAR   From one of the cities she visited, Sue mailed a letter that lacked sufficient postage.

EXERCISE 9. Read each of the following sentences. Take out the misplaced clause, decide what word the clause should modify, and rewrite the sentence, placing the clause near this word. If you find a misplaced phrase, correct it.

1. They drove to the lake in their new car where they always spent their vacations.
2. A large automobile drew up to the curb which was profusely draped with flags.
3. I liked the picture of you on the diving board that you sent me.
4. The new bicycle was standing on the porch which we had ordered from Chicago.
5. I ignored any topics in the book that we covered in class.
6. He gave the letter to the mail carrier that he had just typed.
7. We washed the dishes with sudsy water that had been stacked on the sink all day.
8. We found the book in the attic that had been missing.
9. We caught a dozen fish with the new bait which we fried for supper.
10. Norma showed the photographs to her friends that she had shot in Hawaii.

REVIEW EXERCISE. Most of the following sentences contain errors in the use of modifiers (words, phrases, clauses). Rewrite such sentences, correcting the faulty modifiers. If a sentence is correct, write *C* after its number on your paper.

1. While doing my homework, the telephone interrupted me five times.
2. Two books were discovered by firefighters that could not be identified.
3. Replying to reporters, the coach said that this year's team was better than any other team he had coached.
4. Wilma plans to work before she enters college for a little while.

5. While Percy's essay was the most funniest, it was not written so good as Rita's or Bob's.

6. Listen very careful to the two recordings, and tell me which one you prefer.

7. By working slowly, the job lasted all day.

8. Students are excused from last-period study halls that have a B+ average.

9. An award was presented to Connie Yorita for a job well done by the principal.

10. During the two-week examination period, all extracurricular activities are canceled.

11. Marion can't sing as good as Yvonne because, of the two, Yvonne has the truest voice.

12. Because Jimmy obviously felt bad about his grades, his parents did not scold him severely.

13. Approaching the Capitol from the south, a long flight of stone steps confronts the visitor.

14. Although the captain is faster than any player on the team, he didn't play so good in last night's game.

15. To economize during cold months, weatherstripping should be used for all loose-fitting windows with an adhesive backing.

Chapter 10

Glossary
of Usage

This chapter contains a short glossary of English usage to supplement the material in Chapters 5–9. You may wish to work right through the chapter, using the exercises to test your ability to use these expressions correctly. However, the glossary is intended mainly for reference. Get in the habit of referring to it whenever you are uncertain about a point of usage.

Several kinds of usage problems are treated here. In some, a choice is described between standard and nonstandard ways of phrasing things. In such cases, you will be advised to follow the standard practice. Other choices are between formal and informal usages. Here you should follow the formal practice in doing the exercises. Problems arising from the confusion of similarly spelled words are treated in Chapter 27.

accept, except   *Accept* is a verb; it means "to receive." *Except* may be either a verb or a preposition. As a verb it means "to leave out"; as a preposition it means "excluding."

EXAMPLES   Toby will **accept** the trophy from the principal.
No one will be **excepted** from this assignment.
All may go **except** Anita.

affect, effect *Affect* is usually a verb; it means "to influence." *Effect* used as a verb means "to accomplish," or "to bring about." Used as a noun, *effect* means "the result of some action."

EXAMPLES The tax increase does not **affect** my family.

The antibiotic **effected** a cure immediately.

The **effect** of the coach's pep talk was remarkable.

all the farther, all the faster These expressions are used informally in some parts of the country to mean "as far as" and "as fast as." In formal English, *as far as* and *as fast as* are the correct expressions.

NONSTANDARD That is all the farther the bus goes.

STANDARD That is **as far as** the bus goes.

allusion, illusion An *allusion* is a reference to something. An *illusion* is a "false, misleading, or overly optimistic idea."

EXAMPLES The teacher made many **allusions** to a book she had read.

After the first game, our basketball team had no **illusions** about its chances of winning the championship.

and etc. Since *etc.* is an abbreviation of the Latin "et cetera," which means "and other things," you are using *and* twice when you write "and etc." The *etc.* is sufficient.

anywheres, everywheres, nowheres Use these words and others like them without the *s*.

Anywhere (not *anywheres*) you go in the United States, travelers' checks are accepted.

at Do not use *at* after *where*.

NONSTANDARD Where were you sitting at?

STANDARD Where were you **sitting**?

being as, being that   Use *since* or *because*.

NONSTANDARD   Being that he was in a hurry, he took a non-stop flight to Los Angeles.
STANDARD   **Since** he was in a hurry, he took a nonstop flight to Los Angeles.

NONSTANDARD   Being as she's a senior, she visited colleges.
STANDARD   **Because** she's a senior, she visited colleges.

beside, besides   *Beside* means "by the side of"; *besides* means "in addition to."

EXAMPLES   Nobody sat **beside** him in the auditorium.
Did anybody **besides** you see what happened?

between, among   *Between* implies two people or things; *among* implies more than two. This distinction in meaning is usually observed in formal English; however, use *between* when you are thinking of two items at a time, regardless of whether they are part of a group of more than two. (See the third example below.)

EXAMPLES   The two friends had only twenty-five cents **between** them.
The five committee members shared the work **among** themselves.
What is the difference in meaning **between** *timid, cautious,* and *circumspect?* [*Between* is correct because the speaker is thinking of one word and another word — *two* at a time.]
The rivalry **between** the students at Central and those at North has always been intense. [Although more than two students are involved, the rivalry exists between two groups.]

bring, take   *Bring* means "to come carrying something." *Take* means "to go away carrying something." The situation is complicated by the fact that a speaker sometimes adopts the point of view of the person being spoken to out of politeness: "Shall I bring my bathing suit when I come to your party?" Usually it is helpful to think of *bring* as related to *come* and *take* as related to *go*.

> EXAMPLES   **Bring** your literature books to class tomorrow.
> Please **take** this slip when you go to the principal's office.

bust, busted   Avoid using these words as verbs. Use a form of either *burst* or *break*.

> NONSTANDARD   I busted my arm last week.
> STANDARD   I **broke** my arm last week.
>
> NONSTANDARD   The dress busted at the seams.
> STANDARD   The dress **burst** at the seams.

EXERCISE 1.   Number your paper 1–30. Choose the correct one of the two words in parentheses, and write it after the proper number on your paper.

1. When you visited Louisville, where did you (stay, stay at)?
2. The lawyer (accepted, excepted) our congratulations on winning the case.
3. (Being that, Since) the puppy was only a few weeks old, it needed much care.
4. The speaker made several (allusions, illusions) to the current international situation.
5. The trouble was caused by a water pipe that had (busted, burst).
6. Everyone passed the test (accept, except) Dan.
7. The proceeds from the Community Chest drive will be divided (between, among) several dozen charities.
8. (Bring, Take) your books home with you when you go.
9. This is (all the faster, as fast as) I can go.
10. Ask Ginny to (bring, take) me her new record album.
11. Steady practice has (affected, effected) a marked improvement in his playing.
12. No one (accept, except) Fay will be admitted.
13. Her sudden rise to fame did not (affect, effect) her fundamental modesty.
14. The outdoor chores are shared (between, among) the four children in the family.

15. (Being that, Because) she was in a hurry, she was careless.
16. We could not find you (anywheres, anywhere).
17. When you go shopping, (bring, take) money with you.
18. The "ghost" proved to be a simple (allusion, illusion) caused by the reflection of a distant light.
19. Who (busted, broke) the light bulb?
20. The seniors soon felt the (affects, effects) of the principal's ruling.
21. Has anyone (beside, besides) Brenda finished the assignment?
22. (Everywheres, Everywhere) in Polk County, the dogwoods are flowering.
23. The new coach (affected, effected) a great change in the team's morale.
24. (Bring, Take) your radio with you when you come to my house.
25. This is (all the farther, as far as) I can climb.
26. Tony was (accepted, excepted) from the requirement after he explained his situation to the principal.
27. The rope (busted, broke) and the mountaineer fell.
28. The strain of waiting (affected, effected) Leslie's nerves badly.
29. Who else (beside, besides) you and Daniella bought tickets to the game?
30. The expression "sour grapes" is an (allusion, illusion) to Aesop's fable "The Fox and the Grapes."

can't hardly, can't scarcely   See **The Double Negative** (page 212).

could of   *Could have* sounds like *could of* when spoken. Do not erroneously write *of* with the helping verb *could*. Use *could have.* Also avoid *ought to of, should of, would of, might of,* and *must of.*

   EXAMPLE   Anne could **have** [not *of*] called us earlier.

discover, invent   *To discover* means "to find something that already exists." *To invent* is "to be the first to make something not known before."

EXAMPLES   Margaret Knight **invented** a window frame.
Leif Ericson is said to have **discovered** North America about A.D. 1000.

don't   A contraction of *do not, don't* should not be used with a singular noun or a third person singular pronoun (*he, she, it*). Use *doesn't*. See pages 121–22.

NONSTANDARD   He don't want to go to the movies.
STANDARD   He **doesn't** want to go to the movies.

NONSTANDARD   It don't matter to me.
STANDARD   It **doesn't** matter to me.

effect   See **affect, effect.**

emigrate, immigrate   *Emigrate* means "to go from a country to settle elsewhere." *Immigrate* means "to come into a country to settle there."

EXAMPLES   Catherine's ancestors **emigrated** from Scotland many years ago.
Canadians welcome the many people who **immigrate** to their country every year.

everywheres   See **anywheres.**

except   See **accept, except.**

fewer, less   In standard formal English *fewer* (not *less*) is used before a plural noun. *Less* is used before a singular noun.

There were **fewer** (not *less*) dogs on the lawn.
We took in **less** change this afternoon (but **fewer** dimes).

good, well   *Good* is an adjective. Do not use it to modify a verb.

NONSTANDARD   You sing good.
STANDARD   You sing **well.**

Well is an adverb except in three uses: (1) when used to mean "healthy," (2) when used to mean "neatly groomed" or "attractively dressed," (3) when used to mean "satisfactory." In all of these instances, *well* is an adjective.

EXAMPLES   The band played **well.** [adverb]
You don't look **well.** [adjective]
Some people look **well** in black. [adjective]
All is **well.** [adjective]

had of See **of.**

had ought See **ought.**

hardly See **The Double Negative** (page 212).

he, she, they Do not use unnecessary pronouns. This error is sometimes called the *double subject.*

NONSTANDARD My older brother he goes to college.
STANDARD My older **brother goes** to college.

illusion See **allusion, illusion.**

immigrate See **emigrate, immigrate.**

imply, infer *Imply* means "to suggest something." *Infer* means "to interpret" or "to derive a certain meaning from a remark or an action."

EXAMPLES   In her speech, the candidate **implied** that she was for tax reform.
From other remarks that she has made, I **infer** that she feels that certain taxes are unfair.

EXERCISE 2. Number your paper 1–20. Choose the correct form in parentheses, and write it after the proper number on your paper.

1. Was it Jan Matzeliger or Elijah McCoy who (discovered, invented) the shoe-lasting machine?
2. Mom's remark (implied, inferred) that we soon might get a new car.

3. If you check your answers carefully, you will make (fewer, less) mistakes.

4. If you do (good, well) on this test, you will have a better understanding of usage.

5. Amanda Theodosia (discovered, invented) the principle of the vacuum process for preserving food.

6. During the entire season, the team played exceptionally (good, well).

7. Many Huguenots (emigrated, immigrated) from France to escape religious persecution.

8. Because of the stormy weather, there were (fewer, less) shoppers in the store than usual.

9. By using the newly invented telescope, Galileo (discovered, invented) four moons of Jupiter.

10. (Emigration, Immigration) into the United States reached its peak soon after 1900.

11. In his estimation, nobody does anything as (good, well) as he.

12. (My mother, My mother she) bowls in the 200's.

13. Her band uniform didn't fit very (good, well).

14. He (don't, doesn't) mean to be rude.

15. From what the author said, I (implied, inferred) that he was against a change in the law.

16. If she (don't, doesn't) show up we shall leave without her.

17. Could you (of, have) forgotten our appointment?

18. To avoid getting cavities, one should eat (fewer, less) sugar.

19. People who (emigrate, immigrate) into this country today are just as likely to arrive by plane as by ship.

20. Celia might (have, of) done much better than she did.

invent See **discover, invent.**

kind of, sort of These expressions are often used in informal English to mean "rather" or "somewhat." Avoid them in formal written English.

INFORMAL   She was kind of tired.
FORMAL   She was **rather** tired.

INFORMAL It grew sort of chilly.
  FORMAL It grew **somewhat** [or *rather*] chilly.

kind of a, sort of a The *a* is unnecessary. Leave it out.

EXAMPLE What **kind of** hat did you buy?

learn, teach *Learn* means "to acquire information." *Teach* means "to instruct" or "to give out knowledge."

EXAMPLES She wanted to **learn** how to read music.
The music director **taught** her after school.

leave, let *Leave* means "to go away." *Let* means "to allow" or "to permit."

EXAMPLES **Let** (not *leave*) me show you my new skis.
You should have **let** (not *left*) him go.

lie, lay See Chapter 8, page 169.

like, as *Like* is usually a preposition. *As* is usually a conjunction.

EXAMPLES He cried **like** a baby. [prepositional phrase]
He responds to criticism **as** a baby would. [subordinate clause introduced by a conjunction. In this construction *like* is often used informally, but *as* is preferred in formal written English.]

like, as if Phrases such as *as if, as though* are used as conjunctions to introduce a subordinate clause. In writing, avoid using *like* in place of these conjunctions.

INFORMAL The room looked like a tornado had struck it.
  FORMAL The room looked **as if** [or *as though*] a tornado had struck it.

might of, must of See **could of.**

nowheres See **anywheres.**

of Do not use *of* with prepositions such as *inside, off, outside,* etc.

EXAMPLES   **Outside** [not *outside of*] the house it was cool.
The robber leaped **off** [not *off of*] the roof.

Of is also unnecessary with *had.*

EXAMPLE   If I **had** [not *had of*] remembered my keys, I would
have been able to open this locker.

off of   See **of.**

ought   The verb *ought* should never be used with *had.*

NONSTANDARD   Pam had ought to be finished by now.
STANDARD   Pam **ought** to be finished by now.
NONSTANDARD   You hadn't ought to tease your dog so much.
STANDARD   You **ought** not to tease your dog so much.

respectfully, respectively   *Respectfully* means "with
respect or full of respect." *Respectively* means "each in
the order given."

EXAMPLES   The visiting dignitaries were greeted **respectfully**
by the President.
Susan, Bruce, and Rodney won blue, red, and
white ribbons **respectively.**

EXERCISE 3. Number your paper 1–20. Choose the correct form in parentheses, and write it after the proper
number on your paper.

1. (Leave, Let) me have your answer by tomorrow.
2. Twyla Tharp (learned, taught) me how to dance.
3. The petition was (respectfully, respectively) presented.
4. (Leave, Let) me finish my work.
5. He always drives (like, as if) he were alone on the road.
6. Don't do (like, as) I do; do (like, as) I say.
7. What (sort of, sort of a) movie did you see last night?
8. Simone was hurt when she fell (off, off of) the barn roof.
9. Although we didn't agree with the speaker, we listened to
him (respectfully, respectively).
10. Leave us listen without any interruptions.

11. You can actually (learn, teach) an old dog new tricks if you have the patience.
12. Gentlemen, I regret to say that Secretary Jones will not appear owing to the fact that he feels (kind of, rather) ill.
13. (Leave, Let) sleeping dogs lie.
14. Willy (ought, had ought) to be here by this time.
15. She acted (like, as if) she had seen a ghost.
16. "(Leave, Let) me have some more of that," he said.
17. For two years now, Mr. Bruni has been trying in vain to (learn, teach) me Latin.
18. If you (had of, had) brought your glove, we could have had a game of catch.
19. Vincenta dived (off, off of) the bridge into the river.
20. (Inside, Inside of) the library, all was quiet.

rise, raise   See page 174.

same   *Same* is used as an adjective (the *same* day, the *same* person) and as a pronoun (more of the *same*). In the latter use, *same* should always be used with *the*. Such uses as the following should be avoided:

Four witnesses saw the crime and reported same to the police. [In this sentence, *it* is preferable.]

shall, will   There was a time when careful speakers and writers used *shall* in the first person (I shall, we shall) and *will* in second and third persons (you will, he will, they will). Today, however, this distinction is not observed. *Will* is considered as correct as *shall* in first person.

STANDARD   I **shall** probably be late.
STANDARD   I **will** probably be late.

sit, set   See page 172.

so   In writing avoid using this overworked word as a conjunction meaning "therefore."

POOR The undertow grew very strong, so Kate came out of the surf.

BETTER Because the undertow grew very strong, Kate came out of the surf.

some In writing do not use *some* for *somewhat* as an adverb.

NONSTANDARD This medicine will help your cough some.
STANDARD This medicine will help your cough **somewhat.**

sort of See **kind of, sort of.**

take, bring See **bring, take.**

than, then Do not use *then* in the place of *than*. *Than* is a conjunction used in comparisons.

EXAMPLE She is smarter **than** I.

Then is an adverb telling when.

EXAMPLE Frank added eggs; **then** he stirred the batter.

them *Them* is not an adjective. Use *these* or *those*.

NONSTANDARD Where can I get one of them pens?
STANDARD Where can I get one of **those** pens?

this here, that there *Here* and *there* are unnecessary.

NONSTANDARD This here chair is an antique.
STANDARD **This** chair is an antique.

try and In writing and in formal speaking, the correct form is *try to*.

INFORMAL If you try and relax, you won't be so nervous.
FORMAL If you **try to** relax, you won't be so nervous.

way, ways Use *way*, not *ways*, in referring to distance.

EXAMPLE She stopped a little **way** [not *ways*] down the path.

what   Do not use *what* to mean *that*.

> EXAMPLE   The supplies **that** [not *what*] we carried with us lasted four days.

when, where   Do not use *when* or *where* incorrectly in writing a definition. (See pages 336–39.)

> NONSTANDARD   A doubleheader is when the same two teams play each other twice on the same day.
> STANDARD   A doubleheader is a pair of games played by the same two opposing teams on the same day.

where   Do not use *where* for *that*.

> EXAMPLE   I read **that** [not *where*] the renovation of the town hall was turned down by the voters.

where . . . at   See **at**.

which, that, who   *Which* is used to refer only to *things*. *That* is used to refer to either *people* or *things*. *Who* is used to refer only to *people*.

> EXAMPLES   He sat in a chair **which** was broken.
> She is the girl **who** [not *which*] is the editor of the school paper.
> Here comes the girl **that** is the editor of the school paper.

who, whom   See pages 143–46.

EXERCISE 4.   The following sentences contain examples of the errors listed after Exercise 3. Rewrite each sentence correctly, and then practice saying aloud the corrected form.

1. A peninsula is when a land area is surrounded on three sides by water.
2. I read where they have developed a new kind of engine what uses solar energy, or "sun power."

3. The students which ride this here bus make too much noise in the morning.

4. Them math problems look harder then they really are.

5. I ordered a box of stationery from you two weeks ago, but I have not yet received same.

6. A run-on sentence is where two sentences are erroneously joined as one.

7. Them girls always wear slacks.

8. Sandy read in the paper where it might snow tomorrow.

9. Aline used a lever to get the rock to move some.

10. They were the very ones which complained about the test.

11. Them boys from Boyton live a little ways down this road.

12. After the nurse's visit, Jody felt some better.

13. I'm afraid Carmela is much smarter then I am.

14. Them girls which are wearing corsages are to be ushers for today's assembly.

15. The band members were told to arrive early so they could rehearse in this here hall.

16. The new mayor said that she would try and find a solution to the parking problem.

17. Put three egg whites into the bowl; then whip same into a fine froth.

18. I see in the paper where the mayor wants to hold a special referendum.

19. Myopia is when you can't see distant objects clearly.

20. This here camera makes taking pictures very easy.

REVIEW EXERCISE A. Number your paper 1–10. Choose the correct form in parentheses, and write it after the proper number on your paper.

1. The Bar-H Ranch is (somewheres, somewhere) near Cheyenne.

2. Nora is much taller (than, then) Pauline.

3. Wally read (where, that) the governor had vetoed the bill.

4. Unless you cooperate, I will not be able to (learn, teach) you how to speak French.

5. Every spring we see (fewer, less) bluebirds.

6. You (had ought, ought) to congratulate yourself on your good luck.
7. It was Thomas Edison who (discovered, invented) the electric light bulb.
8. One of us must (of, have) made a mistake, for our answers disagree.
9. It (don't, doesn't) matter to me.
10. The treasurer's responsibilities include collecting dues, paying bills, keeping a running account of expenditures, (and etc., etc.).

REVIEW EXERCISE B. Write twenty original sentences correctly using the following words or phrases.

1. the effect	11. among the three girls
2. as if	12. between the two girls
3. not accepting	13. as though
4. not excepting	14. leave him
5. brought	15. let him
6. taken	16. Mia, Edith, and I respectfully
7. beside Dottie	17. Mia, Edith, and I respectively
8. besides Dottie	18. it affected
9. they emigrated	19. it effected
10. they immigrated	20. like

REVIEW EXERCISE C. Number your paper 1–30. Choose the correct form in parentheses, and write it after the proper number on your paper.

1. When Lincoln was first elected President, many people did not know what (kind of, kind of an) attitude he would take toward slavery.
2. If I could sing as (good, well) as Stephanie, I would (of, have) joined the Glee Club.
3. Tony must (have, of) walked a long (ways, way) in the wrong direction.
4. He (don't, doesn't) give true–false tests.

5. Carla should (of, have) won first prize.

6. She (doesn't, don't) usually like (them, those, that) kind of fish.

7. You shouldn't (of, have) taken advanced algebra when you could (of, have) taken business math.

8. The speakers took their (respectful, respective) places on the stage.

9. (Beside, Besides) being on the track team, Brenda is editor of the school paper.

10. He refuses to be (learned, taught) how to operate the switchboard.

11. Did he really see a ghost, or was it just an (allusion, illusion)?

12. The (affects, effects) of the drought were disastrous.

13. When you go to the game with Aunt Ellen, please act (as if, like) you knew the rules.

14. Please (bring, take) your schedule card with you when you go to your next class.

15. If you (leave, let) me do it, I will finish the posters tonight.

16. How much do you think the poor corn harvest will (affect, effect) the price of beef?

17. None of the wrestlers did very (good, well) in the tournament.

18. She addressed her teacher (respectfully, respectively).

19. "Smoking," said the coach, "will seriously (affect, effect) your performance in a game."

20. I cannot find my books (anywhere, anywheres).

21. (Being that, Because) a strike was called, no trucks went out that day.

22. I hope that you will (accept, except) my advice.

23. Rainy days don't seem to have any (affect, effect) on student attendance.

24. Because my grandmother was weary of the bleak Midlands, she (emigrated, immigrated) from England in 1908.

25. Does his escape (imply, infer) that he is guilty?

26. Virginia refused to (accept, except) the nomination.

27. We divided the duties (between, among) the five of us.

28. The inspector's face was drained of blood; he looked (like, as if) he had seen a ghost.

29. (Inside of, Inside) the cabin were two porcupines.

30. Every year there are (fewer, less) minnows in our streams.

The Double Negative

A *double negative* is a construction in which two negative words are used when one is sufficient. Before the eighteenth century, two or more negatives were often used in the same sentence to make the meaning more emphatic. Standard modern English no longer uses this method of gaining emphasis, and a double negative is generally considered to be nonstandard.

can't hardly, can't scarcely The words *hardly* and *scarcely* should not be used with *not* (or the contraction of *not*, *n't*).

> EXAMPLES **I can** [not *can't*] **hardly** hear you when you speak.
> We **had** [not *hadn't*] **scarcely** enough time to finish our essay test.

haven't but, haven't only In certain uses, *but* and *only* convey a negative meaning and should not be used with *not*.

> EXAMPLES We **have** [not *haven't*] **but** three more days.
> We **have** [not *haven't*] **only** one more chance.

no, nothing, none Do not use these negative words with another negative.

> NONSTANDARD There isn't no reason to be nervous.
> STANDARD There **is no** reason to be nervous.
> STANDARD There **isn't any** reason to be nervous.
> NONSTANDARD At first we couldn't see nothing.
> STANDARD At first we **could see nothing.**
> STANDARD At first we **couldn't see anything.**
> NONSTANDARD We searched the playground for clues but didn't find none.
> STANDARD We searched the playground for clues but **found none.**
> STANDARD We searched the playground for clues but **didn't find any.**

EXERCISE 5. The following sentences contain many of the usage errors covered in this chapter. Rewrite each sentence correctly. Practice saying *aloud* the correct sentences.

1. He might of drowned if it hadn't been for Claudia's clear thinking.
2. He don't know if he should ask Kristan to the dance because she hasn't hardly spoken to him in three days.
3. My grandmother she said that we hadn't ought to use the boat in such bad weather.
4. My grandfather has always been kind of timid.
5. I can't hardly help thinking she don't listen to what I say.
6. My cousins didn't hardly know how to swim, but they wouldn't of missed going to the lake.
7. If you had of been at the meeting, we wouldn't of had no arguments.
8. Pauline don't have nothing to do tonight.
9. The suit didn't fit me no more.
10. The little kitten what we found in the vacant lot didn't hardly seem alive.
11. Hadn't you ought to come to the meeting?
12. Try and remember where you hid them keys at.
13. That there heap of junk is not the kind of a secondhand car that I want.
14. Them apples what you brought were wormy.
15. The people which are in charge of checking the coats don't have no more hangers.
16. A foot fault in tennis is when the server steps over the base line before hitting the ball.
17. I read in the paper where the Dodgers bought them new players from the Giants.
18. These kind of books are the most popular in Mrs. Ito's class.
19. It don't look right to me, but then I don't know nothing about art.
20. She said that she was starting to feel better some.
21. When the sun set, the woods suddenly became sort of gloomy.
22. Because there wasn't no money for new squad cars, there are less cars in the precinct this year.

23. Sarah don't have but three more pages to do.
24. Leave us find out whether she will accept the appointment.
25. When you try and perform, it's not the same as practicing.

REVIEW EXERCISE D. The following sentences contain many of the common errors you have been studying. Rewrite the sentences correctly.

1. That there book isn't no good.
2. She lives a long ways from here.
3. He don't hardly know what he's talking about.
4. I couldn't hardly remember having made them mistakes; my mind must of been a blank.
5. There goes a person what has never done nobody any harm.
6. Being that my sister left for college, I can't borrow her books no more.
7. There isn't no state in this here country that she hasn't visited.
8. My mother she can't hardly help bragging about my brother's winning the four-year scholarship.
9. He fell off of a ladder and busted his leg.
10. You hadn't ought to of walked home in that there rain.
11. You can't hardly smell the smoke from here; the wind must of changed.
12. Because there was so much to do before the holidays, I hadn't hardly no time at all to buy the present what I saw in the catalogue.
13. A haze settled over the town, and you couldn't hardly see where you were going.
14. My baby sister tries to help some, but she's kind of clumsy.
15. Is this all the farther the road goes?
16. If you hadn't only enough books for half the students, you should of gone to the book room for more.
17. Our water pipes they bursted during the cold snap, and when my father he received the repair bill, he almost busted.
18. Being that my mother won't let me use the phone after eight o'clock, my friends they think she is strict.
19. A *tsunami* is when there is a tidal wave caused by an earthquake.

20. In this here paper I read where the mayor has appointed a new member of the park board.

21. You should of received your notice in the mail, since Inez don't never forget to send out the cards.

22. It don't seem right that Mr. Hodson should always pick on Gloria, being that she can't hardly help it if the bus is always late.

23. Here is a person which should try and do better.

24. Hadn't you ought to clean out this here locker?

25. My brother he says he can't hardly carry all them packages by himself.

Composition: Sentence Structure

PART THREE

Chapter **11**

Writing Complete Sentences

Sentence Fragments and Run-on Sentences

Two of the most common errors in student writing result from carelessness in marking the end of one sentence and the beginning of the next. The first kind of error, the *sentence fragment,* occurs when a part of a sentence — a phrase or subordinate clause, for example — is written as a complete sentence. The second, the *run-on sentence,* occurs when two or more sentences are run together with only a comma, or no punctuation at all, between them.

SENTENCE FRAGMENTS

11a. A *sentence fragment* is a group of words that does not express a complete thought. Since it is only a part of a sentence, it should not be allowed to stand by itself but should be kept in the sentence of which it is a part.

A group of words is not a sentence unless it has both a subject and a verb and expresses a complete thought. The following examples are fragments because they fail to meet one or both of these conditions.

FRAGMENT   The referee calling the foul. [The *–ing* form of a
            verb cannot function as the verb in a sentence unless
            it has a helping verb with it.]

FRAGMENT   Because the referee was calling the foul. [The sub-
            ordinating conjunction *Because* signals that what
            follows is only part of a larger sentence. Taken
            by itself, the fragment does not express a complete
            thought.]

Both of the fragments illustrated above are really parts
of a longer sentence:

EXAMPLES   The referee calling the foul was waving her arms in
            the air.

            Because the referee was calling a foul, she was waving
            her arms in the air.

Good writers sometimes punctuate fragments as sentences for stylistic reasons. For example, you may sometimes notice a fragment like this in a story:

FRAGMENT   Paul rides to school every day. *On his younger
            brother's tricycle.*

The second part is not a complete sentence. It is only a
prepositional phrase. The writer used a capital letter at the
beginning and a period at the end of the phrase for humorous effect, thinking that the point would be otherwise lost
to the reader.

> Paul rides to school every day on his younger
> brother's tricycle.

A better solution might have been to use a dash, thus gaining the desired emphasis while remaining within the limits
of conventional punctuation:

> Paul rides to school every day — on his younger
> brother's tricycle.

Although the use of fragments can be justified, the practice requires experience and judgment, and the beginning
writer will do well to avoid it.

The Phrase Fragment

A phrase is a group of words acting as a single part of speech and not containing a verb and its subject.

You will recall from your study of verbals (pages 64–74) that present participles and gerunds are words ending in *–ing*. Words ending in *–ing* cannot be used as verbs unless they follow a helping verb. With a helping verb like *am, are, has been, will be,* etc., they become complete verbs. It is the same with infinitive phrases. Like participial and gerund phrases, infinitive phrases can never stand alone. In order to make sense, they must be attached to a preceding or following sentence or be completed by being developed into a proper sentence.

A participial phrase must not be written as a sentence.

FRAGMENT   The woman giving us directions.   [a phrase; no verb]
CORRECTED   The woman **was giving** us directions.   [The present participle has been made into a complete verb by the addition of the helping verb *was*.]

FRAGMENT   We admired the seascape. Painted and signed by Winslow Homer.   [The participial phrase modifies the word *seascape*. It must be included in the sentence with the word it modifies.]
CORRECTED   We admired the seascape **painted and signed by Winslow Homer.**   [The fragment is corrected by including the participial phrase in the sentence with the word it modifies.]

A gerund phrase must not be written as a sentence.

FRAGMENT   Many of us dislike working in the kitchen. Cleaning and scrubbing objects which in a few hours will be dirty again.   [Here a gerund phrase functioning as an appositive of *working* is cut off from it by the period. It must be reconnected.]
CORRECTED   Many of us dislike working in the kitchen, **cleaning and scrubbing objects which in a few hours will be dirty again.**   [The gerund phrase fragment is corrected by including it in the sentence.]

An infinitive phrase must not be written as a sentence.

FRAGMENT You must first learn to float. To swim properly and with confidence. [The phrase cannot stand alone. It should be attached to the preceding sentence.]

CORRECTED **To swim properly and with confidence,** you must first learn to float.

A prepositional phrase or a succession of prepositional phrases must not be written as a sentence.

FRAGMENT The post office is two blocks from here. Near the corner on the north side of the street. [Here three successive prepositional phrases are isolated. They make sense only when included in the sentence.]

CORRECTED The post office is two blocks from here **near the corner on the north side of the street.**

In each of the examples above, the sentence fragments were cut off from the sentences they were part of by improper punctuation. This kind of mistake is easily corrected: simply attach the isolated phrase to the parent sentence.

EXERCISE 1. Below are ten phrase fragments. Convert each one into a complete sentence by using one of two methods as shown in the example: (1) attach it to an independent clause, or (2) develop the phrase into a complete sentence.

EXAMPLE 1. putting on her jacket
     1. *Putting on her jacket, Cindy left the theater.* [attached]
     or
     1. *Cindy was putting on her jacket.* [developed]

1. standing on the deck beside the captain
2. to make set shots consistently from outside the pivot position
3. on lower Main Street under the Lexington Bridge
4. puzzled by the question
5. to stay alert
6. finishing her assignment

7. murmuring something about a meeting
8. burned and blistered by the sun
9. playing tennis in the hot sun
10. performing the chemistry experiments

The Appositive Fragment

An appositive is a noun or pronoun that follows another noun or pronoun to identify or explain it. An appositive phrase is made up of an appositive and its modifiers; it should not be written as a separate sentence.

EXAMPLES   Mike, **the best mechanic in the garage,** worked on my car. [*The best mechanic in the garage* is an appositive. It is in apposition with *Mike*.]

In two years I will graduate from Madison High School, **a red brick building with a golden dome.** [*A red brick building with a golden dome* is in apposition with *Madison High School*.]

Sometimes a hasty writer will treat an appositive phrase as a complete sentence and leave it standing alone, even though it lacks a verb and subject and does not express a complete thought.

FRAGMENT   The amateur boat-builder was constructing a simple model. A small outboard cruiser of conventional design.

CORRECTED   The amateur boat-builder was constructing a simple model, **a small outboard cruiser of conventional design.** [The appositive phrase has been attached to the sentence in which it belongs.]

EXERCISE 2. Number from 1 to 10. If an item consists of a sentence followed by an appositive fragment, write the last word in the sentence and follow it with a comma and the first word of the appositive. If an item consists of two sentences, write *C*.

1. Before railroads, much inland transportation of freight was done by means of canals. Hand-dug, water-filled ditches that connected natural waterways.

2. Between 1790 and 1850, Americans constructed a canal network totaling 4,400 miles. A distance greater than that between New York and San Francisco.

3. An essential feature of the canals was their locks. Devices by which boats were raised or lowered from one level to another to accommodate changes in the terrain.

4. Where locks were not practical, boats were moved up or down on an inclined plane. A short boat railway on which a boat was raised or lowered by cable.

5. Canal boats were towed by horses walking on towpaths alongside the canals. This was a slow method of transportation.

6. The horses were driven on the paths by youths between the ages of twelve and seventeen. They were called loggees.

7. On the Erie Canal in 1850, a thousand people were employed as loggees. They were exposed to rough weather and if they let their towlines become tangled with those of a passing boat, to the wrath of boat captains.

8. Some boats were passenger boats. The so-called fast packets, which moved at a speed of five miles an hour.

9. In good weather, passengers enjoyed watching the slowly passing landscape from the roof of the boat's cabin. The only suitable deck space.

10. At night the cabin was a common bedroom. The author Nathaniel Hawthorne named it a "chamber of horrors."

The Subordinate Clause Fragment

Although the subordinate clause does have a verb and a subject, it depends upon the independent clause of a sentence to complete its meaning. Standing alone, a subordinate clause suggests a question which it does not answer.

EXAMPLES   Because the machine is so dangerous. [Well . . .?
What will happen?]
If you do not know how to operate it. [Well . . .?
What will happen?]

An isolated subordinate clause must be attached to an independent clause in order to complete its meaning. It should not be written as a sentence.

FRAGMENT   Television make-up differs from stage make-up. Because it must withstand the intense heat from the studio lamps.

CORRECTED   Television make-up differs from stage make-up **because it must withstand the intense heat from the studio lamps.**

FRAGMENT   Lamps that burned fat or olive oil served as the only source of artificial light until 1600. When petroleum was discovered.

CORRECTED   Lamps that burned fat or olive oil served as the only source of artificial light until 1600, **when petroleum was discovered.**

▶ NOTE In combining an adverb clause with an independent clause, the adverb clause may either precede or follow the independent clause.

EXAMPLES   **If you bring your guitar to the picnic,** we can have some music. [adverb clause first]
We can have some music **if you bring your guitar to the picnic.** [adverb clause last]

EXERCISE 3. The following paragraphs contain several sentence fragments. They are all subordinate clauses that should be attached to an independent clause. Copy the paragraphs, changing the punctuation to eliminate the subordinate clause fragments.

Have you ever taken a course in film history? Some film historians believe that Alice Guy Blache was the first person. Who used the medium of motion pictures to tell a story. After she had worked as a director for Gaumont in Paris. She came to the United States. Where she formed her own production company in 1919. When she closed it down and began making films for Metro and Pathé. She returned to France in 1922. Since she was unable to find work in France. She retired from the cinema industry. Still in existence are some of this enterprising woman's American films. Which were made under the Solax company name. Alice Guy Blache died in an American nursing home in 1968 at the age of ninety-five. Her death received little public notice.

In the opinion of many critics, Sarah Maldoror is one of the most important of the film makers. Who are emerging from the Third World. Among her best films is *Sambizanga*. Which is set in Angola during the period before the uprising against Portuguese

rule in 1961. *Sambizanga* deals with the conflicts between the Angolans and the Portuguese.
Do you know what a documentary film is? Have you ever seen one? While some people use the camera to present a fictional story. Others use the camera to try to capture life exactly as it is. In this latter category is Chick Strand, another important film maker. Whose films are part documentary and part personal interpretation of people and events. Her deep concern with anthropology and ethnography is reflected in each of her films. Which attempt to present all of the elements that will enable the viewer to see the people she is filming exactly as they are.

Check your local papers and see if you can find a showing of films by any of these three women.

EXERCISE 4. Add an independent clause either at the beginning or at the end of each of the following subordinate clauses to make ten complete sentences. When an adverb clause comes at the beginning of a sentence, it should be followed by a comma.

1. if we do well on the test
2. when they send the message
3. who can play several musical instruments
4. which I have never read
5. as we shut off the motor
6. what you forgot to say
7. before you do anything impulsive
8. that he was your brother
9. until she has finished her assignment
10. while I was in the dentist's office

EXERCISE 5. Some of the following groups of words are complete sentences. Others are fragments. On your paper, mark the complete sentences with an *S*, and correct the fragments by making them parts of complete sentences.

1. Furnished with beautifully finished cottages, the resort was one of the finest in the area.
2. Running and dodging are features of lacrosse. Whose original

object among its creators seems to have been the development of endurance and agility.

3. If you decide to go.
4. The friends shopped all day at the new shopping mall.
5. Elected by an overwhelming number of the students.
6. As she opened the door and peered out.
7. Because it was foggy and the visibility was poor.
8. Located in the middle of a swamp. The cabin was four miles from the highway.
9. Driving at night can be dangerous. Blinded by the lights of an approaching car. We almost hit a tree.
10. Because they wanted to escape the heat. They left for the mountains. Setting out in the early part of August.
11. To climb up the steep cliff with a heavy pack and camera slung on his back was difficult.
12. He was plagued with difficulties. Losing his way, running out of water, and falling over vines and creepers.
13. How he envied the hawk. Gliding effortlessly high over the tangle of the swamp and thickets.
14. To break through the last thicket of brambles and dwarf cedar into the clearing. This was the hope that drove him on.
15. This was the Maine wilderness. Through which Arnold and his men had dragged cannon and other heavy equipment on their way to Quebec.

THE RUN–ON SENTENCE

11b. Avoid the run-on sentence. Do not use a comma between sentences. Do not omit punctuation at the end of a sentence.

There are two main ways in which independent clauses can be combined in a single sentence: (1) by means of a comma plus a word like *and* or *but;* (2) by means of a semicolon. The following examples illustrate these two methods.

> Peanuts were more than just food to George Washington Carver, and in his laboratory he used them to make such things as ink and shampoo.   [A comma plus *and* is used to join the two independent clauses.]

> Peanuts were more than just food to George Washington
> Carver; in his laboratory he used them to make such things
> as ink and shampoo.   [A semicolon is used to join the clauses.]

Other devices, such as the colon and the dash, are sometimes used, but a comma alone is never enough between
independent clauses. Using a comma or no punctuation at
all in this situation results in the run-on sentence:

> Peanuts were more than just food to George Washington
> Carver, in his laboratory he used them to make such things
> as ink and shampoo.

Like the sentence fragment, the run-on sentence is sometimes used effectively by experienced writers, especially
when its parts are very short. A famous example is the
translation of Julius Caesar's boast "I came, I saw, I
conquered."

An easy test for spotting run-on sentences consists of
simply reading your compositions aloud. The rise or fall of
your voice and the pause you make at the end of a sentence
sound quite different from the intonation and pause that a
comma usually signals.

EXERCISE 6. The following passages contain a number
of run-on sentences. Determine where each sentence properly begins and ends, and write the last word in the sentence
with the proper end mark after it. Then write the first word
of the following sentence with a capital letter.

1. Having been excused early, we hurried to the locker room and
   changed to our uniforms, when the coach called us, we were
   ready to go the big bus drew up in the drive, and just as we had
   done a dozen other times, we piled in and took our usual seats
   this trip was different, however, everybody knew how different
   it was we would return either as champions of the state or as
   just another second-rate team.

2. It was the hottest day we could remember, coming down the
   street, we were sure we could see heat waves rising from the
   sidewalk, we felt as though we'd never get home we ambled
   up the street in a daze, hoping we'd last just one more block,

we knew if we could make it there would be large bottles of ice-cold soda awaiting us.

3. Working on a lake steamer all summer was monotonous, it was also better than any other job I could have obtained, I loved the water and the ships and the rough and ready crew with whom I worked, the food was good the work was not too strenuous, if it hadn't been for the sameness of the routine day after day, I would probably never have left.

REVIEW EXERCISE. Read the following paragraphs carefully. They contain sentence fragments and run-on sentences. Copy the passage, removing all fragments and run-ons by changing the punctuation and capital letters whenever necessary.

Our national bird is the great bald eagle. As most Americans know. Similar to the bald eagle is the golden eagle. Which has a wingspread up to seven-and-a-half feet. The national bird is protected by law, but the golden eagle is not, the result is that hunters are rapidly diminishing the number of these great birds. If the golden eagles are not also given the protection of the law, they may become extinct. In a few years.

The National Audubon Society says that the annual slaughter of golden eagles is a national disgrace. Some hunters bagging hundreds of eagles a year. Texas and Oklahoma are the principal hunting territories, the birds are often shot from airplanes by gunners. Who are paid both by sheep ranchers and by manufacturers. Who want the feathers. Sheep ranchers claim the eagles menace sheep, tourists buy the feathers. Protecting the golden eagle will also provide further protection for the bald eagle. Because hunters often mistakenly kill bald eagles. Which, at a certain stage in growth, resemble golden eagles.

The golden eagle migrates to Texas and Oklahoma from northern regions. Such as Canada, Alaska, and our other Northwestern states. Golden eagles will be protected. If Congress amends the Bald Eagle Act. To include golden eagles.

Chapter 12

Sentence Combining and Revising

Emphasis and Variety in Sentences

Although a knowledge of grammar and punctuation is of obvious help in learning to write correct sentences, there is much more to effective writing than avoiding errors in sentence structure. The main difference between good writing and bad writing is not a matter of correctness, but a matter of *style*.

Style is a hard word to define exactly, but its essential meaning is "a way of doing something." The idea of style can be applied to many other things besides writing. For example, a professional basketball player and an ordinary player perform essentially the same operations in dribbling the ball, yet even a spectator who knows little about the game can usually see a difference. In basketball, and in most other things, there is a difference between doing things well and doing them any old way.

There are probably more ways of writing a sentence than there are ways of dribbling a basketball. Still, from the point of view of style, it is quite easy to tell a good sentence from a bad one. It is considerably harder to write good sentences all of the time. Nevertheless, in the pages which follow, you will find some principles that should help you to write more interesting sentences.

SENTENCE COMBINING

Short sentences are often effective in a composition, but a long series of short sentences tends to irritate readers. Notice how the short, choppy sentences in the following paragraph sound immature and make the paragraph less interesting to read.

> The first person to go over Niagara Falls in a barrel and live was Annie Edson Taylor. She was a schoolteacher. She was from Michigan. On September 24, 1901, she entered the upper Niagara River. She entered the river above the Horseshoe Falls. The Horseshoe Falls drops 51 meters to the lower Niagara River. Seventeen minutes passed. Then Canadian rescuers pulled Annie from the river. She was badly bruised and shaken. She had escaped serious harm. Annie did not gain fame for her dangerous act. She did not gain fortune. Years later she died in a poorhouse.

Notice how the short, choppy sentences in the preceding passage can be combined into longer, smoother sentences.

> The first person to go over Niagara Falls in a barrel and live was Annie Edson Taylor, a schoolteacher from Michigan. On September 24, 1901, she entered the upper Niagara River above the Horseshoe Falls, which drops 51 meters to the lower Niagara River. After seventeen minutes had passed, Canadian rescuers pulled Annie from the river. Badly bruised and shaken, she nevertheless escaped serious harm. Annie did not gain fame or fortune for her dangerous act, and years later she died in a poorhouse.

A number of sentence-combining devices have been used to rewrite the original passage. For example, the first three sentences have been combined through the use of an appositive phrase. Other sentences in the original passage have been combined through the use of coordination and subordination. In this chapter you will study sentence combining, an effective means to achieve a fluent, mature style.

12a. Combine short, related sentences by inserting adjectives, adverbs, or prepositional phrases.

TWO SENTENCES   The coach praised the players.
The coach was delighted.

ONE SENTENCE   The **delighted** coach praised the players.
[adjective]

TWO SENTENCES   The tired fans left the stadium.
The fans left quietly.

ONE SENTENCE   **Quietly,** the tired fans left the stadium.
[adverb]

THREE SENTENCES   The deer were feeding.
The deer were on the hill.
The hill was behind our house.

ONE SENTENCE   The deer were feeding **on the hill behind our house.** [prepositional phrases]

When you join short sentences by inserting adjectives, adverbs, or prepositional phrases, you may invent different ways of combining the same sentences. In such instances, the choice of word order is up to you, the writer. The combined sentences, however, should not change the meaning of the original sentences, nor should adjectives, adverbs, or prepositional phrases be misplaced within the combined sentence.

EXERCISE 1.   Combine each group of short, related sentences into one sentence by inserting adjectives, adverbs, or prepositional phrases. There may be more than one correct way to combine the sentences.

EXAMPLE   1. The basketball game will be televised.
The game is tonight.
The game is in the school gym.

1. *The basketball game tonight in the school gym will be televised.*

1. Basketball has a history.
The history is interesting.

2. The inventor was James Naismith.
He was the inventor of basketball.
He was from Springfield, Massachusetts.

3. In the first games, players shot a soccer ball at a peach
   basket.
   There were nine players on each team.
   The peach basket was suspended.

4. Basketball rules have changed.
   The rules have changed since 1891.
   The rules have changed greatly.

5. Basketball is popular.
   It is popular today.
   It is popular among men and women.
   It is popular all over the country.

6. Women basketball players compete.
   They are professional players.
   They compete before large crowds.
   They compete regularly.

7. The speed of modern basketball is surprising.
   It is often surprising.
   It is surprising to the spectator.

8. Dribbling, leaping, and shooting are the skills players practice.
   Dribbling, leaping, and shooting are skills in basketball.
   Most players practice these skills.
   They practice them for many hours.

9. Players concentrate on passing, shot-blocking, and play-
   making.
   They concentrate during team practice.
   They concentrate under a coach's direction.
   They usually concentrate.

10. Players may organize a play and then execute the play.
    They may organize a play for hours.
    They execute the play during a game.
    They execute the play in seconds.

**12b. Combine short, related sentences by using parti-
cipial phrases.**

A participial phrase (see pages 68–69) is a group of related
words that contains a participle and that acts as an adjective, modifying a noun or a pronoun. In the following examples, all the words in heavy type are part of participial
phrases.

EXAMPLES **Galloping across the meadow,** the horse neared the forest.
Elated by the news, we prepared a celebration.

Two closely related sentences can be combined by making one sentence a participial phrase.

TWO SENTENCES The dogs yelped loudly.
The dogs ran down the trail.

ONE SENTENCE **Yelping loudly,** the dogs ran down the trail.

A participial phrase must be placed close to the noun or pronoun it modifies. Otherwise the phrase might confuse the reader.

MISPLACED Flying overhead, we saw an eagle.
CORRECTED We saw an eagle flying overhead.

EXERCISE 2. Combine each of the following groups of sentences into one sentence by using a participial phrase. There may be more than one correct way to combine the sentences. Add commas where necessary. (See pages 406–07 for the use of commas to set off introductory phrases.)

EXAMPLE 1. He blared his radio.
He woke up the house.
1. *Blaring his radio, he woke up the house.*

1. Music is an ancient word.
It originates in the Greek word *mousikos*.
2. In Greek *mousikos* is an adjective.
It means "concerned with the Muses."
3. The Muses of Greek mythology ruled over the arts.
They inspired artists in their work.
4. The halfback was evading the tacklers easily.
The halfback scored a touchdown.
5. Juanita Platero writes about Navajo culture.
The writing describes the conflict between old and new ideas.
6. Richard Wright was born a sharecropper's son.
He fought valiantly for an education.
7. *Meridian* was written by Alice Walker.
It is a novel about hope and courage.

8. Eudora Welty's stories are full of eccentric characters.
The stories are set in rural places.

9. The memoir *An Unfinished Woman* lay on the table.
It was assigned last week.

10. James Baldwin's essays depict his youth in Harlem.
These essays are very popular.

12c. Combine short, related sentences by using appositive phrases.

Appositive phrases (see pages 77–78) are useful for explaining or identifying nouns or pronouns. The following sentence contains an appositive phrase in heavy type.

EXAMPLE   The poodle, **a very intelligent dog,** is the most popular breed in the United States today.

Two related sentences can be combined by using an appositive phrase.

TWO SENTENCES   The Shetland stands about one-meter tall at the shoulders.
The Shetland is the smallest of ponies.

ONE SENTENCE   The Shetland, **the smallest of ponies,** stands about one-meter tall at the shoulders.

EXERCISE 3.   Combine each pair of sentences by turning one sentence into an appositive phrase. Be sure to put the phrase next to the noun or pronoun it identifies. Punctuate the sentence correctly. (See pages 410–11 for the use of commas to set off appositive phrases.)

EXAMPLE   1. The kiwi has a strong sense of smell.
The kiwi is a flightless bird of New Zealand.
1. *The kiwi, a flightless bird of New Zealand, has a strong sense of smell.*

1. The railroad worm looks like a train with a red headlight.
The railroad worm is actually a light-producing beetle.

2. The weaver may build nests measuring five meters across.
The weaver is a sparrowlike African bird.

3. Koalas carry their young in pouches.
Koalas are living models of the teddy bear.

4. On my travels to South America I saw an Araucana.
   An Araucana is a hen that lays blue and green eggs.
5. The Atlantic bay scallop may have as many as a hundred eyes.
   The Atlantic bay scallop is a delicious shellfish.
6. The flounder is a flat fish that swims on its side.
   The flounder has both eyes on one side of its head.
7. The walking catfish can survive on land for a long time.
   This catfish is a recent import to North America.
8. Prairie dogs greet each other with a kiss.
   The kiss is a touching of their noses and front teeth.
9. The zoo has a colony of animals that never need to drink water.
   The animals are kangaroo rats.
10. That noise sounds like a barking dog.
    It is the voice of a barking frog.

12d. Combine short, related sentences by using compound subjects and verbs.

Compound subjects and verbs (see pages 35–36) are joined by conjunctions such as *and, but,* or *or* and by correlative conjunctions such as *either — or, neither — nor,* or *both — and.*

EXAMPLES   Mom **and** Dad took us to see Williamsburg.
        The committee could **neither** agree on the amendment **nor** vote on the motion.
        Both students **and** teachers arrive early **and** leave late.

Short, related sentences may often be combined by using a compound verb or a compound subject, or both.

TWO SENTENCES   We went to the movie theater.
        We saw the new horror film.
ONE SENTENCE   We went to the movie theater **and** saw the new horror film.
FOUR SENTENCES   The players rushed to home plate.
        The coach rushed to home plate.
        The players protested the umpire's call.
        The coach protested the umpire's call.
ONE SENTENCE   **Both** the players **and** the coach rushed to home plate **and** protested the umpire's call.

EXERCISE 4. Combine the following groups of sentences into one sentence by using compound subjects and verbs. Be sure the subjects and verbs agree in number in each sentence you write.

1. Refined sugar is not necessary in a healthful diet.
   Too much salt is also not necessary in a healthful diet.
2. We should include a food from the bread group in every meal.
   We should avoid overeating carbohydrates.
3. A healthy person eats a varied diet.
   A healthy person gets plenty of exercise.
   A healthy person refrains from too much sugar or bread.
4. Meat provides essential protein.
   Beans provide essential protein.
   Rice provides essential protein.
5. Long-distance runners control their diet.
   Football players control their diet.
   The runners drink plenty of fluids.
   Football players drink plenty of fluids.

REVIEW EXERCISE A. Rewrite the following paragraph by combining short, choppy sentences.

Romeo and Juliet are two young people from rival families. They fall in love. They marry secretly. Romeo is exiled for killing Juliet's cousin in a duel. Romeo returns at night. He finds Juliet lying in a deep coma. Romeo thinks she is dead. Romeo kills himself with poison. Juliet awakens. She discovers Romeo's corpse. She kills herself with his dagger. Their senseless deaths stun the rival families. The deaths bring reconciliation.

12e. Combine short, related sentences by writing a compound sentence.

A compound sentence (see pages 93–94) is really two or more simple sentences joined together by the conjunctions *and, but, or, nor, for,* or *yet.*

EXAMPLE   We started for home, **but** the rain made travel difficult.

When writing a compound sentence, be sure the ideas you connect are related and equal in importance. Unrelated or unequal ideas should not be combined in a compound sentence.

UNRELATED IDEAS The actors rehearsed their lines, and snow fell in record amounts.

RELATED IDEAS The actors rehearsed their lines, and the musicians tuned their instruments.

EXERCISE 5. Five of the following groups of sentences contain two or more closely related ideas. Combine these ideas into a compound sentence, using *and, but, or, nor, for,* or *yet.* Two groups contain unrelated ideas. They should not be combined. Add commas where necessary. (For the use of commas in a compound sentence, see pages 400–01.)

1. The Voyager space probes have discovered much about Jupiter.
   We still have much to learn.
2. Earlier pictures had suggested that Jupiter's atmosphere was calm.
   The Voyager craft uncovered high-speed winds.
3. Voyager photographs showed lightning flashes.
   Scientists detected a new moon orbiting the planet.
4. Jupiter has several moons.
   Scientists are especially interested in the moon named Io.
5. Voyager passed close to Io.
   Scientists wanted a clear look at this small moon.
6. Volcanoes erupt on Io's surface.
   Geology includes the study of volcanoes.
7. Space probes may one day encounter life in another part of the universe.
   So far, there have been no signs of life.

12f. Combine short, related sentences into a complex sentence by putting one idea into a subordinate clause.

A complex sentence (see pages 94–95) has an independent clause and at least one subordinate clause.

(1) Use an adjective clause to combine sentences.

An adjective clause (see pages 84–86) is a subordinate clause which, like an adjective, modifies a noun or a pronoun. In the following example, the adjective clause is in heavy type.

EXAMPLE   We found a book **that had been printed more than two
hundred years ago.**

Adjective clauses begin with one of the relative pronouns: *who, whom, whose, which,* or *that.*

To combine two sentences with an adjective clause, supply the necessary relative pronoun.

TWO SENTENCES   The driver reported the accident.
The accident had blocked traffic in both directions.

ONE SENTENCE   The driver reported the accident, which had blocked traffic in both directions.

EXERCISE 6.   Combine each of the following groups of sentences into one sentence by using an adjective clause. Add commas where necessary. (For the use of commas with nonessential clauses, see pages 403–05).

1. Sacajawea guided Lewis and Clark.
   Lewis and Clark explored the Louisiana territory.
2. Matthew Henson was among the first explorers to reach the North Pole.
   Robert Peary chose Henson as his chief assistant.
3. Margaret Mead studied families in Samoa, Bali, and New Guinea.
   Her books are very popular today.
4. E. A. Martel pioneered in cave exploration.
   He charted deep vertical caves in Europe.
5. Amelia Earhart tried to fly around the world at the equator.
   She crashed into the Pacific Ocean.
6. Silvia Earle tests diving suits.
   The suits enable her to descend 380 meters.

7. Heinrich Schliemann unearthed an ancient city.
   This city, he believed, was the Troy of Homer's *Iliad*.
8. Inez Mexia was a famous botanical explorer.
   She spent months in the jungles of South America.
9. Antarctica has a harsh climate.
   It has never been fully explored.
10. Tenzing Norgay finally scaled Mount Everest.
    He had been climbing mountains for many years.

(2) Use an adverb clause to combine sentences.

An adverb clause (see pages 88–89) is a subordinate clause which, like an adverb, modifies a verb, an adjective, or an adverb.

EXAMPLE   **If the team scores this goal,** it will win the divisional championship.

Adverb clauses, like adverbs, may tell *when, how, where, to what extent,* or *under what condition* an action is done. An adverb clause begins with a subordinating conjunction. Study the following list:

Common Subordinating Conjunctions

after	before	than	whenever
although	if	unless	where
as	since	until	wherever
because	so that	when	while

When you combine two short sentences by turning one of them into an adverb clause, be careful to choose the correct subordinating conjunction.[1] Because a subordinating conjunction shows the relationship between clauses, a poorly chosen conjunction will show a false or meaningless relationship. For example, a number of subordinating conjunctions could be used to join these two sentences, but not all of them would show a relationship that makes sense.

TWO SENTENCES   At camp we get up.
                The sun rises.

[1] Choosing a subordinating conjunction is further discussed on page 252.

UNCLEAR At camp we get up until the sun rises.
CLEAR At camp we get up **when** the sun rises.

EXERCISE 7. Combine each of the following groups of ideas into one sentence by putting one idea into an adverb clause. Refer to the list of subordinating conjunctions on page 240. Vary the conjunctions you choose. Add commas where necessary. (For the use of commas with introductory clauses, see pages 406–07.)

1. A bill begins its passage into law.
   A representative sends a bill to the clerk of the House.
2. The Speaker of the House routes all bills to House committees.
   Relatively few bills pass beyond the committee stage.
3. A committee sends the approved bill to the full House.
   All representatives can have a vote.
4. The House passes the bill.
   It must also win the approval of the Senate.
5. A Senate committee approves or amends a similar bill.
   It moves to the full Senate.
6. The Senate bill is approved.
   The bill must agree with the House version.
7. The two bills go to a House–Senate conference committee.
   A compromise bill is agreed to.
8. A bill passes both the Senate and the House.
   It goes to the President to be signed into law.
9. The bill becomes law.
   The President vetoes it.
10. A vetoed bill can become law.
    A two-thirds majority in both House and Senate can override the President's veto.

(3) Use a noun clause to combine sentences.

Noun clauses (see pages 90–91) are usually introduced by *that, what, whatever, who, whoever, whom,* or *whomever.*

EXAMPLE The jury decided **that the defendant was innocent of the charges.**

Two ideas can be combined by using a noun clause.

TWO SENTENCES   The doctor said something about nutrition.
                 It was important.
ONE SENTENCE   **What the doctor said about nutrition** was important.

EXERCISE 8. Combine each of the following groups of ideas into one sentence by turning one of the ideas into a noun clause.

1. We are going to the fair tonight.
   Nancy told me.
2. The wheel was invented long ago.
   Exactly when is still unknown.
3. The ticket seller refused to admit us.
   My father wanted to know why.
4. Bernie told us something.
   We wanted to hear it.
5. Fifteen players were injured.
   This fact did not affect the coach's game plan.

REVIEW EXERCISE B. Combine each of the following groups of sentences into one sentence. There may be more than one correct way to combine them. Add commas where necessary.

1. American artists have various backgrounds.
   The artists are modern.
   The artists come from many different places.
2. Marisol Escobar spent her childhood in Venezuela.
   She moved at the age of eleven.
   She moved to the United States with her family.
3. Marisol prefers to use only her first name.
   She has displayed her work at the Museum of Modern Art.
   She has displayed her work in a special room at the museum.
4. Gwendolyn Brooks was born in Kansas.
   She was raised in Chicago.
   She was the first black woman to receive the Pulitzer Prize.
   The prize she won was for poetry.

5. Miss Brooks has been recognized as a major American poet.
   She has been recognized for a long time.
   She has been elected to the National Institute of Letters.
6. Hiroko Yajima is originally from Tokyo.
   She is a young violinist.
   She came to New York.
   There she made her professional debut.
7. She has been praised for her sensitivity.
   She has been praised for her agility.
   She has been praised for her accurate pitch.
   She has become a favorite of the critics.
8. Fernando Bujones has lived in New York City.
   He is Cuban-born.
   He has been a dancer with the American Ballet Theater.
9. Cicely Tyson is a native-born American.
   She has appeared on television.
   She appeared as a young African woman.
   This woman refused to adopt Western culture.
10. Miss Tyson is best known for something.
    It is her portrayal of Rebecca.
    Rebecca is the resilient young mother in the movie *Sounder*.

REVIEW EXERCISE C. Rewrite the following paragraph by combining short sentences into longer sentences. There may be more than one correct way to combine the sentences. Add commas where necessary.

The volcanic explosion of Krakatoa produced a noise. Krakatoa is an Indonesian island. The noise was one of the loudest ever heard. People claimed the noise sounded like a cannon. The people were on the island of Rodriguez. Rodriguez is over 5000 kilometers away. The volcanic explosion caused tidal waves. The tidal waves traveled over 1300 kilometers. The tidal waves killed over 36,000 people. For three years people all over the world saw exceptionally brilliant sunsets. Fine dust scattered by the volcano into the atmosphere caused the brilliant sunsets. Krakatoa's explosion, however, had only one-fifth the force of the eruption at Thera. Thera is an island in the Aegean Sea. This eruption probably destroyed the Minoan civilization in 1470 B.C.

VARYING SENTENCE BEGINNINGS

12g. Vary the beginnings of your sentences.

The usual way to form an English sentence is to begin with the subject and end with the predicate. Any piece of writing in which most of the sentences depart from this natural order is certain to strike a reader as artificial. However, an unbroken sequence of subject-predicate sentences may result in another stylistic fault — monotony. Such a sequence is monotonous because it lacks the logical connections and special emphasis that variation in sentence structure can provide.

Compare the following versions of the same paragraph. In the first, each sentence begins in the same way. In the second, an attempt has been made to achieve emphasis and clarity by varying sentence beginnings.

NOT VARIED

The trial had been scheduled for two o'clock. The audience was noisily settling itself in the courtroom for the coming show. The lawyers were quietly talking and shuffling piles of papers at the polished tables in the front of the room. The bell in the courthouse tower struck two in resounding tones. Judge Perez, dignified in her long black gown, walked slowly to her bench. The clerk rasped out, "Everyone rise." The room seemed suddenly to lift for a moment; then it settled back into an ominous silence. The judge opened the case of *The People* v. *John Strong* in a manner which seemed to imply that such trials happened every day of her life.

VARIED

The trial had been scheduled for two o'clock. In the courtroom the audience was noisily settling itself for the coming show. At the polished tables in the front of the room, the lawyers were quietly talking and shuffling piles of papers. When the bell in the courthouse tower struck two in resounding tones, Judge Perez, dignified in her long black gown, walked slowly to her bench. "Everybody rise," rasped the clerk. Suddenly the room seemed to lift for a moment; then it settled back into an ominous silence. In a manner which seemed to imply that these trials happened every day of her life, the judge opened the case of *The People* v. *John Strong*.

You need not avoid the normal order of sentences merely for the sake of variety, but often you can increase the force and clarity of a statement by beginning it with an important modifier.

The exercises that follow are intended to give you practice in using different kinds of sentence openers. Used sparingly, such devices will improve your writing.

(1) You may begin a sentence with a single-word modifier — an adverb, an adjective, or a participle.

EXAMPLES   **Instantly** I felt better.   [adverb]
Thick and slimy, the mud oozed from under the wheels.   [adjectives]
Grinning, Myra tuned in her favorite program. [present participle]
Dejected, the coach sat on the bench and brooded over his team.   [past participle]

EXERCISE 9. The following sentences, all of which begin with a simple subject, each contain a single-word modifier which can be placed at the beginning of the sentence. Find this modifier and rewrite the sentence, placing the modifier first. The sentences in this and the following exercises are good sentences. You are asked to rewrite them so that you will learn a variety of ways of expressing the same idea.

EXAMPLE   1. Our system of measurements will eventually be changed.
1. *Eventually our system of measurements will be changed.*

1. The United States is planning cautiously to introduce the metric system.
2. This system, unfamiliar and different, will change American habits quite a bit.
3. Our vocabulary of measurement will gradually be replaced by a new one.
4. The metric system, tested and refined, has been in use in Europe and most of the rest of the world since the early nineteenth century.

5. The standard unit of measurement until then, surprisingly, was a person's hand or foot.
6. This obviously is not a standard size.
7. The metric system, comprehensive and orderly, includes measurements of length, weight, volume, and temperature.
8. An inch converts metrically to 2.54 centimeters; an ounce to 28.3 grams; a quart to .946 liters; and 32° Fahrenheit to 0° Celsius (or Centigrade).
9. The notion of changing to another system once seemed forbidding.
10. Anyone, informed and willing, can make the conversions with ease.

EXERCISE 10. Write five sentences of your own beginning with single-word modifiers. Include at least one adjective, one adverb, and one participial modifier.

(2) You may begin a sentence with a phrase: a prepositional phrase, a participial phrase, an appositive phrase, or an infinitive phrase.

EXAMPLES **At the sound of the bell,** the teacher collected the papers. [prepositional phrase]
Having examined the records, the lawyer prepared a new deed. [participial phrase]
An excellent example of modern architecture, the new city hall is a favorite tourist attraction. [appositive phrase]
To learn to swim better, we took lessons at the pool. [infinitive phrase]

EXERCISE 11. The following sentences, all of which begin with the subject, each contain a phrase modifier which can be placed at the beginning of the sentence. Rephrase each sentence by placing the modifying phrase at the beginning. Place a comma after each introductory phrase.

1. Pompeii was a well-to-do commercial city at the foot of Mt. Vesuvius.

2. Its population at the time of its destruction was about 30,000.

3. Archaeologists have discovered many facts about the life and times of ancient Pompeii to add to our knowledge of bygone days.

4. Wealthy Romans, attracted by the beauty of the location and healthfulness of the climate, built many villas there.

5. The streets, paved with blocks of lava, were usually wide and straight.

6. The Forum was a square, completely surrounded by temples and public buildings, near the western edge of the city.

7. Mt. Vesuvius had never given any indication of its volcanic character up to the year A.D. 63.

8. The inhabitants, still rebuilding their city from the ravages of earthquakes, were overwhelmed by the sudden eruption of August 24, A.D. 79.

9. The people fled the city to save their lives.

10. The existence of Pompeii was forgotten during the Middle Ages, and it was not until 1763 that excavations of the city began.

EXERCISE 12. Rewrite the following sentences so that each begins with either a word or a phrase modifier. In rearranging the sentences, you may wish to drop some of the words or add others; you may do so provided you keep the original meaning. Hints are given for the first five.

EXAMPLE   1. We were tired and decided to leave the party early.
          1. *Tired, we decided to leave the party early.*

1. Tommy flopped into the nearest chair, kicking off his shoes. [Begin with *kicking*.]

2. He looked through the program to find what songs Chita Rivera would sing. [Begin with *to find*.]

3. The program about Roberto Clemente began at seven o'clock sharp. [Begin with *at*.]

4. We scraped the old bureau down to the natural wood and discovered that it was real mahogany. [Begin with *scraping*.]

5. Our boat, trim and fast, won the race. [Begin with *trim*.]

6. My car was greased last week, and now it runs perfectly.

7. The stage crew, working evenings after school for weeks, completed the sets on schedule.

8. The band marched around the field and entertained the spectators during the half.

9. Garden City High School has good school spirit and always has a large attendance at football games.

10. The light bulb, flickering on and off for several seconds, finally went out.

(3) You may begin a sentence with a subordinate clause.

EXAMPLES I was unable to attend the Junior Prom because I had the flu.
Because I had the flu, I was unable to attend the Junior Prom.
Katsura was interested in joining the Masquers Club and the Film Group, but she did not have time to attend the meetings.
Although Katsura was interested in joining the Masquers Club and the Film Group, she did not have time to attend the meetings.

Subordinate clauses at the beginning of sentences usually begin with a subordinating conjunction. For a list of subordinating conjunctions, see page 240.

EXERCISE 13. Rephrase each sentence so that it begins with a subordinate clause instead of the subject. Place a comma after an adverb clause coming first in the sentence.

1. The praying mantis is a welcome guest in any garden because it destroys many harmful pests. [Because . . .]

2. The insects are not large in this country, but their South American relatives are big enough to devour small birds. [Although . . .]

3. The mantis was once highly regarded, and its landing on any person was considered a token of saintliness and an omen of good fortune. [Since . . .]

4. They watch patiently for their prey, and these creatures hold their claws in a kind of praying position.   [When . . .]

5. Superstitious people believed these insects to be engaged in prayer, and so mantises were often called soothsayers or prophets.   [Because . . .]

6. This insect can fly, but it prefers to wait on shrubs for its unsuspecting dinner to come by.

7. The mantis moves quietly and carefully, and seldom does its prey get away.

8. The forelegs shoot out like lightning, and the victim is caught in the mantis' trap.

9. The female lays small groups of eggs, and she attaches these to boards or twigs.

10. The eggs hatch in May or June, and the small mantises look almost exactly like their parents.

11. The baby mantises develop wings as they mature.

12. The female mantis harbors no love for her mate, and a male mantis may find himself his wife's dinner if he is not fast on his feet.

13. These voracious eaters of destructive pests are protected by law in many areas, and a person may be fined for harming them.

EXERCISE 14.   Change each of the following sentences in the manner suggested.

1. The steak was thick and juicy, and it just seemed to melt in my mouth.   [Begin with single-word modifiers.]

2. The batter swung wildly at the ball.   [Begin with a single-word modifier.]

3. The Student Council elected a parliamentarian to settle all disputes about conducting a meeting.   [Begin with an infinitive phrase.]

4. Myron forgot his lines in the middle of the second act.   [Begin with prepositional phrases.]

5. The house was appraised at $40,000 last year and sold for $45,000 this week.   [Begin with a past participial phrase.]

6. The bookstore in our town gives special discounts at Christmas time. [Begin with a prepositional phrase.]

7. The coach was annoyed at Christine's failure to show up for practice and benched her for two games. [Begin with a past participial phrase.]

8. Ms. Wentworth came into the room and told us to report to the auditorium for our seventh-period class. [Begin with a subordinate clause.]

9. We rowed across the lake and camped at Paradise Point. [Begin with a participial phrase.]

10. I liked *A Separate Peace* very much and have recommended it to all my friends. [Begin with a subordinate clause.]

VARYING SENTENCE STRUCTURE

12h. Vary the kinds of sentences.

You learned in Chapter 4 that, when classified according to their structure, there are four kinds of sentences: *simple, compound, complex,* and *compound-complex.* If you are not sure of the characteristics of each of these, you should turn back to pages 93–95 and refresh your memory before going further.

Just as it is possible to achieve variety in your writing by varying the beginnings of your sentences, it is also possible to achieve variety by varying the kinds of sentences you use. Using simple or compound sentences all the time tends to make your style monotonous. For example, read the following paragraph composed almost entirely of simple and compound sentences.

1. My parents always get a yearning for a family reunion just before Thanksgiving. 2. At this time, the magazines show smiling families sitting around tables laden with the most massive turkeys outside a zoo. 3. I smile bravely at their resolution and resign myself. 4. I sit there and glower. 5. The magazines never really show the "before and after" of sitting down to consume the traditional fare. 6. My parents have a

mania for cleanliness. 7. With company coming, we will turn the house upside down to create a good impression. 8. We will rearrange the house thoroughly and clean silverware and do other odd jobs. 9. These tasks finally completed, we will stagger to the door to greet our guests. 10. Then we will put a sizable dent in the turkey; then we will have endless varieties of leftover food. 11. We will have hot and cold turkey sandwiches, creamed turkey, turkey hash, turkey surprise, and finally turkey soup. 12. Eventually we will throw the skeletal remains out and feel the strangest urge to gobble. 13. I must not forget one thing. 14. I will have a gala time with the pots and pans. 15. I would like to change the routine. 16. I hate drudgery.

Now read the next paragraph, which tells the same tale but contains many complex sentences (the new subordinate clauses are italicized). You will see the superiority of this version over the first one.

1. My parents always get a yearning for a family reunion just prior to Thanksgiving *when the magazines show smiling families sitting around tables laden with the most massive turkeys outside a zoo.* 2. I smile bravely at their announcement and say, "Sounds great." 3. Actually, I sit there and glower. 4. The magazines never really show *what goes on before and after the merry throng sits down to consume the traditional fare. 5. Because my parents have a mania for cleanliness,* we will turn the house upside down to create a good impression for the expected company. 6. We will rearrange the house thoroughly and clean silverware and do other odd jobs. 7. These tasks finally completed, we will stagger to the door to greet our guests. 8. *After we have put a sizable dent in the turkey,* we will have endless varieties of leftover food. 9. We will have hot and cold turkey sandwiches, creamed turkey, turkey hash, turkey surprise, and finally turkey soup. 10. *Before the skeletal remains are thrown out,* we will feel the strangest urge to gobble. 11. I must not forget to mention *that I will have a gala time with the pots and pans.* 12. Do you think for one instant *that I would change the family routine in spite of the drudgery?* 13. You bet your life *I would!*

Actually, all that had to be done to break the monotony of the first version was to change some of the less important ideas from independent clauses to subordinate clauses. A subordinate clause in a sentence makes the sentence complex.

Using subordinate clauses not only gives variety to your writing but also helps you to show how the ideas in a sentence are related. One idea may be the cause or the result of another idea in the sentence, or it may give the time of the other. Study the following pairs of sentences. The first sentence in each pair is compound; the second is complex. Notice that in the second sentence the relationship between ideas is clearer than in the first sentence.

EXAMPLES   Our school is very crowded this year, and most of the study halls are in the auditorium.

Because our school is very crowded this year, most of the study halls are in the auditorium.   [The first idea expresses the *cause* of the second.]

The Cabinet met in emergency session, and the President consulted his staff.

Before the Cabinet met in emergency session, the President consulted his staff. [One idea gives the *time* of the other.]

The band members rehearse every day after school, and then they can give a good performance at their concert.

The band members rehearse every day after school **so that they can give a good performance at their concert.** [The idea in the subordinate clause states the reason for the idea in the independent clause.]

The following words, when used at the beginning of a subordinate clause, help to make clear the relationship between the sentence ideas:

CAUSE   because, since, as
RESULT OR REASON   so that, in order that
TIME   when, while, as, since, until, after, before, whenever

Whenever you are combining ideas, make sure that your connectives are appropriate.

EXERCISE 15. Change each of the following compound sentences into a complex sentence by expressing one of the ideas in a subordinate clause. Begin each subordinate clause with a word which will show how the ideas in the sentence are related: cause, result or reason, time.

1. Last week I visited New York City with my parents, and we saw the Dance Theater of Harlem at the Uris Theater.
2. Melva Murray-White danced in *Don Quixote,* and I was fascinated by her performance.
3. She danced with a powerful grace, and her movements radiated energy and exhilaration.
4. The dancers performed *Romeo and Juliet,* and I became even more entranced.
5. My favorite dance was *Agon,* and I enjoyed its theme of life and combat.
6. It remarkably traced the path of movement in time and space, and I came to admire Balanchine and Stravinsky, who created this dance.
7. Its movements were like flashes of electricity, and the dancers darted back and forth across the stage with computer-like precision and timing.
8. I watched the dances, and I concluded that the group combines jazz movements with classical ballet.
9. I had not known dancers could convey such joy, but then I saw this marvelous group.
10. I will get an advance schedule next year, and I will surely see a dance by Geoffrey Holder.

EXERCISE 16. The following paragraphs consist chiefly of simple and compound sentences. Rewrite them, varying the style by changing or combining some of the sentences into complex sentences. Do not try to make all your sentences complex, for your purpose is to achieve sentence variety.

1. My first day in high school was one of the most hectic days of my life. It all seems ridiculous now, but it was no joke then. With my heart in my mouth, I boarded the school bus that morning. Many of my old friends from junior high days were seated there, but for some strange reason they did not want to talk very much. Everybody was abnormally quiet, and the air was electric with the tension. Gus, the bus driver, must have enjoyed the ride. Usually he has to tell us about twenty times to pipe down.

2. The silent bus soon arrived at the high school, and we filed quickly into the courtyard. For the tenth time in five minutes, I looked at my instructions for the first day. These instructions had come in the mail the week before, and by now I had practically memorized them. Still, I did not want to lose them. "Proceed to the student lobby and check your name on the lists posted there," stated the valuable paper. To make a long story short, I did just that and soon located my name on the bulletin board. The next step was to find Room 134, my official homeroom according to the list on the wall.

3. I wandered all over the school looking for Room 134. I should have asked for directions and saved myself a lot of trouble, but I was too stupid. At least, that's my excuse today. I bumped into Ray and Mike, my best friends last year. They were looking for Room 147. They didn't know the location of 134, but Ray did have a map of the school. I looked at it closely and found that Room 134 was right next to the student lobby.

4. I entered Room 134 slowly and glanced around. There wasn't a familiar face in sight. Where could all these strange people have come from? A short, red-haired man strode toward me and told me to take a seat. Sitting in the front makes me feel very conspicuous, so I selected a choice spot in the back of the room. I just can't stand a million eyes bouncing off the back of my head. The red-haired man was our homeroom teacher, and he explained about fire drills, cafeteria procedure, absentee notes, and countless other school rules. He was wasting his time. It sounded like mumbo jumbo to me, and it went in one ear and right out the other. Soon he distributed the program cards and a map of the school and told us to report to the first class at the ringing of the bell. The bell cut the silence of the room, and off I went on my big adventure.

5. The rest of the day was a real nightmare. I got lost many times, I got pushed around in the halls, and I felt like a rat prowling around in a gigantic maze. Some upperclassmen, chuckling to themselves, tried to sell me a ticket to the swimming pool on the third floor. I didn't fall for that, however. There isn't any swimming pool, and there isn't any third floor. I met all my new teachers, and each one kindly presented me with a book weighing about three pounds. I could hardly walk around. The books kept slipping out of my arms. And so I came to the end of that first day and boarded the bus with my head swimming with *do*'s and *dont*'s. The ride home was just like old times. It wasn't quiet, and sure enough, Gus had to exercise his lungs and tell us to pipe down.

EXERCISE 17. Write a one-page account of one of your own experiences. The purpose of your writing is to show that you can avoid a monotonous style by varying the form of your sentences. Before writing, review the three ways of beginning a sentence. Include some complex sentences in your composition.

Composition

PART FOUR

Chapter 13

The Paragraph

Structure, Unity, and Coherence in Paragraphs

A paragraph is a physical division of a composition, marking a stage in the writer's thought. It is possible for a reader to struggle through a long piece of writing not divided into paragraphs just as it is possible for a motorist to drive over unmarked roads to a destination. But like the motorist, the reader hopes to find an occasional signpost pointing the way. In a composition of several paragraphs, the indention, or spacing, that marks the beginning of a paragraph is a signpost that signals a change in the direction of the writer's thought — a new idea; a change in place, time, or situation; a slightly different point of view.

Paragraphs differ in length, content, and organization, but it is possible to form an idea of the kind of average paragraph that is likely to appear in student writing. It is likely to be from 100 to 150 words long, to consist of a general statement supported by specific statements, and to have a single unifying idea. This chapter provides you with instructions, examples, and practice to help you master the writing of an effective paragraph. The work is important preparation for Chapters 14, 15, and 16, which deal with writing compositions of many paragraphs.

THE STRUCTURE OF A PARAGRAPH

13a. A paragraph is a series of sentences developing a single topic.

The writer of the following paragraph, Martin Luther King, Jr., wanted to establish that violence is both impractical and immoral. He begins with a general statement of this idea and then supports it by giving reasons.

> Violence as a way of achieving racial justice is both impractical and immoral. It is impractical because it is a descending spiral ending in destruction for all. The old law of an eye for an eye leaves everybody blind. It is immoral because it seeks to humiliate the opponent rather than win his understanding; it seeks to annihilate rather than to convert. Violence is immoral because it thrives on hatred rather than love. It destroys community and makes brotherhood impossible. It leaves society in monologue rather than dialogue. Violence ends by defeating itself. It creates bitterness in the survivors and brutality in the destroyers. A voice echoes through time saying to every potential Peter, "Put up your sword." History is cluttered with the wreckage of nations that failed to follow this command.[1]

In this paragraph, after stating the main idea in the first sentence, the writer defends the idea by stating reasons for the impracticality and immorality of violence. The paragraph, which is taken from a longer article on nonviolent resistance, makes a forceful, unified plea against bloodshed. Most of the paragraphs you will study in this chapter are organized around a single, unifying topic.

The Topic Sentence

13b. The sentence stating the topic of a paragraph is called the topic sentence.

[1] From pages 211–14 in *Stride Toward Freedom* by Martin Luther King, Jr. Copyright © 1958 by Martin Luther King, Jr. Reprinted by permission of Harper & Row, Publishers, Inc., and Joan Daves.

Most paragraphs, like the one written by Martin Luther King, Jr., have a general statement, or topic sentence, giving the main idea. (Paragraphs in stories often do not have a topic sentence, but they are a special case.) The topic sentence usually comes at the beginning of the paragraph, so that the reader can immediately tell exactly what the paragraph is about. Notice that the topic sentence comes at the beginning of the paragraph on page 260. Putting the topic sentence at the beginning can be a help to the writer, too, since a clear statement of an idea at the outset can prevent the writer from wandering from the subject.

Occasionally the topic sentence appears in the middle of the paragraph, and sometimes it comes at the end. Coming at the end, the topic sentence often serves as the climax to the series of details that led up to it. It is a conclusion based on the evidence presented in the paragraph.

Read the following paragraphs, noting the topic sentences in bold-faced type.

TOPIC SENTENCE IN THE MIDDLE

Recently, while fishing in a clear stream, I picked a rough twig out of the water. Growing out of the twig were the tightly furled petals of some strange yellow bud. In seconds this "bud" had blossomed into a pale, golden fly with a long, gracefully tapered body and upright wings like sails. As I watched, the wings dried, became taut and fit, and the insect took flight, mounting high over the stream until it disappeared. **Surely there are few stranger creatures in nature than this little mayfly of the order *ephemeroptera*.** The Greeks named it "flower of the river," and the names given to it by trout fishers are no less poetic — "golden drake" and "pale evening sun." The insect spends all but the last few days of its life on the stream bottom where as a nymph it undergoes as many as twenty metamorphoses. Then, in response to some mysterious rhythm of nature, it struggles to the surface, breaks open the nymphal case, and emerges as a winged fly. It is from this instant draining the precious stock of life stored up on the stream bottom, for its mouth has stopped working and it cannot feed again. The insect now has only one function: to mate, to drop eggs into the stream, and then to die.

TOPIC SENTENCE AT THE END

The fourteenth century opened with a series of famines brought on when population growth outstripped the techniques of food production. The precarious balance was tipped by a series of heavy rains and floods and by a chilling of the climate in what has been called the Little Ice Age. Upon a people thus weakened fell the century's central disaster, the Black Death, an eruption of bubonic plague which swept the known world in the years 1347–1349 and carried off an estimated one-third of the population in two and a half years. **This makes it the most lethal episode known to history, which is of some interest to an age equipped with the tools of overkill.**[1]

The Concluding, or Clincher, Sentence

Sometimes a writer may wish to reemphasize the main point of a paragraph by restating it in a concluding sentence. This kind of restatement is sometimes called a *clincher sentence*. It is used to very good effect by skillful writers. A paragraph concluding with a clincher sentence has two statements of its topic: one in the topic sentence and one in the clincher.

Use clincher sentences sparingly. A clincher is unnecessary in a very short paragraph. A poor clincher is one that seems to be tacked on just for its own sake to a paragraph which is complete and effective without it.

In the following paragraph both the topic sentence and the clincher sentence are printed in bold-faced type.

Then in the cool long glade of yard that stretched four hundred feet behind the house he planted trees and grape vines. **And whatever he touched in that rich fortress of his soul sprang into golden life.** As the years passed, the fruit trees — the peach, the plum, the cherry, the apple — grew great and bent beneath their clusters. His grape vines thickened into brawny ropes of brown and coiled down the high wire fences of his lot and hung in a dense fabric upon his trellises, roping his domain twice around. They climbed the porch end of the house and framed the upper windows in thick bowers. And

[1] Excerpt from "History as Mirror" by Barbara Tuchman. "History as Mirror" appeared in *The Atlantic Monthly,* September 1973. Copyright 1973 by Barbara Tuchman. Reprinted by permission of Russell and Volkening, Inc., as agents for the author.

the flowers grew in rioting glory in his yard – the velvet-leaved nasturtium, slashed with a hundred tawny dyes, the rose, the snowball, the red-cupped tulip, and the lily. The honeysuckle dropped its heavy mass upon the fence. **Wherever his great hands touched the earth, it grew fruitful to him.**[1]

EXERCISE 1. The topic sentence in each of the following paragraphs may be at the beginning, middle, or end. Find the topic sentence and the clincher sentence, if any; then copy these sentences.

1. This farm, which was situated two miles west of the village, immediately won our love. It was a glorious place for boys. Broad-armed white oaks stood about the yard, and to the east and north a deep forest invited to exploration. The house was of logs and for that reason was much more attractive to us than to our mother. It was, I suspect, both dark and cold. I know the roof was poor, for one morning I awoke to find a miniature peak of snow at my bedside. It was only a rude little frontier cabin, but it was perfectly satisfactory to me.[2]

2. The number of children under fifteen years old living in poverty in the urban centers of the developing world is now estimated at 156 million, of whom 60 million are under five years old. The basic needs of these children are not being met. Meals are often irregular, accidents are frequent, arrests of older children for delinquency are commonplace. Their environment is often dangerous. Cuts go untreated and untended colds turn into pneumonia. Their mothers usually have to go out to find work to supplement the family income. Many lack the basic physical protection of shoes, a change of clothes, clean, warm blankets to sleep in, or a decent home to shelter them.[3]

3. Greek mythology is largely made up of stories about gods and goddesses, but it must not be read as a kind of Greek Bible,

[1] From *Look Homeward, Angel* by Thomas Wolfe. Copyright 1929 by Charles Scribner's Sons; renewal copyright © 1957 Edward C. Aswell, Administrator, C.T.A. and/or Fred W. Wolfe. Reprinted by permission of Charles Scribner's Sons, and Wm. Heinemann Ltd.

[2] From *A Son of the Middle Border* by Hamlin Garland. Copyright 1917 by Hamlin Garland, renewed 1945 by Mary I. Lord and Constance G. Williams. Reprinted by permission of Macmillan Publishing Co., Inc., and The Bodley Head Ltd., publishers.

[3] Adapted excerpt from "The Situation of Children in the Developing World," a UNICEF publication prepared by *The New Internationalist*, Reprinted by permission of UNICEF.

an account of the Greek religion. According to the most modern idea, a real myth has nothing to do with religion. It is an explanation of something in nature; how, for instance, any and everything in the universe came into existence: men, animals, this or that tree or flower, the sun, the moon, the stars, storms, eruptions, earthquakes, all that is and all that happens. Thunder and lightning are caused when Zeus hurls his thunderbolt. A volcano erupts because a terrible creature is imprisoned in the mountain and every now and then struggles to get free. The Dipper, the constellation called also the Great Bear, does not set below the horizon because a goddess once was angry at it and decreed that it should never sink into the sea. Myths are early science, the result of human beings' first trying to explain what they saw around them.[1]

4. Limiting the field to experienced pilots was the first obvious step. It would be foolish — particularly in a semicrash program — to train astronauts in the basics of flying when a sizable pool of trained pilots was available. But even this limitation left too unwieldy a group from which to winnow the final choices. And at no time was consideration given to throwing Project Mercury open to volunteers from among our considerable number of experienced pilots. Psychologists insisted, with some justification, that many of the men who would blindly volunteer to be fired into orbit would show signs of emotional instability. Thus it was determined to pre-select a rather small group from which volunteers would be sought after the program had been carefully explained to them.[2]

EXERCISE 2. Select one of the following topics and write a paragraph (100–150 words) on it. Underline the topic sentence and, if you use one, the clincher sentence as well. You may choose a topic of your own if you prefer.

1. A visit to an interesting place
2. Things that teen-agers boast about
3. A happy (or unhappy) occasion
4. The best way to solve a dispute
5. Your opinion on a local, national, or international issue

[1] From *Mythology* by Edith Hamilton. Copyright 1942 by Edith Hamilton. Copyright © renewed 1969 by Dorian Fielding Reid and Doris Fielding Reid, Executrix of the Will of Edith Hamilton. By permission of Little, Brown and Company.
[2] From "Selecting the Astronauts" by Joseph N. Bell.

DEVELOPMENT OF A PARAGRAPH

13c. A paragraph is usually developed by means of additional, detailed information given in support of the idea expressed in the topic sentence.

It is easy to make general statements; it is harder to find the specific details, examples, or reasons that are needed to back up such statements. The details may be of many kinds —facts, examples, incidents, or logical arguments. The details, however, must be there, and they must clearly support the topic sentence.

The following paragraph does not develop its topic sentence. Instead, it merely restates its main idea several times in different words. Saying something over and over does not, of course, make it any clearer or truer than saying it once. Details are needed to make a general statement stick. In the absence of details, we are left with an emotional, and not very convincing, repetition of the same theme:

> In my opinion, running daily is the best exercise you can do to become physically fit. People today talk a great deal about physical fitness, but there would not be so many people in poor physical condition if everyone ran a mile every day. It is our responsibility to take care of our bodies. We cannot do this without exercising. No one has found a better or more efficient means of exercising than running. Therefore, everyone should practice running since it is the best exercise you can do to become physically fit.

A paragraph that consists of a series of general statements without supporting information is little better than the one that keeps making the same statement over and over. One topic sentence is enough for a paragraph; once you have stated it, it is up to you to develop it. The following paragraphs deal with the same topic, the duties of a catcher in baseball. Notice that the second one is more convincing and interesting than the first because it is more specific.

I

Baseball demands intelligence, especially behind the plate — because the catcher is the quarterback of baseball. He runs the team and is the one player who can never relax, whether his team is in the field or at bat. He has a wide variety of duties. He must keep track of the tactical situation on the field and see that the rest of the team knows it also.

II

Baseball demands intelligence, especially behind the plate — because the catcher is the quarterback of baseball. He runs the team and is the only man who sees every player on the field and every move that takes place. He calls the pitches and sometimes directs much of the defensive play. He is the one person on the team who can never for a moment relax, whether his team is in the field or at bat. He must know wind conditions in every ball park, and his duties vary from studying the opposing batteries, the mental condition of his own pitcher, and the spacing of the outfielders, watching runners on base, keeping track of the tactical situation and seeing that the rest of the team knows it also, to backing up third and first except when a runner is in a scoring position.[1]

The second paragraph is better because it gives the details that make the general statements interesting and meaningful. Always be specific and illustrate with appropriate details the points you want to make.

Planning a Paragraph

Like most human projects, a paragraph calls for planning. Before you begin to write, make a simple inventory of your ideas on the topic you have chosen. Jot down these ideas in any order they come to mind. The act of setting them down will suggest others, and these may in turn generate still others. Continue until you have a sizable list before you. Next, begin to arrange the ideas into some order, culling out every idea that does not directly pertain to the topic.

[1] From "Who's Catching?" by John R. Tunis from *The Atlantic Monthly*. Reprinted by permission of the Estate of John R. Tunis and the Estate of Lucy R. Tunis.

The Paragraph Outline

When you have decided on the ideas you will include in the paragraph, write a simple outline of it. The following is an outline of a paragraph:

TOPIC SENTENCE People vary a great deal in the conditions they require for efficient study.

DETAILS 1. Some want silence and solitude.
2. Others want noise and company.
3. Some want the radio on.
4. Some want the same conditions day after day.
5. Some can study anywhere.

EXERCISE 3. Make a simple inventory of ideas for a paragraph. The ideas can be written as one-word statements or as complete sentences. When you have compiled a list of ten ideas, stop. Save this list for your own use later.

EXERCISE 4. Make a paragraph outline for each of the following topic sentences. The items in the outline need not be in sentence form. Copy the sentence first; then list the details you would use in your paragraph.

1. Anyone planning a trip from New York to San Francisco finds several ways to make the journey.
2. There are many reasons people would rather attend a spectator sport than watch it on television.
3. In every home certain jobs should be delegated to the children.
4. You will find some of the same types of teachers in any high school.

UNITY IN THE PARAGRAPH

13d. A paragraph should be unified. Unity is achieved by discussing only one topic in a paragraph, the topic stated in the topic sentence.

A unified paragraph is a forceful unit because all of the sentences have a common purpose — to develop or support the general statement made by the topic sentence.

It is possible to measure the unity of a paragraph by testing the relationship of each sentence to the main idea. You should ask this question: "How is each detail related to the topic sentence?" Study the following paragraph, noting how its unity has been broken.

¹One difference between dogs and cats as pets is that dogs can be taught obedience whereas most cats cannot. ²Dogs are easily taught not to get on the furniture and not to steal food left on the kitchen table when no one is around.³ They can be taught to heel, to stay, and to do tricks. ⁴Cats, on the other hand, do just exactly what they want to do in spite of their owners' efforts to discipline them. ⁵Our neighbor has two Siamese cats. ⁶No matter how many times she punishes them for getting on the furniture or stealing food, she knows that at any time she may find them curled up on the easy chair, and she would never dare leave the cats alone in the house with any food lying around. ⁷Many people are fond of cats because cats are beautiful and independent. ⁸As kittens they are more entertaining than they are when full grown. ⁹I have never heard of a cat that had been taught to stay or to sit or to roll over. ¹⁰Dogs make more satisfactory pets because they can be taught to obey.

(1) topic sentence

(2–3) examples of dogs' obedience

(4–6) examples of cats' disobedience

(7–8) unrelated statements break unity

(9) an example related to examples 4–6

(10) clincher sentence

EXERCISE 5. Examine each of the following paragraphs to test its unity. There is one sentence in each that is not closely related to the topic. Find this sentence, copy it onto your paper, and be ready to explain how it breaks the unity of the paragraph.

1

When backpacking in Glacier National Park in northwestern Montana, hikers are advised not to disturb the grizzly bears that live in the park. Because grizzlies have been known to react violently when suddenly surprised by visitors, hikers wear bells which jingle as they march, warning any bears in the vicinity that intruders are coming. The black bears found in Yellowstone Park do not have the same frightening reputation as the grizzlies. Although there are only about two hundred grizzlies in Glacier National Park (the park is larger than the state of Rhode Island) and although the chances of being attacked are about one million to one, visitors are uneasy because the grizzly has traditionally been considered America's fiercest and most dangerous animal. Even today a grizzly will occasionally attack a human being — with painful results.

2

While some parents may be skeptical about the education their children receive at Beeston College and some students may share the attitude of these parents, all have only praise for the college's beautiful campus situated on a wooded hill overlooking Spring Lake. Stand at the edge of the campus and look down at the shimmering surface of the lake. Your eye can follow the graceful curves of a road, obscured here and there by foliage, as it winds to the water's edge. In winter, the dark ribbon of road is visible all the way. Snowmobiles, which are a noisy winter distraction in this part of the country, are forbidden on campus. Now turn about for a view of the campus. All the buildings — dormitories, classroom buildings, the gymnasium, and the student center — have old-fashioned charm. The red and white of the buildings blend easily with the green of lawns and playing fields. Students who are sensitive to beauty say the campus itself is enough to make them glad to return at the beginning of each school year.

3

There are many things to learn about paddling a canoe. Since a canoe can be pushed from its course by a slight breeze, the paddlers must sit in such a way that the bow will not be forced too high out of the water where it will catch too much wind. In calm weather, the canoeists should sit in the stern, but in windy weather, they should kneel just aft of the middle, for in this position they can control their craft with less effort. They should paddle on the side opposite the direction of the wind because the wind then actually helps them to hold to a straight course. A canoe should never be loaded with stones for ballast because the stones will sink the canoe, should it be swamped. Steering is done by a twist of the paddle at the end of each stroke, the extent of the twist depending upon the force of the stroke and the strength of the wind against the bow.

4

If you have read *A Search for the Apex of South America,* you may know something about Annie Peck's career as a mountaineer. This internationally acclaimed climber first became interested in mountaineering when she saw the majesty of the Matterhorn. She climbed Mount Shasta in California and then, in 1895, ascended the Matterhorn. Because she was interested in the terrain of the Americas, she climbed the live volcano Popocatepetl. Climbing Mount Orizaba won her recognition for achieving the highest point in the Americas reached by a woman up to that time. Peck was not satisfied with achieving something no woman had ever achieved before; she wanted to reach a height no person had ever reached before. Some people considered her climbing costume as daring as her accomplishments. She continued searching for the right mountain, and she finally climbed the north peak of Huascarán. This peak was named Huascarán Cumbre Ana Peck in her honor. Peck continued to be an active mountaineer until her death at the age of eighty-four.

5

Walking is more than an everyday necessity — it can be used for all kinds of reasons. As a recreation it serves to pass your leisure time. When you are feeling lonely and depressed, a long walk in the crisp air does heaps of good toward cheering you up. Then again, if you're filled with the glorious feeling that everything is perfect, you enjoy a walk outdoors where everything in nature seems to be happy with you. On hikes through wild country, campers make many wonderful and surprising discoveries. Nervous business people, waiting to hear whether the stock market has gone down another point, put their hands behind them and pace impatiently up and down a room. Riding in a car everywhere you go is faster but not so good for you as walking. Next time you're bored or happy or unhappy or worried, take a walk.

COHERENCE IN THE PARAGRAPH

13e. A paragraph should have coherence; that is, its ideas should be arranged according to a definite plan and should be linked clearly to one another.

Coherent paragraphs are easy to read. The relationship between the sentences is clear, and the train of thought, moving easily and naturally from one sentence to the next, is easy to follow. The two ways to achieve this coherence are (1) to arrange the ideas in a logical order and (2) to provide clear transitions, or links, between sentences. Logical order is explained in connection with the following discussion of paragraph types. Transitional expressions are explained beginning on page 285.

FOUR TYPES OF PARAGRAPHS

13f. Learn to write four types of paragraphs: expository, descriptive, narrative, persuasive.

Like longer forms of writing (which you will study in later chapters) paragraphs can be classified into four types: the expository paragraph, the descriptive paragraph, the narrative paragraph, and the persuasive paragraph. The type of paragraph you write may often depend on your purpose in writing. If, for example, your purpose is to inform, then you will choose the expository paragraph, for it normally gives information or provides explanation. The following presentation of the four types of paragraphs will make familiar to you the ways in which paragraphs may differ according to their purpose.

The Expository Paragraph

As mentioned, the purpose of an expository paragraph is to give information or to explain something, or to do both. The writer of the expository paragraph on page 262, for example, wanted to give information about the fourteenth century. You may notice that her paragraph provides a series of facts all closely related to her topic.

13g. Develop an expository paragraph with facts and specific examples.

The most common way to develop an expository paragraph is to supply facts and examples about a topic. The following paragraph, whose purpose is to give information about the English language, provides a series of facts that develop the idea in the first sentence (the topic sentence). In the paragraph below, these facts are underlined. Some of the facts are, in turn, developed by specific examples.

> The English language has its peculiarities, some of which make the language difficult to learn for speakers of another language. In English, the position of a word is very important. By placing the word *only* before a different one of the seven words in the following sentence, you can change the meaning of the sentence seven times. "She told me that she loved me." English has a number of words that can be used with opposite meanings. *Seeded* rye has caraway seeds in it, but *seeded* raisins have had the seeds removed. A *fast* horse runs, but a *fast* color does not. When plants are *dusted,* chemical dust is sprayed on them, but when furniture is *dusted,* the dust is wiped off. Another source of confusion is the fact that in English the pronoun *I* has the plural form *we,* but the pronoun *you* is the same in the plural as in the singular.

EXERCISE 6. Write an expository paragraph developed by facts that supply information on one of the following topic sentences.

1. One of the greatest problems in the world is the diminishing supply of oil.

2. Many popular beliefs about wild animals are completely wrong.
3. Sports in this country are more popular than ever before.
4. There is evidence suggesting life on other planets.
5. A volcanic eruption is perhaps the most destructive force on earth.

Sometimes a topic sentence states a general idea that can best be supported by a number of specific examples. If carefully chosen, each specific example will make the topic sentence clearer for the reader. In the following paragraph, the writer gives three well-chosen examples to demonstrate the idea in the first sentence, which is the topic sentence. These examples are underlined.

William Golding's *Lord of the Flies* is an interesting book not only because of its unusual plot but also because of the constant suspense Golding creates. For example, there is always the question of whether or not the boys will find adult help before they destroy themselves. Then, too, there is the problem of the beast. Is the beast real or is it imaginary? If real, what kind of creature is it and how should it be dealt with? An event which adds to the suspense is the chase near the end of the book when Ralph is being hunted down by Jack and his fierce band.

EXERCISE 7. Write an expository paragraph developed by examples to illustrate or support one of the following topics.

1. Life in a big city (small town) can be frustrating at times.
2. Haste does not always make waste.
3. "Every neighbor is a teacher." [proverb]
4. Overcoming a physical handicap requires courage and perseverance.
5. Every freedom is a responsibility.

Order of Details in an Expository Paragraph

The arrangement of the sentences in an expository paragraph will determine how easily the reader can follow the writer's train of thought. Without logical organization, the information in an expository paragraph will be difficult to understand.

13h. Arrange the details in an expository paragraph in a coherent, logical order.

There are four common ways of arranging details in an expository paragraph: by order of importance, by chronological order, by comparison, or by contrast.

(1) The facts or details in an expository paragraph may be given in the order of their importance.

Suppose that you are writing an expository paragraph and you have three pieces of information to give in support of your topic sentence. You will have to decide which idea or piece of information to give first and which to give second and third. You may decide to put the most important first, followed by the idea second in importance and the idea that is least important. Or you may reverse this order, placing the most important last, where it will come as a kind of climax. The point is that your paragraph should follow a logical order.

The ideas in the following paragraph are arranged by order of importance, with the most important idea first, directly following the topic sentence.

Specialists in children's television viewing suggest a number of ways parents can control their children's viewing.[1] Most important, they say, is setting time limits such as one hour a day, no viewing on school nights, or two or three hours on weekends.[2] Another suggestion is that parents discuss with the children which television programs to select. It is important that children learn to choose their programs instead of just watching whatever happens to be on.[3] It is generally agreed that parents should watch with their children occasionally. Viewing programs together leads to discussion of the programs and to rating them fairly. It may also bring the family closer together and increase understanding of different points of view.

(2) The details in an expository paragraph may be given in chronological order.

When the purpose of a paragraph is to explain (how to do or make something, or how something works), it is only natural to give the steps of the process in the order in which they must be performed. This is chronological, or time, order. The details in the following paragraph, which tells how the booster and orbiter work in making contact with a space station, are given in chronological order.

After blasting off, the booster rockets the entire double assembly up into the final reaches of the earth's atmosphere.	topic sentence
[1]Having achieved proper altitude and velocity, the booster separates from the orbiter stage.	(1) First step
[2]Then the booster extends its wings and, guided by its two-man crew, returns to earth in normal airplane fashion, using auxiliary jet engines as necessary.	(2) Second step
[3]The second stage, which carries the payload of personnel and supplies, takes up where the booster stage lets off.	(3) Third step
[4]It accelerates on into orbit and makes a rendezvous with the space station.	(4) Fourth step
[5]After transferring its crew and cargo, and picking up whatever personnel or equipment is scheduled for a return to earth, the orbiter casts off for the journey home.	(5) Fifth step
[6]Owing to its unique design, which includes small wings and efficient control surfaces, it is able to spiral downward	(6) Sixth step

and reenter the atmosphere at a safe,
gentle angle, unthreatened by extreme
friction heat.[1]

EXERCISE 8. Decide whether the following two paragraphs are organized by order of importance or by chronological order. Be prepared to explain your answers.

1. Leave the astronauts out of it, and the paratroop teams that free-fall for 10,000 feet or skate down by means of those flattish, maneuverable new parachutes. Leave out the six people who have survived the 220-foot fall from the Golden Gate Bridge, and the divers of Acapulco, who swan-dive 118 feet, clearing outcrops of 21 feet as they plunge past the sea cliff. Leave out even the ordinary high diver, who enters the pool rigid and pointed after a comely jackknife. Come down from such lofty characters to Henri LaMothe — who on his seventieth birthday last April dove from a 40-foot ladder into a play pool of water 12 inches deep.[2]

2. Sometimes a writer will contradict what he has already written, and in that case the only thing to do is to investigate what has changed his point of view. For instance, in 1608 Captain John Smith issued a description of his capture by Powhatan, and he made it clear that the Indian chief had treated him with unwavering courtesy and hospitality. In 1624 the story was repeated in Smith's *General History of Virginia,* but the writer's circumstances had changed. Smith needed money, "having a prince's mind imprisoned in a poor man's purse," and he wanted the book to be profitable. Powhatan's daughter, the princess Pocahontas, had recently been in the news, for her visit to England had aroused a great deal of interest among the sort of people that Smith hoped would buy his book. So Smith supplied a new version of the story, in which the once-hospitable Powhatan would have permitted the hero's brains to be dashed out if Pocahontas had not saved his life. It was the second story that achieved fame, and of course it may have been true. But it is impossible to trust it because the desire of the writer

---

[1] Excerpt on page 117 of *Skylab* by Charles Coombs. Copyright © 1972 by Charles Coombs. By permission of William Morrow & Company.

[2] From "A Low-Water Man" by Edward Hoagland. Copyright © 1975 by Edward Hoagland. Reprinted from *The Edward Hoagland Reader* by Edward Hoagland. By permission of Random House, Inc.

is so obviously involved; as Smith said in his prospectus, he needed money and hoped that the book would give "satisfaction."[1]

(3) The details in an expository paragraph may be given in order of comparison or contrast.

Paragraphs may be developed by offering a comparison or stating a contrast. A comparison shows how two things are alike; a contrast, how they are different. In both cases, facts, incidents, concrete details, or examples may be used to point out the similarities or differences. At times a writer may even wish to use both comparison and contrast to develop a single idea.

In the following paragraph details are given in order of comparison.

> In one way, baby-sitting a two-year-old child is like dog-sitting a two-month-old puppy. You cannot trust either of them out of your sight. Puppies must be watched constantly because their curiosity is endless and their teeth are sharp. Nothing they can reach is safe. They can happily destroy a shoe or a pillow or a book in a few minutes. If you don't know where a puppy is, you had better worry. Silence doesn't necessarily mean sleep. Similarly, two-year-olds are never still. They run, climb, fall down, throw things, disappear suddenly. They try to put everything into their mouth. If you can't see or hear them, you had better investigate. Silence often means mischief.

Not all expository paragraphs, of course, follow these four common orders. A paragraph developed by facts or examples may not follow any particular order if the facts or examples are all of equal importance. Simple, easily understood facts should precede those that are hard to understand. Remember, too, that many writers use not one method, but a combination of methods.

EXERCISE 9. Consider the following topic sentences. Then, next to the proper number on your paper, write down

---

[1] From "Getting at the Truth" by Marchette Chute from *Saturday Review,* September, 1953. Copyright © 1953 by Saturday Review. All rights reserved.

your recommendation for the best method of organizing the details in an expository paragraph developing these topic sentences.

(1) order of importance
(2) chronological order
(3) comparison or contrast

1. Last year the political issues were much less complicated.
2. There are three things that will affect the outcome of this year's election.
3. The process for converting solar energy into electricity is quite complicated.
4. The pollution of our rivers and streams has been easing somewhat.
5. The body needs several basic nutrients for growth.

EXERCISE 10. Select one of the following topic sentences and develop it into an expository paragraph by giving facts or examples to support it. As you plan the paragraph, bear in mind the four common orders of details. If you prefer, you may use a topic sentence of your own.

1. My family enjoys being together.
2. Inflation has affected my current spending habits in several ways.
3. Both wind power and solar power have advantages and disadvantages.
4. Machines and appliances frequently frustrate us.
5. Researching family history can have its rewards.
6. In the long run, what appears to be a tragedy today may turn out to be a blessing tomorrow.
7. Dogs of the same breed may have very different personalities.
8. Changes in our school population have created problems for this community.
9. The success (failure) of our basketball team (or any team) is the result of three causes.
10. A heron (or any other bird) is quite a remarkable creature to watch in flight.

The Descriptive Paragraph

A writer who wants to tell a reader exactly what something looks, tastes, smells, feels, or sounds like uses description, the type of writing that appeals chiefly to the senses. A paragraph-length description usually concentrates on only one subject: a place, an object, a person, or an event.

13i. Develop a descriptive paragraph with concrete (specific) details.

The concrete details that make a description effective are, naturally, details that appeal to the reader's senses. In the following descriptive paragraph, the writer concentrates on bus travel in rural India. As you read, note that the details appeal to the reader's senses of sight and touch, or feeling. In the last sentence, the details appeal exclusively to the sense of touch.

I have not yet traveled on a bus in India that has not been packed to the bursting-point, with people inside and luggage on top; and the buses are always so old that they shake up every bone in the human body and every screw in their own. If the buses are always the same, so is the landscape through which they travel. Once a town is left behind, there is nothing till the next one except flat land, broiling sky, distances and dust. Especially dust: the sides of the bus are open with only bars across them so that the hot winds blow in freely, bearing desert sands to choke up ears and nostrils and set one's teeth on edge with grit.[1]

The following descriptive paragraph portrays a commonplace event, a picnic. As you read, note the number of concrete details and the number of different senses the details appeal to.

Beach picnics come in many shapes and sizes. I like best the evening picnics. The air cools as the lowering sun spreads a gold path across the lake. Someone has started the bonfire,

[1] From *Heat and Dust* by Ruth Prawer Jhabvala. Copyright © 1975 by Ruth Prawer Jhabvala. Harper & Row, Publishers, Inc., and the British publishers John Murray Ltd.

and the bittersweet smoke reaches us as we run across the beach toward the fire. The sand is cold and soft to our bare feet. The small children chase one another in high-pitched, screaming excitement. Breathless from running, they return to the fire to pick up a long-handled fork or a sharply pointed stick to spear a frankfurter for roasting. Those who take up a position on the wrong side of the fire are soon crowding their way around to windward, coughing, eyes smarting from the windblown smoke. Somebody's frankfurter drops into the ashes to roars of laughter. Those too hungry to wait settle for a cold hotdog, while others absentmindedly burn their franks. I like the brittle, burnt skin of a frank that's overdone. On a fresh roll and covered with sharp-tasting mustard and sweet relish, it is irresistible. Plates of fresh green salad are passed around while paper cups of cold drinks suddenly appear. Soon everyone is back at the fire for seconds and thirds. Small groups sit cross-legged on the sand, their faces reflecting the fire's glow. The pungent, sweet smell of roasting marshmallows signals the last course. Talk becomes drowsy. The smaller children, stuffed and sleepy, stagger toward home with their parents. The ring of figures silhouetted around the fire becomes an island in the dark. Someone starts a song; others join in. The evening drifts away.

Order of Details in a Descriptive Paragraph

13j. Arrange the details in a descriptive paragraph in coherent order.

There are two useful ways of organizing a descriptive paragraph: by chronological or by spatial order.

(1) The details in a descriptive paragraph may be given in chronological order.

The details in the description of a beach picnic on page 279 are given in chronological order. A picnic is a series of events, and so it is logical to describe the events in the order in which they happen. The description begins as the picnickers gather on the beach. Following time order, the writer then describes the children's playing while the fire is being built, their gathering around the fire to cook and to eat, the quiet time after the supper as darkness comes, and finally the singing of songs after dark.

(2) The details in a descriptive paragraph may be given in spatial order.

When a place is the subject of a description, the order may be spatial, which means that the writer is careful to give the location of each part of the place. For example, if you were to describe your school building, you might describe first the entrance, and as you enter the building, you would tell what is on your left, on your right, and straight ahead. The following brief description of Samuel Clemens' boyhood home, Hannibal, Missouri, follows spatial order. Phrases used to locate the details in the description are printed in heavy type.

One morning I stood **atop** 200-foot-high Cardiff Hill and surveyed the scene that stretched **before** me. Hannibal—an active town of 20,000 people that today is an agricultural, rail and light manufacturing center—**nestles in** a mile-and-a-half wide fan-shaped valley. It rises gradually **from the river up to residential areas in** the low hills and knolls **a mile or two off to the west. Above** the riverfront's cobblestone levee **below to my left** towered the white silos of the Hannibal Grain Terminal, while directly **in front of me** Main Street passed **through the center** of the grid-like downtown area **on its way toward** Lover's Leap, the high bluff that overlooks the river **to the south.**[1]

EXERCISE 11. Choose one of the following topics and write a descriptive paragraph developed by concrete details. Begin with a general statement of the idea you will develop. If you prefer, write on a topic of your own.

[1] Excerpt from "Paying a Visit to the Boyhood Home of Mark Twain in Hannibal, Missouri" by Tom Weil in New York Times Travel of May 4, 1980. © 1980 by The New York Times Company. Reprinted by permission.

1. A pleasant or an unpleasant place
2. A sight you will always remember
3. The house you live in
4. The view from a vantage point familiar to you
5. A busy air terminal

The Narrative Paragraph

A writer who wants to develop a topic by relating an incident or a series of events uses narrative, the type of writing that tells *what happens.*

A paragraph-length narrative usually focuses on one action or one series of events as it tries to illustrate a single topic.

13k. Develop a narrative paragraph with a brief story.

Notice how the incident in the following paragraph illustrates the point made in the first sentence.

> . . . After a spring tide there was also much high talk of treasure and no little search for it. We lived, indeed, on a coast that nurtured such fancies. Not far from us lay the very island which was rumored to hide within its sands the bulk of Captain Kidd's ill-gotten gains. Moreover, not so many years past, two boys who lived near us, following an old footpath through the woods during a storm, had rested against a small boulder beneath a pine tree. One of them, idly kicking the soft mold at the base of the rock, caught the glint of metal, tarnished yet still bright enough to be distinguished against the black earth. They dug farther, with feet and with hands, to discover at last an iron pot half filled with gold coins, coins marked by strange designs and a strange language. They proved to be French pieces of the seventeenth century, probably buried there, so the learned of our coast surmised, by escaping French traders and settlers of the nearby town of Castine when their fort was captured by the Dutch. What wonder that we scrutinized the wrack of spring tides and dug now and again in likely coves or beneath giant boulders?[1]

[1] From *A Goodly Heritage* by Mary Ellen Chase. Copyright 1932, © 1960 by Mary Ellen Chase. Reprinted by permission of Holt, Rinehart and Winston, Publishers.

The order of ideas in a narrative paragraph is usually chronological, the order in which events occur in time. If you have ever listened to someone tell a joke or relate a story but confuse the proper order of events, you will understand how important chronological sequence can be in a narrative paragraph. Since the narrative paragraph must tell its story briefly, it must never risk confusing the reader.

EXERCISE 12. Write a paragraph in which the main idea or topic is developed with a brief story. Be specific about time, place, and characters. One of the following topics may suggest a story.

1. The best things in life are free.
2. A soft answer often turns away anger.
3. The foolishness of some drivers is beyond belief.
4. About the only thing that makes me really angry is unfair treatment of myself or of others.
5. I usually fail a test of willpower.

The Persuasive Paragraph

Thus far you have written paragraphs in three kinds of discourse: exposition, description, and narration. A fourth kind of discourse, used usually when you are engaged in an argument, is persuasion. The purpose of persuasive writing is to state a view, an opinion, and to support it so effectively that the reader will be persuaded to accept the opinion as correct.

13l. Develop a persuasive paragraph with reasons.

The topic sentence of a persuasive paragraph states an opinion, or point of view, as clearly and succinctly as possible. For example, the writer choosing to state an opinion on the high price of gasoline might write the topic sentence, "The big oil companies are charging too much money for gasoline."

The reasons used to develop a persuasive paragraph explain why the writer holds the view stated in the topic sentence. Reasons are most convincing when they can be supported by facts.

The following persuasive paragraph states an opinion about the future and backs up this opinion with reasons. Because the writer is considering the future, he cannot offer facts to support his reasons, but they remain convincing nevertheless.

> What will be left in a computerized world will be human curiosity and innovation. With the world run by machinery, human beings will be free to follow their interests freely. The leisure will not be that of today, however, when it is possible to watch television in a state of semicoma for six hours a day out of sheer lack of anything else to do. Instead, the availability of computerized education may introduce each individual to complex interests he might otherwise never have known he could have. There will be many human beings who, as a matter of interests, will wish to engage in scientific research, in space exploration, in government, medicine, art, music, or literature — enough of them to help the computers run the world and make it a stimulating place in which to live. Others, on another level, may wish to be involved in entertainment, in sport, in stamp collecting, hiking, or playing chess.[1]

Order of Details in a Persuasive Paragraph

Reasons in a persuasive paragraph may be given in the order of importance. In general, it is better to begin with the least important reason and build up to the most important ones, thus achieving a vigorous conclusion. In some situations, however, especially when the writer may have one very important reason and several less important ones, it may be appropriate to do just the reverse — to give the most compelling fact or reason first and then support it with the less important details.

[1] Excerpt from "Technology and Communication," originally appeared as "Not Enough Information, Too Much Information, and the Information Democracy" in *Dialogues in Technology* #7 by Gould, Inc., from the book *Time and Life* by Issac Asimov. Copyright © 1978 by Issac Asimov. Reprinted by permission of Doubleday and Company, Inc.

Whether the writer chooses one order or the other, the reader must be able to distinguish important from less important details in a persuasive paragraph.

EXERCISE 13. The following sentences could be used to introduce a persuasive paragraph. Select one and write a persuasive paragraph in support of it. You may use a topic sentence of your own if you wish.

1. Pollution control is obviously far from perfect.
2. Young people should have the privilege of changing, if they wish, the names their parents gave them.
3. Interscholastic athletics should be on the same scale for girls as for boys.
4. It is more important that high school graduates be able to qualify for a job than for college.
5. Solving national problems should (should not) take priority over solving international problems.

Transitional Expressions

You have already learned how to achieve coherence by arranging the ideas in the different types of paragraphs in logical order: order of importance, chronological order, and spatial order. Now turn your attention to the use of transitional expressions.

13m. Strengthen a paragraph by using linking expressions and connectives which help the reader to follow the line of thought from one idea to the next.

The most useful words for this purpose are the pronouns: *he, they, this, that, these, those, them, it,* etc. When they appear in the paragraph, they serve to remind the reader of their antecedents — that is, the words, expressions, and ideas to which they refer. As reminders, they help to bind the ideas in the paragraph more tightly together.

(1) Keep the thought of a paragraph flowing smoothly from sentence to sentence by using pronouns which refer to words and ideas in preceding sentences.

As you read the following paragraphs, notice how the words in bold-faced type refer back to an idea that comes earlier in the passage.

A hundred years ago, the average work week in the United States was about seventy hours. Today, **it** is about forty hours — and experts say that in the next decade or so **it** will be cut again, the predictions ranging from thirty-seven hours or thereabouts down to twenty or even less. **This reduction** might come as a shorter workday, or fewer workdays per week, or longer — very much longer — vacations.

What shall we do with all **that free time?** Many people are profoundly troubled about **this question.** They feel that, far from being a blessing, the change may prove a catastrophe. Certainly, the growth of leisure time is an extremely serious matter. It deserves far more attention than **it** is getting.[1]

(2) Keep the thought and purpose of the paragraph flowing smoothly from sentence to sentence by the use of linking expressions.

One infallible mark of a good prose style is care in the choice of linking expressions. Many expressions do approximately the same job. For instance, you can add still another idea to those already mentioned in a paragraph by introducing it with a "furthermore" or an "in addition." You can use "consequently" and "therefore" to show that one idea is the result of the preceding idea. You can use "however" or "nevertheless" to make clear that you are about to introduce a contrasting idea. Which connective you use depends on the logical relationship of the sentences. This relationship must be kept clear and distinct if you are to write well.

Read the following lists of linking expressions. Use the lists for reference when you write paragraphs and longer compositions.

[1] Excerpt from "Using Our Leisure Is No Easy Job" by Bruce Bliven. *New York Times Magazine* of April 26, 1964, © 1964 by the New York Times Company. Reprinted by permission.

Linking Expressions

To add an idea to one already stated:

moreover	likewise	besides	too
further	also	and	again
furthermore	nor	and then	in addition
equally important	in the same fashion		

To limit or contradict something already said:

but	still	although
yet	nevertheless	otherwise
and yet	on the other hand	at the same time
however	on the contrary	

To show a time or place arrangement of your ideas:

first	meanwhile	next	here
second (etc.)	later	presently	nearby
finally	eventually	at length	opposite to
at this point	sooner or later	afterward	adjacent to

To exemplify some idea or to sum up what you have said:

for example	to sum up	in any event
for instance	in brief	in any case
in other words	on the whole	as I have said
in fact	in short	as a result

EXERCISE 14. Read the following paragraph. Select from it (1) all pronouns that you think add to the coherence of the paragraph and (2) all linking expressions. Copy them in order, placing before each the number of the sentence in which it appears.

1. Indiscriminate tampering with the balance of nature has often had unfortunate results. 2. A case in point is the Pacific Islands. 3. On the more remote of these, eons of isolation from the mainland masses had allowed an enormous variety of life forms to evolve. 4. Furthermore, the relationship between these life forms and their environment was precariously balanced. 5. One species of plant, for example, depended upon one species of insect for its pollination. 6. This insect not only served to re-

produce the plant, but by feeding upon competing and more virulent growths protected the plant from being choked out. 7. In a like manner, one species of bird kept the insects in check, and on certain headlands, by its thousands of nests that blanketed the ground, provided the humus for still other varieties of plants. 8. This balance was violently upset by the first Polynesian settlers who brought with them pigs and, accidentally, rats. 9. Within a few centuries thereafter, hundreds of species of birds and plants had become extinct. 10. Later on, mongooses were imported from the East to control the rats which — without natural enemies of any kind — had decimated the bird population and threatened to overrun the islands. 11. These little heroes of Kipling's tales, however, found the ground-nesting birds much easier prey than the rats, and so the carnage goes on unimpeded to this day.

EXERCISE 15. Read the following paragraph. You can see at once that the necessary connectives have been omitted. Consult the list on page 287 and, next to the proper number on your paper, put down your choice for the correct connective.

It is rarely wise for teen-agers to buy a car. (1) ——, average teen-agers cannot pay cash (2) —— they must buy "on time." (3) ——, they must pay far more than merely the value of the car. (4) ——, they must commit themselves to a long series of payments. Without a full-time job, teen-agers find that none of these payments is easy to meet. When, (5) ——, the monthly payment happens to come at the same time as the inevitable and unlooked-for repair bill, then the task of raising the necessary money becomes difficult. (6) ——, this incessant anxiety over money can easily sour whatever pleasure comes from owning the car.

CHECKLIST FOR PARAGRAPH REVISION

Phrasing the Topic Sentence

1. Is it concise, directly to the point? Does it make your topic narrow enough?
2. Will it arouse the reader's interest or curiosity? Will it produce agreement or disagreement?

Developing the Topic

3. Does the paragraph have unity?
4. Have you used good examples, specific facts, sensory details, vivid comparisons, convincing reasons?
5. Does the paragraph have coherence? In what order are the details arranged? Are linking expressions and other connecting devices used properly?
6. Does the paragraph rise to a climax, come to a conclusion, reach a solution? Does it merit a summarizing, or clincher, sentence?
7. Is the paragraph adequately developed? By what method or combination of methods is it developed?

Proofreading Your Paragraph

8. Did you check the spelling of every doubtful word and refer to a list of your own commonly misspelled words?
9. Have you looked for unnecessary words, for trite expressions?
10. Are you confident that the grammatical usage is correct?
11. Have you checked your own error chart, or earlier compositions, to see that your special weaknesses are not being repeated?

Chapter 14

Exposition

Planning and Writing
the Longer Composition

Writing a good expository composition entails many of the same procedures as writing a good paragraph. Like the paragraph, the composition has a central, controlling idea that must be developed by means of smaller, more specific ideas. These specific ideas must be carefully chosen and organized in a logical way, and their relation to each other and to the central idea made clear. Since the idea for a composition is necessarily broader than the main idea of a paragraph, a composition calls for more thought, more planning, and more writing. (A composition is also likely to require reading in books or magazines.)

The main steps in writing a composition are listed below in the order in which they are performed. Each of them is important in successful expository writing. The letters designating the steps correspond to the rules in this chapter.

a. Choosing a subject
b. Limiting a subject
c. Planning the composition
d. Outlining
e. Writing the first draft
f. Revising
g. Writing the final draft

CHOOSING AND LIMITING A SUBJECT

14a. Choose a subject that interests you.

Good writing is possible only when you really know your subject. In addition to what you have learned in school, you have a great deal of knowledge that comes from other sources. Your own special interests have already taught you many things. Your interest in places has acquainted you with the people, the sights, and the experiences associated with another town, city, or country. Your hobbies — collecting stamps, coins, stones, or seashells; practicing a musical instrument, singing, or dancing — all these have developed your interests and increased your knowledge. When the time comes to make a choice, such a familiar subject often makes an ideal place to begin.

You should not, of course, limit yourself to subjects you know well already. In addition to familiar material from your own experience, there may be topics that interest you and arouse your curiosity even though you do not know much about them. Such topics may make excellent material for compositions, providing that you are willing to acquire the information necessary to write about them. Writing is an intense and stimulating activity; new ideas that you have mastered sufficiently to write about are likely to become a permanent part of your stock of knowledge and can extend your interests. In other words, writing a composition is not just a way to show what you know already; it can be a way for you to learn new things.

Some compositions that you write will derive completely from your own experience; others will come mainly from reading and investigation. For your first composition, you will probably wish to choose a familiar topic. But give some thought to the other kind of topic as you read books in English and your other classes. Before long, you should have several interesting possibilities for use in later, more ambitious compositions.

EXERCISE 1. Make a list of ten familiar subjects which you could develop into compositions. (If you wish, turn to the lists on pages 310–314 for ideas.) Submit your list to your teacher for suggestions and comments. Then keep it in your notebook for future use.

EXERCISE 2. Study the following list of subjects. Select five possibilities that you think you would enjoy studying and writing about. You need not limit your selections to this list. For each subject you choose, phrase several questions you think a composition on the subject should answer. Then submit your list to your teacher for suggestions and comments. When you get it back, keep it in your notebook for future use.

EXAMPLE 1. Science fiction writers
1. *a. Who are the most popular science fiction writers?*
   b. Are these writers scientists?
   c. Are they hopeful about the future of humanity?
   d. What were the earliest science fiction stories about? Have science fiction themes changed?

1. The moon's resources
2. Skin diving
3. Two authors with different attitudes toward youth
4. Nobel Prize winners in literature since 1980
5. Modern sculpture
6. The electric car
7. Financing your own college education
8. High school spirit
9. The tragic side of a comic character in a novel or play
10. Origins of place names in your area
11. Collecting records
12. Talking to chimps and dolphins
13. The importance of physical fitness
14. Wildlife conservation
15. Computers for use in the home
16. Characteristics of science fiction
17. Popular novels and the movies made from them
18. New steps in dancing
19. Training for the Olympics
20. New horizons in science
21. The future of the UN
22. How advertisers attract customers

14b. Limit your subject.

Most of your composition assignments will call for a paper of from 300–500 words, four or five paragraphs. You can see that if you choose a subject like "Skin diving" (about which whole books have been written), you must severely limit your treatment of it to some specific aspect of the sport

to avoid uttering meaningless generalities. Even one aspect
— how Jacques Cousteau and Emil Gagnan invented scuba
diving equipment for the French Navy during World War II
— offers more to write about than can be covered by a short
composition.

In fact, whenever possible, choose only a part of the subject. Better still, choose part of that part; then treat the
matter thoroughly, refusing to be content with merely repeating what everybody knows about the subject already.

(1) Limit your topic to one part of the subject.

Notice how the following general topics may be subdivided
into more limited topics. Any of these might be covered
fully in a short composition, whereas the general topic,
before being cut down, would demand several more pages
of development. Think of the general topic as the title of
a book and each of the subtopics as the chapters. Your
composition then would make a very short chapter or even
a part of a chapter.

GENERAL TOPIC   Skin diving

SPECIFIC TOPICS

1. Nitrogen poisoning: what it is and how to avoid it
2. Are sharks really dangerous?
3. The advantages of the wet suit
4. Scuba diving in nearby Marion Pond

GENERAL TOPIC   Movie stars

SPECIFIC TOPICS

1. Have the top movie stars attended drama school?
2. How do movie stars prepare for each movie?
3. How do movie stars feel about their fans?
4. What happens to young movie stars when they grow up?

GENERAL TOPIC   Walking

SPECIFIC TOPICS

1. Walking for exercise
2. What to look for when walking through the woods
3. Last summer's disastrous hike to Elk Creek
4. Walking in the city

EXERCISE 3. For five of the following general topics, write three specific subtopics that are suitably limited for a short composition.

1. Cars	6. Popularity and unpopularity
2. Sports	7. Things I wish were different
3. Family life	8. World leaders
4. Our town	9. Women athletes
5. Clothes	10. Technology

(2) State the purpose of your composition.

You can see from the examples above that it is hard to limit your subject without at the same time indicating what you are going to say about it. Now is the time to make your purpose even clearer and more definite. Since almost every subject can be treated in a number of ways, a clear statement of how *you* intend to treat it helps you choose the ideas to use in your composition. Notice how the following topic admits four different purposes.

GENERAL TOPIC   Jogging

SPECIFIC TOPIC   The popularity of jogging

To amuse   My purpose is to show the ridiculous side of jogging enthusiasts, such as the funny outfits these people wear, the expensive prices they pay for sneakers, and the pain they endure in a "healthful" sport.

To inform   My purpose is to show the difference in the quality and price of running shoes.

To persuade   My purpose is to persuade people that jogging is an easy way to lose weight and get into shape.

To impress   My purpose is to convey the feeling of triumph achieved after jogging farther than expected.

EXERCISE 4. Select five of the following general topics, and list, for each, three limited topics suitable for a short composition. Each of the limited topics should lend itself to a different one of the four purposes: (1) to amuse, (2) to inform, (3) to persuade, (4) to impress. After each topic, write the purpose you would have in writing about it.

EXAMPLE High school [general topic]
How to succeed without trying *to amuse*
The intramural program *to inform*
More privileges for students *to persuade*

1. Money   6. Travel
2. Television   7. Jewelry
3. Books   8. Food
4. Hobbies   9. Movies
5. Politics   10. Pets

(3) Choose a title that reflects your purpose.

Once you have limited your subject to suitable length and drafted your statement of purpose, the title may suggest itself as a matter of course. A good title gives both subject and purpose in one phrase. It excites the reader's interest and suggests what to expect. Take, for example, the sample topic given above, "The Popularity of Jogging." Some possible titles are

1. "Jogging—Flashy Outfits and Sore Feet" [to amuse]
2. "Dollars and Sense About Running Shoes" [to inform]
3. "Run Today for a Healthful Tomorrow" [to persuade]
4. "The Happiness of Long-distance Jogging" [to impress]

If you cannot immediately think of the right title, it is no great matter. You will probably think of a suitable one later. The next step is far more important, for now you are asked to do most of the thinking that will go into your composition.

PLANNING THE COMPOSITION

14c. Plan your composition before writing it.

Planning a composition involves four steps: listing your ideas, grouping them under a few main headings, putting your ideas in proper order, and preparing an outline.

(1) List all the ideas you can think of that bear upon the subject and purpose of the composition.

The first step in planning a composition is to list on paper all the ideas you have on the subject. Write down these ideas as rapidly as they come to you without any regard for their order or importance. Later there will be plenty of time to rephrase and organize them. The important thing at present is to tap the reservoir of the mind for its freshest and most vivid impressions, notions, and memories on the subject and to get these down on paper. At first, the flow of ideas is likely to be strong, but before long—unless you happen to be very well acquainted with the subject—the flow will dwindle and then stop altogether. When this happens, you need not be content with what you have. If the subject is not entirely personal, you can replenish the flow by referring to a good encyclopedia or by reading a magazine article or by talking with your parents or friends or by interviewing a local authority about the subject.

Suppose, for example, you were assigned the topic "My Favorite Outdoor Activity" and asked to write a paper of 300–500 words. With this topic in mind, how would you limit it? What would your purpose be in writing it? Suppose your favorite outdoor activity is exploring caves. Try the title "Exploring Caves Is an Interesting Outdoor Activity." Unfortunately, this title sounds rather commonplace and would probably lead you to list why cave exploration is fun and good exercise—topics that make cave exploring sound like any other outdoor activity. Think more deeply about the uniqueness of cave exploring. What makes it different from other sports and hobbies? Suppose that you are struck suddenly with the fact that the most fascinating aspects of exploring caves are the discomforts and even dangers people risk in order to crawl around in a cave's cramped passageways. Almost immediately you realize that caves hold some sort of unusual attraction for many people, and that writing about this attraction would make an interesting composition topic. Having made this decision, you draft your statement of purpose.

My purpose is to explain why people risk danger to explore the dark, mysterious world of caves.

A title then comes to mind:

Cave Exploring — A Trip into Darkness and Danger

Next you open your notebook and settle yourself to recording every idea, impression, and recollection about exploring caves that bears upon the subject and purpose. This list, which will constitute the raw material of your composition, is not solely the product of one session of silent thought but also grows out of reading, talks with fellow cave explorers, and other investigations (in this case, a trip to the library or a call or letter to an organization of cave explorers). For the sample topic the following list might be jotted down.

PERSONAL IMPRESSIONS
1. The darkness of caves
2. The sense of timelessness in a cave
3. The preservation of footsteps in a cave's protected atmosphere
4. The beauty of cave formations
5. Appeal to the senses — crisp sounds, pure air
6. Animal life in caves — insects and bats
7. Temperature of caves — coldness and dampness
8. Cracks in ceilings — water seeping through
9. Equipment needed for cave exploration
10. Graffiti in caves and my anger at it

INVESTIGATION
1. Formation of caves — geology
2. Limestone mountains in the South
3. The growing popularity of cave exploring and the effect of more people on a cave's ecology
4. Appeal of darkness in caves
5. Stalactites and stalagmites — magnificent formations
6. Dangers — flash floods and unmarked passages
7. Age of caves in the United States
8. Experienced explorers descent in groups
9. Rock-climbing experience a requirement?
10. Physical requirements — strength for climbing and crawling

11. Caving community — national society of cave explorers
12. Common cave accidents

EXERCISE 5. For one of the topics chosen, draft a statement of purpose and select a suitable title. List as many items (facts, details, examples, incidents, impressions, reasons, recollections, etc.) as you can think of to develop the topic into a composition of from 300–500 words. Try to avoid repetition.

(2) Organize your list of ideas under a few main headings.

The second step is to scrutinize your list in order to sort out the three or four major ideas under which everything else may be included. Call these the main headings. These headings will be the major steps in the unfolding of your explanation. Under each of these headings, you will group whatever examples, incidents, facts, or observations are necessary to develop the main heading clearly.

For the sample list on the topic "My Favorite Outdoor Activity," sorting out the main headings is easy because the writer has decided to record every aspect about cave exploration that may appeal to someone. The writer's purpose and sense of what is most appealing and what is least appealing about cave exploration suggest an order of headings.

I. Dangers of caving
II. Cave's beauty and appeal to senses
III. Record of earth's history inside a cave
IV. Appeal of caves to human need for adventure

EXERCISE 6. Examine the list of materials you prepared for Exercise 5. Look for relationships between the items. What general heading is suggested by several specific details? Formulate three or four main headings. If you have difficulty finding or phrasing these, it may be that you do not have enough material to develop your composition. If that is the case, give your initial list of materials more thought.

(3) Place your ideas in their proper order.

The third step is to arrange the main headings into the order in which you will discuss them in your composition. Usually this order will suggest itself merely from an examination of the main ideas in the light of your purpose. An argument, for example, proceeds logically — usually from least important argument to most important or vice versa. An explanation goes from simple to complex, and a description from small to large or from near to far, etc. The idea for the sample topic, an explanation of the appeal of cave exploration, should proceed from the simplest or least important appeal to the most complex or most important appeal. Any composition is clearest when its elements are arranged in the right order; it is your task as the writer to determine what that order is.

Experiment with the raw material of your own list. Rearrange the items under your main topic until each has found its proper place and appears to belong nowhere else. Some will have to be rephrased, others combined, and still others — that cannot be fitted in anywhere or are too long and complicated to be treated adequately — will have to be eliminated entirely.

EXERCISE 7. With the various orders in mind — order of time, order of position, order of simple to complex, and order of importance — examine the main ideas you formulated for Exercise 6, and place them in the most effective order. Be able to explain or to defend the position of each topic.

(4) Make a topic outline.

What you have so far produced is an outline. A formal topic outline differs from this only in form. The various items in a topic outline (main topics and subtopics) are single words or phrases, not complete sentences, and are arranged so that the main ideas stand out.

14d. Observe the rules for form in making a topic outline.

(1) Place the title and the statement of purpose above the outline.

(2) Use Roman numerals for the main topics. Subtopics are given capital letters, then Arabic numerals, then small letters, then Arabic numerals in parentheses, then small letters in parentheses.

Correct Outline Form

I. main topic
    A.⎫
    B.⎬ subtopics of I
         1.⎫
         2.⎬ subtopics of B.
              a.⎫
              b.⎬ subtopics of 2.
                   (1)⎫
                   (2)⎬ subtopics of b.
                        (a)⎫
                        (b)⎬ subtopics of (2)
II. main topic

(3) Indent subtopics. Indentions should be made so that all letters or numbers of the same kind will come directly under one another in a vertical line.

(4) There must always be more than one subtopic because subtopics are divisions of the topic above them. When you subdivide, after all, you must have at least two parts.

If you find yourself wanting to use a single subtopic, rewrite the topic above it so that this "sub-idea" is included in the main topic.

NONSTANDARD D. The study of French culture
                         1. The study of the French language
    STANDARD D. The study of French culture and language

(5) For each number or letter in an outline, there must be a topic.

Never place an *A,* for instance, next to *I* or *1* like this: *1A* or *A1.*

(6) A subtopic must belong under the main topic beneath which it is placed. It must be closely related to the topic above it.

(7) Begin each topic and subtopic with a capital letter. You should not place a period after a topic because it is not a complete sentence.

(8) The terms *introduction, body,* and *conclusion* should never be included in the outline.

Of course, you may have an introduction and a conclusion in your composition, but these terms themselves are not topics you intend to discuss.

EXERCISE 8. Copy carefully the skeleton outline given at the right below and place each of the items in the list at the left in its proper position in the outline.

Greater lung capacity	Bike Riding
No traffic jams	I. Equipment
Locks	A.
Ten-speed bike	B.
No auto pollution	C.
Greater endurance	II. Types of bicycle trips
Races	A.
No wasted energy	B.
Safety helmet	C.
Long tours	1.
Stronger knees and legs	2.
Short errands	III. Advantages of bicycles
Ten-kilometer races	over cars
Five-kilometer races	A.
	B.
	C.
	IV. Healthful benefits of
	bicycling
	A.
	B.
	C.

EXERCISE 9. Prepare a detailed topic outline for the materials you developed in Exercises 5, 6, and 7. If this topic has been unsatisfactory, select a new one from the list in your notebook.

Sample Topic Outline

CAVE EXPLORING — A TRIP INTO DARKNESS AND DANGER

Statement of purpose: To explain why people risk danger to explore the dark, mysterious world of caves

I. Dangers for cave explorers
    A. Unmarked passages
    B. Flash floods
    C. Exploring alone
    D. Being out of condition

II. Cave's appeal to senses
    A. Cool, clean air
    B. Crispness of sounds
    C. Beautiful formations
        1. Stalactities
        2. Stalagmites

III. Geology of caves
    A. Southern caves in limestone mountains
    B. Water tables over centuries
    C. Markings etched onto cave walls by water

IV. Caves as frontiers of exploration
    A. Similarity to astronauts' mission
    B. Similarity to pioneers' adventure

WRITING THE COMPOSITION

14e. With your outline before you, write the first draft of your composition.

If you have been conscientious about the preceding steps, you will find that many of the problems of writing have been solved in advance. You know your topic and your purpose in writing about it. You have assembled the necessary material and have arranged it in the correct order for presentation. Now you can concentrate on the matter of how to say it: paragraphing, word choice, sentence structure, and transitions. These problems can best be understood in relation to the three parts of a composition — *introduction, body,* and *conclusion.*

The Introduction

Neither the introduction nor the conclusion of a composition appears as a heading in a topic outline. The outline is concerned only with the body of a composition. It is important, nevertheless, to make the right kind of beginning and ending.

The introduction should give the reader a preview of what the composition is about. It should clearly indicate the topic and your purpose in writing about it. In a short composition, the introduction may consist of only a sentence in the first paragraph. In longer compositions it is a good idea to allow a short paragraph for this purpose.

The Body

The body is the heart of the composition. It fulfills the promise of the introduction and consists of as many good paragraphs as may be needed to develop the topic. The nature of your subject and your purpose will determine the exact length of the body of your composition. As a general guide, however, you may think of the body as occupying about three fourths of your space and consisting of from two or three paragraphs for a short composition of 250 words to six or eight paragraphs for a longer one of 1,000 words.

In Chapter 13 you considered the paragraph as a single

unit of thought. Except for practice assignments in school, most pieces of writing consist of a number of paragraphs. So it is with the whole composition.

As you write your first draft, you must decide at which points new paragraphs must be started. The way you paragraph should show your reader the successive stages of your thinking. It may be that you can devote one paragraph in your composition to each of the main headings in your topic outline. This simple solution works out well in shorter compositions. In longer compositions, however, you will often find that you need to devote a paragraph to certain important subheadings in your outline. In any case, each of your paragraphs should be built around a single idea or aspect of your main topic. Every time you take up a new idea, begin a new paragraph. Do not start a new paragraph without a good reason for doing so.

The Conclusion

One way to end a composition is simply to stop writing. Although this method is an easy one, it has the disadvantage of suggesting that you have given up. A better way to end a composition is by recalling the purpose of the composition as expressed in the introduction and by summing up the information you have set forth in developing your topic. The conclusion may be only a few sentences or it may be a whole paragraph. In either case, it should tell your reader that you have completed your composition, not abandoned it.

Transitions Between Paragraphs

In a good composition the current of thought flows smoothly from introduction to conclusion. It is not interrupted by the divisions between paragraphs but is helped easily over these divisions by certain transitional devices. By their use, the writer informs the reader how the idea of the paragraph just ended connects to the idea of the paragraph just beginning.

Linking expressions as transitional devices

therefore	furthermore
in spite of this	in the next place
consequently	however
accordingly	as might be expected
as a result of this	an example of this
similarly	finally
besides	lastly
nevertheless	also
on the contrary	meanwhile
on the other hand	soon
after all	in other words
such	in addition
likewise	then again

EXAMPLES   . . . And so day after day the drought continued.

On the thirtieth day, **however,** the wind changed. It blew cool against the face and carried a faint breath of something new . . .

. . . scientists found that dolphins were intelligent.

An example of this intelligence is the way in which dolphins once avenged themselves upon fishermen. A fishing boat in the Pacific had killed several dolphins. The next day about two hundred dolphins surrounded the fishing boat, stranding the fishermen aboard.

. . . it was the hottest day of the year.

The mayor, **accordingly,** declared a heat emergency.

Pronouns as transitional devices

EXAMPLE   . . . The child was overly nervous too. He started violently at unexpected noises and cried piteously when left alone.

This was not the worst burden on **his** mother, however . . .

Repetition of key words

EXAMPLES   . . . What is more, the car will accelerate from 0 to 60 miles per hour in only five seconds.

This blistering acceleration, however, is not its best feature . . .

... A further advantage of using the play by Lorraine Hansberry is that it would require only a small cast of talented actors.

Having a small cast would allow us to increase our profits by at least 10 percent, a major goal since we are donating the proceeds to charity. Since our overhead costs ...

REVISING THE COMPOSITION

14f. Revise your first draft.

Shakespeare is supposed to have written whole plays and changed only a few lines. Unfortunately, that is not the way it goes for most of us. Most of the time, our second thoughts are better than our first ones; a thoughtful and critical reading of our first drafts produces a clearer and stronger final draft.

If possible, lay your first draft aside for a while before you begin the process of revision. Revising is different from writing; it requires a little detachment, which the passage of time helps you to achieve. The object in revision is to see the composition as much as possible through the eyes of a reader. Look for trouble: sentences that are awkwardly constructed; ideas that are not clearly expressed; errors in capitalization, punctuation, and spelling. Make whatever changes seem necessary. Do not hesitate to rewrite or add whole paragraphs. The checklist that follows will serve as a guide for revision. The important matter of writing the final draft is discussed immediately following the checklist for revision.

COMPOSITION CHECKLIST

1. Does your introduction contain a clear statement of purpose?
2. Does each paragraph have only one main idea?
3. Are the main ideas developed by a variety of methods—

factual details, concrete details, examples, reasons, and so forth?

4. Do you use transitions to bridge gaps between paragraphs?

5. Is each main idea in the composition related to the topic as a whole?

6. Does your composition follow a logical order of development?

7. Is your final draft free from errors in capitalization, punctuation, sentence structure, spelling, word choice, and grammar?

8. Is your title interesting and suggestive of the main idea in your composition?

14g. Write the final draft.

A composition requires a considerable amount of effort. By the time you come to the preparation of the final draft, most of this work is behind you. Your main concern now is to put your composition in a neat and attractive form that reflects the thought and care you have devoted to the whole undertaking. Follow the instructions for manuscript preparation in Chapter 23 or the specific instructions that your teacher gives you.

The final draft of the composition you have seen taking shape throughout this chapter is on pages 308–10. Read it through, noting the general organization, the adherence to the outline (page 302), the paragraphing, the use of transitional expressions, and the divisions into introduction, body, and conclusion.

EXERCISE 10. Read the following high school composition and discuss in class the following points:

1. The statement of purpose in the introduction

2. The topic sentence of each paragraph

3. The paragraph divisions. Is each paragraph the development of a main heading in the topic outline, or is the composition differently arranged?

4. The transitional devices that link one paragraph to another

5. The conclusion. What does it accomplish?

CAVE EXPLORING — A TRIP INTO DARKNESS AND DANGER

Caves are dark, cold tunnels inhabited by bats, lizards, insects, and eyeless fish — weird, colorless creatures that have never seen sunlight. Little from the world above can penetrate the black space of caves, except for water that oozes through cracks, occasional threads of light that sneak between rocks — and human beings who descend bravely into the dark. Every year, more and more people become interested in the unique hobby of cave exploring. What lures them into the murky depths? What pleasure do they get from crawling along narrow, jagged passages? As this paper will explain, they are searching for adventure and for a strange beauty unknown in the "upper" world of light. — introduction

statement of purpose

For would-be adventurers, cave exploring offers unusual dangers. Cave passages are seldom marked; therefore, it is quite easy to lose all sense of direction. Water often fills caves during flash floods, drowning anyone inside. Because of these dangers, explorers must never risk entering a cave alone. They also must be in good physical condition because maneuvering inside a cave requires the strength for climbing and crawling.

body

main topic I
dangers

Once the explorer enters a cave's deep vaults, **however,** all the difficulties

transition

seem worthwhile. Cave air is cool and clean. Sounds echo crisply through the vast emptiness. Magnificent rock creations, shaped over centuries by drops of water seeping through the earth, dominate the interior. Like exotic sculptures in a secret museum, formations called stalactites droop ominously from a cave's ceiling, while stalagmites rise in massive pointed shapes from the floor. For the cave explorer, the undergound is a hidden realm of beauty.

main topic II
appeal to senses

Many explorers know another secret hidden inside caves: a sense of intimacy with earth's geologic past. The caves of the Carolinas and Georgia, for example, were originally formed out of limestone mountains. They were created by water tables—levels of water in the ground—that rose and fell over centuries, slowly dissolving the limestone bases of the mountains. The high, dry spaces left when the waters receded are the caves we know today. The explorer sees these water markings etched into the cave's floors and walls. They are vivid reminders of earth's transformation and development.

transition

main topic III
geology

Even more impressive than a cave's beauty or its record of the past is its pull on the human imagination. A cave is a frontier of adventure, a last unexplored wilderness. Like an astronaut, a cave explorer is a wanderer into an alien world.

transition

main topic IV
frontier of exploration

Every "caver" has the pioneer dreams
of being the first to find a new passage-
way, and to take a fresh step into an
undiscovered cavern. It is this call of
the unknown that lures an explorer into
the earth's depths — to enter a world   conclusion
where space, darkness, and the human
imagination join together.

Topics for Compositions

The topics listed below are intended as suggestions. If
you find one that you could use if it were changed slightly,
change the topic to suit your wishes. Word your own title.

The Arts

1. The secret of taking fine photographs
2. Favorite rock groups
3. A good (bad) movie
4. Ceramics
5. How to refinish antique furniture
6. Understanding modern art
7. A musical instrument anyone can learn to play
8. Ballet vs. gymnastics
9. The training of an actor (actress)
10. Designing and building a stage set
11. Lighting principles
12. The dress rehearsal
13. Qualities of a good magazine writer
14. How to listen to music
15. What's great about great painting?
16. The origins of jazz
17. Interior decoration
18. Careers in fashion design
19. The use of watercolor
20. Modern film making
21. The art of sculpture

Literature

1. A great American playwright
2. Antigone and Ismene — sisters but opposites
3. The importance of the minor characters in a Shakespearean play
4. Some differences between Shakespeare's language and today's English
5. Shakespeare's sources
6. Some special features of the Elizabethan stage
7. Two very different poems on the same theme

8. A great American poet
9. Conflicting views of life as represented by two fictional characters
10. The novel as a force for social reform
11. The case against (or for) censorship
12. The qualities of a good short story
13. From book to movie
14. How to read a poem

Personal Opinions and Experiences

1. Moods that I can't help
2. On following the crowd
3. My chief ambition
4. My favorite meal
5. A look at my personality
6. On sophistication
7. Embarrassing experiences
8. The season that best suits my temperament
9. First impressions are rarely the best.
10. What I want to be
11. Sports bore me.
12. I would like to redesign myself.
13. The uses and misuses of make-up
14. What is it to be mature?
15. My finest hour
16. What the UN means to me
17. What does it mean to be true to yourself?
18. Three ways to overcome anxiety
19. Do manners make a difference?

20. The uses of adversity
21. "The world is too much with us . . ."
22. Why I hate winter (etc.)
23. Status-seeking among high school students
24. Three quick and easy routes to unpopularity
25. What is a really *great* person?
26. My bank account problems
27. A pleasant journey
28. My prejudices
29. Some people simply amaze me!
30. My happiest surprise
31. How to endure a terrifying exam
32. On being a big sister (brother)
33. A look into the future
34. The friends around me
35. Dealing with the weather
36. On being a nuisance
37. My greatest triumph
38. Daydreaming and the troubles it has caused me
39. The person I admire most

Right Around Home

1. Our family customs
2. Why my parents annoy (or criticize) me
3. Sunday dinner
4. Our favorite family holiday
5. Wait till I have my own family!
6. The family car
7. Trials and tribulations of moving

8. Discipline and what it does to (or for) me
9. Two relatives too many
10. Ancestors as only I could know them
11. Chores that bore me
12. Guests who I wish would stay longer
13. Street games
14. "To Grandmother's house we go . . ."
15. My dream house
16. Waiting for the doctor
17. Our worst accident
18. Our furniture
19. Backyard pests
20. Our family album
21. Landlords are often human
22. A room of my own
23. Our block is a tight little world.
24. Educational television
25. Things that get lost around the house
26. Network television
27. Neighborhood sounds

School

1. Fighting your way up the ladder
2. How to make grades and lose friends
3. Teachers' problems
4. My favorite seat
5. A trip to the infirmary
6. Waiting in line
7. "Miles to go before I sleep . . ."
8. On spelling
9. Suggested changes in the curriculum

10. Winning an election
11. Schools I have attended
12. My favorite subject
13. Arguments for (or against) studying foreign languages
14. Advantages of the honor system
15. Once I tried to bluff . . .
16. Trying out for the class play
17. Teachers' odd habits
18. A system for homework
19. My locker
20. High schools in the U.S. and in another country
21. Students come in three varieties.
22. Appropriate school dress
23. Who can determine what is proper?
24. My happiest (unhappiest) school experience

Hobbies and Leisure Time Activities

1. Raising hamsters
2. Collections and how to arrange things
3. Just loafing around the house
4. An educational hobby
5. Small repairs that become big headaches
6. Bicycling
7. My favorite animal
8. Church work
9. How to spend a rainy Sunday
10. Friendship by mail
11. On learning to play chess
12. The game I play best

13. The do-it-yourself craze
14. What I do in my spare time
15. Training a dog
16. Low-cost cameras
17. The fascination of bird watching
18. Fun on water-skis
19. Ham radio
20. Teaching karate
21. Horror movies, or why is it fun to be scared?
22. The discriminating window-shopper
23. Television commercials
24. The unobserved observer
25. Organize your own rock group.
26. Quick and easy ways to spoil a child
27. A lexicon of high school slang
28. On collecting a library of classical music
29. Profitable activities
30. On tour with the family
31. Wind surfing

Far and Wide

1. The country fair
2. On the boardwalk
3. Customs I have observed in other people
4. Our strange neighbors
5. Virtue is rewarded.
6. How to enjoy an illness
7. To the moon and beyond
8. On borrowing and lending
9. On being lost
10. The art of fishing
11. On mountain climbing
12. Outdoor decorations
13. On looking up at the stars

Science

1. Pollution control
2. The Ice Age in North America
3. To Mars and beyond
4. Oceanography — an exciting new science
5. Why birds migrate
6. Rocks — the record of the earth's history
7. The exploding universe
8. The possibility of life in outer space
9. The uses of the laser beam
10. The dangers of insecticides
11. Easy experiments for the home workshop
12. Hybridization — a way to bigger crops
13. A conservation project
14. The great sequoias of California
15. Landing on the moon
16. An endangered species

Social Problems

1. The threat of war
2. The Peace Corps
3. The balance of trade
4. Why vote?
5. The move to small cars
6. Air pollution
7. Stream pollution
8. How to improve our schools
9. What is inflation?
10. Fewer and fewer farm jobs
11. The blessing (curse) of presidential primaries
12. Discrimination

13. The need for more city parks
14. How Congress passes a law
15. Teen-agers and cars
16. The age of anxiety
17. Overcrowded schools
18. The continuing fight for civil rights
19. The nonmedical and scientific uses of drugs
20. The promise of urban renewal
21. Our plundered natural resources
22. The future of Africa
23. Are demonstrations effective?
24. Juvenile delinquency
25. The chief problem of my home town
26. Population control
27. A bigger defense budget
28. Problems of welfare
29. Family size
30. Freedom of the individual
31. A cure for unemployment
32. Our changing cities
33. Why we have strikes

Chapter 15

Specific Writing Assignments

Explanations, Essay Answers, Character Descriptions, Critical Reviews, Essays of Opinion, Definitions

The general principles of exposition discussed in Chapter 14 apply to most of the writing assignments you are likely to be given in school. There are, however, certain specific kinds of composition which come up often enough to require special treatment. Except possibly for the description of a character, the kinds of composition discussed in this chapter will play an increasingly important part in your classroom assignments from now on. Concentrate on one type at a time, always remembering that the general rules for planning and organizing a composition apply to all expository writing.

EXPLAINING A PROCESS

Explanation differs from description by focusing on a process or series of steps. The writer of a society column may *describe* a wedding cake. The writer of a cookbook must *explain* how to make one. Your local library probably offers how-to books on many different subject.

Hints for Writing the Explanation of a Process

1. Choose a subject that lends itself to explanation. Make sure it is a subject about which you are fully informed.

2. *Keep your reader in mind.* Don't assume the reader knows much, but don't go to the other extreme and "talk down." Try to anticipate questions. Define briefly any terms that might not be understood.

3. *Be clear, accurate, and complete.* Don't omit any necessary step, or allow anything irrelevant to intrude.

4. *Begin effectively.* Identify the process you will explain; explain its purpose; explain when and by whom it is performed; clarify what value it will have when performed.

5. *If you are explaining how to make something, make clear to the reader what will be needed to carry out the process (equipment, ingredients, skills, etc.).* You may use one paragraph to list and explain these materials all at once, or you may explain them as they come up naturally in the process.

6. *Break down the process into steps, and present these steps in chronological order.* Provide easy transitions between the steps, and put in whatever cautions are needed where missteps might normally occur ("Don't let the two wires touch").

7. *Conclude this type of composition by explaining what the results will be if the steps have been followed carefully.*

Read the following explanation of the process of carving an egg from a block of wood. Note the step-by-step organization and the clear instructions. The author leaves the final step to the reader, but until that point, everything is patiently explained.

CARVING A WOODEN EGG FOR PRACTICE

Whether or not you have carved wood before, this practice project is a good way to begin. — introduction

Use a block of wood of any kind (without knots) about $1\frac{1}{2}$ inches thick by $1\frac{1}{2}$ inches wide by $2\frac{1}{2}$ inches long, with the grain running the long way.

materials needed

If you cannot find wood this thick, you can make such a block from two pieces of standard $\frac{3}{4}$-inch board, each

$2\frac{1}{2}$ inches long. [1]Measure and mark with the ruler and pencil the $2\frac{1}{2}$-inch lengths. Clamp the board in the vise or C-clamps, and with the crosscut saw cut off the measured pieces, then glue them with the flat sides together, using a thin coat of the white glue. Press them in the vise or clamp them together, but not *too* tightly or all the glue will squeeze out. Let them dry for at least an hour, then use the piece exactly as if it were a single solid block. This method of gluing is called *laminating* wood, and although the joint may show a little, it will give you no trouble in carving if the two pieces are of the same kind or hardness of wood. All wood can be glued easily and permanently with the *flat sides* (long grain) together, but it is almost impossible to glue two cut *ends* (end grain) together to stay.

    [2]Now you need to make a simple pattern for the wooden egg. On a piece of the cardboard measure off and mark with ruler and pencil the $1\frac{1}{2}$-inch by $2\frac{1}{2}$-inch rectangle of one side of your block. In that rectangle, draw freehand the shape of an egg that almost touches each of the four sides. Now, using the scissors, cut out the cardboard-egg pattern and draw around it with the pencil on each of the four sides of your wooden block. [3]To start work on the egg, first shave away with the knife the four corners of the block outside the drawn lines and then

(1) first step

(2) second step

(3) third step

slowly shape the piece into an egg just like those in the refrigerator. We are not going to give you a single further hint or bit of instruction. You are on your own to experiment and to learn some of the things about using your knife and about carving wood that you must find out for yourself. Try using first one blade and then the other to discover how your knife works. <u>This practice is more important than it is to make a perfectly oval-shaped egg, so don't worry too much if the wood splits, or if you finally wind up with nothing but a scrap of wood. This is an important way to learn — to do a project by yourself in your own way.</u>[1]

conclusion—
final advice

CHECKLIST FOR EXPLANATIONS

1. Is the explanation complete and clear? If carried out, is it likely to give the desired results?
2. Are the steps easy to follow from one to the next? Have you cautioned against missteps?
3. Did you list and explain unfamiliar terms and mention all of the materials needed?
4. Do the introduction and conclusion identify the process and define the end product?
5. Has the writer adapted the explanation to the intended audience? Is the writing itself interesting to read?

[1] Text of "Carving a Wooden Egg for Practice" from *HOW TO MAKE WHIRLIGIGS AND WHIMMY DIDDLES and Other American Folkcraft Objects*, by Florence H. Pettit. Copyright © 1972 by Florence H. Pettit. By permission of Thomas Y. Crowell, Publishers.

EXERCISE 1. (Suggested writing assignments)

1. *How to make something:* a birthday cake, a cement walk, a model airplane, a rock garden, a sweater, a sailor's knot, a bookcase, a clay pot.
2. *How to do something:* organize a club, buy stereo equipment, build a library of your own, redecorate your room, write a news story.
3. *How a process works:* how green plants manufacture sugars, how lenses invert images, how storekeepers arrive at the price of their stock, etc.
4. *A humorous essay or explanation:* how to forget an important birthday, how not to meet people, how to study without trying, how to miss a train.

WRITING THE ESSAY ANSWER

Most of the classroom tests you have taken so far have probably required one-word or short-paragraph answers. As you continue in school, however, you will find that you are more and more frequently asked to write longer essay answers to test questions. While the specific techniques will vary, there are some general techniques which it will be helpful to learn.

The essay answer is really an impromptu composition written under time pressure about a specific subject. All that you have learned about writing compositions, therefore, can be brought to bear on the writing of the essay answer. In addition, the following suggestions should be of help.

Hints for Writing the Essay Answer

1. Read the test question slowly and carefully. Watch for key terms used in the question and follow them exactly.

EXAMPLES   *compare:* find likenesses
               contrast: point out differences
               criticize: find faults and merits
               discuss: examine, analyze carefully, and come to a conclusion

> *explain:* spell out the how and why
> *summarize:* condense the main points
> *trace:* give a description of progress, sequence, or development

2. Plan your time and your answer. Calculate on the basis of the point value of the question and the total time of the test. Then jot down your ideas in a simple outline with usually not more than three or four major points.

TOTAL TEST TIME   40 minutes
Question 1. (60 points) allow 24 minutes

Discuss the question: Who is the real tragic hero of *Julius Caesar* — Brutus or Caesar?

OUTLINE   (1) Brutus in all five acts; Caesar dies in third.
(2) Brutus, not Caesar, is lamented at the end — "The noblest Roman of them all."
(3) Inner conflict occurs in Brutus, not in Caesar.

3. Write a good introductory paragraph in which you refer directly to the question, and state the main point, or thesis, of your answer.

4. Devote one paragraph to each main point, and begin it always with a topic sentence. In this way your main points will stand out for the teacher who is reading your answer quickly.

5. Illustrate and support what you say by specific details, examples, and references. Teachers are not likely to admire unsupported generalities.

6. Summarize what you have said in a good concluding paragraph.

7. Allow yourself a few minutes to proofread what you have written, checking carefully for spelling and usage errors.

There is room for much honest debate as to whether Caesar or Brutus is the real tragic hero of Shakespeare's *Julius Caesar.* | reference to the test question

In my close reading of the play, however, I found three com- | statement of answer pelling reasons for believing that Brutus is the protagonist.

The first reason is that Brutus has a much bigger role than Caesar. Caesar dies in Act III; Brutus is present in every act. It has been argued that Caesar's ghost continues to make his presence and influence felt throughout the rest of the play. Such an influence is not evident in the number of lines reserved for the ghost, who speaks only three times, a total of sixteen words. Even a master dramatist like Shakespeare cannot build a successful final two acts with the hero offstage. By the mere reason of his presence on the stage, it is Brutus' play.

first main point

supporting facts

The second reason is also concerned with this matter of structure and presence. When the play ends, it is Brutus to whom Antony and Octavius pay tribute. Antony's final speech is especially significant here:

second main point

specific example

> This was the noblest Roman of them all.
> . . . Nature might stand up
> And say to all the world, 'This was a man.'

The most compelling reason of all is found in Brutus' own nature. It is he in whom the moral issue of the play is fought out. He is the person in the play who experiences the most intense inner

third main point

conflict—and inner conflict in the tragic hero is the essence of all great tragedy. There is little of this in Caesar; he is a man with few doubts and uncertainties, a character who undergoes no change. Brutus, on the contrary, is torn with doubt and pulled apart by the moral issue. The tragedy is the chronicle of his rise and fall.   *specific details*

   By reason of what happens on the stage and what takes place inside the characters, Brutus is the tragic hero of *Julius Caesar*.   *summary*

CHECKLIST FOR ESSAY ANSWERS

1. Does the introductory paragraph make direct reference to the question and state the main thesis of the answer?
2. Are the key points referred to in the topic sentence of each paragraph?
3. Are the main points of the answer supported and illustrated by details and references to the text?
4. Does the concluding paragraph summarize what has been said?
5. Does the answer follow the directions of the question exactly?

EXERCISE 2. (Suggested writing assignments)

1. Compose your own essay question on a subject in the field of English, social studies, or science. Then write an essay answer for the question you have composed.
2. Ask your science or social studies teacher to give your class a practice essay question. When you have written your answer, submit it to both your English teacher and to the teacher who assigned it.

DESCRIPTION OF A CHARACTER

If you wanted to know what someone looked like and was like, the best way would be to meet the person. The second best way would probably be to see a motion picture of the person in action. The third best way would be to read a character sketch that would show how the person speaks and acts.

Hints for Writing the Character Description

1. Select an interesting character to describe. Although a skilled writer can make any character interesting, you will do well to choose a character who, because of appearance, idiosyncrasies, characteristics, or occupation, is intrinsically interesting. Observe closely before you begin to write; get to know the character so well that you can see beneath the surface. Try to understand and reveal not just what the person *seems* to be like but what he or she really *is* like.

2. When you begin your description, place the character in a setting that either reflects personality or that serves as an effective contrasting background. Don't describe the setting in too much detail; a few brief strokes should suffice. Whenever possible, details of setting should be woven naturally into the rest of the sketch.

3. Decide on the dominant impression you wish to create. Since you will ordinarily not be able to develop a character as fully in a 300-word sketch as a novelist would in an entire story, you can avoid painting a jumbled and confused picture by emphasizing one chief impression. Your character sketch thus becomes a study in depth of the outstanding quality of the subject.

4. Show your character in action. Remember we mentioned a moving picture, not a still life. Since action reveals character, show us, for example, how the person walks, sits, gestures, and expresses anger, amusement, love, dislike, confusion, and so on.

5. Use dialogue to contribute to the total picture. What does the subject's voice sound like? What characteristic idioms and expressions are used? Does the character slur endings, drop sounds from words, or enunciate with exaggerated precision? What does the character say when upset, happy, moody, angry, or depressed?

6. Select vivid details of physical appearance that will portray an individual. Since it is impossible to say everything about a person's appearance, selection becomes necessary. Two principles will help you determine which details to select. Select those which contribute most to the dominant impression you are trying to create; select those which will best individualize and differentiate. In describing features, use striking comparisons whenever possible, but avoid clichés like "a nose like an eagle's," "waddled like a duck."

7. Use sensory details for vividness. In describing details both of the setting and the appearance of the character, choose sensory details that will help the reader see, hear, feel, and smell. Since we apprehend experiences through the senses, it is essential that any re-creation of experience rely heavily on depictions of these sense impressions.

8. Pay special attention to word choice. Always important in writing, word choice is crucial to good description. Use specific and concrete nouns (not "he wore a sweater," but "he wore a red wool cardigan"). Use active and sharp verbs (not "walked," but "ambled" or "strode" or "paced"). And use vivid adjectives too, but don't overuse them.

The family was at the very core and ripeness of its life together. Gant lavished upon it his abuse, his affection, and his prodigal provisioning. They came to look forward eagerly to his entrance, <u>for he brought with him the great gusto of living,</u> of ritual. They would watch him in the evening as he turned the corner below with eager strides, follow carefully the processional of his movements from the time he flung his provisions upon the kitchen table to

character placed in a setting

dominant characteristic

character in action

the rekindling of his fire, with which he was always at odds when he entered, and onto which he poured wood, coal, and kerosene lavishly. This done, he would remove his coat and wash himself at the basin vigorously, rubbing his hands across his shaven, tough-bearded face with the cleansing and male sound of sandpaper. Then he would thrust his body against the door jamb and scratch his back energetically by moving violently to and fro. This done, he would empty another half can of kerosene on the howling flame, lunging savagely at it and muttering to himself.

Then, biting off a good hunk of powerful apple tobacco, which lay ready to his use on the mantel, he would pace back and forth across the room fiercely, oblivious to his grinning family who followed these ceremonies with exultant excitement, as he composed his tirade. Finally, he would burst in on Eliza in the kitchen, plunging to the heart of denunciation with a mad howl.

His turbulent and undisciplined rhetoric had acquired, by the regular convention of his usage, something of the movement and directness of classical epithet: his similes were preposterous, created really in a spirit of vulgar mirth, and the great comic intelligence that was in the family — down to the

details of physical appearance

vivid diction

vivid diction

vivid diction

youngest — was shaken daily by it. The children grew to await his return in the evening with a kind of exhilaration.

As he stormed through the house, un-   *vivid diction*
leashing his gathered bolts, the children
followed him joyously, shrieking exult-   *vivid diction*
antly as he told Eliza he had first seen
her "wriggling around the corner like a
snake on her belly," or, as coming in
from freezing weather, he had charged
her and all the Pentlands with malevo-
lent domination of the elements.

"We will freeze," he yelled, "we will   *quotation*
freeze in this . . . cruel and God-for-
saken climate. . . . Merciful God! I
have fallen into the hands of fiends in-
carnate, more savage, more cruel, more
abominable than the beasts of the field.
. . . They will sit by and gloat at my
agony until I am done to death."

As his denunciation reached some
high extravagance, the boys would
squeal with laughter, and Gant, in-
wardly tickled, would glance around
slyly with a faint grin bending the
corners of his thin mouth.[1]

EXERCISE 3. (Suggested writing assignments)

1. Take a character from fiction whom you know well. Write a character sketch as if you were describing a real person.

---

[1] From *Look Homeward, Angel* by Thomas Wolfe. Copyright 1929 by Charles Scribner's Sons; renewal copyright © 1957 Edward C. Aswell, Administrator, C.T.A. and/or Fred W. Wolfe. Reprinted by permission of Charles Scribner's Sons, and Wm. Heinemann Ltd.

2. Write a character sketch of yourself, but write it in the third person, as if you were looking at yourself from a detached point of view.
3. Write a character sketch of yourself—as you think your mother or father sees you.
4. Write a character sketch of a close friend.
5. Write a sketch of a town "character" who interests you.

CHECKLIST FOR CHARACTER DESCRIPTIONS

1. Do we see the character in action? Are gestures, movements, and responses vividly pictured?
2. Do we hear the character speaking? Is there effective use of speech to reveal character and feeling?
3. Is the setting sketched in so that it helps us see the character? Is the setting readily visualized?
4. Are the details of the description skillfully chosen so that we get a clear sense of the dominant characteristic of the character?
5. Does the description make an effective appeal to the senses? How do the sensory images contribute to the total effect of the description?
6. To what extent do word choice and diction contribute to the success of the description? Are there striking comparisons? Is there good use of precise, specific, and vivid nouns, verbs, and adjectives?

THE CRITICAL REVIEW

Reviews of nonfiction books (biography, history, science, current affairs) are written to enable other readers to decide whether or not they would enjoy a particular book. Your review, therefore, must summarize clearly the theme of the book, examine a few of the major arguments, and comment upon the author's conclusion.

While none of these jobs is easy, the last is hardest of all because you are expected to make impartial judgments upon matters you are likely to know little about. Under these circumstances, the only thing to do is to evaluate as best you can the author's reliability. If the author seems—either through experience or the use of sources—to be in a position to know what is being talked about, then the conclusions of the book demand respect. To be modest in your appraisals is surely the wisest course.

Hints for Writing the Critical Review

1. Begin the review by identifying the title, author, and publisher, and by indicating the book's general nature.

2. In the library look up the author's background, and from the information given there, discuss the author's qualifications in the early part of your review. What else has the author written? Does the author's background afford any particular insight into the matter of the book, or, on the contrary, is it likely to be a source of prejudice?

3. Summarize—usually in not more than one or two paragraphs—the content of the book. Focus particularly on those sections of the book that might be controversial.

4. Discuss the author's purpose in writing the book. For what kind of audience was the book intended—young readers, college students, the general public, teachers, or specialists in the field? Is the book broad or limited in coverage?

5. Describe any special features of the book. Is it well illustrated? Does it have a good index, a complete bibliography? Do the footnotes add interest or distract? Are there illustrations or charts in the text?

6. Evaluate the overall effectiveness of the book. Is it timely? Is it reliable; that is, are the generalizations supported by convincing evidence?

7. End your review by giving your individual response to the spirit of the book. Are you now aware and alive to things that formerly you did not know? Would you recommend the book to a friend?

In the book review which follows, note how each of these hints for writing is smoothly and effectively woven into the text.

Shinohata
by Ronald P. Dore
Pantheon © 1978

title, author, and
publisher

The Western vision of Japanese society rarely goes much further than picturing the entire nation uniformly dressed in dark suits and shiny slim ties, walking submissively behind a tour leader with a pennant in his hand. The other more congenial, but equally superficial, impression of the Japanese comes from the foreign traveler who has returned home laden with gifts, praising Japanese hospitality, the Tokyo taxi drivers who refuse tips, the friendly natives who ever so politely offer directions at Ginza street corners. Excluded, coddled, taunted, charmed, confused, Westerners shift between enchantment at the warm mysteries of the Japanese sensibility and anger at what frequently seems a spitefully unapproachable, thoroughly hermetic society.

introduction

audience

In his chatty, friendly description of life in the village of Shinohata, Ronald P. Dore has done much to give us the brains and blood and humor of the puzzling Japanese. When Dore, an eminent Japanologist, visited Shinohata in 1955,

purpose

author's
qualifications

the villagers were finally recovering from the ravages of the war, and upon his return in 1975, he found the people prospering from the Japanese industrial boom. Tracing the effects of the development upon his old friends, Dore makes a fascinating exploration of the changes in farming techniques, transportation, land ownership, and family life. Economic well-being has brought farm machinery, color televisions, indoor toilets, and automobiles to many Shinohata families, but some old-timers complain that wealth has destroyed the reverence for small, lovingly tended details: There is a particularly Japanese regret for the loss of "the preciousness of things." summary of contents

Shinohata lives most vividly in the talk of the villagers, which Dore has transcribed verbatim. We hear the lament of the mother-in-law, once the all-powerful tyrant over her daughter-in-law's existence, who complains about the disobedience of the new, independent brides. Or the modern farmer, his nose too sensitized to bear the smell of cow manure ("The stink gets into your clothes and into your hair. . . ."), now completely dependent upon manufactured chemical fertilizer. Comfortable with the Japanese and their language, Dore has combined the precision of a scholar, the anecdotal talents of a novel- general evaluation ist, and the heart of a humanist. He could have given his hosts in Shinohata no greater gift than this affectionate and informative portrait of their lives.[1]

personal
evaluation

CHECKLIST FOR REVIEWS

1. Is the reader given an accurate idea of the book's contents? Does the review give the overall theme of the book as well as discuss its specific parts?
2. Is the reader given enough information about the author's background and qualifications?
3. Does the review seem fair, and are the reviewer's judgments supported by quotations from the text?
4. Is the review well written?
5. Does the review help the reader decide whether the book is worthwhile? Is the review well written?

EXERCISE 4. (Suggested writing assignments)

1. Write a review of a nonfiction work that will prove to your teacher that you have read and understood the book.
2. Suppose you have been appointed to a committee to award a prize to the best nonfiction work written for high school students in the past year. Write a report to the committee in which you indicate your selection and defend your choice.

THE ESSAY OF OPINION

A familiar sort of essay of opinion is the "letter to the editor." It is a written statement of the writer's belief about an arguable subject, supported by evidence, and written to convince.

---

[1] From a review by Phyllis Birnbaum of *Shinohata* in *Saturday Review,* March 3, 1979. Copyright © 1979 by Saturday Review. All rights reserved. Reprinted by permission.

Hints for Writing the Essay of Opinion

1. Choose a debatable subject, one that permits of constructive controversy and disagreement. Be sure that it is clearly stated, is concerned with only one issue, and is sufficiently limited in scope. A formal statement of the subject of an argument is called a "proposition"; for example, "All drivers of motor vehicles should be required to pass a physical examination."

2. Jot down a list of the arguments that support your stand. Cross out any that are self-evident, trivial, or irrelevant. The ones that remain should have two genuine sides to them. They are called "issues." In dealing with the issues, you should (if you have the time) anticipate and refute every argument unfriendly to your point of view.

3. Begin effectively.
Catch the reader's interest.
State the proposition fairly and clearly.
Define any terms likely to be misunderstood.
Indicate the issues to be discussed.
Consider (if important) the history and significance of the question.

4. Support your point of view with evidence.
When you quote from an authority, identify the authority.
If you cite facts, give the source.
When you use an example, do not claim that one example establishes a general rule.
Be logical and fair.

5. Conclude your essay by summarizing your main arguments and indicating a future course of action.

DRIVER TRAINING FOR ALL

On a single weekend last month, there were three serious highway accidents in this county that involved teenage drivers. One of the results of this tragic weekend was a renewed public demand that high school students should be required to take a course in driver training before receiving their driver's licenses. True, most of the high schools in this area have offered driver-training courses for many years. But these courses have always been elective, rather than required; and sometimes only a small fraction of the student body has actually been enrolled in the course. It would be an excellent idea, as I see it, to make driver training a required course.

The opponents of this idea have argued that providing driver training for every student would be very expensive and that the results would not be worth the price. It is true that the courses would be costly. Our town school board has estimated that in order to provide driver training for every high school student, the school would need at least two more full-time instructors and two additional training cars, as well as extra lab space and equipment. While the cost of this program would be large, it must be weighed against the much greater cost—both in money and in human suffering—of continuing to allow inexperienced and poorly trained people to join the ranks of licensed drivers. An effective driver-training program would certainly be worth the expense.

consideration of opposing views

I think there is little question that the driver-training course now offered at our school has been effective. According to Ms. Shue, the instructor in charge of the course, only two of the forty-three students who took and passed the course last year failed to pass the state driver's-license examination on the first try; both of them passed on the second try. This compares very favorably with the statewide average of nearly twenty percent failures on the examination. Furthermore, Ms. Shue reports that only one of the students who has completed the course during the past five years has been involved in a serious accident since getting a license, and that in this case the other driver was judged at fault. Although Ms. Shue does not have figures for accidents involving students who have *not* taken the course, she says that each year at least three or four such students from our school have been arrested for speeding, while no student who has completed the course has been arrested for any traffic violation.

Some people grant that driver-training courses are effective, but still do not feel that driving instruction should be a required subject in a public high school. I think, on the contrary, that if we are to turn out a future generation of well-trained drivers, the public school is

first argument supported by evidence

second argument supported by reasons

the logical place to provide the training. Sixty years ago, driving an automobile may have been a hobby of the rich, but today it is an essential part of nearly every adult's workaday life. It would be in the public interest to train all citizens to drive well and wisely. The only present alternative to teaching driving in the schools is to continue the haphazard practice of leaving the instruction to parents or older friends, a system that in too many cases has proved ineffective.

The schools have shown that they can train good drivers. Let's give them the job of teaching all students to drive well.

short summary statement

CHECKLIST FOR ESSAYS OF OPINION

1. Is the question truly debatable; that is, are there genuinely two sides to it?
2. Does the writer take a definite stand, while still remaining fair to the contrary point of view?
3. Does the opening paragraph arouse the reader's interest, state the proposition, and provide the necessary background?
4. Are the arguments supported by ample evidence?
5. Does the writer refute evidence to the contrary?
6. Is the essay well written?
7. Does it convince?

EXERCISE 5. (Suggested writing assignments)

1. Write an imaginary letter to the editor of a school newspaper on some school issue. The following examples may suggest a topic:

       Enlarged powers for the student government
       Freedom for the student press
       Class elections
       Greater freedom for students in choosing their courses

2. Write an essay of opinion on some community issue. The following examples may suggest a topic:
       A youth recreation center should be established.
       Schools should be open six days a week, all year long.
       A teen-age curfew should be enacted.
       Traffic regulations should be changed.
       The community should set up collection centers for bottles, cans, and other trash that can be recycled.

3. Write an essay of opinion about some historical issue. The following examples may suggest a topic:
       The Revolutionary War should not have been fought.
       The U.S. should have joined the League of Nations.
       The Great Depression could have been prevented.

4. Select a candidate in a school, local, or national election, and try to convince your readers that they should support this candidate.

THE DEFINITION

Frequently larger issues cannot be debated until the contestants have first agreed on the meaning of certain terms. That is why definitions are so important and why it is necessary to take such care in composing them. A definition may be one sentence long or it may require a long essay.

Limited Definition

A short definition in a single sentence follows a definite pattern:

EXAMPLE   A taxicab is a public vehicle, usually equipped with a meter, for carrying passengers.

In this sentence definition, taxicab is the *term;* the broad class into which the term is placed is called the *genus* (public vehicle); and the properties which differentiate the term from others in the genus are called the *differentiae* (equipped with a meter, for carrying passengers). These parts of a definition always occur in a specific order: the term, followed by *is* or *are;* the genus; and the differentiae.

EXAMPLE   A captain _{term} is a commissioned officer next in grade _{genus} above a first lieutenant. _{differentiae}

Avoid the following errors in sentence definitions:

(1) Irrelevant material

EXAMPLE   A taxicab is a vehicle for carrying passengers, usually wealthier people.

(2) Circular definitions (defining the term by using a different form of the same word)

EXAMPLE   Freedom is the state of being free.

(3) Differentiae that do not really set apart the term

EXAMPLE   Democracy is a form of government used in modern times.

(4) Differentiae that restrict the term too much

EXAMPLE   A university is an advanced school for liberal arts students.

(5) Differentiae just as puzzling as the term

EXAMPLE   Sapremia is a state resulting from the products of putrefaction in the blood.

Extended Definition

Complex terms or concepts are best defined by compositions which explore every aspect of the idea. You may begin with a sentence definition, but in all likelihood you will use the rest of your composition to explain why you have chosen the differentiae you have cited. In such an extended definition, you might use the following methods:

(1) Citing authority

EXAMPLE   Maria Tallchief once defined grace as . . .

(2) Using a dictionary definition (give title and publisher)
(3) Discussing the origin of the term
(4) Discussing the history of the term

EXAMPLE The word *nice* once referred to someone who was "ignorant." Then it came to mean "stupid" or "foolish." Today the word means "agreeable" or "pleasing."

(5) Using comparison and contrast

EXAMPLE Hockey is a game similar in some ways to soccer . . .

(6) Using an anecdote

EXAMPLE To define what I mean by a "good neighbor," let me cite the parable of the Good Samaritan . . .

(7) Defining by telling what it is *not*

EXAMPLE A *ballerina* is not merely a dancer who can stand on her toes. She is not merely someone who can point her feet . . .

(8) Defining by citing many examples

EXAMPLE A young mountain range is, for example, the Rockies or the Alps or the Himalayas . . .

A [1]melodrama is a kind of [2]play, usually with a happy ending, [3]in which the interest centers in the exciting and unusual things that happen fast and mysteriously. [4]The characters are likely to be stock figures — that is, types rather than strongly marked individualities — moved by elementary motives. [5]The good people in such a play are very good and very brave, qualities which they need if they are to survive the dangers into which they are plunged for no plausible reason except to provide another thrill for the audience.

(1) term (2) genus

(3–4) differentiae

(5) supporting details

The bad people are very bad, with no redeeming feature unless tenacity of purpose may be so called. [6]Melodrama pays almost no attention to human values, and its object is to give a thrill. It is not to be judged too seriously. If it supplies harmless entertainment, like *Broadway,* for instance, its purpose is achieved. The plot of *Hamlet,* as it originally existed, is melodramatic, but Shakespeare transformed the leading character from a figurehead of blood-and-thunder melodrama to a genuinely tragic human being.[1]

(6) differentiae continued

CHECKLIST FOR DEFINITIONS

1. Does the definition place the subject in its class or genus?
2. Does the definition sufficiently distinguish the term from others similar to it?
3. Is the definition sufficiently clear so that no ambiguity remains and all exceptions are accounted for?
4. Is the definition sufficiently complete and inclusive so that no essential ideas or concepts are overlooked?

EXERCISE 6. (Suggested writing assignments)

1. Without consulting a dictionary, write a one-sentence definition for the following nouns: wristwatch, shoe, cup, match, chair, glove, fountain pen.

---

[1] Somewhat adapted from *The Enjoyment of Literature* by Ralph Boas and Edwin Smith, copyright, 1934, by Harcourt Brace Jovanovich, Inc.; renewed, 1962 by Edwin Smith and Louise Schutz Boas. Reprinted by permission of the publishers.

2. Demonstrate your knowledge of any one of the following literary terms by showing how it is used in several literary selections: simile, metaphor, irony, alliteration.

3. Define the following pairs of words so that the difference between them is clear: conservative — reactionary; liberal — radical; farce — comedy; city manager — mayor.

4. Use a combination of methods to define as completely as possible any one of the following abstract terms: wit, progress, faith, success, common sense, courage, love, intelligence.

Chapter 16

Creative Writing

All writing is creative in the sense that any piece of writing is a creation; it is something that never existed before. However, the term "creative writing" has a special meaning. It usually means a more personal kind of writing than the kind normally required in school courses and in life after you graduate. It includes stories, personal essays, and poems. Creative writing is literary writing as distinguished from practical workaday writing. It is imaginative rather than factual. It attempts to involve readers, to stir their feelings, and to amuse and entertain them, rather than merely to inform or to explain.

Many of the skills of the creative writer, however, may be used to good advantage in any kind of writing. Some of these skills are explained in the following pages. Study them and practice them. They will enable you to add interest and color and life to all your writing; furthermore, creative writing is fun for both writer and reader.

DEVELOP THE HABIT OF CLOSE OBSERVATION

Because creative writers are mainly concerned with describing the people around them and the world they live in, they must learn to describe accurately whatever they perceive. They must be very close observers of life.

In the following paragraph Annie Dillard shares with us an experience she enjoyed when visiting the Atlantic coast of Florida. Standing on the shore, she saw a group of sharks. Because she observed closely and remembered what she observed in accurate detail, she is able to convey to us the full excitement of her experience.

EXERCISE 1. Read the passage; visualize the scene; prepare answers to the questions following the passage.

Another time I saw another wonder: sharks off the Atlantic coast of Florida. There is a way a wave rises above the ocean horizon, a triangular wedge against the sky. If you stand where the ocean breaks on a shallow beach, you see the raised water in a wave is translucent, shot with lights. One late afternoon at low tide a hundred big sharks passed the beach near the mouth of a tidal river, in a feeding frenzy. As each green wave rose from the churning water, it illuminated within itself the six- or eight-foot long bodies of twisting sharks. The sharks disappeared as each wave rolled toward me; then a new wave would swell above the horizon, containing in it, like scorpions in amber, sharks that roiled and heaved. The sight held awesome wonders: power and beauty, grace tangled in a rapture with violence.[1]

1. What details does the author include to indicate time and place?
2. What accurate details specify size and shape?
3. Point out a verb and an adjective that you think were particularly well chosen.
4. What comparison does the author use to make the experience vivid?

EXERCISE 2. Write a paragraph in imitation of Annie Dillard's, in which you describe a simple childhood experience, perhaps an exploration of your own, and make clear to your reader what you saw and how you felt.

To sharpen your powers of observation, jot down in your notebook, every day for a week, brief detailed descriptions of things you see, preferably ordinary, unimportant things you may not have observed closely before or

---

[1] From "Heaven and Earth in Jest" in *Pilgrim at Tinker Creek* by Annie Dillard. Copyright © 1974 by Annie Dillard. First appeared in *Harper's Magazine,* October, 1973. Reprinted by permission of the author and her agent, Blanche C. Gregory, Inc.

indeed even noticed at all. Your descriptions need not be written in sentence form. Think of them simply as the part of a sentence following "I saw. . . ." It is your ability to observe details, not the quality of their expression, that is important in these descriptions. The following examples, all written about things observed on the way to school, will make clear this kind of recording of observations.

1. water standing in the gutter, a film of oil reflecting in rainbow swirls
2. a worker—big stomach like a basketball above his belt— drinking coffee from a white cup held with both enormous hands
3. a metal garbage can, dented, leaning drunkenly by the curb, a greasy bag thrown on top like an afterthought, spilling bits of lettuce, dried bread, coffee grounds
4. the driver of a car that stopped below my window on the bus, grim, unshaven jaw holding a big black pipe, hairy elbow resting on the window frame
5. Jane, bent nearly double by the load of books in her arms, running for the bus, books slipping, long black hair waving
6. a discarded aluminum can on the school lawn, its silver end reflecting in the sun, like a bright flashlight
7. a little whirlwind skittering across the parking lot, a funnel of leaves, papers, and dust

EXERCISE 3. Bring to class five observations from the week's recording in your notebook. Share them with your classmates. Evaluate one another's observations for their accuracy and the effectiveness of the details.

An example of the effective use of detailed observation is the following description of an old-fashioned oil lamp, the kind of table lamp found in most houses before the advent of gas and electric lighting. The style of this passage is "literary"; you should read slowly and attempt to see the lamp exactly as it is. The author supplies enough details. Prepare answers to the questions below the passage.

1. It is late in a summer night, in the room of a house set deep and solitary in the country; all in this house save

myself are sleeping; I sit at a table, facing a partition wall; and I am looking at a lighted coal-oil lamp which stands on the table close to the wall, and just beyond the sleeping of my relaxed left hand; with my right hand I am from time to time writing, with a soft pencil, into a school-child's composition book; but just now, I am entirely focused on the lamp, and light.

2. It is of glass, light metal-colored gold, and cloth of heavy thread.

3. The glass was poured into a mold, I guess, that made the base and bowl, which are in one piece; the glass is thick and clean, with icy lights in it. The base is a simply fluted, hollow skirt; stands on the table; is solidified in a narrowing, a round inch of pure thick glass, then hollows again, a globe about half flattened, the globe-glass thick, too; and this holds oil, whose silver line I see, a little less than half down the globe, its level a very little — for the base is not quite true — tilted against the axis of the base.

4. This "oil" is not at all oleaginous,[1] but thin, brittle, rusty feeling, and sharp; taken and rubbed between forefinger and thumb, it so cleanses their grain that it sharpens their mutual touch to a new coin edge, and the odor is clean, cheerful, and humble, less alive by far than that of gasoline, even a shade watery; and a subtle sweating of this oil is on the upward surface of the globe, as if it stood through the glass, and as if the glass were a pitcher of cool water in a hot room. I do not understand nor try to deduce this, but I like it; I run my thumb upon it and smell of my thumb, and smooth away its streaked print on the glass; and I wipe my thumb and forefinger dry against my pants, and keep on looking.

5. . . . In this globe, like a thought, a dream, the future, slumbers the stout-weft strap of wick, and up this wick is drawn the oil, toward heat; through a tight, flat tube of tin, and through a little slotted smile of golden tin, and there ends fledged with flame, in the flue; the flame, a clean, fanged fan.[2]

---

[1] oily

[2] Abridged from *Let Us Now Praise Famous Men* by James Agee and Walker Evans. Copyright 1939 and 1940 by James Agee. Copyright 1941 by James Agee and Walker Evans. Reprinted by permission of Houghton Mifflin Company, and the British Publishers, Peter Owen Ltd., London.

1. Following the details given in the third paragraph of the description, draw in rough outline a picture of the lamp. Compare your picture with those of your classmates. What information that would be helpful did Agee omit?

2. From paragraph 3, select three or four descriptive details that were most helpful to you when you were drawing the lamp.

3. In paragraph 3 Agee appeals to the sense of sight. To what senses does he appeal in paragraph 4?

4. Is Agee's description of the lamp limited to the nature of the lamp and oil, or does it include his feelings about them? Explain.

5. Explain the meaning of the following pieces of description:

   paragraph 3   "solidified in a narrowing"

   paragraph 4   "it sharpens their mutual touch to a new coin edge"

   "as if the glass were a pitcher of cool water in a hot room"

   paragraph 5   "In this globe, like a thought, a dream, the future, slumbers the stout-weft strap of wick"

6. Find evidence in the selection to support the following statement: In his description of the lamp, Agee shows that he is a close observer.

EXERCISE 4. Take any object that interests you, observe it closely, and write a detailed description of it. Make your description so accurate that a reader could draw a picture of the object. If you can, let the reader know your feelings about the object, as Agee let you know his feelings about the lamp. Your description will be easier to write and more effective if you choose a small object like the lamp, rather than a large object like a car or a plane or a building. You might write about a ball-point pen, a light fixture, a beat-up book bag, or a classmate's shoe.

IN DESCRIPTIVE WRITING, SELECT WORDS THAT APPEAL TO THE SENSES

Everything we experience, we experience through our senses. It is impossible to write a description of anything without appealing to at least one of the five senses: sight, hearing, smell, touch, and taste. The sense most commonly appealed to, of course, is the sense of sight. But because most experiences involve more than one of the senses, skillful writers study how other senses are affected by what they observe. They increase the effectiveness of their descriptions by referring to as many senses as they can.

To appeal to the senses, writers use words that describe, or identify, the various sights, sounds, smells, tastes, feelings (touch) that they wish their readers to experience.

EXERCISE 5. Copy on your paper the following list of words. After each word, write the sense to which it refers. Some may refer to two senses.

1. hot	6. salty	11. whisper	16. glassy
2. spicy	7. icy	12. bitter	17. glittering
3. sour	8. bright	13. tart	18. thump
4. loud	9. roar	14. coarse	19. empty
5. green	10. moist	15. smoky	20. burnt

Describing the Sense of Sound

Most of the words we use to describe sounds are words that suggest in themselves the sounds to which they refer. *Clang,* for example, suggests the sound of metal striking metal; *bong* suggests the sound of a large bell, while *jingle* suggests the sound of a small bell. The use of words of this kind is called onomatopoeia, and the words are said to be onomatopoetic.

EXERCISE 6. Supply an onomatopoetic, or sound-imitating word, for the blank in each item. Copy the entire item on your paper. You may, if you wish, qualify the words with adjectives; thus "the crash of thunder" might become the "ear-splitting crash of thunder."

1. the —— of pages being turned
2. the —— of footsteps in the corridor
3. the —— of the wind

4. the ——— of wheels on gravel
5. the ——— of water dripping
6. the ——— of a fire
7. the ——— of a piano
8. the ——— of distant rifle fire
9. the ——— of a door opening
10. the ——— of a jet plane

Describing the Senses of Smell and Taste

Since smell and taste are closely related, the same words may be used to describe both. For example, the word *pungent* may be used to describe both taste and smell. Similarly, the words *bitter, musty, sweet,* and *stale* may describe both sensations.

EXERCISE 7. Supply an adjective you think appropriate for each blank.

1. the ——— taste of coffee
2. the ——— odor of strong cheese
3. the ——— taste of pickles
4. the ——— aroma of fresh bread
5. the ——— smell of pizza

In the following paragraph, Thomas Wolfe describes the sounds and smells he associated with the arrival of the circus at the railroad station-yard when he was a young boy. Discuss with your classmates the effectiveness of Wolfe's descriptions of smells.

> And to all these familiar sounds, filled with their exultant prophecies of flight, the voyage, morning, and the shining cities — to all the sharp and thrilling odors of the trains — the smell of cinders, acrid smoke, of musty, rusty freight cars, the clean pineboard of crated produce, and the smells of fresh stored food — oranges, coffee, tangerines and bacon, ham and flour and beef — there would be added now, with an unforgettable magic and familiarity, all the strange sounds and smells of the coming circus. The gay yellow sumptuous-looking cars

in which the star performers lived and slept, still dark and silent, heavily and powerfully still, would be drawn up in long strings upon the tracks. And all around them the sounds of the unloading circus would go furiously in the darkness. The receding gulf of lilac and departing night would be filled with the savage roar of the lions, the murderously sudden snarling of great jungle cats, the trumpeting of the elephants, the stamp of the horses, and with the musty, pungent, unfamiliar odor of the jungle animals: the tawny camel smells, and the smells of panthers, zebras, tigers, elephants, and bears.[1]

Describing the Sense of Touch, or Feeling

The sense of touch applies to two kinds of feelings. One kind is the sensation of actually touching a surface or being touched by something. Such words as *smooth, rough, icy,* and *slimy* describe the feeling of a surface when we touch it or are touched by it.

In the following passage Lois Hudson recalls the sensations she experienced as a young girl on a North Dakota farm when the temperature one winter night dropped to 50° below zero.

I was well acquainted with the shock of stepping from the warm kitchen into a winter night. But none of the freezing memories of the past could prepare me for the burning air that night. It was like strong hot smoke in my nostrils, so that for one confused instant I thought I was going to suffocate with the cold that was so cold it was hot. I gasped for breathable air, and my father said, "Don't do that! Breathe through your nose—your breath is warmer that way when it gets to your lungs."

[1] From "Circus at Dawn" copyright 1934, 1935 Modern Monthly, Inc., from *Death to Morning* by Thomas Wolfe. Reprinted by permission of Charles Scribner's Sons and the British Publishers, William Heinemann Ltd.

We walked carefully down the hill to the barn; then I slithered down the steps, chopped in a snowdrift in front of the door, and slid it open. The barn was very old, but, always before, it had been warm with the heat of the animals kept in it all day long. But that night being inside didn't seem to make any difference. I still had the kind of ache in my temples and cheekbones that I always got when I took too big a mouthful of ice cream.[1]

The other kind of feeling is internal, a feeling like nausea or weakness or sensations of fear — a rapid heartbeat, breaking out in perspiration. The following passage describes how a boy felt after having been critically ill with a high fever that finally broke. The sensations are not those of touch as we usually think of touching something, but they are internal sensations closely related to the sense of feeling.

After fever my body and head felt light, like a piece of dew-damp vegetable. The illness had emptied me so completely, now I seemed bereft of substance. Being so long in that sunless, fever-spent room, I was filled with extraordinary translations.[2] I felt white and blood-drained, empty of organs, transparent to color and sound, while there passed through my flesh the lights of the window, the dust-changing air, the fire's bright hooks, and the smooth lapping tongues of the candle. Heat, reflections, whispers, shadows, played around me as though I were glass. I seemed to be bodiless, printed flat on the sheets, insubstantial as a net in water.[3]

EXERCISE 8. Write an adjective or a phrase that describes the sensation of touching the following.

1. velvet
2. marble
3. silk
4. corduroy
5. denim
6. earthworm
7. fish
8. fur
9. baseball
10. tire

---

[1] From "The Cold Wave" from *Reapers of the Dust* by Lois Phillips Hudson. Reprinted by permission of Atlantic-Little, Brown and Company.
[2] Mr. Lee means that he feels his body has been changed.
[3] From *The Edge of Day* (English title: *Cider with Rosie*) by Laurie Lee. Copyright © 1959 by Laurie Lee. Reprinted by permission of The Hogarth Press Ltd.

EXERCISE 9. Write a paragraph (approximately 100 words) in which, by appealing to as many senses as you can, you convey your feelings at a time when you were under a strain, or the opposite – a time when you were feeling especially relaxed and happy. You could, like the author of the preceding description, tell how you felt when you were ill or were convalescing. You might describe your nervousness before an examination or a public performance, the sensation of fear or anger, the feeling of complete physical well-being or of complete laziness. You should make clear in the beginning exactly where you are and what the general circumstances are.

FILL YOUR WRITING WITH VIVID DETAILS

Most writing, no matter what kind it is, goes from the general to the particular. Whether you are writing a description or telling a story, you make general statements and then back them up with supporting details. Writing shorn of its details is dull and lifeless. Although it is important to give many details, quantity is never so important as quality. Through close observation, a skillful writer sees the details needed to convey a picture clearly.

In the following selection, which describes the reaction of an observer watching from the sideline at a basketball game, the author supports the opening generalization with details. Which senses are appealed to?

Gayforth became bewildered by the confusing swiftness and wild intensity of the play. He heard the constant thud of soft-shod feet striking the hard floor, the dull clang of the basket frame as the ball hooked itself down into the net, and the instant sharp yell that followed from the onlookers. Two men, colliding, fell at his very feet. He glimpsed the contortion of pain that flashed across the face of one; he saw the shine of the lights on their wet faces and shoulders, and caught the sharp odor from their hot, sweating bodies. The whole floor was a maze of moving legs and arms, a bewildering kaleidoscope of shifting pose, with the ball making long arcs across from man to man, or curving through the air toward the basket.[1]

In the following paragraph, Edmund G. Love recalls the barber to whom he and his brother went when they were children. Find two general statements about Joe Gage and point out the details that support the general statements.

I do not think that Joe Gage overcharged for his haircuts. A boy certainly got his money's worth. He was the first barber I ever knew who gave away lollypops to his customers. He also gave balloons, tops, kites, and baseballs. He entertained his customers as he cut their hair. He would stop in the middle of whatever he was doing and put on the boxing gloves and go a quick round with a boy. He would Indian-wrestle, play mumblety-peg, or teach a boy how to whittle. He would repair a coaster wagon or paint a name on a sled. He was a talented man in many ways. He was the best whistler who ever came to Flushing. He could imitate birds or whistle a song. He could sing. He could tell stories. Sometimes in the middle of a haircut he would get so engrossed in one of his own stories that he would draw up a stool and sit down. When my brother Walter stalked into his shop and asked for a shave, a shave was forthcoming. Joe lathered Walter's face, used the back of a comb to shave off the lather, applied a hot towel, and finished off with a generous application of witch hazel and lilac water.[2]

EXERCISE 10. Each of the following places has its own atmosphere. Select one place — or, if you prefer, a place not listed here — and write a one-paragraph (approximately 150 words) description conveying its atmosphere. Support your general statements with as many appropriate details as you can. Appeal to as many of the senses as possible. Let your reader know your feelings in this place.

[1] From *Prose Specimens* by C. S. Duncan, E. L. Beck and W. L. Graves. D. C. Heath: Boston, 1913.
[2] Excerpt from in *The Situation in Flushing* by Edmund G. Love. Copyright © 1965 by Edmund G. Love. Reprinted by permission of the author and his agent, Blanche C. Gregory, Inc.

pizza parlor	library
greenhouse	schoolroom
automobile repair shop	zoo
city playground	restaurant
city street	indoor swimming pool

USE COMPARISONS TO MAKE YOUR WRITING CLEAR AND INTERESTING— SIMILES AND METAPHORS

Skillful writers give full play to their natural tendency to think in terms of comparison. In the models of good writing in this chapter, we have seen many examples of the use of comparisons. In Annie Dillard's description of an encounter with sharks, you noticed her use of comparison. She writes of "scorpions in amber" when referring to the sharks inside the waves, and she refers to a wave as a "triangular wedge against the sky."

In his description of a glass lamp, James Agee said its base was a "fluted, hollow *skirt*," thus drawing a comparison between the lamp base and a skirt. He says that the lamp wick *slumbers* in the oil, comparing the wick to a live thing asleep, and he describes the flame at the top of the wick as a "clean, fanged fan."

In his description of how he felt after a severe illness, Laurie Lee writes of a candle flame as "the smooth lapping *tongues* of the candle." You may remember that he used other comparisons when he wrote, "I seemed to be bodiless, *printed* flat on the sheets, *insubstantial as a net in water*."

Comparisons like those you have been reading are called figures of speech, and the language in which they are expressed is called figurative language. A figurative expression is the opposite of a literal expression. An expression is literal when it is completely factual. It is figurative when it is imaginative rather than factual, when it compares things that are not alike in reality but are alike in the writer's imagination. For example, a writer describing the sensations of a passenger on the bow of a ship at sea on a winter night might say, "The wind in her face was strong and cold."

This would be literal, not figurative, description. On the other hand, the sentence might read, "The wind cut her face like a knife." While there is really no similarity between wind and a knife, the comparison does make sense imaginatively. It is a figurative expression, a figure of speech.

Comparisons are common features of your speech and writing. Often you use them without thinking: "busy as a bee," "hard as a rock," "straight as an arrow." We speak of a person as "a good egg," and we talk about a "flood of words" and "death's door." Such everyday comparisons as these are to be avoided in writing because they are "tired" and commonplace. They have lost their effectiveness as description. But the ability to fashion fresh, original comparisons is a very important writing skill.

The two most common figures of speech are simile and metaphor. A simile is a comparison between things essentially unlike, expressed directly through the use of a comparing word such as *like* or *as:*

> They slept *like* the dead all day.
> The flame rose *like* a pointed flower.
> She is as quick *as* a rabbit.

A metaphor is a comparison between things essentially unlike, expressed without a comparing word such as *like* or *as.* The comparison is suggested, not directly stated:

Between steep walls flowed the swollen *stream* of rush-hour traffic.
The sun *hammered* at our uncovered heads.
The blooming orchard *was a pink cascade* on the hillside.

EXERCISE 11. Identify each of the following as simile or metaphor by writing *S* or *M* after the proper number. Be prepared to state what things are being compared and to evaluate the effectiveness of the figure of speech.

1. Buildings are waterfalls of stone. —Louis Ginsberg
2. The modern racehorse, inbred for speed, carrying the maximum amount of muscle on the minimum amount of bone structure, is as frail as a pastry shell. —Ernest Haveman

3. A tree of pain takes root in his jaw. —John Updike
4. I could not bear to see her dimmed. —Mary Renault
5. Her face was deep-carved stone. —Maurice Walsh
6. I felt their eyes directed like burning-glasses against my scorched skin. —Charlotte Brontë
7. An island [Manhattan] uttered incandescent towers like frozen simultaneous hymns to trade. —Malcolm Cowley
8. The Possible's slow fuse is lit/By the Imagination! —Emily Dickinson

EXERCISE 12. Using your imagination, complete the following similes in as fresh and original a way as you can. Take time to wait for your imagination. Don't write down the first comparison that comes to mind; it may be a well-known, worn-out expression.

1. Cars climbing the distant hill looked like . . .
2. He had a chin like . . .
3. Bright beach umbrellas like . . .
4. To press his hand was like . . .
5. Trees outlined against the sky like . . .
6. The heavy fog was like . . .
7. High above us a jet plane moved across the sky like . . .
8. The room was as quiet as . . .
9. The clouds were like . . .
10. She looked as happy as . . .

EXERCISE 13. Write a three-paragraph composition (approximately 300 words) describing the experience of waking up in the morning or falling asleep at night. Whichever you choose, your experience will certainly not be lacking in things and people to describe.

Show by your use of specific details that you have observed closely. As you describe your sensations, appeal occasionally to senses other than sight. Include at least three figures of speech: similes or metaphors. You will probably want to consult your notebook in which you have recorded your observations. (See Exercise 3.)

A MODEL NARRATIVE

Narrative writing is the art of storytelling. Good storytellers use all of the elements discussed in this chapter: accurate details, words that appeal to the senses, and comparisons. To these ingredients they add the elements of plot, or action: characters, conflict, and outcome.

Narratives can be as long as a thousand-page novel or as short as a paragraph. A narrative need not be long to be effective; many excellent stories have been written with very few words, as the model narrative that follows will demonstrate.

A narrative, however, usually contains the following three elements:

Characters. Every story normally has at least one leading character. This hero or heroine of the story is called the *protagonist.* Often another character, called the *antagonist,* opposes the plans or wishes of the hero or heroine. A narrative many include other characters, of course, depending upon the writer's plan.

Conflict. Something has to happen in a story. There must be a problem or situation that challenges the leading character. In other words, the protagonist must be *in conflict* with someone or something.

Outcome. The outcome of the story resolves the conflict facing the leading character. The resolution may be either good or bad for the protagonist. The story may end either happily or unhappily.

In the following short narrative, observe these three elements of narrative writing: characters, conflict, and outcome. The story is told by one of the characters, Death.

An Appointment in Samarra

There was a merchant in Bagdad who sent his servant to market to buy provisions, and in a little while the servant came back, white and trembling, and said, "Master, just now when I was in the marketplace I was jostled by a woman in the crowd, and when I turned I saw it was Death that jostled me. She looked at me and made a threatening gesture; now, lend me your horse, and I will ride away from this city and avoid my fate. I will go to Samarra and there Death will not find me." The merchant lent him his horse, and the servant mounted it, and he dug his spurs in its flanks and as fast as the horse could gallop he went. Then the merchant went down to the market-place and he saw me standing in the crowd and he came to me and said, "Why did you make a threatening gesture to my servant when you saw him this morning?"

"That was not a threatening gesture," I said, "it was only a start of surprise. I was astonished to see him in Bagdad, for I had an appointment with him tonight in Samarra."[1]

EXERCISE 14. Write a short narrative that includes conflict, characters, and outcome. Discuss your story idea ahead of time with your teacher or classmates.

---

[1] Adapted excerpt from "An Appointment in Samarra" from *Sheppy* by W. Somerset Maugham. Copyright 1933 by W. Somerset Maugham. Used by permission of Doubleday and Company, Inc., A. P. Watt Ltd., and the Estate of W. Somerset Maugham.

Chapter 17

The Business Letter

A letter speaks for you in your absence. To do its job of representing you well, it must be clear, appropriate in tone, and attractive in appearance. Let us consider these three important qualities individually.

Clarity. Remember that you will not be present when your letter is being read to explain what you mean. The reader will not be able to ask you to clarify. Obviously, then, you must make your message unmistakably clear. It goes without saying that your letter should be easily legible, whether handwritten or typewritten.

Tone. When speaking face-to-face with someone, you use your tone of voice to reflect shades of meaning and attitude. Writing, too, has a tone, reflected largely in the words you choose. What will your letter sound like to the recipient? First, be sure that it sounds like *you*—that it speaks with your voice. Second, be sure that the tone will neither anger nor offend. Unlike spoken words, which are often readily forgotten, letters are permanent records of what you have said. An angry letter may make you feel better at the time of writing, but a few weeks later you may be sorry that you mailed it.

APPEARANCE AND FORM OF A BUSINESS LETTER

Appearance and form. Appearance and form are the "good manners" of letter writing. This chapter explains the conventions of letter-writing form. If you follow them carefully, even though they may seem unimportant to you now, your letter will have a much better chance of making a good impression. A letter that is neat, free of errors, and in good form will do a fine job of representing you—just as your speech and personal appearance do in a face-to-face relationship.

17a. Observe standard practice in writing business letters.

A business letter is usually written to a firm or an individual in a firm. It must be a combination of clearness, brevity, and courtesy.

Appearance and Stationery

Proper stationery is the first important consideration in a business letter. You should type your letter, if possible, on the usual $8\frac{1}{2} \times 11$-inch plain white paper. The typewritten letter is more legible and therefore more quickly read than a handwritten one. If you write the letter by hand, use the same stationery as for a typewritten letter. Also, remember to write carefully; your best penmanship is a courtesy you owe to anyone to whom you are writing.

Form

The form of a business letter follows a certain pattern. Whether your letter is typewritten or handwritten, the pattern is the same. The semiblock form is used in the illustrations which you will find later in this chapter; however, the full block and the block forms are also acceptable, and an illustration of these forms is also given.

The Letter Picture

Three frequently used forms for the business letter are the full block, the block, and the semiblock. In the full block all typed material is flush with the left-hand margin, and para-

Model Business Letter Forms

graphs are not indented. Such a form is easiest for the typist, since there is no indention to worry about. Some object to it, however, because it seems unbalanced to the left. The only difference between the block and the full block is the placement of the heading, closing, and signature; in the block style these are placed just to the right of the center. The semiblock style is similar to the block except that it uses paragraph indention.

Before beginning your letter, judge the amount of space it will occupy on the page you are using. Center it as nearly as possible by making sure you have approximately the same margin at the top of your page as at the bottom, and the same margin on both the left- and right-hand sides. Never run your letter off the page at the right-hand side, and never finish the body of your letter at the end of a page so that you have nothing left for the second page except the complimentary close and your signature. If the letter is to be very short, it will look better on smaller stationery. Use the 5½ × 8½-inch size, which is also acceptable for business letters. For a model letter, see page 361.

1. Heading

To begin your business letter, always put your *complete* address and the full date in the upper right-hand corner, beginning no less than one inch from the top of the page. It is better to write this heading without abbreviations.

EXAMPLES

49 Surrey Lane
Clinton, Iowa 57232
June 4, 1981

RFD 4
Cross Corners, Oklahoma 73028
September 27, 1981

2. Inside Address

Business firms file copies of the letters they write. Since the copies are filed under the name of the person or firm to which they are written, standard form requires an inside address on every business letter.

The inside address should be placed at the left-hand side of the page, flush with the margin and several spaces (at least four, if the letter is typewritten) lower on the page than the heading. It should include the full name of the company to which you are writing, as well as its full address. If you are writing to an individual in the firm, use the full name and title, with a comma between the two if they are on the

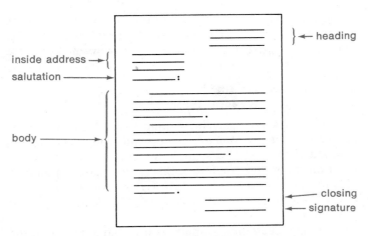

The Parts of a Business Letter

same line; if the name and title are too long to be put on one line, put the title on the next line.

EXAMPLES

The Helen Mills Company
220–224 Center Street
Waukegan, Illinois 60085

Ms. Marjorie Berg, Vice-President
Newland and Company
40 Fifth Avenue
Lewiston, Maine 04240

Mr. Reginald B. MacPherson
Secretary to the President
Wilbur Field and Sons
218 South Street
Fort Hamilton, Virginia 24437

Mrs. Susan Barlow, Principal
Lakeview High School
Lakeview, Michigan 48850

3. Salutation

The salutation is placed two spaces below the last line of the inside address and flush with the margin. When writing to an individual within the firm, the correct salutation is *Dear Mr. . . . (Mrs., Ms.,* or *Miss)* followed by a colon. If you are writing to a professional man or woman, use the title instead:

EXAMPLES   Dear Dr. Grayce:
            Dear President Tyson:

Sometimes you may be writing to an entire group or company, or to an officer whose name you do not know. You may have just "Personnel Department," "President," or "Editor" on the first line of the inside address. You may use an impersonal salutation (*Editor, Personnel Department*) or the traditional salutation (*Dear Sir, Gentlemen*) followed by a colon.

In using traditional salutations it is understood that the group you are writing to may be composed of both men and women.

4. Body

The form of the body of a business letter is the form followed in the body of any letter. A double space is used between paragraphs of a typed letter. If your typewritten letter is short (7 lines or less), you may either put it on a smaller sheet of stationery or double space the entire body of the letter on $8\frac{1}{2} \times 11$-inch stationery.

5. Closing

The closing of a letter comes between the body of the letter and the signature. In business letters, appropriate closings are limited. *Very truly yours, Yours truly,* and *Yours very truly* are the ones most frequently used. *Sincerely yours* and *Yours sincerely* are also correct. The closing is placed just to the right of the center of the page, two spaces below the last line of the body of your letter. It is followed by a comma.

Avoid ending your letter with an outmoded phrase such as "I beg to remain," "Hoping to hear from you soon, I am," or "Thanking you in advance, I am . . . ." End the body of your letter with a *period,* and then begin your closing.

EXAMPLES   Very truly yours,
            Yours truly,
            Sincerely yours,

6. Signature

Sign your full name to your letter. Do *not* put *Mr.* or *Mrs.* or *Ms.* before your name. An unmarried woman writing to a stranger may choose to put *Miss* in parentheses before her signature.

EXAMPLE   (*Miss*) *Margaret Hoyt*

A married woman signs her full name, and if she wishes, she may put her married name in parentheses directly below her signature.

EXAMPLE   *Elsie M. Rhoad*
           (*Mrs. Robert L. Rhoad*)

A signature should always be handwritten. If your letter is typewritten, type your name below your written signature, flush with the first letter of the closing and far enough below to allow room for your signature.

7. Envelope

For a letter on small stationery, use a small envelope (be sure the letter fits it). A letter on small single-sheet stationery is usually folded twice unless it fits into the envelope without any folding. The folds are made in this way: up from the bottom about a third of the way, then down from the top, so that when it is unfolded it will be right side up for the reader. Note paper or personal stationery is usually folded in half and inserted into the envelope with the fold at the bottom.

Either a small or a large envelope may be used for a letter on large single-sheet stationery. If a large envelope is used, the folding is the same as that of a small sheet for a small envelope. If the envelope is small, fold your letter up from the bottom to within a quarter of an inch of the top; then fold the right side over a third of the way; finally, fold the left side over. Insert in the envelope with the fold at the bottom of the envelope.

Your envelope should carry the same address as the inside address of the letter and also your own name and full address. You may put your return address on the back of the envelope, but the Post Office prefers that you put the return address in the upper left-hand corner of the envelope on

Folding the Letter

Model Envelope

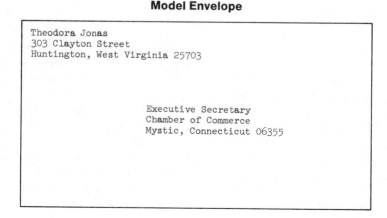

```
Theodora Jonas
303 Clayton Street
Huntington, West Virginia 25703



            Executive Secretary
            Chamber of Commerce
            Mystic, Connecticut 06355
```

the same side as the address to which it is going. Unless the address to which a letter is being sent is very long, you should start it about halfway down the envelope and place it midway between the ends.

The Post Office also requests that you use your zip code number in both the address to which the letter is going and in your return address. The zip code should appear on the last line of the address, following the city and state, with a double space left between the last letter of the state and first digit of the code. A comma should *not* be inserted between the state name and zip code. Note the examples in the models shown on pages 364 and 366.

CONTENT OF THE BUSINESS LETTER

Clarity, tone, and form are important in the business letter, since business letters are customarily sent to firms or individuals who do not know you and who have a large bulk of mail to handle. No matter how routine your communication is, be sure that your letter speaks well of you.

Even though the tone will be formal, you still should strive for naturalness and simplicity of expression. Come right to the point in your letter; avoid wordy beginnings. Make sure you have supplied all the necessary information. Never use the old-fashioned clichés of business correspondence. Be very certain that you don't close with the expression, "Thanking you in advance." Such a phrase presumes that the recipient will grant your request and seems to indicate that you are too lazy to write a separate thank-you note if some special favor is received.

TYPES OF BUSINESS LETTERS

The Request Letter

You have had and will continue to have many occasions to write letters of request: sending for a college catalogue, requesting a free pamphlet, arranging for a speaker to talk to your club. First, be reasonable in your requests. If you are asking for information, be very specific about what you want. Don't make yourself look ridiculous by asking, "Please send me all you have about national parks and camping grounds." If asking for a free pamphlet, request only that number which you personally can use. If arranging for a speaker, be sure to write in plenty of time and give all the information necessary about time, place, type of audience, etc.

Second, be courteous in the phrasing of your request. While you should avoid the "thanking you in advance" expression discussed above, it is good form to conclude the request letter with a polite acknowledgment like: "I shall certainly appreciate any help you can give me with this request." Finally, make your request simple and clear. Since the company to which you are writing is probably handling a large volume of mail, their employees cannot afford to waste time reading lengthy, chatty letters.

Model Request Letter

---

76 Brixton Place
Phoenix, Arizona   85008
July 8, 1981

Model Airways, Inc.
410-12 Second Avenue
Flagstaff, Arizona   86001

Mail Order Department:

    Will you please send me a copy of your latest catalogue on model planes? I have three of your models and would like to add some of the later ones to my collection.

Very truly yours,

Frank Tyndall

Frank Tyndall

EXERCISE 1. Write to a college, asking for their catalogue. If you think the catalogue may not include all the information you need, ask specifically for whatever you wish to know.

Another type of request letter is the kind you write when you ask a firm to send a representative to your school for some purpose or other. This kind of letter is a little more complicated to write, because it is *you* who have to give the company information before they reply. Remember to include all the details necessary for the company's complete understanding of the situation.

EXERCISE 2. Copy in proper form the business letter given below.

420 Jackson Avenue, Iola, Texas 77861, January 8, 1981. Miss R. F. Hawkins, Business Manager, Perry and Company, 480–96 Fuller Street, Fort Worth, Texas 76104. Dear Miss Hawkins: Our junior class of 170 pupils in the Iola High School is to decide this month on our class rings and pins. We expect to have representatives from several companies here on Monday, January 21, to show us samples of the rings and pins their firms make, together with price lists. We'd like very much to have someone from your company here on that date, if possible. Your representative should come to Room 31, any time after 2:45. Very truly yours, Sarah Porter, Secretary of the Junior Class, Iola High School.

EXERCISE 3. Using the following information, set up this material in the form of a business letter. You must compose the letter.

Ms. Elsie Dowing of 222 Twin Oaks Road, Carlsburg, Ohio 43316, writes on April 6, 1981, to the George C. Buckeye Company, 240 Lexington Avenue, Cleveland, Ohio 44102, stating that while shopping there the week before, she lost a valuable gold ring. It contained a diamond and two pearls in an old-fashioned setting. She would like to know if it has been found and if so, where she may call for it.

EXERCISE 4. As head of the student assembly program,

you wish to have a neighboring high school send its glee club to perform in one of your assembly periods. Give the time, date, place, length of program, type of song selection (if you wish), and any other information you think is necessary.

EXERCISE 5. You are interested in art. There is an exhibit to be given in the high school auditorium of a nearby city. Write to the art department of the high school, requesting information. Ask specific questions about what you want to know — time, admission price, dates the exhibit will be displayed, etc.

The Order Letter

If you are writing an order letter, you should list the items you wish, one below the other, with complete information (catalogue number, style, size, price, etc.) about each item. The price should be put at the right-hand side (flush with the right-hand margin) and each amount should be placed directly under the one above, to make it easier to add the prices. List the cost of shipping, if you know it, and include it in the total, unless you know the firm pays for it. Be sure to specify how the articles are to be paid for — check, C.O.D., etc.

EXERCISE 6. Write a business letter to Marshall Field and Company, Chicago, ordering 2 long-sleeved cotton blouses, size 14, 1 plain white, the other French blue, at $10.98, 1 green "Betty Gaye" dress, size 13, at $17.95. Have them sent C.O.D.

EXERCISE 7. Write to Ritz Camera Center, 1147A Sixth Avenue, New York, N.Y. 10036, an order letter ordering the following: 1 Star D Model D–18 tripod, price $19.75; 3 rolls 35 mm. Kodachrome film at $3.50 a roll. Include $1.50 postage. You are enclosing a money order for the amount.

Model Order Letter

---

58 Crane Street
Canton, Iowa 52542
December 1, 1981

Webb and Sons
140-156 Seventh Avenue
Des Moines, Iowa 50311

Gentlemen:

    I should like to order the following arti-
cles, as advertised in the Des Moines Register
of November 29.

2 white silk scarves, fringed, one with black
   initials A.J., the other with red initials
   M.W., @ $7.98 $15.96
1 size 15-34 Supercron white shirt,
   collar attached   16.50
                               Postage   1.20
                               Total $33.66

    I am enclosing a check for $33.66 to cover
the total amount.

Very truly yours,

Amy Ladd
Amy Ladd

The Letter of Application

The letter of application is one with which you have no
doubt had very little experience to date. However, you soon
may find that it is one of the most important types of business letters, for it is in the application letter that you try to
convince an employer to hire you.

Model Letter of Application

---

98 Oxford Street
St. Cloud, Minnesota   56303
April 2, 1981

Mrs. O. A. Lester, Director
Camp Carlson
Oneidaga Lake
Big Pines, Minnesota   56680

Dear Mrs. Lester:

Ben Nichols, one of your regular campers, told me this week that you have a vacancy for a swimming counselor on your camp staff this summer, and I would like to apply for the position.

I am a senior at St. Cloud High School and am eighteen years old. For the last two years I have been the junior swimming counselor at Camp Winnebega, Cauhoga Falls, Wisconsin. I have just received my Examiner's badge in lifesaving and am now certified for the position of senior swimming counselor. If you have junior or senior lifesaving classes, I am also qualified to direct them.

The following people have given me permission to use their names as references:

Mrs. J. B. Morse, Director, Camp Winnebega, Cauhoga Falls, Wisconsin.

Mr. Chester Roberts, Principal, St. Cloud High School, St. Cloud, Minnesota.

I will be glad to come for a personal interview at your convenience.

Sincerely yours,

Francine Larson

Francine Larson

When you apply for a position, your letter of application comes before your personal interview with your prospective employer. It is the first contact the two of you have. Therefore, you must "put yourself across" in a way which will suggest confidence that you can do the job called for. You will also have an added advantage if you can put some original, personal touch into your letter (but only if it comes naturally to you) to distinguish you, favorably, from the rest of the applicants this employer may be considering.

Remember to include the following:

1. Include a statement of the position you are applying for and how you learned about it.

2. Show that you know what qualifications are needed and that you believe you can fill them. State your age, experience, and education.

3. Give references as to your character and ability.

4. Request an interview at the employer's convenience.

EXERCISE 8. You have learned from a friend that a couple she knows in another city are looking for a high school student to spend the summer with their family at their summer home. They want the student to take care of three children, ages two, four, and six. Write to the couple (make up a name and address) and apply for this job. State your qualifications. Try to make your letter interesting as well as informative.

EXERCISE 9. A drugstore in a neighboring town needs someone to deliver orders from 4:00 to 6:00 schooldays and all day Saturdays. Write your letter of application.

► NOTE   The United States Postal Service recommends the use of two-letter codes for states, the District of Columbia, and Puerto Rico. The service also recommends the use of nine-digit zip codes. When you use these codes, the address on business correspondence should look like this:

EXAMPLE   Ms. Laura Braverman
               72 White Plains Blvd.
               Dallas, TX   75231–2424

The two-letter code is in capital letters and is never followed by a period. Refer to the following list of two-letter codes.

Alabama	AL	Montana	MT
Alaska	AK	Nebraska	NE
Arizona	AZ	Nevada	NV
Arkansas	AR	New Hampshire	NH
California	CA	New Jersey	NJ
Colorado	CO	New Mexico	NM
Connecticut	CT	New York	NY
Delaware	DE	North Carolina	NC
District of Columbia	DC	North Dakota	ND
Florida	FL	Ohio	OH
Georgia	GA	Oklahoma	OK
Hawaii	HI	Oregon	OR
Idaho	ID	Pennsylvania	PA
Illinois	IL	Puerto Rico	PR
Indiana	IN	Rhode Island	RI
Iowa	IA	South Carolina	SC
Kansas	KS	South Dakota	SD
Kentucky	KY	Tennessee	TN
Louisiana	LA	Texas	TX
Maine	ME	Utah	UT
Maryland	MD	Vermont	VT
Massachusetts	MA	Virginia	VA
Michigan	MI	Washington	WA
Minnesota	MN	West Virginia	WV
Mississippi	MS	Wisconsin	WI
Missouri	MO	Wyoming	WY

Mechanics

PART FIVE

Chapter 18

Capitalization

Standard Uses of Capitalization

Capital letters are used mainly to individualize what we are writing about. When we capitalize a word, we serve notice on the reader that we are referring to some *particular* person, place, or thing rather than to the general class. Custom determines the use of capital letters, and it is the wisest course to conform to customary or standard usage.

Occasionally, however, publications adopt slightly varying styles of capitalization to serve their own purposes. Newspapers may use the "down" style, in which words like *avenue, river, county,* etc., are not capitalized as they are in standard usage when used with a particular name. In the columns of your newspaper, you might see *Fifth avenue, Bergen county,* and *Red river;* and in some publications which condense much information into very small space, you might note even fewer capital letters. Advertisers, on the other hand, frequently use capital letters for every word of their messages. It is clear, therefore, that styles of capitalization do indeed differ, but in ordinary writing we are justified in hewing to the rules of standard usage that are outlined in the following chapter. It is useful to know the rules, of course, but nothing can replace the habit of carefulness. Always read over your written work to check for correct use of capitals.

Take the following diagnostic test to see how much you have to review.

Diagnostic Test

If you can make 100 per cent on the following quiz, you may work through this chapter very rapidly. If you make a lower score, you should learn the uses of capital letters and do the exercises so that you will be able henceforth to use capital letters correctly.

Number your paper 1–25. In each of the following items, you are to choose the correct one of two forms. After the proper number on your paper, write the letter of the correct form (*a* or *b*).

1. a. Last summer we hiked along the Adirondack Trail.
   b. Last Summer we hiked along the Adirondack Trail.
2. a. the Amazon River
   b. the Amazon river
3. a. the Morrison Hotel
   b. the Morrison hotel
4. a. They took the wrong exit on San Mateo Boulevard.
   b. They took the wrong exit on San Mateo boulevard.
5. a. Hofstra university is in Hempstead.
   b. Hofstra University is in Hempstead.
6. a. Is she a Senior this term?
   b. Is she a senior this term?
7. a. The junior prom was a huge success.
   b. The Junior Prom was a huge success.
8. a. My sister thinks that Reed is a fine college.
   b. My sister thinks that Reed is a fine College.
9. a. I enjoy french and trigonometry.
   b. I enjoy French and trigonometry.
10. a. the Mediterranean sea
    b. the Mediterranean Sea
11. a. She graduated from high school last year.
    b. She graduated from High School last year.
12. a. a bottle of Tropicana orange juice
    b. a bottle of Tropicana Orange Juice
13. a. a speech by the President of the United States
    b. a speech by the president of the United States
14. a. Miss Lee, the director of that department
    b. Miss Lee, the Director of that Department

15. a. They prayed to God for guidance.
    b. They prayed to god for guidance.
16. a. the Bijou Theater
    b. the Bijou theater
17. a. Minerva was a Roman Goddess.
    b. Minerva was a Roman goddess.
18. a. Are you Canadian?
    b. Are you canadian?
19. a. We import tea from Asia.
    b. We import tea from asia.
20. a. a german shepherd puppy
    b. a German shepherd puppy
21. a. Seventy-Second Street
    b. Seventy-second Street
22. a. They drove West for twenty miles
    b. They drove west for twenty miles.
23. a. We spent our vacation in the Far West.
    b. We spent our vacation in the Far west.
24. a. The National Audubon Society
    b. The National Audubon society
25. a. Everyone feared a civil war.
    b. Everyone feared a Civil War.

18a. Capitalize the first word in every sentence.

This is one of the first rules a schoolchild learns. It is usually broken only by students who have trouble telling where one sentence ends and another begins.

INCORRECT   Roald Amundsen and Robert Scott challenged each other in a race to reach the South Pole. with careful planning Amundsen easily won.

CORRECT   Roald Amundsen and Robert Scott challenged each other in a race to reach the South Pole. With careful planning Amundsen easily won.

INCORRECT   After studying reports on new cars, Mother said, "the models with front-wheel drive have improved."

CORRECT   After studying reports on new cars, Mother said, "The models with front-wheel drive have improved."

▶ **NOTE** The first word in a line of poetry is often capitalized.

EXAMPLE Cast a cold eye
On life, on death.
Horseman, pass by! — W. B. YEATS

18b. Capitalize the pronoun *I* and the interjection *O*.

INCORRECT The line i translated was "Hear us, o Zeus."
CORRECT The line I translated was "Hear us, O Zeus."

The common interjection *oh* (Oh, yes!) is capitalized only when it appears at the beginning of a sentence.

18c. Capitalize proper nouns and proper adjectives.

A *proper noun* is the name of a particular person, place, or thing.

How a proper noun differs from an ordinary, common noun, which is not capitalized, can be seen from the following lists.

COMMON NOUN	PROPER NOUN
city	Miami
river	Colorado River
mountain	Lookout Mountain
woman	Sarah Bernhardt

Do not confuse proper nouns, which are *names,* with nouns which merely state kind or type. For instance, *subcompact* is not the name of a particular automobile company (like Ford or General Motors) or of a particular automobile model (like Impala, Thunderbird, Model T). The word *subcompact* is merely a general name for a type of automobile, one that is smaller than a compact.

INCORRECT When I had a car, it was a Ford Subcompact.
CORRECT When I had a car, it was a Ford subcompact.
INCORRECT The deer hunter has a Winchester Carbine.
CORRECT The deer hunter has a Winchester carbine.

A *proper adjective* is an adjective formed from a proper noun.

PROPER NOUN	PROPER ADJECTIVE
England	English literature
America	American people
Ireland	Irish linen

Compound adjectives are frequently a source of trouble. In most cases, only that part of a compound adjective is capitalized which is itself a proper noun or adjective.

EXAMPLES   French-speaking Canadians, God-given liberty
pro-Western alliance, anti-British, pro-American
Italian-American, Anglo-Saxon

Study carefully the list which follows. It classifies under seven headings the most frequently used kinds of proper nouns and adjectives.

(1) Capitalize the names of persons.

GIVEN NAMES   James, Evelyn, Aime
SURNAMES   Johnson, Powers, Goldstein, Mangano

In some surnames, another letter besides the first should be capitalized. This practice varies; to be sure you are right, check a reference source.

EXAMPLES   MacReady, O'Donnell, LeClerc, O'Casey

The abbreviations *Jr.* and *Sr.* (*junior* and *senior*) should always be capitalized when they follow a name.

EXAMPLES   Gregory E. Burke, Jr.
Warren Grattan, Sr.

(2) Capitalize geographical names.

Cities and Towns   Detroit, Perryville, Carson City
Counties and Townships   Hamilton County, Atlanta County, Oyster Bay Township
States   Georgia, Arizona, California
Countries   France, United States of America, Mexico
Continents   Africa, Asia, South America
Islands   Catalina Island, Key West
Bodies of Water   Caribbean Sea, Atlantic Ocean, Nile River
Mountains   Sangre de Cristo Mountains, Mount Everest, Rocky Mountains

Streets Grand Street, Post Avenue, Northern State Parkway, Thirty-second Street [In a hyphenated number, the second word begins with a small letter.]

Parks Sequoia National Park, Hamilton County Park, Jones Beach State Park

Sections of the Country the East, the Middle West, the Great Plains

► NOTE Do not capitalize *east, west, north,* and *south* when they merely indicate direction. Do capitalize them when they refer to commonly recognized sections of the country. The modern tendency is to write nouns and adjectives derived from capitalized *East, West, North,* and *South* without capital letters (a *southerner, southern fried chicken*).

EXAMPLES We headed west for five miles and then turned north.
My grandmother spends the winter in the South.

When an adjective indicating direction is *part of the name* of a recognized region or political unit, capitalize it. When such an adjective merely indicates some portion of a region or political unit, do *not* capitalize it.

EXAMPLES South America [a continent], Eastern Samoa [a territory], southern Mexico, northern Idaho

EXERCISE 1. Copy the following, using capital letters wherever they are required.

1. yellowstone national park
2. bering sea
3. pro-canadian
4. a bracelet of mexican silver
5. at eagle lake
6. a house on block island
7. beside the chattahoochee river
8. in schurtz county
9. the oklahoma oil fields
10. the bay of fundy
11. an east wind
12. danish pastry
13. pennsylvania farmers
14. on fifty-third street
15. gerald brill, jr.
16. the east side of the canyon
17. the pacific northwest
18. the rocky mountains
19. some swedish glassware
20. spanish-american

EXERCISE 2. Copy all words requiring a capital, and be sure to capitalize them. Before each word, write the number of its sentence.

1. My brother, who lives on the eastern coast of florida, asked us to visit his home in the south.

2. We planned to leave manhattan island, turn south on the newest turnpike, bypass the pocono mountains and spring lake, and let the road map guide us to kenansville, florida.

3. With my dad's sense of direction, east, west, north, and south are all the same; if you told him westbury pond was great salt lake, he might almost believe it.

4. He often has trouble finding his way through new york city to the george washington bridge.

5. Usually he does not drive to manhattan at all; instead, he catches a train which takes him to pennsylvania station on thirty-third street.

6. Dad kept insisting that he had to visit washington, d.c., situated on the banks of the potomac river, and that from there he wanted to drive through some of the mountains in virginia.

7. Mother said that if he was so interested in mountains, he should take a cruise up the hudson river to visit bear mountain in the catskills.

8. She added that she wanted to spend some time with her cousin in nichols, south carolina.

9. We decided to cross from new jersey to delaware over the delaware memorial bridge, cross the chesapeake bay bridge in maryland, and then continue into the south.

10. Incidentally, we never did drive to florida; we drove to kennedy airport and took a plane from there.

11. From the air i was able to recognize the washington monument and the lincoln memorial.

12. While we were flying over cape hatteras in north carolina, we were served lunch.

EXERCISE 3. Read the following paragraphs, which begin on the next page. List in a column all words requiring capital letters. When two or more capitalized words belong together, list them together: *East Shore Drive, Windsor Square, Dawson Lake,* etc. Number your list according to the numbers of the sentences in each paragraph. Do not list words already capitalized.

EXAMPLES   1. Our dog ran away from our home on east shore
drive, and somebody found him wandering around
windsor square.
1. *East Shore Drive*
Windsor Square

2. How he ever got across fulton street and park
boulevard without being hit by a car is a mystery
to me.
2. *Fulton Street*
Park Boulevard

1. Our school is located in the heart of macon county, but the
exact location really isn't very important. 2. The students and
teachers could be dropped into any school in the north or the
south, the east or the west; and, except possibly for regional accents, nobody would notice the difference. 3. There are students,
teachers, and coaches whose ancestors have come from europe,
asia, or africa. 4. There are some who live on farms on the west
side of town, and there are others who live in apartments on
franklin avenue. 5. There are some whose parents take them
camping in the rocky mountains or alaska, and there are others
who have never been farther north than tanners pond or farther
south than winslow park. 6. A few of us may become captains
of industry and work in san francisco or new york, and some might
even become celebrities on broadway or in hollywood. 7. Even
our homes could be found anywhere in the u.s.a.
8. Stroll along cherry street, and you will notice cape cod
cottages that look as if they were transplanted from a new
england village overlooking an atlantic beach. 9. Turn left on
smith street, and you will see ranch houses that would look right
at home in nevada or texas. 10. In short, we are a cross section
of the united states.

**(3) Capitalize the names of organizations, business firms,
institutions, government bodies.**

Organizations and Clubs Jericho Country Club, Elks Club,
National Organization for Women, National Honor Society.

► NOTE Do not capitalize such words as *democratic, republican,
socialist,* etc., when these words refer only to types of societies
rather than to specific parties. The word *party* in the name of a

political party may be capitalized or not; either way is correct: *Republican party, Republican Party.*

EXAMPLES Mr. Jones, formerly a Democrat, has now joined the Republican party.

Most of the new African nations have adopted republican forms of government.

The democratic nations of the West cherish many of the same ideals.

Business Firms Eastman Kodak Company, Ford Motor Company, Aluminum Greenhouses, Inc., United Aircraft Corporation

Institutions and Buildings St. Charles Hotel, the Empire State Building, Rivoli Theater, Colby College, Chester High School, Friends Academy, St. Mary's Hospital

▶ NOTE Do not capitalize such words as *hotel, theater, college, high school* unless they are part of a proper name.

EXAMPLES Carroll College   a college in Wisconsin
Eastland Hotel   a hotel in Portland
Great Falls High School   a high school in Montana
Helen Hayes Theater   a theater in New York

Government Bodies House of Representatives, the Supreme Court, Congress, the Securities and Exchange Commission

(4) Capitalize the names of historical events and periods, special events, and calendar items.

Historical Events and Periods the Renaissance, World War II, the Battle of Gettysburg, the Middle Ages, the San Francisco Conference, the Atomic Age

Special Events the Junior Prom, the Mercy League Ball, the Meadowbrook Dog Show, the National Amateur Tennis Championships, the World Series

Calendar Items Wednesday, February, Easter, Labor Day, Fourth of July

▶ NOTE Do not capitalize the names of the seasons: summer, winter, spring, fall.

(5) Capitalize the names of nationalities, races, and religions.

EXAMPLES Japanese, Hungarian, Indian, Roman Catholic, Methodist

(6) Capitalize the brand names of business products.

EXAMPLES a Toyota automobile, Pepperidge Farm rolls, a Nikon camera

► **NOTE** Do not capitalize the nouns which often follow a brand name.

EXAMPLES Sunbeam toaster, Kroflite golf balls, Vicks cough drops, Apple computer

(7) Capitalize the names of ships, planes, trains, monuments, awards, heavenly bodies, and any other particular places, things, or events.

EXAMPLES the *Queen Elizabeth 2* (a ship), Constellation (a plane), the Purple Heart (a medal), *Mariner II* (a space vehicle), Jupiter, Orion (heavenly bodies)

► **NOTE** Planets, constellations, asteroids, stars, and groups of stars are capitalized. However, do not capitalize *sun, moon,* or *earth* unless they are used in conjunction with other heavenly bodies which are all capitalized.

18d. Do *not* **capitalize the names of school subjects, except names of languages and course names followed by a number.**

English, Spanish, Latin, French, mathematics, social studies, history, Mathematics II, History II

► **NOTE** Do not capitalize *senior, junior, sophomore,* and *freshman* unless these words are part of a proper noun or are used to designate a *specific* organization.

EXAMPLES The juniors invited the seniors to the Junior Prom. The Freshman Class cordially invites all sophomores to its first play.

EXERCISE 4. List in order all words requiring capitals. When two capitalized words belong together, list them together. Number your list according to the numbers of the paragraphs. Do not list words already capitalized.

1. The state of florida, one of the most popular vacation areas in the united states, has thousands of kilometers of coastline. The state is bounded by the atlantic ocean, the gulf of mexico, and the straits of florida.

2. Whether you travel on a daily nonstop flight aboard a delta airlines' jet or on a cruise ship such as the *queen elizabeth 2*, or on a train such as the *broadway limited*, the florida tourist's bureau will be delighted to welcome you.

3. Central florida abounds in lakes, with lake okeechobee being the largest.

4. In florida history, an important role belongs to osceola, a powerful leader of the seminole indians, who guided his people through a long and costly war from 1835 to 1837. One of the most important battles of the war occurred in the everglades, a huge wilderness region.

5. The everglades national park, which includes big cypress swamp, is today a major tourist attraction. Beautiful beaches, such as those at daytona, miami, and fort lauderdale, also draw large crowds of visitors.

6. The second-largest city in the state is miami, the seat of dade county and one of the most famous resort areas in the eastern united states. Miami beach is on an island between biscayne bay and the atlantic and is connected to the city of miami by four causeways.

7. Visitors to miami may be interested in biscayne boulevard, the route to miami beach, or they may be interested in the orange bowl, the home of the city's football team.

8. Thousands of students each year attend the university of florida, located in gainesville. The university offers degrees in engineering, french, english, and many other fields.

9. Many space flights, including some to the moon, have been launched from cape canaveral, the site of the john f. kennedy space center.

10. Florida has one of the fastest-growing populations in the country. Many retired persons have settled in the state, particularly in the area near st. petersburg.

EXERCISE 5. Follow the instructions for Exercise 4.

1. Stella is a senior at calhoun high school and expects to attend a university in the west next fall.

2. Every thursday the club meets at winthrop hall on chestnut street.

3. The painting was shipped from the louvre, a museum in paris, to the National art gallery in Washington, d.c.

4. Will the kiwanis club hold its halloween party in the Salisbury theater or at the herrick country club?

5. The hilton fife and drum corps will lead the parade down main street on memorial day.

6. The wilton memorial library is on the corner of fulton avenue and jefferson street, near a baptist church.

7. Last tuesday, march 8, I stayed after school for extra help in french and english; but I really should have stayed for help in geometry and social studies.

8. The century theater, located on Sheridan road just outside evansville, shows the latest pictures from hollywood as well as films from europe.

9. Every morning for breakfast, Hank has some danish pastry and a bowl of cornflakes.

10. Johnson & jackson, inc., buys most of its office supplies from Hillman's Supply company.

EXERCISE 6. As you did in Exercise 3, list all words requiring capitals in the following sentences. Do not list words already capitalized.

1. Last fall Fred came to midville high school from a small town in the midwest. 2. On labor day his family said farewell to oak falls, indiana, and moved to wilson avenue in midville. 3. It wasn't easy to start his senior year in high school without knowing anybody, but if the Carter manufacturing company had sent his father to the shores of crater lake in oregon or to a sledding camp in alaska, Fred would have had to go along, of course.

4. Fred spent a day or so being interviewed by the guidance counselor in our school and was assigned to classes in intermediate algebra, social studies, physics, and english. 5. That's not exactly the easiest program in the world, but since he wants to go to the United States Military Academy at west point, he needs to concentrate on math and science. 6. Although a member of the Varsity club showed Fred around school the first day, he ended up in latin class when he should have been in physics. 7. Now that he's

been here a few months, he could take a member of the Midville Board of education on a tour and even give a declamation on the monument in memorial park that was built after world war I.
8. Fred was in for a surprise when he saw the peach trees behind the brentwood arena. 9. Fred is now thoroughly accustomed to midville life, even though for him the spanish moss in baker park can never replace the oak and hickory forests of indiana.

18e. Capitalize titles.

(1) Capitalize the title of a person when it comes before a name.

EXAMPLES   General Lee, Dr. Foster, President Reagan

(2) Capitalize a title used alone or following a person's name only if it refers to a high official or someone to whom you wish to show special respect.

EXAMPLES   The President spoke from the White House. [When it refers to the highest official of the United States, *President* is capitalized.]

Charles Evans Hughes, Chief Justice of the Supreme Court from 1930 to 1941, served during one of the most interesting periods of the Court's history. [The office of Chief Justice is a high one.]

Who is principal of your school?

Mr. Montgomery is president of the new firm.

The new traffic commissioner will be sworn in tomorrow.

Mrs. Deering, chief dietician for the city's junior high schools, has her office in Elm Street School.

► NOTE   When an official is directly addressed by title, it is customary to capitalize it.

EXAMPLES   Do you intend, Captain, to lead your troops?
Mr. Secretary, will you read the minutes?

(3) Capitalize words showing family relationship when used with a person's name but *not* when preceded by a possessive.

EXAMPLES   Grandfather Scott, Aunt Martha, Uncle Chet, my
sister Mara

► NOTE   When family-relationship words like *aunt, cousin,* and
grandfather are customarily used before a name, capitalize them
even after a possessive noun or pronoun.

EXAMPLES   My Grandmother Finch is going to retire to Florida
next month.

Did you notice Aunt Carmen's picture in the paper?
[You customarily call these persons *Grandmother
Finch* and *Aunt Carmen.*]

My sister Claire graduates from high school next
June. [You do not customarily call her *Sister
Claire.*]

► NOTE   Words of family relationship may be capitalized or
not when used *in place of* a person's name.

EXAMPLES   Hello, Mother. *or* Hello, mother.   [Mother is used
in place of the woman's name.]

**(4) Capitalize the first and last word and all important words
in titles of books, periodicals, poems, stories, movies, paintings, and other works of art.**

Unimportant words in a title are *a, an,* and *the,* short prepositions (usually those under five letters long), and coordinating conjunctions.

EXAMPLES   *Harper's Bazaar* (magazine), Turner's *Crossing the
Brook* (painting), *Pride and Prejudice* (novel), Treaty
of Versailles, the Charter of the United Nations, the
Talmud, "Under the Lion's Paw" (short story), "The
Tuft of Flowers" (poem)

The words *a, an,* and *the* written before a title are capitalized only when they are part of the title. In a composition
they are usually not capitalized before the names of magazines and newspapers.

EXAMPLES   *The Mayor of Casterbridge* (book), *A Nation of
Sheep* (book)
Mimi reads the *Times* and the *Reader's Digest.*

(5) Capitalize the word God except when it refers to the gods of ancient mythology.

► NOTE   Other words referring to God are usually capitalized as well.

EXAMPLES   Father   Lord God   His will

EXERCISE 7. List all words requiring capitals. Number your list according to the numbers of the sentences. Do not list words already capitalized.

1. One of georgia o'keeffe's finest paintings, *cow's skull, red, white and blue,* hung in the hirshhorn museum in washington, d.c.
2. In the january edition of the *reader's digest,* annette read an article called "the crisis in u.s. transportation."
3. Miss west, the chairperson of the music department, told us that a play produced on broadway in 1931 called *green grow the lilacs* was turned into the musical *oklahoma!*
4. Annette enjoyed dorothy sayers' *gaudy night* more than she did *murder must advertise.*
5. Last christmas aunt harriet, the family sculptor, gave my grandmother a statue called *the captive warrior;* but this statue will never be a serious threat to *the thinker* by rodin.
6. I enjoyed reading annie dillard's *pilgrim at tinker creek,* and I particularly liked the chapter "the horns of the altar."
7. Mr. commissioner, would you care to confirm the report that mayor douglas and senator giacomo have asked you to resign?
8. The president has invited protestant, catholic, and jewish leaders to a conference in the White House.
9. Bill Gomez, president of our high school's conservation club, introduced deputy inspector rogers of the new jersey fish and game commission.
10. In the school auditorium, while the principal introduced the winner of the american legion award, I spotted commissioner murphy, superintendent adams, and mayor briggs.

REVIEW EXERCISE. List all words that should be capitalized. Number your list according to the numbers of the sentences.

1. Because I don't know a waltz from a tango and am not in the least ashamed of my ignorance, I refused to take lessons at the diane dance studio on maple avenue.

2. "One in a million" is the title song of her new album, which was recorded at carnegie hall in new york city.

3. Twice a year, dr. carter, the dentist whose office is on butler street, reminds me to pay her a visit; and twice a year, I read old copies of the *national geographic* in her waiting room and hope that daily brushings with zing toothpaste have prevented any new cavities.

4. The *nina II,* a replica of christopher columbus' smallest ship, was towed to nassau from san salvador last tuesday.

5. After world war II thousands of veterans flocked to colleges and universities all over the country.

6. Whether you want japanese cultured pearls or norwegian skis, you will find these items at perkins & company's new store, located at the corner of twenty-first street and maple avenue.

7. In her last lecture in hadley hall, professor jennings said that human beings, from the dawn of history to the present, have always been able to laugh at themselves.

8. Without looking up a copy of the declaration of independence, I cannot name five of the original signers; but I do know that the document was first signed at independence hall in philadelphia.

9. The president left the white house early and drove to the capitol to deliver his address to congress.

10. The lutheran minister who spoke at our christmas program reminded us to give thanks to god.

11. I enjoyed reading *to kill a mockingbird,* a novel about life in a small town in maycomb county, alabama.

12. *The harvesters* is a painting by pieter brueghel, a sixteenth-century artist.

13. One of the cities of the incas, machu picchu, lay hidden among the peaks of the andes in peru and was never discovered by the spanish conquerors.

14. Each year more than a million visitors flock to holland state park, a preserve on lake michigan, west of grand rapids.

15. Last saturday a fire, fanned by a brisk northwest wind, destroyed the meadtown lumber company.

16. Traffic along powell avenue had to be rerouted when a gray lincoln sedan rammed a truck.

17. Julie anderson, the president of her class, joined the peace corps last july and is now working as an engineer in pakistan.

18. Because paula took advanced courses in english, chemistry, and mathematics at washington high school in st. paul, minnesota, she had little difficulty with her freshman courses at duke university.

19. When my grandmother retires, she expects to spend her winters at sea island, georgia, and her summers at lake manota in the northern part of minnesota.

20. Between halves of the football game between lincoln high school and milbridge academy, the band marched down the east side of the field, played stirring marches composed by john philip sousa, and exited through the main gate.

SUMMARY STYLE SHEET

Names of Persons

Shirley, Shirley O'Neil	the girl next door
Mrs. William McAndrew, Jr.	a family friend

Geographical Names

Carson City	a city in Nevada
Yosemite National Park	a national park
the San Mateo Mountains	a mountain in New Mexico
the Pacific Ocean	an ocean voyage
the Savannah River	the banks of a river
living in the South	the south side of town
the Caribbean Sea	a sea voyage
the Gaspé Peninsula	a long peninsula

Organizations, Business Firms and Products, Institutions, Government Bodies

the Press Club	a club for writers
the Union Coal Company	a coal company
the Commodore Hotel	the newest hotel
Chevrolet	an automobile
Midwood High School	a large high school
the Supreme Court of Nebraska	a Nebraska court

Historical Events and Periods, Special Events, Calendar Items

the French and Indian War	wars on the frontier
the Renaissance	the sixteenth century
Memorial Day	a day in May
the Junior Prom	a junior in high school
the Winter Carnival	in the winter

Nationalities, Races, Religions, Languages

Canadian	a nationality
Caucasian	a race
Lutheran	a religion
Spanish	a language

Ships, Planes, Trains, Monuments, Awards, Heavenly Bodies, and Particular Places, Things, or Events

the *Mary Deere*	a schooner
the *Orient Express*	a train
the P-51 Mustang	a fighter plane
the Washington Monument	a monument in Washington, D.C.
Saturn and Venus	the sun, earth, and moon
the Congressional Medal of Honor	the highest award of the nation
Friendship VII	a space vehicle

Titles

Mayor Winthrop	Mr. Winthrop, the mayor
the President, the Chief Justice (high government officials)	the president of the club, a senator's duties
Praise God for His blessings	the gods of the ancient Greeks
Aunt Sarah	his aunt
Go with Grandfather.	my grandfather
A Tale of Two Cities	a novel
"Ode on a Grecian Urn"	a poem
"America the Beautiful"	a song

Chapter 19

Punctuation

End Marks and Commas

The sole purpose of punctuation is to make clear the meaning of what you write. When you speak, the actual sound of your voice, the rhythmic rise and fall of your inflections, your pauses and hestitations, your stops to take breath—all supply a kind of "punctuation" which serves to group your words and to indicate to your listener precisely what you mean. Indeed, even the body takes part in this unwritten punctuation. A raised eyebrow may express interrogation more eloquently than any question mark, and a knuckle rapped on the table shows stronger feeling than an exclamation point.

In written English, however, where there are none of these hints to meaning, simple courtesy requires the writer to make up for the lack by careful punctuation. Examine the sentences below. If you heard them spoken, you might know exactly what was meant; but as they stand, with no punctuation to show where one thought ends and another begins, they are confusing.

Into the new washing machine he put the clothes and Jim then turned the water on.

The children munched happily on the various courses soup vegetables and meat salad rolls and butter pie and ice cream.

He settled wearily onto the first chair which was not strong enough to hold him.

Don't overpunctuate. A sentence that bristles with commas, colons, dashes, and brackets within parentheses doesn't need the services of a punctuation expert. It needs to be rewritten. Use a mark of punctuation for only two reasons: (1) because the meaning demands it, or (2) because conventional usage requires it. Otherwise do not use punctuation.

The rules for the correct use of end punctuation and commas are listed on the following pages. Learn the rules. Do the exercises. Read over carefully whatever you have written once or twice before handing it in, each time inserting whatever punctuation is necessary to make the writing clear and taking out those marks that are unnecessary. Above all, *apply what you learn about punctuation to everything you write.*

PERIODS, QUESTION MARKS, AND EXCLAMATION POINTS

19a. A statement is followed by a period.

EXAMPLES   Margaret Walker has written many beautiful poems.
From out of the cave came a low growl.
"Yes, I'll be there," Barbara said.

19b. A question is followed by a question mark.

EXAMPLES   Where are you going?
Who broke my record?
What did you say?

Sometimes the way in which a writer intends a sentence to be read determines whether it is a statement or a question.

STATEMENT   You mean you are not going. [Read with falling inflection.]

QUESTION   You mean you are not going? [Read with rising inflection.]

19c. An exclamation is followed by an exclamation point.

EXAMPLES   Great shot!
How wonderful!
Whew, isn't it hot!

**19d. An imperative sentence is followed by either a
period or an exclamation point.**

EXAMPLES   Put the book down, please.   [calmly]
Put the book down!   [with strong feeling]

It is not hard to use the question mark and the exclamation
point correctly. The sound of your own voice as you read
your sentences under your breath gives you sufficient clues
to where these marks go. It is much harder to know where
to put the period. You can never be certain of this until
you are certain of what a sentence is and where it ends.
(Chapters 1–4 and Chapter 11 of this book should help you
to recognize a sentence and therefore to know where to put
the period.)

Perhaps the most common cause of end-mark errors,
however, is simply carelessness. There is only one cure for
this. Always take time to read over everything you write.

EXERCISE 1. In this exercise all end marks have been
omitted. On your paper, write the final word of the sentence
with the proper end mark, followed by the first word of
the next sentence, if any.

EXAMPLE   1. Miriam Colon, a native of Puerto Rico, is an accomplished actress using her own experience, she
wished to acquaint Americans with the art and
culture of Puerto Rico to that end she founded
and directed the Puerto Rican Traveling Theatre

    1. *actress. Using*
Puerto Rico. To
Theatre.

1. Gail was assigned a report on knighthood, and she undertook
the assignment eagerly she knew from the stories she had read
that knights were spotless champions of God and humanity
she knew also that a long apprenticeship preceded the honor of

knighthood, and that young boys of the nobility entered upon this training as soon as they were able to wield a sword or draw a bow

2. When a lad completed his training as a page, he was promoted to the rank of squire in this capacity he accompanied his lord into battle, fighting at his side and caring for the knight's horse and equipment at long last the squire himself was deemed fit to become a knight he was accorded this honor, however, only after several honorable wounds and some show of gallantry on his part had impressed the sovereign with the lad's readiness to uphold the code of chivalry

3. When the sovereign considered him ready, a day was appointed for the ceremony how long had the youth waited for this glorious hour how many times had he rehearsed in his fancy every step in the stately ceremony now that it was at last at hand, he could scarcely believe his good fortune he resolved to conduct himself always as a perfect knight — to bear true and faithful allegiance to his lord, to bow his head meekly before misfortune, to help the weak, to punish the wicked, and to answer any insult to his honor with terrible, swift power

4. These things about knighthood Gail knew already as she entered the library and opened the encyclopedia what a surprise lay in store for her she found first of all that the chivalry of Europe arose from a simple economic circumstance the first chevaliers were those rich enough to afford horses *chevalier* in French and *Ritter* in German mean "knight," but these words also mean "rider" this fact suggests that the first knights were merely those Frankish warriors who rode into battle while their humbler fellows walked behind in the dust

5. When the cavalry of Charlemagne became the foremost military force in Europe, his way of ordering the forces was adopted by all other nations the class of soldiers composing the cavalry became, therefore, an elite class or an aristocracy with special privileges but also with special obligations they were supported in peacetime, for example, by the labor of the rest of the population however, when the state was in danger, they were obliged to rally immediately underneath the royal standard and there to offer their courage, their property, and their lives to the royal cause

19e. An abbreviation is usually followed by a period.

EXAMPLES   Gen.   General
            Fla.   Florida
            A.D.   *anno Domini*
            Feb.   February
            oz.   ounce
            T. S. Eliot   Thomas Stearns Eliot

► **NOTE**   Abbreviations of government agencies are often written without periods.

FBI   Federal Bureau of Investigation
HUD   Department of Housing and Urban Development

Abbreviations in the metric system are often written without periods, especially in science books.

km   kilometer
ml   milliliter

Most abbreviations are capitalized only if the words they stand for are capitalized.

COMMAS

Commas are necessary for clear expression of ideas.

Items in a Series

19f. Use commas to separate items in a series.

WORDS IN SERIES   The examination proctor distributed scrap paper, test booklets, blotters, and copies of the test.   [nouns]
The cat spits, bites, scratches, and sheds.   [verbs]

PHRASES IN SERIES   We have a government of the people, by the people, and for the people.

SUBORDINATE CLAUSES IN SERIES   I can go camping in Yellowstone National Park in June if my grades are high, if I save enough money, and if my parents approve.

► **NOTE**   When the last two items in a series are joined by *and*, you may omit the comma before the *and* if the comma is not necessary to make the meaning clear.

CLEAR She made, painted and sold the table. [clear with comma omitted]

UNCLEAR The following courses will be added next year: Physics II, Composition II, conversational French and French literature. [Not clear with comma omitted. How many courses, three or four?]

CLEAR The following courses will be added next year: Physics II, Composition II, conversational French, and French literature.

Some words appear so often paired with another that they may be set off in a series as one item.

EXAMPLES bacon and eggs, lox and bagels, bread and butter

(1) If all items in a series are joined by *and* or *or* (*nor*), you need not use commas to separate them.

EXAMPLES We danced and sang and listened to records.
A volunteer addresses envelopes or answers phones or files correspondence.

(2) Independent clauses in a series are usually separated by semicolons. Short independent clauses, however, may be separated by commas.

EXAMPLES We played records, we danced, and we watched television. [short clauses]
I finished my examination in forty minutes; I checked my answers carefully; and I handed my paper in to the proctor in the front of the room.

19g. Use a comma to separate two or more adjectives preceding a noun.

EXAMPLE Sally was an energetic, mischievous girl.

When the last adjective before the noun is thought of as part of the noun, the comma before the adjective is omitted.

EXAMPLE We found an old wooden chest in the attic.

Here the adjective *wooden* is so closely associated with the noun *chest* that the two words are considered a unit, a single word, or what is called a *compound noun*. Therefore, the adjective *old* modifies not just *chest,* but *wooden chest,* and is not to be separated from it by a comma.

To determine whether it is right to put commas between two adjectives in a series of adjectives modifying a noun, substitute the word *and* for the doubtful comma. If the *and* sounds wrong, then you don't need a comma.

PROBLEM   A single electric bulb illuminated the long hallway.
[comma before *electric?*]

USE <u>AND</u>   A single and electric bulb illuminated the long hall-way. [obviously wrong!]

SOLUTION   A single electric bulb illuminated the long hallway.
[no comma]

EXERCISE 2. On your paper, copy each word after which a comma is needed and then add the comma. Some sentences will not need commas.

1. Rita Lil Rosa and I played ice hockey last winter.
2. A picturesque old riding stable was torn down and replaced by a new macadam parking lot.
3. Give your money to the treasurer today tomorrow or Wednesday.
4. The dusty sore and weary hikers returned about 7 P.M.
5. We need a person who can sing dance and act.
6. Ella sharpened her pencil took out a clean sheet of paper made a few notes and finally started the first draft of her composition.
7. Irving was a tall lean clean-shaven young man.
8. The conductor took my ticket punched it and handed me the stub as a receipt.
9. Neither wind nor rain nor sleet nor snow keeps the mail carrier from delivering the mail.
10. The following people will report to the main office at the end of the period: Peter Wong Jessica White Linda Gelder Alice Ortiz and Erica Robinson.
11. You can't eat drink and be merry when you are on a diet.
12. My hands were cold my feet were cold and my ears were cold.
13. In a bulky winter coat Norma was muffled against the strong March wind.

14. Beneath it she wore a blue summer dress.
15. For the outing she had washed her hair scrubbed her face pressed her dress and polished her shoes.
16. At the gymnastics meet Les performed on the parallel bars the rings and the high bar.
17. A blond little child in faded blue jeans emerged from the shrubbery to stare at the mail carrier.
18. The mail carrier came to an abrupt halt cleared his throat nervously and finally muttered, "Sorry, mister, no mail for you."
19. Sylvia is a fan of the great women novelists: Jane Austen the Brontë sisters Virginia Woolf Willa Cather Elizabeth Bowen George Eliot and many others.
20. In the meadow were an amazing number of wild flowers: red and yellow columbines black-eyed Susans purple asters buttercups Indian paintbrush sweet peas pink wild roses Queen Anne's lace and tall tiger lilies.

EXERCISE 3. Write ten sentences, illustrating each of the following uses of the comma twice.

1. Two or more adjectives preceding a noun
2. Nouns in a series requiring a comma before the *and* between the last two items
3. Phrases in a series
4. Short independent clauses in a series
5. A sentence containing a series joined by conjunctions, requiring no commas

Comma Between Independent Clauses

19h. Use a comma before *and, but, or, nor, for,* **and** *yet* **when they join independent clauses.**

EXAMPLES   Do your homework every day, and you certainly will pass the course.

There wasn't much to be done, but there wasn't much time in which to do it.

► NOTE   Independent clauses joined by *and, but, or,* or *nor* need not be separated by a comma when they are very short. If the clauses are joined by the conjunctions *yet* or *for*, they must be separated by a comma.

EXAMPLES   We knocked and Nilda opened the door.   [Clauses are too short to require commas.]

Laura pulled hard, yet the lid stayed on the jar. [Clauses are short but are separated by the conjunction *yet*. Therefore, a comma is required.]

I remained there, for Gwen hadn't come.   [Comma is needed because clauses are joined by *for*.]

Do not be misled by compound verbs, which often make a sentence look as though it contained two independent clauses.

SIMPLE SENTENCE   Russ took the makeup examination and passed it with ease.   [one independent clause with a compound verb]

TWO CLAUSES   Russ took the makeup examination, and he passed it with ease.   [two independent clauses]

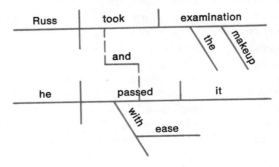

EXERCISE 4. The sentences in this exercise contain independent clauses joined by the conjunctions *and, but, or, for, nor,* or *yet.* Number your paper 1–15. Decide where the commas should go, and write on your paper after the proper number the word preceding each comma. Add the comma and the conjunction following it. Do not be misled by compound verbs.

EXAMPLE   1. Earvin Johnson tossed the ball neatly into the basket and the crowd went wild with excitement.
         1. *basket, and*

1. All students must arrive on time for no one will be admitted late.
2. The newspaper review complimented every performance in the movie but the leading character received the strongest praise.
3. A few spectators tried to climb over the fence but the police ordered them back.
4. Environmentalists who try to prevent the destruction of valuable land and water areas must stay alert or their efforts may be frustrated by their opponents.
5. The Nature Conservancy raises money through donations from concerned citizens and it uses these funds to buy and preserve wilderness areas.
6. Land developers sometimes overlook the importance of ecology but environmentalists persuade them to act more responsibly.
7. In general, people today work fewer hours than their grandparents did yet for some the difference is not that great.
8. The cost of living is rising for consumers must pay higher prices for gasoline and other products.
9. Our guide led and we followed closely.
10. Although the manager had signaled for a bunt, Patricia hit a home run and later the manager said nothing about disobeying instructions.
11. This television program will probably appeal to everyone but parents will find it especially interesting.
12. She said she did not like the story in the science fiction magazine nor did she enjoy the illustrations.

13. Robert knew how long we had waited for he kept looking at his watch.

14. High school graduates may go on to college or they may prefer to begin a career immediately.

15. Manhattan's theater district is only twelve blocks long and two blocks wide but every year ten million people go there to be entertained in its theaters.

EXERCISE 5. Write six compound sentences each illustrating the use of a different one of the following six conjunctions to join independent clauses: *and, or, but, nor, for,* and *yet.* Punctuate your sentences correctly before handing them in.

19i. Use a comma to set off nonessential clauses and nonessential participial phrases.

A nonessential[1] clause is a subordinate clause that is not essential to the meaning of the sentence. Such clauses serve only to add some extra information or to explain something further; they could be omitted without altering the fundamental meaning of the sentence. An essential[2] clause, on the other hand, is one that cannot be omitted without changing the meaning of the sentence.

NONESSENTIAL Robert Brill**, who lives across the street,** graduated from Mepham High School three years ago.

Since you know without the clause who it was that graduated from Mepham High School three years ago, the clause is not necessary to identify Robert Brill. It merely adds information about him. It is a nonessential clause and should be set off by commas. *Most adjective clauses which modify proper nouns are nonessential and require commas.*

ESSENTIAL All girls **that march with the honor guard** are required to be members of the senior class.

The clause *that march with the honor guard* is essential

---

[1] A nonessential clause is sometimes called a nonrestrictive clause.

[2] An essential clause is sometimes called a restrictive clause.

because it tells which girls are required to be members of the senior class. Omitting the clause would change the meaning of the sentence into something absurd. Since the clause is an integral, or essential, part of the sentence, it is not set off by commas. (Adjective clauses introduced by *that* are almost always essential.)

EXAMPLES   The girl **whom we saw last week** drives the delivery truck for the florist.   [essential]
Coral Sing, **whom we saw last week,** drives the delivery truck for the florist.   [nonessential]
The bold sea raider **who helped destroy the Spanish Armada** was Sir Francis Drake.   [essential]
Sir Francis Drake, **who was a bold sea raider,** helped destroy the Spanish Armada.   [nonessential]
A magazine **that has good news coverage** helps me in social studies.   [essential]
Newsweek, **which has good news coverage,** helps me in social studies.   [nonessential]
The subject **that I like best** is biology.   [essential]
Biology, **which I like best,** will be my major in college. [nonessential]

Sometimes the writer of a sentence is the only one who knows whether the clause used is nonessential (commas) or essential (no commas). Accordingly, the writer will either make use of commas to enclose the clause or abstain from their use in order to make the meaning clear.

NONESSENTIAL   My aunt, **who lives in Mississippi,** sent me a check for my birthday.   [The clause is not needed to identify this aunt. Since it is nonessential, it requires commas.]

ESSENTIAL   My aunt **who lives in Mississippi** sent me a check for my birthday.   [I have several aunts. The clause is necessary to tell which aunt I am talking about. It should not be set off by commas.]

The same principles govern participial phrases. You will remember that participles are of two kinds: present participles ending in *-ing* and past participles ending usually in *-ed*. A participial phrase is a group of words in which a participle is the chief word. When such a phrase is non-essential — not necessary to the sentence — the phrase is set off by commas. When it is essential, no commas are used.

NONESSENTIAL   Esther**, running at a slow, leisurely pace,** easily finished the marathon.

ESSENTIAL   The woman **running at a slow, leisurely pace** easily finished the marathon.

NONESSENTIAL   Vicky's silkscreen**, wrapped carefully inside a cardboard box,** arrived today.

ESSENTIAL   The silkscreen **wrapped carefully inside a cardboard box** was not damaged.

EXERCISE 6. After the proper number, write all words in the sentence that should be followed by a comma. Write the comma after each word. Be prepared to explain your answers. Some sentences do not need commas.

1. The heavenly event winning most of the public's attention at the beginning of 1974 was the visit of Kohoutek.
2. Kohoutek which is a large and visible comet visited our sun during the holidays.
3. The turn about the sun that gained Kohoutek such recognition was actually a fizzle as far as most people were concerned.
4. Most comets covered as widely by the news media of the past were much more exciting and easier to see than Kohoutek.
5. Kohoutek eagerly awaited after weeks of publicity came and left invisibly in the poor weather.
6. Only the sophisticated telescopes which were focused upon it with scientific accuracy managed to record the event.
7. Unaided eyes which after all have fairly limited vision proved incapable of seeing Kohoutek.
8. Comets which are identified by serial numbers as well as names may be composed of the oldest materials in the solar system.
9. The ancients seeing only the brightest comets with the largest tails named them after the Greek word *kometes,* meaning "hairy."
10. *Neighbors of the Earth* which is a valuable book on astronomy offers a good deal of interesting information on comets.

EXERCISE 7. Write three sentences containing nonessential clauses, three containing essential clauses, two containing nonessential phrases, and two containing essential phrases. Label each sentence according to the kind of phrase or clause it contains.

Introductory Elements

19j. Use a comma after certain introductory elements.

(1) Use a comma after words such as *well, yes, no, why,* **etc., when they begin a sentence. Exclamations like** *wow, good grief, gee whiz,* **etc., if not followed by an exclamation mark, must also be set off by commas.**

EXAMPLES   No, you can't go.
Well, I've heard that story before.
Why, he isn't old enough to drive!
Wow, this pavement is hot!

(2) Use a comma after an introductory participial phrase.

EXAMPLES   Calling for a timeout, the referee began waving her arms.
Exhausted after three hours of continuous swimming, Diana emerged from the water.

(3) Use a comma after a succession of introductory prepositional phrases.

EXAMPLE   At the next ring of the bell on the timer, you may start the examination.   [Three prepositional phrases precede the comma.]

A single introductory prepositional phrase does not usually require a comma unless the comma is necessary to make the meaning of the sentence clear.

EXAMPLES   At dawn the hikers set out.
In our library, books are arranged according to the Dewey decimal system.   [The comma is needed so that the reader does not read "our library books."]

(4) Use a comma after an introductory adverb clause.

An introductory adverb clause is a subordinate clause preceding an independent clause.

EXAMPLES **Although the Winnebagos are now in Nebraska,** they first lived on the shores of Lake Michigan.

If you read the accounts of early travelers to the West, you will learn of their productive life.

Population in the area increased; and **after the tribe ceded their land,** they moved westward.

EXERCISE 8. The sentences in this exercise contain introductory clauses and phrases. Decide where a comma should be used. After numbering your paper, copy the word preceding each comma, and place the comma after it. Some of the sentences may not require commas.

EXAMPLE 1. During the morning classes will be shortened by ten minutes.
1. *morning,*

1. When the price of oil started to rise the oil-importing countries began looking for other sources of energy.

2. While these countries search for a new and renewable source of energy they need an oil substitute to tide them over until the new source has been developed.

3. As might have been expected they found a practical substitute in the world's vast coal deposits.

4. According to the World Coal Study the mining and distribution of coal and the building of facilities for burning it may cost the nations as much as a trillion dollars.

5. Since coal is so much cheaper than oil the oil-importing countries could probably spend such a large sum and still save money.

6. In a worldwide substitution of coal for oil, however, may lie serious dangers.

7. Because burning coal sends large amounts of carbon dioxide into the atmosphere there is the possibility of causing irreversible harm to the environment.

8. Owing to the present use of both coal and oil the amount of carbon dioxide in the atmosphere is already quite large.

9. Over a period of time the increased burning of coal might double this amount.

10. In large quantities carbon dioxide causes a rise in the temperature of the earth's atmosphere.

11. As a result of the higher temperature weather patterns could change and affect the growing of crops.

12. Melting under the higher temperature the polar ice cap could add enough water to the oceans to raise their level twenty feet.

13. While admitting the possibility of these dangers scientists say that they cannot predict the effects of an increase of carbon dioxide in the atmosphere.

14. Until a safer source of energy is developed, however, coal may still be the most practical temporary substitute for oil.

REVIEW EXERCISE A. This exercise covers all uses of the comma that you have studied so far. Decide where commas should be used in these sentences. Copy on your paper the word preceding the comma. Place the comma after the word. Number your answers according to the numbers of the sentences.

EXAMPLE 1. In her lecture on cities Professor Gonzales who is an expert in her field suggested that the development of towns might have had as much to do with self-defense as with commerce.
1. *cities, Gonzales, field,*

1. The English word *weapon* is related to the Old English *waepen* the Dutch *wapen* the German *Wappe* and some earlier common root.

2. Sticks stones and poisons were among the weapons of primitive humanity.

3. Modern weapons which are produced by sophisticated people like ourselves are more fully developed.

4. Weapons that were produced in early times were not that developed nor were they distinct from each other in appearance function or design.

5. An object found in an archaeological dig might be an eating

utensil a tool for the hearth a farming implement or a weapon of war.

6. Coming upon such an ancient object diggers might not be able to identify its function with immediate instinctive accuracy.

7. The old Assames *dao* which was a sharp knife-like object was used to chop plants fell trees kill animals threaten enemies and carve wood.

8. The cord sling which is easily the most familiar sling was used all over the world for it was easy to put together and not too difficult to master.

9. When he slew Goliath David used a simple sling.

10. The boomerang which is a flat stick that can be thrown with accuracy was developed into a weapon by the people of Australia and the western Pacific.

11. Although they were both used as weapons the fighting boomerang and the returning boomerang are not the same.

12. Among the many kinds of weapons the stick thrown by hand became one of the most heavily specialized.

13. In many cases clubs were thrown even though they were not particularly designed for the purpose but design played an important role in the history of most weapons.

14. The dart the arrow the spear the lance and the javelin all developed from the plain stick thrown by hand.

15. The simplest earliest development was the addition of a head to the stick transforming the stick itself into a shaft.

16. The plainest and least developed was the stick that was hardened by fire at one end and often pointed.

17. Being among the more unusual weapons the *bolas* consisted of weighted balls of stone wood or metal tied together with thongs.

18. Its purpose which was somewhat different from that of most other weapons was to entangle the victim without inflicting pain injury or death.

19. Primitive undeveloped straightforward weapons like all these are somewhat easier to contemplate than the intricate devious modern weaponry of our own day.

20. As anyone can see the purpose of both kinds of weapons is identical and the end results have not altered in the least.

19k. Use commas to set off expressions that interrupt.

There are three kinds of "interrupters" which you should be able to recognize and punctuate properly.

(1) Appositives and appositive phrases are usually set off by commas.

An appositive is a word or group of words which follows a noun or pronoun and means the same thing as the noun or pronoun. An appositive usually identifies or explains the noun or pronoun that precedes it.

EXAMPLES   Nancy Landon Kassebaum, the **senator** from Kansas, was the principal speaker.
The Aegean Sea, the **highroad** of ancient Greece, is sprinkled with small islands.
I lost my watch, a **present** from my mother.

In these sentences *senator, highroad,* and *present* are appositives.

When you set off an appositive, you include with it all the words which modify it. An appositive, together with its modifiers, is an appositive phrase.

EXAMPLES   Julio Falabella, **a rancher near Buenos Aires,** raises miniature horses that are only thirty-six inches high at maturity.
I enjoyed *At Home in India,* **a book by Cynthia Bowles.**
An intelligent girl, Jennifer Goodfellow was the winner of a scholarship.

Sometimes an appositive is so closely related to the word preceding it that it should not be set off by commas. Such an appositive is called a "restrictive appositive." It is usually a single word.

EXAMPLES   my sister **Gail**
the writer **Doris Lessing**
my dog **Gypsy**
Catherine **the Great**

EXERCISE 9. Copy the following sentences containing appositives, inserting commas where needed.

1. The *Mona Lisa* a painting by Leonardo da Vinci is a prize possession of the Louvre.
2. The painting a portrait of a young Florentine woman is slightly cracked from temperature changes.
3. In 1911 an Italian house painter Vincenzo Perugia stole the painting from its frame.
4. For two years the Paris police some of the cleverest detectives in the world were baffled by the crime.
5. Since its recovery the painting one of the most valuable portraits in the world has been carefully protected.

(2) Words used in direct address are set off by commas.

EXAMPLES   **Tina,** shut the window.
Yes, **Virginia,** there is a Santa Claus.
Won't you run for office, **Mrs. Perkins?**

(3) Parenthetical expressions are set off by commas.

These expressions are often used parenthetically: *I believe (think, suppose, hope,* etc.*), on the contrary, on the other hand, of course, in my opinion, for example, however, to tell the truth, nevertheless, in fact.*

EXAMPLES   The movie, **in my opinion,** was terrible.
The book, **on the other hand,** was excellent.

These expressions are not *always* used as interrupters.

EXAMPLES   She promised **to tell the truth.**   [not used as an interrupter]
I don't remember, **to tell the truth,** what she was talking about.   [used as an interrupter]
I think Fran was elected.   [not used as an interrupter]
Fran, **I think,** was elected.   [used as an interrupter]

▶ NOTE   A contrasting expression introduced by *not* is parenthetical and must be set off by commas.

EXAMPLE   Emily Brontë, **not Charlotte Brontë,** was the author of *Wuthering Heights.*

EXERCISE 10.   Number your paper 1–10. Copy after the proper number the words in each sentence that should be followed by a comma, placing a comma after each word.

1. Francoise Giroud the Secretary of State for the Condition of Women under President Valery Giscard d'Estaing was called the "star" of the French Cabinet.

2. Mrs. Giroud who was a co-founder of the popular weekly *L'Express* asked Presidential candidate d'Estaing on television, "How much Mr. Giscard d'Estaing does a Paris subway ticket cost?"

3. To his embarrassment Giscard d'Estaing who went on to win the election did not have the vaguest idea.

4. Although she had publicly endorsed his opponent Mrs. Giroud was asked by the victorious candidate to create her new Cabinet post but at first she refused.

5. The attempt to deal with women in any separatist way was she thought a matter of "Let's be kind to the natives."

6. Among her public statements many of which became instant classics were these.

7. Theories about women are one thing in my opinion and practice is another especially when one is a woman.

8. You don't become Brigitte Bardot I suspect by using the same beauty cream she does.

9. It would be funny I think if suddenly the primitive woman were to reemerge the woman who had to be subjugated so that men could concentrate on creating civilizations.

10. Her autobiography *I Give You My Word* was published in the United States.

19l. Use a comma in certain conventional situations.

(1) Use a comma to separate items in dates and addresses.

In addresses the street number and the name of the street are not separated from each other by a comma. Neither are the name of the state and the zip code number which follows it. Similarly, in dates the day of the month and the month itself are considered one item. Commas do go between the date and the year and the city and the state.

EXAMPLES On June 30, 1981, my father's business moved to 837 Main Street, Seattle, Washington 98104.

Send your check or money order to Dorothy Stevenson, 981 Dartmouth Street, Newport News, Virginia 23602.

Our trip last summer to Tucson, Arizona, was most enjoyable.

On Wednesday, January 20, I shall be sixteen years old.

Our address is 718 Alvern Street, Los Angeles, California 90045.

(2) Use a comma after the salutation of a friendly letter and after the closing of any letter.

EXAMPLES   Dear Delia,   Dear Aunt Martha,
            Affectionately yours, Sincerely yours,
            Yours truly,

(3) Use a comma after a name followed by *Jr., Sr., Ph.D.,* **etc.**

EXAMPLES   Dr. Juanita Montez, Ph.D.
           John Q. Adams, Jr.
           Daniel Hale Williams, M.D.

19m. Do not use unnecessary commas.

Too much punctuation is a greater impediment to easy reading than too little. Do not use a comma unless a rule specifically calls for it or unless the sentence would be unclear without it. When in doubt, leave it out.

EXERCISE 11.   Number your paper 1–10. Copy after the proper number the words in each sentence that should be followed by a comma, placing a comma after each word.

1. We drove one hundred miles to visit my cousin at 418 Glendale Street Dayton Ohio.
2. On June 27 1981 the firm moved from 44 Rush Drive to a new building on Center Street.
3. We flew to Seattle Washington on September 9 1980 and flew back on October 9 1981.
4. Our friends sold their home at 237 Liberty Avenue Glens Falls New York and rented an apartment at 19 Circle Drive New York New York 10010.

5. The building at 29 Victory Drive Butte Montana was destroyed by an explosion on August 10 1980.
6. Address your letters to Ms. Violet Lee 18 Third Avenue San Francisco California 94118.
7. The letter from J. D. Harriman 16 Melbourne Road Seattle Washington 98177 was dated January 28 1980 but did not arrive until February 15 1981.
8. After baking John gave his sister Betsy a piece of bread.
9. To tell the truth Jeanne's resolution was prompted by her fear of being caught in an embarrassing white lie.
10. After the mutiny Captain Bligh the tyrannical master of the *Bounty* was put adrift in a boat with those of the crew who had remained loyal to him.

REVIEW EXERCISE B. Number your paper 1–12. After the proper number, rewrite the sentence, inserting commas where necessary. Do not use unnecessary commas.

1. Last Tuesday we learned about the Pharos at Alexandria one of the wonders of the ancient world. It was I believe one of the largest lighthouses ever built.
2. The lighthouse situated on an island two hundred yards from the mainland was one of the tallest buildings of its time.
3. The rulers of Alexandria then one of the most powerful cities in the world built the lighthouse at the entrance of the city's harbor.
4. This magnificent lighthouse built entirely of marble stood for sixteen hundred years.
5. The Pharos a blocklike structure contained a military barracks at its base. Its huge lamp which was fueled by wood or oil cast a powerful beam far away into the night.
6. Donkeys carried a daily supply of fuel up the broad ramps that rose at an easy grade from one story to another. These animals so we are told often carried visitors who were anxious to view the huge beacon.
7. In the fourteenth century an earthquake destroyed the lighthouse.
8. Archaeologists tell us that traces of the lighthouse remained for centuries; but we could not I suppose reasonably expect to see signs of the ancient ruin today.

9. Yes Patty today there is a lighthouse at Alexandria.

10. The city itself as its name suggests was founded by Alexander the Great in 332 B.C.

11. The Heptastadium a mile-long jetty connecting the island of the Pharos to the mainland provided a way of escape for Caesar when after a furious battle he was driven out of the city by the mob.

12. Alexandria became a great and prosperous city rivaling Rome itself in magnificence and far surpassing it as a center for learning.

REVIEW EXERCISE C. Select from the following sentences all words which should be followed by a comma. List these words on your paper, placing a comma after each. Number your answers according to the numbers of the sentences.

EXAMPLE 1. We all of course make mistakes once in a while.
1. *all, course,*

1. Yes as a matter of fact Belinda does have a cold.

2. As the season progressed the team piled up one victory after another.

3. Diane send this letter to the Allied Chemical Corporation 61 Broadway New York New York 10006.

4. We watched the parade for an hour but couldn't decide which one of the floats was the best for they all looked beautiful to us.

5. Take the garbage out Barbara and be sure to put the cover back on the pail.

6. Alan Bev and Mercedes served as ushers at the graduation exercises last year.

7. On June 6 1980 we closed the doors of our house at 16 Washington Street St. Paul; and on June 8 1980 we opened the doors of our new home in Durham North Carolina.

8. As soon as we heard the crunch of the tires on the gravel in the driveway we rushed out to inspect the new car a Pontiac station wagon.

9. Although it was four years old the car had been very well cared for by its former owner a seventy-year-old man.

10. That at least was the story the salesclerk told.

SUMMARY OF THE USES OF THE COMMA

19f. Use commas to separate items in a series.
  (1) If all items in a series are joined by *and* or *or* (*nor*), do not use commas to separate them.
  (2) Independent clauses in a series are usually separated by semicolons. Short independent clauses may be separated by commas.

19g. Use commas to separate two or more adjectives preceding a noun.

19h. Use commas before *and, but, or, nor, for,* and *yet* when they join independent clauses.

19i. Use commas to set off nonessential clauses and nonessential phrases.

19j. Use commas after certain introductory elements.
  (1) Use a comma after such words as *well, yes, no, why,* etc., when they begin a sentence.
  (2) Use a comma after an introductory participial phrase.
  (3) Use a comma after a succession of introductory prepositional phrases.
  (4) Use a comma after an introductory adverb clause.

19k. Use commas to set off expressions that interrupt the sentence.
  (1) Appositives and appositive phrases are usually set off by commas.
  (2) Words used in direct address are set off by commas.
  (3) Parenthetical expressions are set off by commas.

19l. Use commas in certain conventional situations.
  (1) Use a comma to separate items in dates and addresses.
  (2) Use a comma after the salutation of a friendly letter and after the closing of any letter.
  (3) Use a comma after a name followed by *Jr., Sr., Ph.D.,* etc.

19m. Do not use unnecessary commas.

REVIEW EXERCISE D. Copy after the proper number the words in each sentence that should be followed by a comma, placing a comma after each word.

1. Whenever Veronica watches Lily Tomlin she doubles up with laughter.

2. In past years Broadway has exported a number of hit plays and musicals to London. This year strangely enough many shows are playing on Broadway that originated on the other side of the Atlantic.

3. As knives forks and spoons clattered to the floor Mother raced from the living room to see what had happened to Dad in the kitchen.

4. Dad who was discharged from the army on January 30 1966 celebrates his release from the service each year by trying to squeeze into his old uniform.

5. My sister Anna is in her own opinion a genius in science. The teachers oddly enough do not share her opinion about her scientific aptitude.

6. "Doris for pity's sake," Mother shouted, "turn down the television sound or the neighbors will be banging on the walls again!"

7. "Yes Ruth Aunt Carolyn is a professor of English literature at Hofstra University, which is in Hempstead New York," said my father.

8. We intend to stay in Portland Oregon from Monday June 2 to Saturday June 7.

9. Broiled on the new grate the steak looked and smelled delicious..

10. An athlete who breaks the coach's training rules soon slips from the peak of condition a lapse which is hardly fair to the rest of the team.

11. Aristophanes whom the ancient Greeks considered the greatest of comic dramatists wrote *The Clouds* and *The Frogs*.

12. Sophocles often regarded as the greatest dramatist of all times is credited with almost a hundred plays of which only eight have been recovered.

13. Although the play was acclaimed by the critics the public did not like it and refused therefore to recommend it to their friends.

14. Leaning over the ship's rail Mel the cabin attendant idly watched the flying fish playing among the waves.

15. Of course if you find it impossible to attend the Student Council meeting Anita who was elected an alternate delegate will take your place.

REVIEW EXERCISE E. *End Marks and Commas.* Copy the following sentences, inserting end marks and commas as needed. Remember to capitalize the first word of any sentence.

1. What else I wondered could possibly happen

2. Buzzy the cook on our camping trip liked ham and eggs every day; therefore we had no choice about what we would have for breakfast

3. Christie rose to her feet was recognized by the president and asked what had happened to the treasury

4. Why Antony how fantastic you look with your new haircut

5. On Friday April 10 the sophomores will have a special assembly program on Monday April 13 the juniors will I understand report to the gym for a class meeting

6. Despite a winning streak of seven games Mrs. Miles the softball coach thought we had a good chance of losing the next game

7. At the barbecue Vivian and Fred served a green salad baked potatoes hamburgers and rolls and berry pie

8. I who am supposed to be on a diet had second helpings of rolls and pie and ice cream

9. The old gypsy who read my palm at the fair in St Cloud Florida said that I would be taking a journey I never suspected however that it would turn out to be a trip to the principal's office

10. If you have some writing ability if you are willing to work and if you are interested in the school paper the staff of the *Echo* can use you

11. Of course I don't know a thing about wiring but if somebody would teach me I could learn

12. Quentin Bell wrote an excellent biography of Virginia Woolf an outstanding novelist essayist and critic of British literature during the twentieth century

13. If you can't sing or dance or act you can make yourself useful by selling tickets to the play

14. When Louise had collected her prize a sporty new bicycle she and Maria departed quickly for 670 Church Avenue Lake Forest Illinois their home

15. Imprisoned without warning or explanation the two reporters were held if I remember correctly for two months in spite of the efforts by England France and the United States to win their release

Chapter 20

Punctuation

Semicolons and Colons

THE SEMICOLON

The semicolon [;] is a very useful mark of punctuation. It says to the reader, "Pause here a little longer than you do for a comma, but not so long as you do for a period."

20a. Use a semicolon between independent clauses in a sentence if they are not joined by *and, but, or, nor, for, yet.*

EXAMPLES   The President was concerned about the international situation; he called a special meeting of his Cabinet.

Martha Graham must have enjoyed teaching my friend dancing; I never knew a more talented student.

When the thoughts of the clauses are *very closely connected,* a semicolon is better than a period.

20b. Use a semicolon between independent clauses joined by such words as *for example, for instance, that is, besides, accordingly, moreover, nevertheless, furthermore, otherwise, therefore, however, consequently, instead, hence.*

EXAMPLES   We waited in line for an hour; **however,** the movie was exciting and well worth the wait.

The game progressed slowly; **for example,** the second inning lasted nearly forty-five minutes.

Wanda does not want to be president; furthermore, she refuses to take any part in the nominations.

The principal was a fine speaker; **therefore** she was often invited to address civic groups.

When the connectives mentioned in this rule are placed at the beginning of a clause, the use of a comma after them is frequently a matter of taste. When they are clearly parenthetical (interrupters) they are followed by a comma. The words *for example, for instance,* and *that is* are always followed by a comma. The word *however* is usually followed by a comma.

20c. A semicolon (rather than a comma) may be needed to separate the independent clauses of a compound sentence if there are commas within the clauses.

EXAMPLES My parents bought our home ten years ago, but now they have decided to sell it.   [A comma between the clauses is sufficient.]

My parents bought our home, a modified Cape Cod cottage, ten years ago; but since they now need more room, they have decided to sell it. [Additional commas make the semicolon preferable.]

20d. Use a semicolon between items in a series if the items contain commas.

EXAMPLES The volcano has erupted three times: January 2, 1610; March 15, 1823; and May 8, 1945.

The meeting was called by Gina Cusco, president of the senior class; Nancy Blake, president of the junior class; and Marvin Celler, president of the sophomore class.

EXERCISE 1. List on your paper (in the order in which they appear in the sentences below) all words you think should be followed by a semicolon or a comma. After each word, place the mark of punctuation you decide on. Number your list by sentences, keeping the words from each sentence together.

1. The scientific names of animals are often informative for example *Procyon lotor,* the scientific name for the raccoon, names two traits of the animal.

2. *Lotor,* which means "washer," refers to the raccoon's habit of dunking its food in water and *procyon,* which means "before the dog," indicates that the animal is a favorite quarry for hunters and their hounds.

3. Weighing about twenty-five pounds at maturity, the raccoon looks like a little bear indeed, "little bear" is precisely what some Native Americans call it.

4. The raccoon is usually a nocturnal animal that is, it begins to prowl for food at sundown and hunts only at night.

5. If the suburbs encroach upon the ponds and streams where it finds food, it rapidly adjusts to the changed environment for instance, it will make its home in attics, boathouses, and garages when it cannot find other suitable lodgings.

6. The raccoon's preferred diet consists of crayfish, frogs, mice, birds' eggs, fruit, and corn however, when these are in short supply it will not hesitate to raid garbage cans and hen houses.

7. Raccoon fur coats, once very popular, have gone out of style consequently, the raccoon population has increased greatly in recent years.

8. Baby raccoons make excellent pets they are easily tamed and rarely bite or scratch.

9. Older animals are usually surly and ill-tempered accordingly it is very unwise to attempt to pet a grown raccoon.

10. The raccoon's front paws are marvelously dexterous in fact, its tracks along the muddy banks of streams look exactly like the prints of a baby's hands.

11. Raccoons are common in the woods nearby otters, however, are very rare in these woods.

12. Most wild animals are very businesslike their search for food is almost incessant, interrupted only by the need to sleep.

13. Otters, on the contrary, do not spend all their waking hours hunting for food instead, they prefer to spend most of their time amusing themselves.

14. Unlike raccoons, otters detest civilization therefore, they are very rarely seen except in the deep woods.

15. Carol has seen them on only three occasions: on a fishing trip to Port Kent, Maine on a vacation trip to the Okefenokee

Swamp in Georgia and on a canoe trip through Superior National Forest, Minnesota.

16. On the last occasion Carol had an odd assortment of gear in the canoe: a feather-light nylon sleeping bag a Hudson's Bay ax three new, valuable fishing rods a map case and compass a brass-bound grub box and a newly bought, expensive gasoline stove.

17. When a large otter surfaced suddenly in the water beside the canoe, Carol was so startled she upset the canoe luckily the water was shallow and none of her gear was lost.

18. Otters build long mud slides along the banks of streams then, having polished the slides to a perfect slickness, whole families of otters gather and pass the day in wild merriment.

THE COLON

The usual purpose of the colon is to call the reader's attention to what comes next. A colon means "notice the following."

20e. Use a colon to mean "note what follows."

Use a colon before a list of items, especially after expressions like *as follows* or *the following*.

EXAMPLES   We visited four states last year: Nevada, Idaho, Montana, and Colorado.

My little sister's vocabulary is limited to four words: "no," "daddy," "out," and "scram."

For her science project Juanita built the following: a solar-heat collector, a thermostat, and a small model of a house designed for solar heat.

► NOTE   When a list comes immediately after a verb or preposition, do not use a colon.

INCORRECT   In the zoo can be seen: an Indian elephant, two giraffes, four gnus, and a rare Himalayan snow leopard.

CORRECT   In the zoo can be seen an Indian elephant, two giraffes, four gnus, and a rare Himalayan snow leopard. [The list follows the verb *can be seen.*]

CORRECT   Most interesting to me were the sea lions, the pandas, the chimpanzees, and the snakes.

CORRECT   Letters of congratulations came from relatives, friends, business associates, and government officials.

20f. Use a colon before a long, formal statement or quotation.

EXAMPLE   Thomas Paine's first pamphlet in the series *The American Crisis* starts with these famous words: "These are the times that try men's souls. The summer soldier and the sunshine patriot will, in this crisis, shrink from the service of their country; but he that stands it *now* deserves the love and thanks of man and woman."[1]

20g. Use a colon in certain conventional situations.

(1) Use a colon between the hour and the minute when you are writing the time.

EXAMPLES   8:45 P.M.
3:07 this afternoon

(2) Use a colon between chapter and verse in referring to passages from the Bible.

EXAMPLES   Proverbs 15:3
Romans 2:11

(3) Use a colon after the salutation of a business letter.

EXAMPLES   Dear Mrs. Raymond:
Dear Sir:

Use a comma after the salutation of a friendly letter.

EXAMPLE   Dearest Janice,

EXERCISE 2. Decide where colons should be used in the following sentences. On your paper, write the word pre-

---

[1] For further discussion of the use of long quotations in a composition, see pages 429–30.

ceding the colon; then add the colon. If a sentence needs no colon, write *C* for correct after its number. Be able to explain your answers.

1. Mrs. Bryant wanted a report on one of the following women Ida B. Wells, Buffy St. Marie, Anne Bradstreet, or Ynes Mexia.
2. Look, Sally, if you want to do well in her class, take my advice hand in your homework on time, take notes, pay attention, and keep quiet.
3. The following students will report to the principal at the end of the first period Anna Crossan, Nelson Finn, Mary Aspland, and Sonia Cortez.
4. The performance was scheduled to start at 8 10, but technical difficulties held up the opening until 8 45.
5. At the picnic everybody enjoyed the French fries, the potato salad, the corn, and the hamburgers.
6. The story of Moses and the Pharoah's daughter is told in Exodus 2 5–10.
7. The president of the Student Council opened the special meeting with these words "It has been brought to my attention that many of the students are dissatisfied with the ban on senior privileges."
8. There are three reasons why we have chicken for dinner so often Dad likes it, Mom likes it, and it's cheap.
9. The principal began her announcement as follows "Good afternoon. Here is a list of the afternoon activities for Green Bay High School."
10. Liz's favorite authors are Gloria Gonzalez, Willa Cather, N. Scott Momaday, and James Baldwin.

Chapter 21

Punctuation

Underlining (Italics) and Quotation Marks

UNDERLINING (ITALICS)

Italics are printed letters which lean to the right, such as the following:

> *These words are printed in italics.*

When you are writing or typing, indicate italics by underlining the words you want italicized. If your composition were to be printed, the typesetter would set the underlined words in italics. For instance, if you typed

> All sophomores in our school read The Good
> Earth, by Pearl Buck.

your sentence would be printed like this:

> All sophomores in our school read *The Good Earth*, by Pearl Buck.

21a. Use underlining (italics) for titles of books, periodicals, works of art (pictures, musical compositions, statues, etc.), planes, trains, and so on.

EXAMPLES   The Red Badge of Courage
the Mona Lisa
the Reader's Digest
the Santa Maria

► NOTE The words *a, an,* and *the* before a magazine or news-paper title are not underlined. Notice, however, that in titles of books these words are underlined if they are part of the title.

EXAMPLES the Runner's World   [magazine]
the Washington Post   [newspaper]
The Wings of the Dove   [book]
The Return of the Native   [book]

21b. Use underlining (italics) for words, letters, and figures referred to as such, and for foreign words.

EXAMPLES How many and's are there in this sentence?
There is only one c in the word recommend.
His phone number has three 7's in it.
Common poison ivy (Rhus toxicodendron) is to be avoided.

EXERCISE 1. List on your paper all words and word groups which should be italicized. Underline each.

1. In Arts Club we have no program; we just talk about things that are crafted. By this word crafted we mean not only works of art but also useful things that happen to be beautiful.

2. This definition admits things like the ship Old Ironsides on the same basis with works like the abstract sculpture Hudson River Landscape by David Smith.

3. Many of us think that mechanical things are beautiful — for example, the train El Capitan. Some admire things for the romance that surrounds them — for example, Mississippi steam-boats like the Grey Eagle, The Maid of New Orleans, and the doomed Robert E. Lee or clipper ships like the Cutty Sark, the Nightingale, and the Thermopylae.

4. Books, however, are usually the chief topic of our talks. Some students vote for adventure — books like Guthrie's The Big Sky, Ernest Thompson Seton's Two Little Savages, Willa Cather's Death Comes for the Archbishop, Defoe's Robinson Crusoe, and Johann Wyss's The Swiss Family Robinson.

5. Others prefer books of another sort — books like Emily Brontë's Wuthering Heights, Edna Ferber's Showboat, Marjorie Kinnan Rawlings' The Yearling, and Jessamyn West's The Friendly Persuasion.

6. Notice that Ms. West spells her first name with a y rather than an i. This practice is now widely adopted: Alice becomes Alyce and Caroline becomes Carolyn.

QUOTATION MARKS

Quotation marks are used mainly to show the reader that someone's *exact words* are being reproduced. Accordingly, quotation marks come in pairs — one set marking the beginning of the quotation and the other the end.

21c. Use quotation marks to enclose a direct quotation — a person's exact words.

Do not use quotation marks to enclose an indirect quotation — not a speaker's exact words.

DIRECT QUOTATION	Marie said, **"**I have an hour's detention for being late for homeroom.**"** [Marie's exact words]
INDIRECT QUOTATION	Marie said that she had an hour's detention for being late for homeroom. [not Marie's exact words]

► NOTE Place quotation marks at both the beginning and the end of a quotation. Omission of quotation marks at the end of a quotation is a common error.

INCORRECT	"I can't budge this piano alone, said Dan. [second set of quotation marks left out]
CORRECT	**"**I can't budge this piano alone,**"** said Dan.

21d. A direct quotation begins with a capital letter.

EXAMPLE Ed asked, "What time does the bus leave?"

► NOTE If the quotation is only a fragment of a sentence, not intended to stand alone, do not begin it with a capital letter.

EXAMPLE He resented Bob's remark that he was "never there when needed."

21e. When a quoted sentence is divided into two parts by an interrupting expression such as *he said* or *she replied,* the second part begins with a small letter.

EXAMPLES   "I know," said Joan, "the solution to our problem."
"All we have to do," she continued, "is raise some
money."
"Let's hear your ideas," replied Ann, "because the
treasury is sadly depleted."

If the second part of a broken quotation is a new sentence,
it begins with a capital.

EXAMPLE   "Start from the beginning," said Greg. "The joke
doesn't make sense to me."

**21f. A direct quotation is set off from the rest of the
sentence by commas or by a question mark or an exclamation point.**

EXAMPLES   "Where will it all end?" asked Eileen.
"Let me do that!" exclaimed Helen.
"There is no specific homework assignment for this
weekend," announced Mrs. Levitt, "but remember
that your term papers are due next Friday."
"Has anyone in this class," asked Mrs. Lukas, "seen
a performance of *Raisin in the Sun?*"
Of the Spitfire pilots the Prime Minister said, "Never
in the field of human conflict was so much owed by
so many to so few."

► NOTE   A long quotation in your composition is usually introduced by a colon and is set off by itself from the text by wider
margins and by single spacing instead of double spacing (unless
your teacher instructs otherwise). This practice so clearly identifies the passage as a quotation that no quotation marks are needed.

After the collapse of Europe and the tragedy

of Dunkirk, the German dictator thought he had

penned the British lion in its home islands

and that, weakened as it was by its losses on

the continent, it would easily succumb to an

invasion. The British Prime Minister, voicing

the grim resolve of the whole nation, warned

him against such a move:

> We shall defend every village, every town
> and every city. The vast mass of London
> itself, fought street by street, could
> easily devour an entire hostile army;
> and we would rather see London laid in
> ruins and ashes than that it should be
> tamely and abjectly enslaved.

21g. Other marks of punctuation when used with quotation marks are placed according to the following rules.

(1) Commas and periods are always placed inside the closing quotation marks.

EXAMPLE   "I've got a report due tomorrow," she said, "so don't count on my being at the meeting tonight."

(2) Colons and semicolons are always placed outside the closing quotation marks.

EXAMPLES   Miss Kendall said, "Write your answers on one side of the page"; however, I wasn't paying attention and put mine on both sides.

The following students in our homeroom have, according to Mr. Cahill, "hit the honor roll jackpot": Vic Chapman, Mary Arnold, and Olga Martinez.

(3) Question marks and exclamation points are placed inside the closing quotation marks if the quotation is a question or an exclamation. Otherwise, they are placed outside.

EXAMPLES   Maria asked, "What time is the game tomorrow?"
Why did you yell, "It doesn't matter"?
On the last lap Vicky said, "Do your best!"
Don't say, "I quit"!

EXERCISE 2.   Copy the following sentences, inserting the necessary punctuation. Watch carefully for the placement of commas and end marks in relation to quotation marks, and capital letters for the beginning of direct quotations.

1. I'm afraid said the woman you've made the wrong turn.
2. You're headed toward Newton now she added, but if you make a right turn on Route 200, you'll come to your destination.
3. Did you say I should turn right on 200 asked Jake.
4. Wow, look at that house exclaimed Sue. Did you ever see anything spookier?
5. You shouldn't read only fiction said Mrs. Werner. You should try an occasional biography.
6. The following sophomores have, in the words of Coach Balcolm, brought honor to their class and school: Al Hawthorne, Eunice McCarthy, and Edith Levine.
7. Did you hear Mrs. Lopez say hand in your papers?
8. Yes, I heard her say that answered Sheila I wish I hadn't because I'm far from finished.
9. In a crowded place never shout fire! unless you mean it.
10. Ms. Timpanaro asked if anyone knew the beginning of Alexander Pope's line which ends with the words where angels fear to tread.

21h. When you write dialogue (two or more persons having a conversation), begin a new paragraph every time the speaker changes.

EXAMPLE   "Hello, mates," said Captain Handy softly, "what can I do for you now?"

"You can turn over the ship to me," replied the first mate, his voice filled with tension.

Handy looked with deliberation at the crowd of mutineers. "So it's mutiny, is it, you cowards? You can't get away with it!" he roared.

"We have got away with it, sir," replied the mate.

21i. When a quoted passage consists of more than one paragraph, put quotation marks at the beginning of each paragraph and at the end of the entire passage.

EXAMPLE   "Fellow sophomores," said Theresa, opening the meeting, "permit me first of all to thank you for turning out in such good numbers. Despite our dismal showing so far, I think this packed room proves beyond any doubt that the Sophomore Class is determined not to take second place to the freshmen.

"Up to now, we have simply not been ourselves. As you know, the freshmen have more people on the honor roll than we. More freshmen than sophomores play on all school teams. Perhaps we are ready to change all that."

21j. **Use single quotation marks to enclose a quotation within a quotation.**

EXAMPLES   Margaret whispered, "Mr. Burns just said, 'Do the first three examples.'"
Laura said, "I don't understand the poem 'My Last Duchess' very well."

21k. **Use quotation marks to enclose titles of short stories, poems, songs, chapters, articles, and other parts of books and periodicals.**

EXAMPLES   "The Steeple-Jack" is my favorite poem by Marianne Moore.
Did you read the article "America on Ice" in *American Heritage?*
The assignment for Wednesday is Chapter 16, "Women in Literature."

► NOTE   The length of a written work determines whether the title should be italicized or enclosed in quotation marks. Book-length works are italicized; shorter works usually are not. However, the titles of poems long enough to be divided into books, cantos, or sections—like Longfellow's *Evangeline,* Coleridge's *The Rime of the Ancient Mariner,* and Hardy's *The Dynasts*—are italicized.

21l. **Use quotation marks to enclose slang words, technical terms, and other expressions that are unusual in standard English.**

EXAMPLE   Esther's taste in clothes was "way out."

Putting slang expressions within quotation marks amounts to apologizing for them. If you are doubtful about the appropriateness of a word, do not use it.

EXERCISE 3. Using quotation marks correctly, write one original sentence containing each of the following:

1. A direct quotation beginning with *he said*
2. A direct quotation ending with *she asked*
3. An indirect quotation
4. A direct quotation not beginning with a capital letter
5. A direct quotation interrupted by *he replied*
6. A question mark inside quotation marks
7. A question mark outside quotation marks
8. The title of a short poem within a direct quotation
9. The title of a novel within a direct quotation
10. A slang expression used in directly quoted conversation

Chapter 22

Punctuation

Apostrophes, Hyphens, Dashes, Parentheses

APOSTROPHES

The possessive case of a noun or a pronoun is used to indicate ownership or relationship.

OWNERSHIP   the **girl's** motorcycle

                his record   [The record is *his*.]

RELATIONSHIP **her** suggestion

                this **evening's** program

In the English language the possessive case of nouns is formed by adding an apostrophe and an *s* or, with some words, merely an apostrophe, to the noun.

EXAMPLES   a **child's** toy

             Bert's paper

             two **ladies'** umbrellas

Making a word possessive is very easy. *Remembering* to do so, however, may be hard. When you are in doubt whether or not to use an apostrophe, try an "of" phrase in place of the word. If the "of" phrase makes good sense, then an apostrophe is called for.

EXAMPLE   a half hours work   [An apostrophe in *hours?*]

work "of a half hour" [This makes good sense,
therefore . . .]
a half hour's work

22a. To form the possessive case of a singular noun, add an apostrophe and an *s*.

EXAMPLES a day's work
Eva's sculpture
cat's whiskers

▶ NOTE A proper name ending in *s* may add only an apostrophe if the name consists of two or more syllables and if the addition of *'s* would make the name difficult to pronounce (Artemis' death, Themistocles' oration). Some singular nouns ending in *s* need the apostrophe and the *s* since the added *s* must be pronounced as a separate syllable to make the meaning clear (waitress's uniform). In general, adding an apostrophe and an *s* is a correct way to make any singular noun possessive.

22b. To form the possessive case of a plural noun ending in *s*, add only the apostrophe.

EXAMPLES boys' club
turkeys' feathers

▶ NOTE The few plural nouns that do not end in *s* form the possessive by adding an apostrophe and an *s*.

EXAMPLES women's hats
children's games

Take care not to use an apostrophe to form the *plural* of a noun.

INCORRECT The four hour's passed swiftly.
  CORRECT The four hours passed swiftly.
INCORRECT The runner's ran all afternoon.
  CORRECT The runners ran all afternoon.

Study the following examples of the application of these rules for forming the singular and plural possessives of nouns. Be able to explain how each possessive was formed.

SINGULAR	SINGULAR POSSESSIVE	PLURAL	PLURAL POSSESSIVE
girl	girl's ticket	girls	girls' tickets
Mr. Jones	Mr. Jones's house	the Joneses	the Joneses' house
ox	ox's hoof	oxen	oxen's hooves
nurse	nurse's uniform	nurses	nurses' uniforms
baby	baby's gloves	babies	babies' gloves
clerk	clerk's desk	clerks	clerks' desks
monkey	monkey's paw	monkeys	monkeys' paws
lawyer	lawyer's office	lawyers	lawyers' offices

EXERCISE 1. On your paper, make a four-column chart listing the singular, singular possessive, plural, and plural possessive of the following words:

1. army
2. florist
3. governor
4. baby
5. mouse
6. book
7. press
8. deer
9. rose
10. man

Pronouns in the Possessive Case

22c. Possessive personal and relative pronouns do not require an apostrophe.

The lists below show the nominative and possessive forms of personal and relative pronouns. Note that there are no apostrophes.

NOMINATIVE CASE	POSSESSIVE CASE
I	my, mine
you	your, yours
he	his
she	her, hers
it	its[1]
we	our, ours
they	their, theirs
who	whose

[1] The common form *it's* is not possessive; it is a contraction meaning *it is* or *it has*. See page 540.

22d. Indefinite pronouns in the possessive case require an apostrophe and an *s*.

EXAMPLES   everyone's books
nobody's name

If you need to review indefinite pronouns, see the list on page 6.

Compounds in the Possessive Case

22e. In compound words, names of organizations and business firms, and words showing joint possession, only the last word is possessive in form.

COMPOUND WORDS   sister-in-**law**'s office
commander-in-**chief**'s order
board of **directors**' report
NAMES OF BUSINESS FIRMS   Heywood and **Bigalow**'s Department Store
Remson and **Doyle**'s office
JOINT POSSESSION   Doris and **Walter**'s boat
Jill and **Barbara**'s house
Pamela's and my car   [exception: noun and possessive pronoun]

22f. When two or more persons possess something individually, each of their names is possessive in form.

EXAMPLES   **Art**'s and **Chuck**'s report cards
Sally's and **Jane**'s toothbrushes

EXERCISE 2. Some of the following expressions need apostrophes; some are plurals that do not need apostrophes. Copy each expression, inserting apostrophes where needed.

1. a months delay
2. two cars in the garage
3. three pairs of gloves
4. a childs toy
5. a peoples choice
6. curtains in the breeze
7. a candidates speech
8. among four boys
9. the girls gym
10. seven loaves of bread
11. the sound of trumpets
12. two days work

13. the hands of the clock
14. Ulysses travels
15. two pairs of glasses
16. a ships cargo

17. Two cars collided.
18. Elaines keys
19. rivers of mud
20. my mothers cooking

EXERCISE 3. List on your paper in the order in which they appear in the numbered sentences the words requiring apostrophes. After each word with an apostrophe, write the thing possessed. Remember that plural nouns ending in *s* require an apostrophe only.

EXAMPLE   1. At Stellas request we decided to visit George Washingtons home.
　　　　　1. *Stella's request*
　　　　　George Washington's home

1. At Midges party last week, my friends plan for this summers vacation didn't receive everyones approval. 2. Jills brother had been on a three weeks trip with the American Youth Hostels, and her brothers enthusiasm had infected Jill.

3. For this years trip somebodys suggestion was to go to Fishers Lake; but since nobody greeted this with shouts of approval, we listened to more of Jills idea. 4. She recognized the fact that a bicycle trip wasn't some peoples idea of fun, but it was at least something new and different. 5. Jill said that all one needed to do was to drag out the kid brothers bicycle, invest a few dollars in camping equipment, and pedal off to see our countrys scenery. 6. I agreed to go along with her suggestion, provided that first we all take a days bicycle trip to nearby Orchard Beach as preparation for the long trip.

7. I thought that after five years neglect my bike would probably need some repair, and a trip to the cellar soon confirmed this surmise. 8. Hidden behind my sisters old wagon, the bike looked rusty and in need of a mechanics skilled touch. 9. Dads tool kit was nearby, and with a little elbow grease and my mothers advice, I made the old heap look like a cyclists dream.

EXERCISE 4. List in order after the number of the section the words requiring apostrophes. After each word with an apostrophe, write the thing possessed.

1. With my mothers advice and my fathers laughter ringing in

my ears, I was at Joes house at the crack of dawn. The suggestion that we meet there was his. 2. Soon the whole gang arrived. Everyones bike was in good working order. 3. Helens idea that we stay off main thoroughfares met with everyones approval.

Before long we left the Greens house and started the first lap of the sixteen-mile round-trip. 4. Our groups spirit was high. Since everyones intention was to make the trip pleasant, we started to sing some of our schools songs. 5. There wasn't much traffic to worry about at that hour, and we soon passed the mens club building, Harris and Cosgroves store, and the police officers booth on the outskirts of town. 6. Of course, we had a long way to go, but sixteen miles seemed like childs play. 7. Luckily, no ones bike developed mechanical difficulties. Even Davids and Julies bicycles held together, which surprised us because theirs were old models.

8. After about five miles of steady pedaling, my legs began to get tired, and somebodys suggestion that we take a short break seemed like a good idea. 9. The girls stamina proved to be equal to the boys. 10. We all raided Julies supply of candy, and after a few minutes we were off again. 11. Before we reached our destination, Midges face was beginning to get a little sunburned, and Mikes brow was damp with perspiration. 12. Tired and dusty, we finally arrived at Orchard Beach and had a swim, a lunch, and a few hours relaxation. 13. The groups plan was to leave at two o'clock. If my legs had been tired early in the morning, now they were ready to fall off.

14. When we arrived at Pegs house late that afternoon, everyones muscles were aching, but everybodys spirits were still high. 15. At Pegs house Davids bicycle at last collapsed. 16. Its front wheel detached itself suddenly from the frame and wobbled away. Davids weariness overcame him and he began to laugh. 17. Soon everybodys restraint dissolved, and we all laughed so hard that the tears rolled down our faces. 18. After a while, Jo offered to alternate walking and riding with David, using her bike, while Peters bike carried the broken parts of Davids bike. This arrangement of theirs worked nicely, and eventually everyone got safely home. 19. If your club decides on a days bicycle trip, I hope yours is as much fun as ours was.

Contractions

Contractions are shortened forms of certain words or certain word groups that commonly go together. The apostrophes in contractions are to indicate that letters have been left out.

22g. Use an apostrophe to show where letters or numbers have been omitted in a contraction.

EXAMPLES you have   you've
we are   we're
it is   it's

What words or figures have been contracted, and what letters or numbers have been omitted from the following?

Readin', 'ritin', and 'rithmetic are the three R's.

You're too young to drive.

It's a long story.

The winter of '78 set records for cold weather.

EXERCISE 5. Study the following contractions. Be able to write them when your teacher dictates to you the uncontracted expressions.

1. shouldn't	should not	11. she'll	she will
2. they've	they have	12. he's	he is
3. o'clock	of the clock	13. I'm	I am
4. isn't	is not	14. they'll	they will
5. they'd	they would	15. let's	let us
6. haven't	have not	16. who's	who is
7. we're	we are	17. she'd	she would
8. weren't	were not	18. they'd	they had
9. that's	that is	19. doesn't	does not
10. hasn't	has not	20. didn't	did not

REVIEW EXERCISE A. Copy the following sentences, inserting apostrophes wherever necessary.

1. Youve got to finish todays assignment.
2. Theyre going to the principals office.
3. The girls gym wasnt painted this year.
4. One cats whiskers werent singed.
5. Im not so sure you cant do it.

6. Certainly hed met Jerrys uncle, but he didnt remember his name.

7. Youll have to pay a fine if your book isnt found.

8. At four oclock, lets see if theyre still in the gym.

9. Vivians sister wont be able to attend Elsies party.

10. Dont you want to tell us whos going to be there?

Do not confuse possessive pronouns with contractions.

POSSESSIVE PRONOUNS	CONTRACTIONS
its roof	it's = it is *or* it has
your house	you're = you are
their house	they're = they are
whose house	who's = who is

EXERCISE 6. This exercise is to give you practice in distinguishing between possessive pronouns and contractions. You should be able to do the exercise perfectly. After each number, write the correct word from the pair (or pairs) in parentheses.

1. (Its, It's) true the plant has already lost (its, it's) leaves.

2. (Whose, Who's) the girl (whose, who's) record player you borrowed for the party?

3. (Their, They're) not really very suitable records for a party.

4. (You're, Your) sure (they're, their) not too loud?

5. (Who's, Whose) the vocalist on this one? (Its, It's) not labeled.

6. (Its, It's) one of the best songs by a new group of five young singers. (Their, They're) very good.

7. (You're, Your) sure to like it. (Their, They're) accompanied by seven drums and a bass.

8. (Whose, Who's) orchestra do they use?

9. (Your, You're) parents may not like the record. (Its, It's) sound is something (they're, their) not used to at all.

10. (Whose, Who's) (your, you're) favorite singer?

22h. Use an apostrophe and an *s* to form the plural of letters, numbers, signs, and words referred to as words.

EXAMPLES   There are two *m*'s, two *t*'s, and two *e*'s in *committee.*
There are four *3*'s in my phone number.
The +'s and 0's belong on your paper, not in the book.
Your sentences have too many *and*'s.

EXERCISE 7. List on your paper all words and symbols needing apostrophes. List them according to the sentences in which they appear. Supply the needed apostrophes.

1. Youre sure they have two *t*s in their name?
2. The Moraleses mill burned down in 29, the year of the crash.
3. Youve forgotten the childrens shoes.
4. Deers and goats hooves are cloven.
5. Whose car did you say this was, your sister-in-laws?
6. So far Ive got six 90s on these spelling tests; I mightve done better on this one.
7. The speakers delivery was marred by too many *ah*s.
8. His is red, ours is green.
9. Youve not told me whos coming.
10. *Aint* is in the dictionary, but its considered nonstandard by most people.
11. Whos going to cook the babies dinner?
12. The equation contained two ∞s, which my glossary told me were symbols for infinity.
13. Theyre not nearly as good as they pretend to be.
14. Georgias dog wags its tail continuously; its very friendly.
15. *So*s occur too often in students compositions.
16. Beth shouldve recognized the handbag as Judy Johnsons; after all, its monogrammed with two *J*s.
17. *Oh*s and *ah*s greeted the winners appearance on the stage.

HYPHENS

22i. Use a hyphen to divide a word at the end of a line.

Division of words at the end of a line in order to maintain an even margin should be avoided but is sometimes necessary. A hyphen is used between parts of words divided in this way. Never divide one-syllable words. When you divide a word of more than one syllable, follow these rules:

1. Divide a word between its syllables.

INCORRECT   Katherine, the captain, is a fo-
             rceful speaker.
  CORRECT   Katherine, the captain, is a force▪
             ful speaker.

2. Words containing double consonants should be divided between the double consonants.

  ban▪nister, recom▪mend

See Rule 3 for exceptions like tell-ing and call-ing.

3. Words with a prefix or suffix should usually be divided between the prefix and root or the root and suffix.

  per▪form, tell▪ing, call▪ing, accept▪able

4. Divide an already hyphenated word only at the hyphen.

INCORRECT   She is also quite self-reli-
             ant.
  CORRECT   She is also quite self▪
             reliant.

5. Divide a word so that at least two of its letters are carried forward to the next line.

INCORRECT   Dave always takes his camer-
             a with him.
  CORRECT   Dave always takes his cam▪
             era with him.

6. Do not hyphenate a proper name or separate a title, initials, or first name from a surname.

INCORRECT   At the end of the period, Mrs. Led-
             better collected the papers.
  CORRECT   At the end of the period,
             Mrs. Ledbetter collected the papers.

EXERCISE 8. Assume that the following words come at the end of a line and have to be divided. Copy each word, indicating by the use of hyphens how it might be divided.

1. ravioli	6. delicious
2. inexplicable	7. accompaniment
3. squirrel	8. happy-go-lucky
4. anti-British	9. recognize
5. approximately	10. beginning

Compound Words

Hyphens are used to join together the parts of some compound words. There are three kinds of compound words in our language: solid compounds (bookkeeper), hyphenated compounds (self-satisfied), and open compounds (disc jockey). Every year a great number of new compound words come into the language.

Most new compounds are first written as two words (*nose cone, launching pad*). Often, as they become more familiar, they begin to be written with hyphens and then as single words.

Only dictionary makers can keep track of this progression from open to solid compounds. Therefore, to be sure about the correct form, consult an up-to-date dictionary.

22j. Use a hyphen with compound numbers from *twenty-one* to *ninety-nine* and with fractions used as adjectives.

EXAMPLES   seventy-six trombones
a two-thirds majority [*Two-thirds* is an adjective modifying *majority.*]
two thirds of the boys [*Two thirds* is used as a noun.]

22k. Use a hyphen with the prefixes *ex-*, *self-*, and *all-*, with the suffix *-elect*, and with all prefixes before a proper noun or proper adjective.

EXAMPLES   self-assurance,   all-encompassing,   ex-champion, president-elect, mid-July, post-Reformation, late-Renaissance, anti-American

22l. **Hyphenate a compound adjective when it precedes the noun it modifies. Do not use a hyphen if one of the modifiers is an adverb ending in** *-ly.*

EXAMPLES   a well▪planned campaign (But: "The campaign was well planned.")
an after▪school job
a heavily laden burro

EXERCISE 9.   In the following sentences many compound words need hyphens. Find the words that should be hyphenated, and list them, correctly punctuated, after the proper number on your paper.

1. The self confidence of a scout comes from deliberately cultivated self reliance.
2. Suzy played the piece in three quarter time.
3. The mayor elect was a forty eight year old ex senator.
4. Two thirds of the vote was in favor of antitrust legislation.
5. Janet chipped a neatly hit shot directly onto the green.
6. Anti French sentiment was strong in nineteenth century England.
7. The self taught cabinetmaker finished the piece in mid July.
8. A well known ex champion is Billie Jean King.
9. Her love of Europe was all embracing: she was pro British, pro French, pro Spanish, and pro Italian.
10. A well rehearsed minuet was staged by the French Club.

DASHES

22m. **Use a dash to indicate an abrupt break in thought.**

EXAMPLES   I invited Margie━ she's the new girl in town━ to the Winter Carnival.
The dog skidded on the floor━ his nails acted like ice skates━ and crashed into the kitchen table.

22n. **Use a dash to mean** *namely, that is, in other words,* **etc., before an explanation.**

EXAMPLES The newspaper deliverer is the best we've ever
had━━she always puts the paper inside the door on
rainy days. [*that is*]

The roses looked beautiful but were expensive and
impractical━━they lasted only two days before the
petals began to fall. [*in other words,* or *that is*]

We visited three national parks━━Grand Canyon,
Yosemite, and Yellowstone. [*namely*]

► **NOTE** The dash and the colon are frequently interchangeable
in this type of construction.

In typewritten work you indicate a dash by striking the
hyphen key twice.

PARENTHESES

**22o. Use parentheses to enclose matter which is
added to a sentence but is not considered of major
importance.**

EXAMPLES Mrs. Henderson works all day long in her garden
(she is a very particular gardener) and is forever
pruning, mulching, and weeding.

Several of the speaker's stories (they were very dull)
pointed out the need for a good memory.

Put punctuation marks within the parentheses when they
belong to the parenthetical matter but outside the parentheses when they belong to the sentence as a whole.

EXAMPLES Charlie's exclamation when the gorilla came on the
screen ("Oh, look, a monkey!") amused us all.

When the king met Bolingbroke (afterwards Henry
IV), he charged him with treason.

► **NOTE** Commas, dashes, and parentheses may all be used to
enclose incidental words or phrases that interrupt the sentence
and are not considered of major importance. Commas are much
more commonly used in this way than dashes or parentheses.

EXAMPLES We fished in the muddy stream, a brown torrent
after the downpour. [a slight pause]

We fished in the muddy stream━━a waste of time!
[a stronger break in the sentence]

We fished (or should I say drowned worms?) in the muddy stream. [a strong interruption]

EXERCISE 10. Colons, dashes, and parentheses are omitted in the following sentences. To show where each mark of punctuation belongs, copy the word or number that should precede the mark, write the mark, and then write the word or number that should follow it.

1. If anybody ever asked me what I wanted to do, I'd say this I want to make the world a better place in which to live.

2. Ted has heard a great deal about the Peace Corps a fine organization from all reports and hopes to join this group.

3. The dance committee always has one big problem everybody wants to decorate, but nobody wants to clean up later.

4. Rushing to catch the 3 45 train, Betsy broke the heel on her shoe she always leaves at the last minute and didn't arrive at the meeting in Greensville until 5 07.

5. Pacing up and down, Mark Antony addressed the people of Rome "Friends, Romans, countrymen, lend me your ears."

6. Harriet has a beautiful speaking voice Mrs. Jeffers raves about it in speech class but she can't sing a note.

7. Frank had many things to do yesterday buy the tickets, rent a tuxedo, arrange transportation, and order the flowers.

8. Hank agreed to serve on the committee what a surprise! if we really needed him.

9. Many spring flowers tulips, hyacinths, daffodils, crocuses should be appearing soon.

10. We approached the dog what an ugly looking hound it was! with caution.

11. My scores in gymnastics the best results of anyone on the team are much higher than I expected.

12. I received the following gifts for my birthday two shirts, a pair of cuff links, three books, and ten dollars.

13. Doreen's parents bought her a car something I've wanted for years as a graduation present.

14. Emory is on a diet and has stopped eating candy, cake, ice cream, and potatoes.

15. If you miss the 3 05 bus after school, you can take a later one at 4 05 or 5 10.

16. I found my other gym shoe good grief, how long had it been missing? in the next locker.

17. There are many more people backstage than the average audience knows electricians, prop people, scenery movers, prompters, wardrobe assistants, and stand-ins.

18. Clearing her throat, the speaker began to quote "Ladies and gentlemen, we are here today for a serious purpose . . ."

19. Many imported products English bicycles, Italian motor scooters, Japanese cars are now available.

20. We grabbed our hats somebody had thoughtfully mixed them all up on the piano and ran out the door.

REVIEW EXERCISE B. Copy the following sentences on your paper, inserting all necessary punctuation and any necessary capital letters.

1. Last weeks edition of the Echo our school newspaper contained a review of the play

2. Every morning I wake up at six o clock every morning I hate to get out of bed

3. Yes the first bus to Midvale leaves at 10 15 but you can always catch a later one at 11 10

4. Do you asked Mother always have to do what Anne Charlotte and Carol do

5. Bowers Candy Store our gangs meeting place is always crowded however Mr. Bower wont tolerate much noise

6. If you wash the dishes Matthew Ill dry them I promised before we sat down to dinner

7. Whats the rush Steve I asked youve still got plenty of time before youre marked late

8. To tell the truth Eddies favorite flowers are roses not carnations

9. Why Gene exclaimed Mimi I havent seen you for ages where have you been

10. Right here in town he mumbled looking at the ground who wants to know

11. My cousin Harold who must be at least seventeen years old lives in Torrance California

12. The letter was dated August 15 1981 it was addressed to Cindy Melton 1163 High Street Tulsa Oklahoma

13. Scratching your head wont help you Charles said Mrs. Marshal the French teacher what you need is a little more study

14. Frightened by the sound of the explosion the dog ran under the table and all the coaxing in the world couldnt persuade him to come out

15. Students who are taking examinations in the gym must bring the following items with them pens pencils rulers and compasses

16. An article entitled Three Steps to Happiness appeared in last months Readers Digest

17. A list of those students who made the honor roll was posted in the lobby last week the list of seniors with special privileges will be posted today at 3 10

18. Give the winner a great big hand urged the master of ceremonies then he handed Rose her prize a transistor radio

19. Racing down the hall Ken was stopped by a monitor stuttering and stammering he tried to explain that he was late for class but the excuse fell on deaf ears

20. Your penmanships terrible Beth exclaimed Mr Mann who is very particular I cant tell your es from your is or your ts from your ls please rewrite your book report on Austens novel Pride and Prejudice.

REVIEW EXERCISE C. Copy the following paragraph, inserting all necessary punctuation and capital letters.

Frankly if Mrs Lawrence hadnt forgotten to collect todays compositions my average in English would have hit a new low her unnatural lapse of memory I thought was the miracle of the century for shes the type who never forgets to dot is and cross ts all during homeroom period which had been extended until 9 30 because of some special announcements I had worked on an outline but the outline was far from perfect science French and social studies came the following periods and you know that it is impossible to do homework in those classes how I regretted reading my new detective story The Strange Case of the Missing Sub last night homework forgotten I had been lost in the terror laden spine tingling story and before you could say outline rough draft and finished copy it was 12 o clock what a lucky break for me that Mrs Lawrence a strict teacher forgot to collect the themes

REVIEW EXERCISE D. Copy the following sentences, inserting capital letters and punctuation as needed.

1. Diane Johnston who is our homerooms representative to the student council read the minutes of last tuesdays meeting

2. The warm waters of the gulf stream from the south eventually meet the cold waters of the labrador current from the north and the result is that some areas of the north atlantic are covered with fog

3. The sinking of the titanic off the grand banks of newfoundland on april 15 1912 at 2 20 am has been described in Walter Lords book a night to remember

4. On my last trip to Joffones grocery store I bought several items that were on sale tomatoes pears eggs and coffee

5. Tiny belgium which has only about ten million people is bounded on the north by the netherlands and the north sea on the southwest by france and on the east by germany

6. To tell the truth I dont remember what she looked like said the witness all I can recall is that she was wearing a black persian wool coat however I do think that she had a scar on her cheek

7. The hamilton nurseries on jericho turnpike always sell the finest shrubs each plant according to the coltsville gazette is guaranteed to grow or youre given a refund

8. If alice arrives promptly at 6 30 in her new plymouth station wagon we should be at your house by 7 oclock and have plenty of time to drive to the rivoli theater to see a movie

9. In spite of last summers heat wave we thoroughly enjoyed visiting the grand canyon yellowstone national park and a hopi indian reservation

10. Having graduated from ford high school with a straight a average maria melendez who won every award in science last year thought she would find college a snap

REVIEW EXERCISE E. Copy the following, inserting all necessary punctuation and capital letters.

1. when my sister Ada got her drivers license last fall she became the fourth licensed driver in our family 2. the women in our family are I think better drivers than the men

3. Carl my older brother does a lot of thinking but he doesnt always think about what hes doing in my mothers opinion he is a daydreamer the rest of us think hes absent-minded 4. he wasnt thinking about what he was doing yesterday when he failed to stop at a stop sign and a police officer saw him the officer asked are you blind and gave him a summons 5. just my bad luck Carl complained my father a common-sense type said that passing a stop sign wasnt likely to lead to much good luck

6. Ada has been learning about winter driving one dark freezing day a thin glaze of ice formed suddenly on Mountain Avenue a very steep street 7. Ada had never driven on ice she wondered why traffic had slowed when she jammed on the brakes the car started down the hill sideways spun completely around missed a school bus by inches and bounced over the curb onto the sidewalk 8. after driving carefully down the walk she took the first cross street and headed for home as she handed Carl the car keys she exclaimed Carl stay off Mountain Avenue its covered with ice

9. my mother I believe is the best driver in the family she never speeds never gets impatient like my father and can park better than the others 10. of course she misplaces the car keys cuts corners too short and honks the horn a lot nevertheless I feel safe when shes at the wheel

Chapter 23

Manuscript Form

Standards for Written Work

A *manuscript* is any typewritten or handwritten composition, as distinguished from a printed document. More and more frequently in your school years ahead, you will be asked to hand in well-prepared manuscripts. Therefore, you should learn correct form for your written work now, and prepare all future written work accordingly.

23a. Follow accepted standards in preparing manuscripts.

Your teacher will find it easier to read and evaluate your papers if they are properly prepared. Although there is no single way to prepare a paper correctly, the rules given below are widely used and accepted. Follow them unless your teacher requests you to do otherwise.

1. Use lined composition paper or, if you type, white paper 8½ by 11 inches in size.

2. Type on only one side of a sheet of paper. Follow your school's policy about writing on both sides of composition paper.

3. Write in blue, black, or blue-black ink, or typewrite. If you type, double space the lines.

4. Leave a margin of about two inches at the top of a page and margins of about one inch at the sides and bottom. The left-hand margin must be straight; the right-hand margin should be as straight as you can make it.

5. Indent the first line of each paragraph about one-half inch from the left.

6. Write your name, the class, and the date on the first page. Follow your teacher's instructions in the placement of these items. You may put them on three separate lines in the upper right-hand corner of the sheet, or write them in one line across the top of the page. Either way, they should begin about an inch down from the top of the page.

7. If your paper has a title, write it in the center of the first line. Skip a line between the title and the first line of your composition. (Double space twice if you are typing.)

8. If the paper is more than one page in length, number the pages after the first, placing the number in the center of the line, about one-half inch down from the top.

9. Write legibly and neatly. If you are using unlined paper, try to keep the lines straight. Form your letters carefully so that your *n*'s do not look like *u*'s, *a*'s like *o*'s, and so on. Dot the *i*'s and cross the *t*'s. If you are typing, do not strike over letters or cross out words. If you have to erase, do it neatly.

23b. Learn the rules for using abbreviations.

In most of your writing, you should spell out words rather than abbreviate them. A few abbreviations, however, are commonly used.

The following abbreviations are acceptable when they are used with a name: *Mr., Mrs., Ms., Dr., Jr.,* and *Sr.* If they do not accompany a name, spell out the words instead of using abbreviations.

EXAMPLES   **Mr.** Rugelli   **Dr.** Loesster
            Mrs. Corning   John S. Wilbur, **Sr.**
            She has an appointment with the **doctor.**
            The **senior** law partner was consulted.

The abbreviations A.M. (*ante meridiem* — "before noon"), P.M. (*post meridiem* — "after noon"), A.D. (*anno Domini* — "in the year of the Lord"), and B.C. (*before Christ*) are acceptable when they are used with numbers.

EXAMPLES The *Queen Elizabeth 2* is scheduled to sail at 9:00 A.M.

Octavian (63 B.C.–A.D. 14) is now known as Augustus Caesar. [Notice that the abbreviation *A.D.* precedes the number, while *B.C.* follows it.]

Abbreviations for organizations are acceptable if they are generally known.

EXAMPLES My sister and I joined the Y.W.C.A. [or YWCA]

Thousands visit the U.N. headquarters.   [or UN]

The **FBI** cooperates closely with state police agencies. [Abbreviations for government agencies are usually written without periods.]

23c. Learn the rules for writing numbers.

Numbers of more than two words should be written in numerals, not words. If, however, you are writing several numbers, some of them one word and some of them more than one word, write them all the same way.

EXAMPLES Edith traveled **675** kilometers on her trip to Texas.

Marlene weighs **ninety-seven** pounds.

To the north we have **750** acres, to the south **340**, to the west **182**, and to the east only **47**.

A number at the beginning of a sentence should be written out.

EXAMPLE **Thirty-five hundred** pairs of terns were counted on the shore.

Write out numbers like *eleventh, forty-third,* and so on. If they are used with a month, however, it is customary to use numerals only.

EXAMPLES My brother came in **eleventh** [not *11th*] in the race.

School closes on **June 6.**   [or **the sixth of June;** not *June 6th*]

23d. Learn the rules for dividing words at the end of a line.

Sometimes you do not have room to write all of a long word at the end of a line. It may look better to start the word on the next line; however, if doing that would leave a very uneven right-hand margin, you should divide the word, using a hyphen after the first part. Learn the rules for dividing words (see pages 442–45). Remember that you should try to avoid dividing words if possible. A slightly irregular margin looks better than a word which is hyphenated.

23e. Learn the standard correction symbols.

In correcting your papers, your teacher may use some or all of the following symbols. If you memorize these symbols, you will understand at once what is wrong in your paper. What you are to do about each marked error is explained after the given meaning of the symbol. If you are not sure how to correct your error, use the index of this book to find the section that you need to review.

All errors requiring rewriting of one or more sentences should be numbered (1, 2, etc.) in the margin where the symbol occurs. Then on a separate "correction sheet" (or on the final page of your composition if there is room), you should rewrite the incorrect sentence, numbering it to correspond with the numbered symbol. Errors that do not require rewriting a whole sentence are to be corrected on the composition itself at the place where the error appears.

Correction Symbols with Instructions

ms   *error in manuscript form or neatness*
Rewrite the sentence or paragraph neatly on correction sheet.

cap   *error in use of capital letter*
Cross out the incorrect letter, and write the correct form above it.

p   *error in punctuation*
Insert punctuation, remove it, or change it as required.

sp *error in spelling*
  Cross out the word; write the correct spelling above it; write the word five times correctly spelled on your correction sheet.

frag *sentence fragment*
  Correct the fragment by changing punctuation and capital or by rewriting on correction sheet.

rs *run-on sentence*
  Correct it by inserting the necessary end mark and capital.

ss *error in sentence structure*
  Rewrite the sentence on your correction sheet.

k *awkward sentence or passage*
  Rewrite the sentence or passage on your correction sheet.

nc *not clear*
  Rewrite the sentence or sentences on your correction sheet.

ref *unclear reference of pronoun*
  Cross out the error, and write the correction above it.

gr *error in grammar*
  Cross out the error, and write the correct form above it.

w *error in word choice*
  Cross out the word, and write a better one above it.

¶ *Begin a new paragraph here.*
  This cannot be corrected but should be carefully noted.

t *error in tense*
  Cross out the error, and write the correct form above it.

∧ *You have omitted something.*
  Insert omitted words above the line.

COMPOSITION PASSAGE MARKED BY THE TEACHER

p   "All is grass, said Heracli-

tus." By this he meant that

gr

p

sp p
w

all animals and people depends
upon green plants to store up
the suns energy in forms they
can use. The sun shines on all
equally, but it's energy would be
quickly dissipated (unless) the
green leaves of plants did not
take the three inorganic materials—water, carbon dioxide,
and sunlight—and transform them

r s

into food even electricity is a
form of energy first trapped and
stored in green leaves. Coal

nc, k

is burned to make steam to drive
generators is energy stored
by the leaves of now petrified car-
boniferous plants.

COMPOSITION PASSAGE CORRECTED BY STUDENT

p

gr

p

sp p
w

"All is grass," said Heracli-
tus.⋏ By this he meant that
all animals and people depends
upon green plants to store up
the sun's energy in forms they
can use. The sun shines on all
~~equaly~~ *equally*, but it's energy would be
quickly dissipated *if* (unless) the
green leaves of plants did not

r s

take the three inorganic materials—water, carbon dioxide,
and sunlight—and transform them
into food$_\odot$ $\overset{E}{\cancel{e}}$ven electricity is a
form of energy first trapped and
stored in green leaves. Coal

nc, k

(1)

is burned to make steam to drive
generators is energy stored
by the leaves of now petrified car-
boniferous plants.

equally, equally, equally, equally,
equally

(1) The energy of coal, which is
burned to make steam to
drive generators, is energy ...

Aids to
Good English

PART SIX

Chapter 24

The Library

Arrangement of the Library; Important Reference Books

During the Renaissance, some scholars set themselves the task of mastering all knowledge. Today no one imagines that one person can know all there is to know. There is simply too much information. As a result, modern scholars are not expected to know all of the answers, but they are expected to know how to find the answers that they need.

You can find the answers to a great number of questions in a library. Books, pamphlets, and other sources of information record knowledge for you to use. To take advantage of these resources, however, you must know what your library contains and how it is arranged.

ARRANGEMENT OF BOOKS IN THE LIBRARY

24a. Learn the arrangement of books in your library.

Libraries are sufficiently alike so that when you are familiar with one library you can find your way in others.

Fiction

The fiction section contains novels and stories about imaginary people, places, and things. Here the books are arranged alphabetically according to the author's last name. Jane Austen's famous novels, for example, will come near the beginning of the section. If the library has several of her novels, they will be arranged under *Austen* alphabetically by *title.* For example, *Pride and Prejudice* will come before *Sense and Sensibility.*

Nonfiction

Since nonfiction includes so many kinds of books on so many subjects, the simple method used for arranging fiction will not do. Instead, most libraries use a system invented by an American librarian named Melvil Dewey.[1]

The Dewey decimal system classifies all nonfiction under ten major subject areas. Each of these ten classifications is assigned an identifying number which is printed on the spine of the book near the bottom.

The classifications and the numbers that stand for them are as follows:

000–099 General Works (encyclopedias, periodicals, etc.)
100–199 Philosophy (psychology, behavior, etc.)
200–299 Religion (including mythology)
300–399 Social Sciences (communication, economics, government, law, etc.)
400–499 Language (dictionaries, grammars, etc.)
500–599 Science (mathematics, chemistry, physics, etc.)
600–699 Technology (agriculture, engineering, aviation, etc.)
700–799 The Arts (sculpture, painting, music, etc.)
800–899 Literature (poetry, plays, orations, etc.)
900–999 History (geography, travel, etc.)

Within each of the ten major classifications, there are an unlimited number of subdivisions. A work of history, for example, bears a number in the 900's. Since, however, history is such a vast field and even a small library might well contain several hundred books on history, the 900's must be further broken down.

[1] Many larger libraries use a somewhat different method of classification developed by the Library of Congress. This system is not described here, but if a library in your area uses this system, the librarian will tell you how it works.

The Dewey decimal system accomplishes this by creating many subdivisions within each major class. For example, it breaks down the general class *History* in the following way:

900–999 History
   910–919 Geography, Travel
   920–929 Biography (arranged alphabetically according to the name of the person written about)
   930–939 Ancient History
   940–949 European History
   950–959 Asian History
   960–969 African History
   970–979 North American History
     971.0–971.99 Canadian History
     972.0–972.99 Mexican History
     973.0–979.99 United States History
       974.0–974.99 History of the Northeastern States
       975.0–975.99 History of the Southeastern States
       976.0–976.99 History of the South Central States
          etc.

Therefore, a book bearing the number 972 will be generally a work of history (900), specifically a work on North American history (970), and still more specifically a work on Mexican history (972). This number, called *the call number,* may include a decimal point and additional identifying numbers to indicate a smaller division of the subject, such as a particular period of history. Large libraries find it necessary to use many numbers after the decimal point, but in smaller libraries the author's initial is usually printed under the call number to distinguish the book from other works on the same subject. For example, the call number $\frac{972}{P}$ may be used to designate William Prescott's famous history, *The Conquest of Mexico;* it will appear not only on the spine of the book itself, but also on every card in the card catalogue referring to it.

Once you have learned the call number, you may either go directly to the proper shelf and pick out the book; or, if the stacks are inaccessible to the public, have the librarian get the book for you.

LOCATING INFORMATION IN THE LIBRARY

The Card Catalogue

24b. Learn the uses of the card catalogue.

In every library there is a cabinet of small drawers containing cards. These cards list every book in the library alphabetically. In the average library there are usually three cards for each book: a *title card,* an *author card,* and at least one *subject card.*

1. *The author.* On the *author card,* as you can see on page 465, the author's name appears on the top line, last name first. If you wanted a book by a particular writer, you could look it up in the card catalogue under the author's last name. All books by an author are listed on similar cards and are arranged under the author's name in alphabetical order of their *titles.* All books *about* an author (critical studies of the author's work, biographies, etc.) are listed on cards coming after the cards for the author's own books.

2. *The title.* The title of the book is printed at the top of the *title card.* Title cards are arranged alphabetically according to the first letter of the title. If this first word is an article, however—an *a, an,* or *the*—then the card is filed according to the second word of the title. Jack London's novel *The Call of the Wild* would come under the *C*'s, not the *T*'s.

3. *The subject.* The subject is printed at the top (usually in red) on the *subject card.* This kind of card is a great timesaver when you come into the library to look up information on a general topic with no particular book in mind. Subject cards direct you to whatever books in the library deal with your topic. Among the subject cards, you frequently find still other subject cards dealing with different aspects of the main topic. For example, under the subject "Languages," you may find cards labeled "Linguists," "Orthography," "Composition," as well as "see" or "see

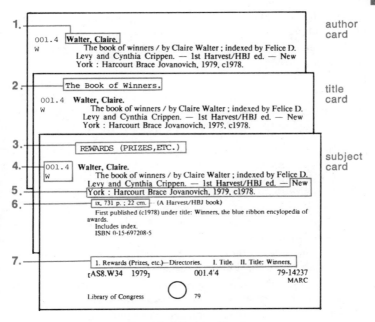

Sample Library Cards

also" cards. These "see also" cards refer you to yet another part of the catalogue for the information you are seeking. Under the topic "Ellis Island" you might find a card saying, "See United States – Immigrant Station, Ellis Island"; or under "Democracy," another card saying, "See also Politics."

4. The call number. This Dewey decimal number appears on every catalogue card referring to the book.

5. The publisher and the date of publication. This information is important to students who wish to make sure they are consulting the latest information on any subject. A book on atomic physics published in 1980 would be vastly different from one published in 1930.

6. The description of the book. Claire Walter's book, for example, has 9 pages of introductory material and 731 pages of text. It is not illustrated, nor does it have maps or

charts, for these would be noted here. Twenty-two centimeters gives the length of the book's spine.

    **7. *The subject headings in the card catalogue under which
the book is listed.***

EXERCISE 1. Remembering that books are catalogued
by title, author, and subject, answer the following questions by using the card catalogue in your library.

1. Does the library have these books?
   The Good Earth   *Jane Eyre*
   To Kill a Mockingbird   *The Complete Adventures of*
   The Swiss Family Robinson   *Sherlock Holmes*

2. Does your library have any books written by Virginia Woolf,
   Thomas Mann, Marjorie Kinnan Rawlings, and John Dos
   Passos? If it does, write the title of one book by each.

3. Give the title, author, publisher, and publication date of a
   book about Martin Luther King, Jr.

4. Does your library have any books by Margaret Mead? If
   so, give the title and call number of one of them.

5. What is the most recent book about computers in your library?
   Give the call number.

6. Find the author, title, publisher, and call number of the following books:
   a. A book about American artists
   b. A book about the American frontier
   c. A book by George Eliot
   d. A book giving information about George Eliot
   e. A book about photography

The Parts of a Book

Once the card catalogue has helped you find your book on
the shelves, and you have it in hand, a quick glance at
certain standard parts will tell you if it contains the information you seek.

24c. Learn the parts of a book.

    Not every book has all the parts described here, but all
books have some of them. They are very useful in that they

enable you to get acquainted with a book with no loss of time. Every careful reader should be familiar with them.

1. *The frontispiece.* A full page illustration usually facing the title page.

2. *The title page.* A page giving the complete title of the book, the complete name of the author (or authors), the name of the publisher, and the place of publication.

3. *The copyright page.* A page on the reverse side of the title page telling when the book was listed at the United States copyright office to protect the author's rights of ownership. The copyright page also tells by whom the book was copyrighted (sometimes the author, sometimes the publisher).

The copyright date is important when you want to know if the book's information is up-to-date. A book may be many times reprinted (each time with a new publication date) and yet be unchanged in form and content. A new copyright date, on the other hand, informs you that new material has been added. Do not confuse the copyright date with a date of reprinting. Copyrights often appear as a list of dates.

EXAMPLE   Copyright © 1982, 1977, 1969

4. *The preface, foreword,* or *introduction.* A section at the beginning of a book in which the author speaks directly to the reader. In this place the author may comment about the writing of the book, acknowledge help received from others, indicate the purpose of the book, and generally prepare the reader for what is to come.

5. *The table of contents.* A table at the beginning giving, usually, the title of chapters, their subdivisions, and the number of the page on which each begins. The table of contents gives a general view of the book. Accordingly, it enables you to determine whether the book contains the information you want without leafing through the entire book. Works of fiction usually have no table of contents.

6. *List of illustrations.* A list telling what graphic materials (maps, diagrams, charts, etc.) are provided in the book and where they are found.

7. *The appendix*. A section containing material not included in the body of the book which the author nevertheless considers relevant. The appendix may include charts, maps, lists, statistics, or even long quotations from other works on the same subject. A text on American history might include the *Declaration of Independence* and the *Constitution* in the appendix.

8. *The glossary*. A dictionary section, usually at the end of the book, in which technical or difficult words and expressions are explained.

9. *The bibliography*. A list of books, periodicals, films, and other sources which the author has consulted in preparing the text. Many books have bibliographies at the end of each chapter listing books which the author recommends. Others have a single bibliography at the end of the book.

10. *The index*. A guide to all information in the book. It lists alphabetically the topics treated in the book. It is much more detailed than the table of contents and gives the exact page on which a topic is discussed. For those in search of specific information, it is doubtless the most important part of the book other than the text itself.

11. *The end papers*. Pages pasted inside the front and back covers of the book. Maps, diagrams, charts, and illustrations are sometimes printed there. For example, the end papers of a history of California might have a map of the state.

EXERCISE 2. Write on your paper the answers to the following questions.

1. List the parts of a book of nonfiction that you would probably not find in a work of fiction.
2. Explain the importance of the copyright date.
3. Why is a glossary more useful in a book about stagecraft than in a collection of modern plays?
4. What is the difference between a table of contents and an index?
5. Would a typical novel be likely to have an index?
6. By what company was this textbook published?
7. How many pages are devoted to the main index of this book?

8. What copyright dates are given for this book?
9. How many pages are devoted to the table of contents of this book?
10. Skim the preface of this book, and briefly explain its main purpose.

The *Readers' Guide*

24d. **Learn to use the** *Readers' Guide to Periodical Literature.*

Often in writing a report or in doing an assignment for one of your other subjects, you will have occasion to use a story, article, or poem published in a magazine. To find it conveniently, you will need to use the *Readers' Guide to Periodical Literature,* an index to the contents of more than one hundred and fifty magazines. The *Readers' Guide* is published roughly twice a month — twenty-two times a year — and at regular intervals these booklets are combined into a cumulative volume.

Magazine stories are listed in the *Readers' Guide* by title and author; poems and plays are listed by author and under the headings POEMS and DRAMAS. A sample excerpt from the *Readers' Guide* is reproduced on page 470. You can probably figure out the meaning of the various abbreviations. If not, all of them are explained in the front of the *Readers' Guide* itself.

EXERCISE 3. Using the *Readers' Guide* in your school or public library, look up the answers to the following questions.

1. Choose one of the topics and look up in the *Readers' Guide* three recent articles about it. Give complete information: title and author, magazine, date, and page numbers.

France	Poetry
Horses	Football
Photography	Solar energy

2. Select one of the topics above, look it up in the *Readers'*

BEAR hunting — subject entry
Four-toed bear [black bear hunting] E. A.
Bauer. il Outdoor Life 165:114+ Mr '80
My 40 years with bears [ed by J. Rearden] C. — title of article
Williams. il Outdoor Life 165:82-5+ F '80
Yellowstone grizzly hunts foreseen. J. Weiss.
il Outdoor Life 165:44+ Mr '80
BEARAK, Harold
Sensuous sipping. il Essence 10:109+ F '80
BEARDS
Why men wear beards [opinions of black men]
il Ebony 35:94-6+ Mr '80 — title and issue of magazine
BEARNAISE sauce. See Sauces
BEARS
See also
Cooking—Game
Bear attack! [grizzlies] E. Wiseman. il por map — secondary subject heading
Outdoor Life 165:45-7+ Ja '80

Training
Though she barely survived three close mauls,
it's still love among the bruins for Ursula
Bottcher [polar bear trainer] D. M. Clayton. — description of article
il por People 13:128-9 Ap 21 '80
BEASON, S. T.
Diesel power invades the lawn. il Mech Illus
76:66+ Mr '80
BEATITUDES
Prickly pair. J. A. Tetlow. America 142:inside
back cover F 9 '80
BEATTIE, Ann — author entry
Learning to fall [story] il Ms 8:54-5+ Ja '80
BEATTIE, Bob — article by author (interview)
Bob Beattie [interview by C. Bentsen] pors
Sports 70:24+ F '80

about
Coaching or kibitzing on the Olympics, Bob
Beattie is America's indomitable snowman.
F. W. Martin. il pors People 13:86+ F 18 '80 * — article about author
BEATTIE, L. Elisabeth
What happens when you do stop the world and
try to get off? Glamour 78:100+ Mr '80
BEAUBOURG Center. See Paris—Georges Pom-
pidou Center
BEAUJOLAIS (wine) See Wine
BEAUPRE, Lee
Grosses gloss: breaking away at the box-office.
il Film Comment 16:69-73 Mr/Ap '80
BEAUTICIANS
See also
Hairstylists
BEAUTY. See Aesthetics — cross reference
BEAUTY, Personal
See also
Exercise
Hair
Hairstyling
Make-up
Manicuring
Skin — list of related entries
Ask the expert. V. Sassoon and B. Sassoon. pors
Mademoiselle 86:50 F '80 — volume number
Beautiful time of life [excerpt from Newborn
beauty: a complete guide to beauty, health and
energy for the nine months of pregnancy and
the nine months after] W. D. Gates and G.
M. Meckel. il McCalls 107:96-7+ F '80
Beauty. il N Y Times Mag p 56 Ja 20; p66 F 10; — page reference and date of issue
82 F 24; 84 Mr 23 '80

Guide, and list on your paper three articles *that you could get in your library* on the subject.

3. Choose a prominent man or woman whom you admire, and in the *Readers' Guide* look up an article about the person. Give author, title, and source.

4. Suppose you are writing an essay on the President of the United States. List three articles about him that you could get in your library and give the information from the *Readers' Guide.*

5. How many articles about motorcycles are listed in the *Readers' Guide* you are using? List three of them.

The Vertical File

24e. Learn the nature and proper use of the vertical file.

Useful information on current topics is often to be found in pamphlets — brief treatments of a subject, usually bound in paper covers. They are published by government agencies, industrial concerns, museums, colleges and universities, radio stations, welfare organizations, etc. The librarian files pamphlets in a special cabinet, usually referred to as the vertical file, and can help you to find material on your subject, especially if it is of contemporary interest.

In the vertical file the librarian also stores interesting pictures and important clippings from newspapers.

REFERENCE BOOKS IN THE LIBRARY

24f. Acquaint yourself with the reference books in your library.

In every library there is a section known as the reference section. Here the librarian keeps together those ready reference volumes which are designed to help you look up brief articles giving various kinds of information. You will find acquaintance with certain of these reference books to be very valuable.

Special Dictionaries

Belonging to the reference section of a library are various dictionaries of the English language such as those described on pages 482–84. In addition, there are many special dictionaries written to help you with specific problems of word choice, correct usage, etc. Very often a writer has some trouble thinking of the exact word with which to express a given meaning. Often, too, a writer has used the same word so many times in a composition that it is desirable to find a synonym for it to avoid repeating. The two books described below, as their titles suggest, will help you to find the right words.

Roget's Thesaurus of English Words and Phrases

The word *thesaurus* derives from a Latin word meaning "treasure," so that literally a thesaurus is a storehouse or treasury. The contents of this storehouse are synonyms and antonyms. While the thesaurus can be useful to a writer, it is also a dangerous book to use. Since the synonyms are listed without definitions or other indication of differences in meaning, it is easy to choose an inappropriate word. For example, all of the following synonyms are given for the verb *change: alter, modulate, veer, swerve,* and *deviate.* All of these synonyms have something to do with the general idea of change, but each has a specific shade of meaning that would make it unsuitable for most of the contexts in which *change* appears.

Make it a rule to use a thesaurus only as a memory aid— a reminder of words you already know. Do *not* use an unfamiliar synonym you find in a thesaurus without checking its meaning in a reliable dictionary. A strange word that you hope will sound impressive is likely to strike your reader as absurdly inappropriate.

Webster's New Dictionary of Synonyms

Much safer to use because of its detailed distinctions between synonyms, *Webster's New Dictionary of Synonyms* can be a great help to a writer in search of a word.

Encyclopedias

An encyclopedia offers informative articles on a wide range of subjects. The articles in an encyclopedia are arranged alphabetically, but many facts and references can be found only by using the index. For example, the *Encyclopedia Americana* has a long entry on the "Olympic Games," but there are a number of references to this topic elsewhere in the encyclopedia which you can find only by using the index.

The *Encyclopaedia Britannica* now has a different shape than most encyclopedias have. The first volume is an introduction to the rest of the encyclopedia, and can be used like an alphabetically ordered table of contents or index. The rest of the encyclopedia is divided into a "Macropaedia" (*makro* is from the Greek for *big*) and a "Micropaedia" (*mikro* is from the Greek for *small*). The Macropaedia has long articles and the Micropaedia has shorter articles. When you use the new *Britannica,* you can look up what you want in the first volume, and it will tell you where to look in the rest of the encyclopedia. When you are familiar with the rest of the encyclopedia, you will ordinarily look up things first in the Micropaedia, which takes up ten of the volumes. Once you have found what you are looking for in the Micropaedia, you will also find very generous cross-references to spots in the rest of the encyclopedia that deal with the same subject. This way of arranging the information in an encyclopedia is interesting; it has only been in use since 1974, but it seems to be helpful in our trying to cope with the rapidly growing, vast amounts of knowledge.

Encyclopedias are designed for quick reference. Because they give a general background in a subject, they are a good place to begin research on an unfamiliar subject. Remember, however, that encyclopedias should be the starting point, not the end, of research. Limitations of space prevent encyclopedias from treating their topics in depth. A report based entirely on encyclopedia entries is likely to be too general to be of any real merit.

Most reliable encyclopedias are kept up-to-date through frequent revisions. In addition, yearbooks are published to supply information on important developments of the preceding year.

The following encyclopedias are well known and widely used:

General Encyclopedias

Collier's Encyclopedia
> 24 volumes
> Bibliography and Index in Volume 24
> Publishes *Collier's Yearbook*

Encyclopaedia Britannica
> 30 volumes
> Cross-referencing throughout *Micropaedia*
> Publishes the *Britannica Book of the Year*

Encyclopedia Americana
> 30 volumes
> Index in Volume 30
> Publishes the *Americana Annual*

World Book Encyclopedia
> 22 volumes
> Research Guide and Index in Volume 22
> Publishes an annual supplement

Biographical Reference Books

Besides the standard encyclopedias there are many reference books which give biographies of famous persons.

Webster's Biographical Dictionary

A one-volume work with very short entries giving the basic facts of the person's life.

The New Century Cyclopedia of Names

A three-volume work, the *Century Cyclopedia* contains short biographies as well as information about all sorts of proper names: people, places, things, works of art, events, literary and mythological characters.

Current Biography

Published monthly, *Current Biography* is the best source of information about prominent people in the news. A picture of the subject usually heads the biography. The monthly pamphlets are bound together into a book each year, and a cumulative index is provided. Using these indexes, the student can often follow the career of an important person from early issues of *Current Biography*, at which time the celebrity first attracted public attention, to the latest issues of the magazine, in which later achievements are reported. A separate index covers the years 1940 through 1970. The cumulative index runs from 1971 on.

Who's Who and Who's Who in America

These volumes give important data about prominent *living* persons. *Who's Who* is a British publication dealing mainly with famous English people; *Who's Who in America* provides similar information about famous Americans. In both works the biographical entries are fairly short, giving such data as parentage, date of birth, positions held and honors received, principal achievements, names of immediate family, and present address. *Who's Who* is published annually; *Who's Who in America*, every two years.

Reference Books About Authors

Some books are devoted exclusively to literary men and women. In the "author" books by Stanley Kunitz, the biographies are headed with a picture of the subject. *The Writers Directory*, which comes out every two years, lists about 18,000 writers living today.

> *British Authors of the Nineteenth Century* by Kunitz and Haycraft
> *British Authors Before 1800* by Kunitz and Haycraft

American Authors 1600–1900 by Kunitz and Haycraft
European Authors 1000–1900 by Kunitz and Colby
The Writers Directory, St. Martin's Press, N.Y.
Contemporary Authors, and Contemporary Authors, First
  Revision

Atlases

An atlas is chiefly a collection of maps, but it may contain, as well, a wealth of statistical material about industries, raw materials, trade routes, rainfall, air and sea currents, and many other kinds of information. Any of the following are good atlases and are likely to be found on the shelves of your library.

Goode's World Atlas
Hammond Contemporary World Atlas
New York Times Atlas of the World
National Geographic Atlas of the World

Four historical atlases of particular interest to students of world history are listed below. These atlases represent graphically historical changes from earlier times, showing the rise and fall of empires, the movement of peoples, and the spread of culture.

Heyden's Atlas of the Classical World
The American Heritage Pictorial Atlas of United States History
Rand McNally Atlas of World History
Shepherd's Historical Atlas

Almanacs and Yearbooks

For factual information on the world today, the most useful of all reference books are the almanacs. Two popular ones are the World Almanac and Book of Facts and the Information Please Almanac. All are published annually and are full of information and statistics about current events — sports, industry, agriculture, science, entertainment, and census information. In addition, almanacs contain articles on significant events and issues of the past year. They also contain much historical information. Indeed, in these handy volumes you can find items as diverse, for example, as the lifetime batting average of Henry Aaron and the names of the original signers of the Magna Charta.

The Statesman's Yearbook

This fat volume is published annually and contains a compilation of statistical information about the world and its nations. Most of the information is in quantitative form (i.e., number of bales of cotton produced, balance of foreign payments, etc.), but some of the information is political, governmental, etc., and can be understood without much knowledge of economics. It begins with information about international organizations like the United Nations and the World Council of Churches, and goes on to cover individual nations and other more limited organizations.

Literature Reference Books

Bartlett's *Familiar Quotations*

Occasionally you will need to know a quotation or the author of a quotation. In such a case, the place to look is the famous Bartlett's *Familiar Quotations*.

The quotations in Bartlett's are arranged chronologically by author; that is, Emily Dickinson comes before Robert Frost. At the end of the work, there is a huge index in which every quotation is listed alphabetically by its first (and every important) word. Suppose you wished to find out who wrote

> Know then thyself, presume not God to scan;
> The proper study of mankind is man.

You would find this quotation by Alexander Pope indexed under the words *know, presume, God, scan, study, mankind,* and *man.*

Stevenson's *The Home Book of Quotations*

Used for somewhat the same purpose as Bartlett's, Stevenson's *The Home Book of Quotations* is, however, arranged differently. The quotations in this book are arranged by subjects. You can also find the author of a quotation, although, since the book is not arranged by authors, you will find the book less efficient for this purpose than Bartlett's. Stevenson's book is especially helpful if you want a quotation on a certain subject. For instance, if you want one on love or happiness or Christmas, you will find many listed under each of these topics.

Granger's *Index to Poetry*

Granger's *Index* contains no poems. It tells you in what books you can find almost any poem or recitation (popular prose passage) you wish. If you know the title of a poem or its author, yet do not know in what books you will find the poem, look it up in Granger's. There you will find a list of books in which, for example, "The Listeners" can be found. The names of these books, however, are abbreviated; and in order to make sense of them, you must consult the list of abbreviations in the front of Granger's. Suppose, for example, that you find "The Listeners" listed as appearing in BLV. A glance at the key to abbreviations tells you that BLV means the *Book of Living Verse*. Then it is a simple matter to check the card catalogue to see whether the library has the book. Granger's also indexes poems and recitations by their authors and by the first word in the line.

Stevenson's *The Home Book of Verse* and Stevenson's *The Home Book of Modern Verse*

These anthologies, containing well-known poems, are so large that you are almost certain to find the poem you wish in any one of them. They are indexed in three ways — by title, by author, and by first word. The poems themselves are collected under general headings like *Poems of Youth and Age, Poems of Nature, Familiar Verse,* and *Poems,*

Humorous and Satiric. These headings are useful to students in search of a suitable poem on certain subjects.

EXERCISE 4. You may be asked to give a brief description of the books in the following list with which your teacher thinks you should be familiar. Tell what sort of material the book contains, how the material is arranged, and how best to use the book.

Special Dictionaries
> *Roget's Thesaurus of English Words and Phrases*
> *Webster's New Dictionary of Synonyms*

Encyclopedias
> *Collier's Encyclopedia*
> *Encyclopaedia Britannica*
> *Encyclopedia Americana*
> *World Book Encyclopedia*

Biographical Reference Books
> *Webster's Biographical Dictionary*
> *The New Century Cyclopedia of Names*
> *Current Biography*
> *Who's Who*
> *Who's Who in America*

Reference Books About Authors
> *British Authors of the Nineteenth Century*
> *British Authors Before 1800*
> *European Authors 1000–1900*
> *American Authors 1600–1900*
> *Contemporary Authors*
> *Contemporary Authors: First Revision*
> *The Writers Directory*

Atlases
> *Goode's World Atlas*
> *Hammond Contemporary World Atlas*
> *New York Times Atlas of the World*
> *National Geographic Atlas of the World*

Historical Atlases
> Heyden's *Atlas of the Classical World*

> *Rand McNally Atlas of World History*
> Shepherd's *Historical Atlas*

Almanacs and Yearbooks
> *World Almanac and Book of Facts*
> *Information Please Almanac*
> *The Statesman's Yearbook*

Literature Reference Books
> Bartlett's *Familiar Quotations*
> Stevenson's *The Home Book of Quotations*
> Granger's *Index to Poetry*
> Stevenson's *The Home Book of Verse*
> Stevenson's *The Home Book of Modern Verse*

EXERCISE 5. Disregarding dictionaries and encyclopedias, decide what reference book would be the best in which to look up the following items of information. Number your paper 1–10, and after the corresponding number, write the title or titles of the reference book.

1. A profile of the modern author Ursula LeGuin
2. The population of important world cities
3. A biography of someone recently in the news
4. Facts about the president of CBS News
5. The poem "Patterns"
6. Several quotations from Eleanor Roosevelt
7. A number of quotations about loneliness
8. The title of a book containing Christina Rossetti's poem "Goblin Market"
9. Results of the 1980 census
10. A map showing the first centers of civilization in the Near East

EXERCISE 6. Follow the directions for the preceding exercise.

1. A brief biography of Ethel Kennedy
2. A list of the Presidents of the United States

3. The gross national product of France
4. Some interesting information about the poet Edith Sitwell
5. The rest of the quotation beginning "A robin redbreast in a cage . . ."
6. The author of the poem "Abraham Lincoln Walks at Midnight"
7. A biographical sketch of the twentieth-century American poet Countee Cullen
8. The name of the present governor of the state of Oklahoma
9. A record of the last five annual games in the Rose Bowl
10. The titles of several books in which the poem beginning "All I could see from where I stood . . ." can be found

EXERCISE 7. Name the reference books best suited as sources for the following information. You may include the dictionary and the encyclopedia. Be prepared to explain your choice.

1. A list of words meaning *knowledge*
2. An account of the construction of the Panama Canal
3. A very short biographical sketch of Shirley Chisholm
4. An explanation of the difference in meaning between two common words often used interchangeably—*pretty* and *beautiful*
5. A number of pictures of San Francisco
6. The years American tennis teams won the Davis Cup
7. The site in Asia Minor of ancient Troy
8. The average annual precipitation in Ghana
9. A clear explanation of Johann Kepler's laws of planetary motion
10. The principal exports of Argentina
11. A detailed map of Israel
12. A detailed map of the Holy Roman Empire in 1500
13. The meaning of the Latin phrase *carpe diem*
14. An account of the gold rush of 1849
15. The history of the environmental movement in the United States

Chapter 25

The Dictionary

Arrangement and Content of Dictionaries

A dictionary is a report on words and their uses. In a sense, a good dictionary is also a report on the civilization of the users of the language it deals with. "Languages," observed Dr. Samuel Johnson, "are the pedigrees of nations." A good dictionary gives a complete account of that pedigree. In addition to the present meaning and spelling of a word, dictionaries tell what a word has meant in the past, how it came to be a part of English, what other words it is related to, and other useful facts about its history. For those who know how to use it, a good dictionary contains a wealth of information about the history of English and attitudes of English-speaking people over the centuries.

In earlier years you learned how to find words in a dictionary by means of the alphabetical arrangement and the guide words at the top of each page. Being able to find a word is an essential dictionary skill, but it is not the only one. It is equally important to know how to interpret the information a dictionary gives you about a word. This chapter is intended to help you develop this second important skill.

KINDS OF DICTIONARIES

25a. Know the kinds of dictionaries.

Dictionaries have been prepared for many special purposes: for specialists in history, the sciences, and other special studies; for crossword puzzle enthusiasts; for poets and others with special interests. This chapter deals only with general dictionaries — those intended for the general public. There are two main kinds of general dictionaries: *unabridged* and *college* dictionaries.

The Unabridged Dictionary

An unabridged dictionary is one that is not based on a still larger dictionary. Although a large library may have several different unabridged dictionaries, the one that is best known and is most likely to be found in even the smallest library is *Webster's Third New International Dictionary,* which has been kept up-to-date through recent revisions. The newest unabridged dictionary is the *Random House Dictionary of the English Language, Unabridged Edition.*

An unabridged dictionary may contain almost a half million words. For many words, it gives uncommon or historical, but now old-fashioned, meanings. It clarifies some of the meanings of a word by quoting examples of its use by prominent writers of the past and present. It contains fuller discussions of the distinctions in meaning between words whose meanings may seem to be very similar.

To see how unabridged and college dictionaries differ, compare the two entries reproduced on page 484.

The College Dictionary

A college dictionary is a shorter work, designed for quicker and more convenient reference. Such a dictionary may contain from 125,000 to 150,000 words, as well as some special sections giving abbreviations, biographical information of famous people, articles on spelling and punctuation, and other useful information. As the sample entries reproduced on page 484 suggest, a college dictionary does not attempt to report as fully on a word as an unabridged dictionary does. On the other hand, college dictionaries are likely to be revised more frequently and consequently are often better able to give up-to-date information on the meaning and uses of words.

¹**ten·sion** \'tenchən\ *n* -s *often attrib* [MF or L; MF *tension,* fr. L *tension-, tensio,* fr. *tensus* (past part. of *tendere* to stretch) + *-ion-, -io* -ion — more at THIN] **1 a :** the act or action of stretching or the condition or degree of being stretched to stiffness **:** TAUTNESS ⟨to install the belt, slip it over the pulleys and adjust its ∼ —H.F.Blanchard & Ralph Ritchen⟩ **b :** STRESS ⟨arterial ∼⟩ ⟨muscular ∼⟩ **c :** a momentary state of muscular tautness in dance technique that inevitably resolves into relaxation **2 a :** either of two balancing forces causing or tending to cause extension **b :** the stress resulting from the elongation of an elastic body — contrasted with *compressive stress* **c** *archaic* **:** PRESSURE **3 a :** inner unrest, striving, or imbalance **:** a feeling of psychological stress often manifested by increased muscular tonus and by other physiological indicators of emotion ⟨went back to bed and dropped asleep suddenly with the release of ∼ —Mary Austin⟩ ⟨∼s distort personality —Bruce Bliven b. 1889⟩ **b :** a state of latent hostility or opposition between individuals or groups (as classes, races, nations) ⟨there is bitter ∼ between them —Bernard De Voto⟩ ⟨a lessening of minority-group ∼s —J.A.Morris b. 1904⟩ ⟨mob insanity explodes when ∼ reaches the flash point —*New Republic*⟩ **c :** a balance maintained in an artistic work (as a poem, painting, musical composition) between opposing forces or elements **:** a controlled dramatic or dynamic quality ⟨the ∼ which makes his sonata . . . so compelling —Stephen Spender⟩ ⟨the poetry of Dryden and Pope is characterized by the ∼ between its constituent elements —F.W.Bateson⟩ **4 :** ELECTRIC POTENTIAL **5 :** any of various devices in textile manufacturing machines or sewing machines that are used to control the tautness and movement of thread or material passing through **syn** see BALANCE, STRESS

From *Webster's Third New International Dictionary* © 1976 by G. & C. Merriam Co., Publishers of the Merriam-Webster Dictionaries. Used by permission.

¹**ten·sion** \'ten-chən\ *n* [MF or L; MF, fr. L *tension-, tensio,* fr. *tensus,* pp.] **1 a :** the act or action of stretching or the condition or degree of being stretched to stiffness **:** TAUTNESS **b :** STRESS 1b **2 a :** either of two balancing forces causing or tending to cause extension **b :** the stress resulting from the elongation of an elastic body **c** *archaic* **:** PRESSURE **3 a :** inner striving, unrest, or imbalance often with physiological indication of emotion **b :** a state of latent hostility or opposition between individuals or groups **c :** a balance maintained in an artistic work between opposing forces or elements **4 :** electrical potential **5 :** a device to produce a desired tension (as in a loom) — **ten·sion·al** \'tench-nəl, -ən- l\ *adj* — **ten·sion·less** \'ten-chən-ləs\ *adj*

From *Webster's New Collegiate Dictionary* © 1980 by G. & C. Merriam Co., Publishers of the Merriam-Webster Dictionaries. Used by permission.

Since all dictionaries must pack a great deal of information into relatively little space, they make extensive use of abbreviations, special signs and symbols, and other shortcuts. These space-saving devices are always explained in the front part of a dictionary and are usually easy enough to understand. However, each dictionary has its own system of abbreviations and symbols, and you cannot always assume that you know what one of them means because you once looked it up in a different book.

EXERCISE 1. Open to the table of contents at the front of your own dictionary. Notice where to find the introductory notes, the beginning of the definitions, and the special tables, charts, and illustrations. Then on your paper, write down the page numbers on which each of the following items of information can be found.

1. An explanation of the way syllables are divided in the dictionary entries
2. The meaning of the abbreviation *SALT*
3. The pooulation of Tampa
4. The capital of Uruguay
5. The dates (birth and death) of Jane Addams
6. An explanation of the metric system
7. The meaning of the abbreviations *n., adv., v.t.,* and *v.i.*
8. The meaning of the word *slalom*
9. A guide to capitalization
10. An explanation of the treatment of prefixes

KINDS OF INFORMATION IN DICTIONARIES

25b. Become familiar with the kinds of information in your dictionary and the method by which the information is presented.

As you study the following kinds of information that dictionaries contain, examine the sample column from a college dictionary on page 487.

Spelling

The bold-faced word at the beginning of a dictionary entry gives you the spelling. If there are two or more accepted spellings for a word, the various spellings are given. If one spelling is more common than another, the common one is given first. When in doubt, you will always be safe in using the first spelling given.

EXAMPLES   judgment, judgement   theater, theatre

If some grammatical change in the form of a word is

likely to create a spelling problem, this form is given. For example, a dictionary gives the plural of a word if the plural is formed irregularly—*hero, heroes;* it gives the present and past participle forms of *refer,* showing that the final *r* is doubled—*referring, referred;* it gives the comparative form of *funny,* with the *y* changed to *i*—*funnier.*

Capital Letters

Proper nouns and proper adjectives are given with capital letters in college dictionaries. If a word is capitalized in certain meanings only, a dictionary labels these meanings *cap.*

EXAMPLE

pres·i·dent (prĕz′ə-dənt, -dĕnt′) *n. Abbr.* **p., P., pres., Pres.**
1. One appointed or elected to preside over an organized body of people, as an assembly or meeting. **2.** *Often capital* **P.** The chief executive of a republic, especially of the United States. **3.** The chief officer of a branch of government, a corporation, a board of trustees, a university, or any similar body. [Middle English, from Old French, from Latin *praesidens,* present participle of *praesidēre,* PRESIDE.] —**pres′i·dent·ship′** *n.*

© 1980 by Houghton Mifflin Company. Reprinted by permission from *The American Heritage Dictionary of the English Language.*

Division of Words into Syllables

When it is necessary to divide a word at the end of a line, the word should be divided between syllables. Most dictionaries indicate a break between syllables with a centered dot (el•e•va•tor). Syllable division is indicated in the boldfaced entry word.

Pronunciation

Dictionaries indicate the pronunciation of words by means of accent marks and respellings which show clearly how the words should sound. The respellings are necessary because our alphabet uses more than two hundred combinations of letters to represent the forty-two or -three sounds of English. Each letter or special symbol used in the respellings always stands for the same sound. The sounds represented by the

in·fec·tive (in fek′tiv) *adj.* [ME. *infectif* < OFr. < L. *infectivus*] likely to cause infection; infectious — main entry

in·fe·cund (in fē′kənd, -fek′ənd) *adj.* [ME. *infecunde* < L. *infecundus*] not fecund; not fertile; barren —**in·fe·cun·di·ty** (in′fi kun′də tē) *n.* — pronunciation respelling

in·fe·lic·i·tous (in′fə lis′ə təs) *adj.* not felicitous; unfortunate or unsuitable —**in′fe·lic′i·tous·ly** *adv.*

in·fe·lic·i·ty (-tē) *n.* [L. *infelicitas* < *infelix*, unfortunate: see IN-² & FELICITY] **1.** the quality or condition of being infelicitous **2.** *pl.* **-ties** something infelicitous; unsuitable or inapt remark, action, etc. — part of speech, spelling of verb forms

in·fer (in fur′) *vt.* **-ferred′, -fer′ring** [L. *inferre*, to bring or carry in, infer < *in-*, in + *ferre*, to carry, BEAR¹] **1.** orig., to bring on or about; cause; induce **2.** to conclude or decide from something known or assumed; derive by reasoning; draw as a conclusion **3.** *a)* to lead to as a conclusion; indicate *b)* to indicate indirectly; imply: in this sense, still sometimes regarded as a loose usage —*vi.* to draw inferences —**in·fer′a·ble** *adj.* —**in·fer′a·bly** *adv.* —**in·fer′rer** *n.* — numbered definitions

SYN.—**infer** suggests the arriving at a decision or opinion by reasoning from known facts or evidence [from your smile, I *infer* that you're pleased]; **deduce**, in strict discrimination, implies inference from a general principle by logical reasoning [the method was *deduced* from earlier experiments]; **conclude** strictly implies an inference that is the final logical result in a process of reasoning [I must, therefore, *conclude* that you are wrong]; **judge** stresses the careful checking and weighing of premises, etc. in arriving at a conclusion; **gather** is an informal substitute for **infer** or **conclude** [I *gather* that you don't care] — synonyms with illustrative examples of usage and meaning

in·fer·ence (in′fər əns) *n.* [ML. *inferentia*] **1.** the act or process of inferring; specif., the deriving of a conclusion in logic by either induction or deduction **2.** something inferred; specif., a conclusion arrived at in logic

in·fer·en·tial (in′fə ren′shəl) *adj.* [< ML. *inferentia* + -AL] based on or having to do with inference —**in′fer·en′tial·ly** *adv.*

in·fe·ri·or (in fir′ē ər) *adj.* [ME. < L., compar. of *inferus*, low, below < IE. **ṇdheros*, whence UNDER] **1.** lower in space; placed lower down **2.** low or lower in order, status, rank, etc.; subordinate **3.** lower in quality or value than (with *to*) **4.** poor in quality; below average **5.** *Anat.* located below or directed downward **6.** *Astron.* between the earth and the sun [Mercury and Venus are *inferior* planets] **7.** *Bot.* having the sepals, petals, and stamens attached at the apex: said of the ovary of an epigynous flower **8.** *Printing* placed below the type line, as 2 in NO₂ —*n.* an inferior person or thing —**in·fe′ri·or′i·ty** (-ôr′ə tē, -är′-) *n.* — etymology, restrictive label, illustrative example

inferiority complex 1. *Psychol.* a neurotic condition resulting from various feelings of inferiority, such as derive from real or imagined physical or social inadequacy and often manifested through overcompensation in excessive aggressiveness, a domineering attitude, etc. **2.** popularly, any feeling of inferiority, inadequacy, etc.: *cf.* SUPERIORITY COMPLEX — cross reference

in·fer·nal (in fur′n′l) *adj.* [ME. < OFr. < LL. *infernalis* < L. *infernus*, underground, lower, infernal < *inferus*: see INFERIOR] **1.** *a)* of the ancient mythological world of the dead *b)* of hell **2.** hellish; diabolical; fiendish; inhuman **3.** [Colloq.] hateful; outrageous —**in·fer′nal·ly** *adv.* — usage label, derived form with label

infernal machine *earlier name for* a booby trap or time bomb

in·fer·no (in fur′nō) *n., pl.* **-nos** [It. < L. *infernus:* see INFERNAL] hell or any place suggesting hell, usually characterized by great heat or flames —[I-] that section of Dante's *Divine Comedy* which describes hell and the sufferings of the damned various letters and other symbols in the respelling are shown in a key that usually appears at the front of the dictionary and at the bottom of every pair of facing pages. Since different dictionaries use different systems of indicating pronunciation, it is essential that you familiarize yourself with the key and notes on pronunciation in your own dictionary. The more detailed presentation of pronunciation which begins on page 494 of this book shows several different systems in wide use.

Part of Speech

After each word listed in the dictionary, an abbreviation tells what part of speech the word is.

noun	*n.*	adjective	*adj.*
verb	*v.*	preposition	*prep.*
adverb	*adv.*	conjunction	*conj.*
pronoun	*pron.*	interjection	*interj.*

Since many words may be used as more than one part of speech, some entries will contain several part-of-speech labels. In the sample column on page 487, for example, the first eight definitions for *inferior* are labeled *adj.* (for *adjective*) and the last one is labeled *n.* (for *noun*). Verbs have, in addition to the label *v.*, the labels *v.i.* and *v.t.* (See the entry for *infer* on page 487.) The label *v.i.* stands for "intransitive verb," and *v.t.* stands for "transitive verb."

Meaning

The principal function of a dictionary is to give the meaning of words. Since a single word may have many different meanings, many dictionary entries contain a number of different definitions, which are distinguished from one another by means of letters and numbers. Numbers usually indicate important differences in meaning, and letters indicate differences within the numbered definitions.

In some dictionaries, these separate meanings are listed in historical order—the earliest recorded meaning first, the latest last. Other dictionaries give meanings in order of the frequency of their use — from the most common meaning to the least common. The following definitions illustrate these two methods of ordering meanings. The first is in historical order, and the second in order of use.

hec·tic \'hek-tik\ *adj* [ME *etyk,* fr. MF *etique,* fr. LL *hecticus,* fr. Gk *hektikos* habitual, consumptive, fr. *echein* to have — more at SCHEME] **1** : of, relating to, or being a fluctuating but persistent fever (as in tuberculosis) **2** : having a hectic fever **3** : RED, FLUSHED **4** : filled with excitement or confusion <the ~ days before Christmas> — **hec·ti·cal·ly** \-ti-k(ə-)lē\ *adv*

From *Webster's New Collegiate Dictionary* © 1980 by G. & C. Merriam Co., Publishers of the Merriam-Webster Dictionaries. Used by permission.

hec·tic (hek′tik), *adj.* **1.** characterized by intense agitation, feverish excitement, confused and rapid movement, etc.: *The period preceding the trip was hectic and exhausting.* **2.** marking a particular habit or condition of body, as the fever of phthisis (**hec′tic fe′ver**) when this is attended by flushed cheeks (**hec′tic flush′**), hot skin, and emaciation. **3.** pertaining to or affected with such fever; consumptive. —*n.* **4.** a hectic fever. **5.** a hectic flush. **6.** a consumptive person. [< LL *hectic(us)* < Gk *hektikós* habitual, equiv. to *hekt-* (s. of *hēxis*) state, condition + *-ikos* -IC; r. ME *etyk* < MF] —**hec′ti·cal·ly**, **hec′tic·ly**, *adv.* —**hec′tic·ness**, *n.*

From the unabridged *Random House Dictionary of the English Language.* Copyright © 1966, 1967, 1969, 1970, 1971 by Random House, Inc. Reprinted by permission.

Derivation

Most dictionaries indicate the history of a word. They show by means of abbreviations what language the word originally came from and what its original meaning was. English is unusual among languages for the vast number of words it has taken from other languages. The source of newly coined words is also given. Knowing the source and original meaning of a word is often a great help to you in understanding the word's present meaning and correct use.

The abbreviations used to indicate the languages from which words derive are explained in front of your dictionary under the heading "Abbreviations Used in This Book" or another heading of essentially the same meaning. The derivation of *curfew* is given as follows in *Webster's New World Dictionary:*

cur·few (kur′fyo͞o) *n.* [ME. *curfeu* < OFr. *covrefeu,* lit., cover fire < *covrir* (see COVER) + *feu,* fire < L. *focus,* fireplace (see FOCUS)]

From Webster's *New World Dictionary of the American Language,* Second College Edition. Copyright © 1980 by Simon & Schuster. Reprinted by permission of Simon & Schuster, a Division of Gulf and Western Corporation.

The symbol < means "from" (abbreviated *fr.* in some dictionaries). If written out, this etymology would read "derived from Middle English *curfeu* from Old French *covrefeu,* literally "cover fire," from *covrir* (see COVER) + *feu,* "fire," from Latin *focus,* "fireplace" (see FOCUS).

Restrictive Labels

Most of the words defined in a dictionary belong to the general vocabulary of standard English. Some words, as well as some special meanings of otherwise standard words, require special treatment, and these usually appear with a label. There are three main kinds of labels: *subject* labels, which specify that a word has a particular meaning in a certain field: *Law, Med., Aeron.* (Aeronautics), etc.; *geographical* labels, which indicate the area in which a particular word, meaning, or pronunciation is principally used: *Brit., SW U.S.* (Southwest U.S.); and *usage* labels, which characterize a word as to its kind of usage: *informal, slang, nonstandard,* etc. As the following examples show, however, different dictionaries may not agree about giving a usage label:

> **glitch** \'glich\ *n* [prob. fr. G *glitschen* to slide, slip; akin to OHG *glitan* to glide — more at GLIDE] **1 a** : an unwanted brief surge of electric power   **b** : a false or spurious electronic signal   **2** : MALFUNCTION <a ~ in a spacecraft's fuel cell> **3** : MISHAP; *also* : a minor technical problem

From *Webster's New Collegiate Dictionary* © 1980 by G. & C. Merriam Co., Publishers of the Merriam-Webster Dictionaries. Used by permission.

> **glitch** (glich) *n.* [< G. colloq. *glitsche,* a slip < *glitschen,* to slip, slide, intens. of G. *gleiten:* see GLIDE] [Slang] a mishap, error, malfunctioning, etc.

From *Webster's New World Dictionary of the American Language,* Second College Edition. Copyright © 1980 by Simon & Schuster. Reprinted by permission of Simon & Schuster, a Division of Gulf & Western Corporation.

Usage labels provide a good general guide to usage, but all writers should learn to make their own judgments. Assigning a label such as *slang* or *informal* is necessarily a subjective judgment on the part of the definer, and not all dictionaries agree about labeling the same word. (For instance, the first example has no label.)

Synonyms and Antonyms

For some entries in the dictionary, synonyms or antonyms, • or both, are given. A synonym is a word having nearly the same meaning as the word being defined: *brave — courageous.* An antonym is a word having the opposite meaning: *brave — cowardly.* See the entry for *infer* on page 487.

Illustrations

If the meaning of a word can best be shown by a picture, the dictionary may give an illustration. While you, of course, cannot depend on finding a picture of the thing you may be looking up, there is a chance that you might find one, especially if the object cannot be easily described.

OTHER INFORMATION IN THE DICTIONARY

Biographical Entries

Who was Clara Barton? When did Pablo Casals die? What was Chopin's nationality? What were the dates of Queen Elizabeth I's reign? For what is Thurgood Marshall famous? What was George Eliot's real name? How do you pronounce Persephone? The answers to such simple fact questions about famous persons can probably be found in your dictionary.

Some dictionaries devote a special section called *Biographical Names* to famous persons. Others give names of persons and places in a section called *Proper Names.* Sometimes these names are included in the body of the book. You can easily discover which method your dictionary uses.

The following common pieces of biographical information are usually given in a dictionary:

1. *Name:* spelling, pronunciation, first name
2. *Dates:* of birth and death and of reign if a king or queen, or term of office if head of a government
3. *Nationality*

4. Why famous

The following is a typical dictionary entry for a famous name.

King (kiṅg), *n.* **1. Ernest Joseph,** 1878–1956, U.S. naval officer. **2. Martin Luther,** 1929–68, U.S. Baptist minister: civil-rights leader; Nobel peace prize 1964. **3. Rufus,** 1755–1827, U.S. political leader and statesman. **4. William Lyon Mackenzie,** 1874–1950, Canadian statesman: prime minister 1921–26, 1926–30, 1935–48. **5. William Rufus De·Vane** (də vān′), 1786–1853, vice-president of the U.S. 1853.

From the unabridged *Random House Dictionary of the English Language.* Copyright © 1966, 1967, 1969, 1970, 1971 by Random House, Inc. Reprinted by permission.

Mythological and Biblical characters, as well as some literary characters, are often listed in the body of the dictionary: *Ruth, Lancelot, Naomi, Juno,* etc.

Geographical Entries

Like the biographical entries in the dictionary, the geographical entries are sometimes given in the body of the book and sometimes in a special section. This section may be called a gazetteer – a geographical dictionary.

In general the following information is given about a place:

1. Name: spelling, pronunciation

2. Location

3. Identification: whether a city, country, lake, mountain, river, etc.

4. Size: population, if a city or country (often given in thousands – 225 = 225,000); area in square miles, if a country or territory or body of water; length, if a river; height, if a mountain, etc.

5. Importance: If a city is the capital of a state or country, this will be indicated by a star or an asterisk. The capital city of a country or state will also be given under the name of the country or state.

6. Historical or other interesting information of importance: Thus for Hampton Roads, Virginia . . . "battle of *Merrimack* and *Monitor,* March 9, 1862." For Lake Mead, formed by Hoover Dam in the Colorado River,

one dictionary says "the largest artificial lake in the world."
  7. *Governed or controlled by what country:* For Guam,
the dictionary says "belonging to the U.S."

Miscellaneous Information

Most good dictionaries include the following kinds of information, either in separate sections or in the body of the dictionary itself:
  1. *Foreign words and phrases:* spelling, pronunciation, meaning
  2. *Abbreviations:* a list of abbreviations of all kinds, giving the words in full

An unabridged dictionary and some of the larger student dictionaries include
  3. *Signs and symbols:* Not all dictionaries include a section of this kind, but some do, and if yours does, you should study the section to familiarize yourself with its content.
  4. *Spelling rules*
  5. *Punctuation rules*
  6. *New words*

REVIEW EXERCISE A. When your teacher gives the signal, look up the answers to the following questions in the dictionary you have. Write the answers on your paper. Accuracy is more important than speed, but speed *is* important.

1. Who was Ann Lee and for what is she famous?
2. When did Sir Francis Bacon live?
3. Give the meaning of the abbreviation UNESCO.
4. Copy the pronunciation of *de facto* and *de jure,* and distinguish between the meaning of these two Latin phrases.
5. Who was Julia Howe?
6. What is the derivation of *hippopotamus?*
7. What is the height of Mont Blanc and where is it?
8. What is the area of Lake Erie?
9. What is the capital of Mali?

10. Where is the island group called the Hebrides and to what country does it belong?

REVIEW EXERCISE B. Look up in your dictionary the answers to the following questions.

1. Give the pronunciation and meaning of *dolce far niente*.
2. Who was Eurydice?
3. Give the more usual pronunciation of *apparatus*.
4. Of what country is Kabul the capital?
5. What is the population of Copenhagen?
6. What is the length of the Rhine River?
7. What is the derivation of *Gypsy?*
8. What country governs the Falkland Islands?
9. Who was Mrs. Malaprop? For what is she famous?
10. What is the meaning of the abbreviation CIF?

PRONUNCIATION

25c. Use your dictionary for pronunciation.

You learn the pronunciation of most words from your parents, your teachers, and the other people you talk with. Ordinarily, you consult a dictionary only for the pronunciation of words that you encounter in books but do not hear in normal conversation.

Dictionary makers try to provide a suitable pronunciation for every word, but since the same word may be pronounced quite differently in various parts of the country, this task is not always easy. The sound represented by the *a* in *water* is pronounced one way in Boston, another way in New York, and in still other ways in Richmond, Chicago, and Portland. There is no one correct way of making that sound — each different version of the vowel *a* is the right one for that area. For this reason, you may sometimes find that your dictionary tells you one thing about the sound of a word and that you hear it spoken quite differently in your part of the country. In such a case, ask your teacher about the acceptable pronunciation of the word in your area. Do not assume that the pronunciation you hear is wrong just because you cannot find it in the dictionary.

Because the actual spelling of many English words does not clearly indicate how they are pronounced, dictionaries use simplified respellings to indicate the sound of a word. Moreover, since there are more sounds in English than there are letters to represent them, special symbols called *diacritical marks* must be used to show different speech sounds represented by the same letter. The following pair of words illustrates both respelling and the use of diacritical marks:

knit (nit)   knife (nīf)

Notice that in both respellings the silent letters are dropped—both silent *k*'s and the *e*. Notice also that the different sounds of the *i*'s are distinguished. The *i* in *knit* is unmarked, and the *i* in *knife* is written with a straight line above it.

Indicating pronunciation is one of the dictionary maker's most difficult tasks, and it is not surprising that there is some disagreement as to how it should be done. The systems used in various dictionaries differ in a number of details. You will see some of these differences in this chapter. However, when you have need of a pronunciation, you will not need to know all the different ways of indicating it. What you will need to know is how to interpret the pronunciation given in your own dictionary. To do this, you must familiarize yourself with the explanatory notes dealing with pronunciation and with the pronunciation key. Most dictionaries explain in the introductory pages the system they use. A full key is usually given inside the front cover. Many dictionaries print a shorter key on each page or each set of facing pages. The key illustrates the use of each letter and symbol used, by means of simple examples that everyone knows how to pronounce.

Consonant Sounds

The sounds that a speaker makes by squeezing or cutting

off the stream of breath are called *consonants*. The last sounds in *with, this,* and *itch* are made by forcing the breath through a narrowed passage at one point or another between the throat and the lips. The last sounds in *first, wasp,* and *break* are made by cutting off the breath momentarily.

Consonants present few problems in representing pronunciation because most of them are pronounced in essentially the same way in all words. In some cases, ordinary English spelling uses one letter for two different consonant sounds. For example, the letter *c* stands for two quite different sounds in *cake* and *cell*. In giving the pronunciation of these words, the dictionary would spell the first with a *k* and the second with an *s*.

Two closely related sounds, the sound of the *th* in *thin* and its sound in *then*, are distinguished in different ways in different dictionaries. For example:

	WNC	RHC[1]
thin	\thin\	(thin)
then	\then\	(then)

Vowel Sounds

The sounds that a speaker makes when not squeezing or stopping the flow of breath are called *vowels*. Although we use five letters (*a, e, i, o, u*) and sometimes a sixth (*y*) in representing vowel sounds in writing, there are actually nine different vowels that are used by most speakers of English in America. To indicate these sounds, dictionary makers use the letters above in combination with diacritical marks.

Long Vowels

The long straight mark over a vowel is called the macron. When the macron appears over a vowel, the vowel is said to have the sound of its own name. Such vowels are called *long vowels*.

[1] The abbreviations stand for *Webster's New Collegiate Dictionary* and *The Random House College Dictionary*, respectively.

EXAMPLES late (lāt)
          sheep (shēp)
          tide (tīd)
          bone (bōn)
          cube (kūb)[1]

Short Vowels

The vowels in the words *hat, bed, pig, odd,* and *up* are called *short vowels*. There are two common methods of showing the sound of short vowels. One uses this symbol (˘), the breve, over the vowel; the other method leaves the short vowels unmarked:

EXAMPLES **add** (ăd) or (ad)
          end (ĕnd) or (end)

Other Vowel Sounds

The remaining vowel sounds, which cannot be classified either as long or short, are represented by the letter and one of several other diacritical marks:

KEY WORD	WNC	RHC
order	ȯ	ô
urge	ǝ	û
took	u̇	o͝o
pool	ü	o͞o

In addition, a number of sounds usually considered to be a single unit are in fact combinations of two other vowel sounds. Such combinations are usually represented by two letters:

KEY WORD	WNC	RHC
oil	oi	oi
house	au̇	ou

The Schwa

Modern dictionaries use an *e* printed upside down (ǝ) to represent the indistinct sound of vowels in unaccented

---

[1] The long *u* sound is also represented by *yo͞o* or *yü:* kyo͞ob, kyüb.

syllables. This symbol, called the *schwa* (shwa), is used in such words as the following:

against	(ə·genst′)
banal	(bā′nəl)
correct	(kə·rekt′)

Some dictionaries make more use of the schwa than others. Those that do, use this symbol for the same sound when it appears in accented as well as in unaccented syllables:

bun	(bən)
serpent	(sər′pənt)

EXERCISE 2. Look up the pronunciation of each of the following words. On your paper, copy the word after the proper number, enclosing the respelling in parentheses.

1. consummate	6. irrevocable
2. cultural	7. Themistocles
3. genuine	8. thistle
4. hog	9. those
5. hypothetical	10. Worcester

Accent

In words of more than one syllable, one syllable is pronounced louder than the other or others. The syllable stressed in this way is said to be *accented* and is marked with an *accent mark*. Dictionaries mark accents in two main ways: with a heavy accent mark (′) after the accented syllable or with a mark (ˈ) before the syllable.

KEY WORD	WNC	RHC
compete	kəm-ˈpēt	kəm·pēt′
pony	ˈpō-nē	po′nē

Some longer words have two accented syllables — one receiving a heavy, or primary, stress and the other receiving a light, or secondary, stress. The following example illustrates ways of showing this difference in accent:

KEY WORD	WNC	RHC
elevator	ˈel-ə-ˌvāt-ər	elˈə·vāˈtər

Sometimes the same word may be accented in different ways, depending upon how the word is used. The listed words are examples of how the accent shifts when the words are used as different parts of speech.

com'pact (noun)	com·pact' (adjective)
con'duct (noun)	con·duct' (verb)
con'tent (noun)	con·tent' (adjective)
pro'test (noun)	pro·test' (verb)

EXERCISE 3. Rewrite each italicized word, showing the accented syllables and the part of speech as given in your dictionary.

EXAMPLE   1. I *refuse* to carry out the *refuse.*
            1. (*re fuse'*) *v.,* (*ref'use*) *n.*

1. One cannot *object* to the *object* of trial by jury: to allow the guilt of an accused person to be judged by peers.
2. The new track *record* was duly *recorded* in the book.
3. The Stamp Act caused the colonists to *rebel;* still, few of them yet considered themselves *rebels* against duly constituted authority.
4. Jeeves, *conduct* this gentleman to the door. His *conduct* has been intolerable.
5. To *console* her invalid sister, Victoria bought her a huge mahogany *console,* housing both a TV and a record player.
6. The less-developed countries have often arranged to *import* consumer products from the major powers. The *import* of these products has been undertaken to raise the standard of living in smaller nations.
7. Of all my *subjects* I dislike algebra most. My total lack of comprehension *subjects* me to much ridicule in that class.
8. Although the police did not *suspect* him, the thief sensed that to Sherlock Holmes he was already a *suspect.*
9. Intense cold caused the plastic parts to *contract,* cracking many of them. A new *contract,* therefore, had to be negotiated with the supplier for better plastic.

10. The queen's *consort* was known to *consort* openly with enemies of the crown.

EXERCISE 4. Using the pronunciation key in the front part of your dictionary, write the vowel markings above the vowels in the following common words. Place accent marks in the words of more than one syllable. The final silent *e*, of course, should not be marked.

1.	prod	11.	far
2.	old	12.	fur nish
3.	tame	13.	re make
4.	like	14.	pro tect
5.	rib	15.	rob in
6.	eve	16.	com ment
7.	lend	17.	loop hole
8.	boil	18.	cook ing
9.	us	19.	un til
10.	mood	20.	out cast

EXERCISE 5. Using the pronunciation key inside the front cover of your dictionary, respell the following words according to the system used by your dictionary. Make use of accent marks, diacritical markings, and divisions between syllables. When you have finished, check your work against the word as it actually appears in the dictionary.

1.	beautiful	6.	unnecessary
2.	Chicago	7.	apparatus
3.	conduit	8.	sough
4.	bathe	9.	sought
5.	llama	10.	rough

Chapter 26

Vocabulary

Learning and Using New Words ·

More and more these days, tests of one kind or another play an increasingly important role in our lives. They are used to measure success in school and often to decide who is accepted into a particular college or kind of job. These tests differ, but most of them place great importance upon vocabulary. To prepare for these tests, you will find it well worthwhile to take stock of your vocabulary right now and to consider ways of improving it.

The best way to increase your vocabulary is to read widely and thoughtfully. There is no other way of doing the job successfully. There are, however, ways in which to add to your vocabulary more of the new words you encounter than you may be adding now. This chapter will give you experience in using these techniques of word study.

Before you begin the chapter, take the following test to get a rough idea of how good your vocabulary is right now. Sixteen correct answers is about average for students of your age. Can you do better?

Diagnostic Test

Number your paper 1–25. After the proper number, write the letter of the word which is nearest in meaning to the italicized word at the left. Do not try to guess the correct answer.

1. *affluent*	a. verbose	b. wealthy	c. friendly
2. *assuage*	a. relieve	b. rub	c. make brighter
3. *brevity*	a. position	b. goodness	c. shortness
4. *circumvent*	a. evade	b. surround	c. open
5. *denizen*	a. lair	b. inhabitant	c. bear
6. *explicit*	a. proud	b. apologetic	c. definite
7. *flay*	a. arrange in line	b. cast a rod	c. strip off skin
8. *gregarious*	a. sickly	b. sociable	c. cheerful
9. *hierarchy*	a. system of ranks	b. sound of music	c. ancient manners
10. *indolent*	a. unrefined	b. sorrowful	c. lazy
11. *jeopardize*	a. risk	b. assist	c. stripe
12. *lucrative*	a. profitable	b. bright	c. creative
13. *miscreant*	a. sneak	b. hobo	c. villain
14. *nebulous*	a. indistinct	b. difficult	c. villainous
15. *onerous*	a. rich	b. burdensome	c. poor
16. *plebeian*	a. aristocratic	b. common	c. military
17. *preclude*	a. prevent	b. preview	c. prevail
18. *quaff*	a. guffaw	b. drink	c. tremble
19. *repugnance*	a. dislike	b. insolence	c. desire
20. *sinecure*	a. easy job	b. hard job	c. technical job
21. *subjugate*	a. sublet	b. submit	c. subdue
22. *turgid*	a. cloudy	b. unusual	c. swollen
23. *vacillate*	a. waver	b. impart	c. empty
24. *wreak*	a. destroy	b. inflict	c. stretch
25. *zenith*	a. heavenly body	b. highest point	c. tower

WAYS TO LEARN NEW WORDS

You have learned some of the words you know by looking them up in the dictionary, but the number of words you can learn this way is usually quite limited. Most of the words that you have in your vocabulary have come to you in other ways. You are constantly meeting new expressions in the course of your schoolwork and your conversations, but you will never be able to make them a part of your own word list unless you become *word conscious*. Keep on the alert for new words, and when you meet them you will be able to add them to your collection.

26a. List new words with their meanings in your notebook, and use them in your speech and writing.

Set aside a special part of your notebook for new words. Write down every new word that you find, together with its meaning. Thereafter, try to use it in speech and writing as often as you can in order to make it a permanent part of your vocabulary. Begin now. Enter every word you missed on the Diagnostic Test, and to these add the new words you learn from day to day.

Context

26b. Learn new words from their contexts.

If your teacher asks you what *cumulative* or *exotic* means, or if your younger brother looks up from a book and asks if you know what *grotesque* means, you won't be able to answer their questions unless the words are already in your vocabulary. However, most of the words you encounter will not be isolated; instead, you will find them surrounded by other words and used in specific situations that will help you guess their meaning. The total situation in which a word is found is called its *context*. The *verbal context* refers to the other words in the sentence or phrase, and the *physical context* refers to the circumstances in which the word is used.

By paying careful attention to the context of a word, you can probably make an accurate guess about its meaning.

Verbal Context

The words accompanying the new word usually provide plenty of "context clues" to its meaning. For example:

> Bills relating to taxation must originate in the House of Representatives.
> The dust particles gravitated slowly to the bottom of the pool.

In the first example the verbal context clues (*relating to taxation, House of Representatives*) tell us that *bills* must certainly refer to laws or legislative acts and not some other meaning of the word such as "part of the head of a bird" or "a statement of debt." Likewise in the second example, it is not hard for us to think of what dust particles would naturally do in a pool and arrive at a good idea of the meaning of *gravitate* — something like "to move slowly downward."

Frequently the context clues missing in the sentence are contained in the paragraph. For example, read the following two passages. Do not look up the meanings of the words in bold-faced type, but try instead to guess their meanings from the clues given in the selections.

1. Some people call them nature's thermometers.

They are rhododendrons, the **nondeciduous** broad-leaved plants that decorate thousands of suburban yards with their greenery in both the winter and summer. But when the temperature drops below freezing, their normally flat leaves become **mercurial thermal sensors,** varying their shape according to the temperature.

As a result, a veteran rhododendron watcher can peer through a frost-rimmed window and **gauge** the approximate outdoor temperature by observing how tightly curled the leaves are.[1]

2. Somewhere in the **annals** of American folklore there is a tale about the farmer who made a scarecrow so fearsome in appearance that crows not only left his crops alone but brought back corn they had stolen years before. It is the kind of story that appeals to those who **wage** continuous battle against not only crows but other garden pests as well.

From Man's earliest efforts to protect his crops he has relied upon scarecrows. Created in his own image and more often than not dressed in his own cast-off clothing, these intimidating **minions** stand guard while he is attending to other chores. They range from simple stick figures draped with old gunny sacks to elaborate **sartorial** masterpieces, some of them fit for display in a museum.

---

[1] Excerpt from "Plant Thermometer" by Bayard Webster in New York Times of March 11, 1980. © 1980 by The New York Times Company. Reprinted by permission.

There is evidence to show that when Columbus set foot on this continent, Indians were using scarecrows to keep **vigil** over their cornfields. The Colonists used them extensively as they heeded the planter's **adage** and dropped five kernels into each hill of corn, "one for the woodchuck, one for the crow, one for the cutworm and two to grow."[1]

EXERCISE 1. Copy the italicized word in each of the following sentences. Then examine the context clues, and write down what you think the word means. Check your answers in your dictionary.

EXAMPLE   1. The scientific report was so abstruse that even Professor Bowen had trouble comprehending it.
  1. *abstruse — difficult to understand*

 1. This word is *ambiguous;* it can have two meanings.
 2. *Oblivious* of the terrible danger threatening her, she sauntered along absent-mindedly.
 3. He was a very *astute* buyer, estimating values very carefully and never allowing himself to be deceived.
 4. They wanted no *remuneration* in money or gifts; their only reward would be the knowledge that they had saved the child.
 5. Although she profited greatly by the action, the queen could not *condone* the murder of the baron.
 6. The fearful crowd watched with great *trepidation* as the rescuers inched their way along the ledge.
 7. The *epitaph* on her tombstone was brief: "Here lies one who died for her country."
 8. After what seemed to the impatient children an *interminable* time, the boring hour came to an end.
 9. The trapped animal struggled for hours but could not *extricate* itself from the snare.
10. After a *cursory* examination of only a minute or so, the doctor said that the child probably had not been seriously hurt.

[1] From "Scarecrows Provide an Antic Art Form" by Avon Neal from *Smithsonian,* September 1976. Copyright 1976 by the Smithsonian Institution.

EXERCISE 2. Follow the directions for Exercise 1.

1. He was a *fastidious* dresser, always very neat and very particular about what he wore.
2. The business was an extremely *lucrative* one; in their first year their profits were five times the amount of their original investment.
3. The fire threatened to spread to the *adjacent* houses.
4. To drive home his accusation by repetition, he *reiterated* that he thought Smithers was a liar.
5. Such an ointment is likely to *mitigate* the pain of the burn.
6. Smoking is likely to have a *pernicious* effect on one's health.
7. Michael looked at the dead roach on the shelf without trying to conceal his *repugnance*.
8. Wasting no words at all and being very brief, she gave a *succinct* account of her adventures.
9. He wanted to meet the new girl, but he was too *reticent* to try to speak to her without having been introduced.
10. The overpowering odor of roses spread from room to room, *permeating* the whole house.

Kinds of Context Clues

There are a number of kinds of verbal context clues, but three in particular are extremely useful, clear, and helpful. Writers are often aware that some of their words may not be immediately clear to all of their readers, and they insure complete understanding by adding little definitions or shorter synonyms. Usually these little definitions or synonyms are preceded by *or*. A writer may put down "the person's irascibility, or *bad temper*" or something similar. Sometimes wording like *that is* or *in other words* is used. A person writing about first aid may say "a tourniquet may be used to stop excessive bleeding." On reconsideration this may be changed to "a tourniquet, that is, *a tightly twisted bandage applied above the wound,* may be used to stop excessive bleeding." Sometimes these explanations are made by the use of appositives or appositive phrases (see pages 77–78). Appositives that define are often punctuated with commas, as in the sentence "The opprobrium, *the deep public disgrace*, of his treason stayed with him all the years of his life." Here the word *opprobrium* is made clear by the following appositive.

EXERCISE 3. Number your paper 1–10. Copy after each number the italicized word in the corresponding sentence. Then after it write the context clue that helps you to know what it means.

1. Many of the Romans were quite willing to *deify* their Caesars, to make gods of them.
2. Then the old mansion split apart and fell into the widening *abyss*, into the yawning chasm developing before it.
3. Baltimore County and the city of Baltimore are *coterminous;* that is, they have a common boundary.
4. Such preparations will *depilate* the skin; in other words, they will remove the hair.
5. She gave us the most *succinct,* or brief, answers that she possibly could.
6. The others questioned the *veracity* — the truthfulness — of these reports.
7. Ms. Jenkins was too *hypercritical,* too given to constant fault-finding, to be a very good teacher.
8. These medical students have decided to become *pediatricians;* that is, doctors specializing in the care and diseases of children.
9. The *nomenclature,* or system of naming, now used in botany is in part the work of Linnaeus.
10. The explorers were all afflicted with *nostalgia*, a yearning to return home.

Physical Context

To know the actual circumstances surrounding the use of a word, that is, its *physical* context, is often essential in distinguishing between two meanings of the same word. Take the word *foul*, for instance. If you are watching a baseball game, the word *foul* means one thing; if the game is basketball, it means something else. The word *cell* has one meaning in a biology laboratory and another in the city jail. Both kinds of context—verbal and physical—should be carefully noted, for both help you to discover the meaning of unfamiliar words.

EXERCISE 4. Following are ten words. After each one are given two different physical contexts, labeled *a* and *b*. Arrange your paper with numbers 1a, 1b, 2a, 2b, etc., along the left side. After each of these numbers, write the meaning that the word in question will have in the physical context given.

EXAMPLE   1. cast   a. a fishing trip
                         b. a theater
         1a. *the throwing of a fishing line into the water*
         1b. *the entire group of performers in a show*

1. *delta*   a. a Greek class
             b. a geography
               class

2. *bench*   a. a park
             b. a court

3. *drill*   a. carpentry
             b. the army

4. *carrier* a. a health
               department
             b. a naval base

5. *switch* a. a railway
               yard
             b. a hair-
               dresser's

6. *coach*   a. a railway
               station
             b. a gymnasium

7. *colony*   a. a history
               class
             b. a bacteriology
             laboratory

8. *secretary* a. a business
               office
             b. a furniture
             store

9. *bridge*   a. a dentist's
               office
             b. a naval
             vessel

10. *jacket*   a. a metal-
               worker's
             shop
             b. a book shop

26c. Learn to find the meanings you want in the dictionary.

To build up your vocabulary systematically, do not rely entirely on context clues—as helpful as they are. Track down the word further in the dictionary.

Very few nonscientific words in English have a single meaning. Most have many meanings, often entirely different when the context is different. Therefore, the first step in finding the meaning of any new word is always to determine how it is being used when you read it or hear it for the first time in conversation.

To help you in this way, dictionaries often provide sample contexts. One dictionary, for example, lists twelve definitions of the word *bond* when it is used as a noun. The list begins with the most common use, "that which binds or holds together; a band; tie," and proceeds through more and more specialized contexts, for example, the meaning of *bond* in law, in finance, in insurance, in commerce, in building, etc., and ends with its very specialized meaning in chemistry. This arrangement of definitions allows you to find quickly the one that best suits the context of your word.

Some dictionaries may enter definitions in the order of frequency or importance. In this type the first meaning given will be the one considered the most common and the one given last will be considered the least common. A dictionary using historical order, for example, would give as the first definition of the word *forum* the notion of a Roman marketplace or other open public area and would list the idea of a public meeting much later. A dictionary that arranged its definitions in terms of contemporary importance would reverse this procedure.

EXERCISE 5. Number your paper 1–10. The italicized words in the following sentences all have a number of different meanings. Consult your dictionary to find the meaning that best fits the context of the word in the sentence. Then write the meaning after the proper number on your paper.

1. The pasture creek was fed by three tiny *affluents*.
2. Mr. Yamamoto was a teacher of high *caliber*.
3. At the bottom of the *defile,* the river appeared like a silver thread.

4. The image on the screen *dissolved* from a tube of toothpaste to a panorama of giant cacti.
5. Pails and buckets are *galvanized*.
6. The cold-induced *inertia* of grasshoppers allows anglers to catch them easily in the early morning.
7. The imprint of the huge scorpion was found in a *matrix* of Devonian sediments.
8. Joanne *executed* a series of elaborate dance steps on her skates.
9. At the bottom of the jar was a peculiar purple *precipitate*.
10. To defend her interests in the suit, Ms. Jones *retained* a young attorney.

Finding the Right Word

26d. Select the word that conveys the precise meaning and impression you want to give.

You cannot use the dictionary for very long before discovering that there are many words meaning approximately the same thing. The distinctions in meaning between synonyms, though sometimes very slight, are important and are carefully preserved by people who want their speech to be as lively and expressive as possible. Consider, for example, the multiple ways a person can *say* something:

utter	query	expostulate	hint	declare
whisper	question	vociferate	drawl	enunciate
grate	probe	insinuate	plead	state
lisp	asseverate	intimate	demand	respond
roar	aver	opine	threaten	announce
coo	argue	insist	proclaim	preach
reiterate	retort	descant	answer	perorate
recite	observe	comment	expatiate	deliver

As you can see, none of these verbs are interchangeable, but some are nearly so. Remember that a useful vocabulary is one that for every common word has a good stock of synonyms but preserves the differences between them.

EXERCISE 6. Number your paper 1–10. For each sentence below, choose from the list the most appropriate synonym for the word *say*. Use a different synonym for every sentence, and change the tense of the verb to suit the context. Write the word next to the proper number on your paper.

1. Asked for the fifth time, Ted —— angrily that he had no more.
2. Endlessly, Mrs. Bronson —— the rule until the class knew it by heart.
3. Reminded of his oath, the witness —— that he had heard nothing.
4. Quick-witted Marie —— instantly to the taunt by her brother.
5. The subject was complex and difficult; accordingly, Mr. Ives —— on it slowly and methodically.
6. Told that promptly on February 2 the woodchuck comes out of its burrow to calculate the length of its shadow, Ms. Ranby, our biology teacher, removed her glasses and —— that there was more fancy than fact in that story.
7. Lucy was not bold enough to state her suspicions openly; she merely —— that our dog was guilty.
8. The President —— that henceforward the day would be dedicated to the memory of the war dead.
9. The civil authorities —— that the rioting stop.
10. Unwilling at first to announce her candidacy, Ms. Dixon —— that at a later date she would announce her intentions.

EXERCISE 7. Write the letter for the synonym nearest in meaning to the words in the list at the left below.

1. *abut*	a. ram	b. adjoin	c. hint
2. *allay*	a. soothe	b. befriend	c. juggle
3. *anneal*	a. toughen	b. cancel	c. recover
4. *cajole*	a. heal	b. calculate	c. coax
5. *decimate*	a. operate	b. destroy	c. decide
6. *encumber*	a. burden	b. consume	c. undermine
7. *enervate*	a. soar	b. strengthen	c. weaken
8. *espouse*	a. marry	b. comb	c. respond
9. *fabricate*	a. butcher	b. make	c. descend
10. *furbish*	a. darken	b. sign	c. brighten
11. *gird*	a. plow	b. release	c. encircle
12. *imbibe*	a. bribe	b. sponsor	c. drink

13. *mollify*	a. reduce	b. soothe	c. repair
14. *ossify*	a. harden	b. classify	c. restore
15. *preclude*	a. prevent	b. pray	c. foreclose
16. *prevaricate*	a. anticipate	b. sicken	c. lie
17. *recant*	a. argue	b. disavow	c. republish
18. *ruminate*	a. meditate	b. enlarge	c. belittle
19. *simulate*	a. enliven	b. imitate	c. discourage
20. *vacillate*	a. anoint	b. inject	c. waver

PREFIXES AND ROOTS

Many words now part of the English language have been "borrowed" from another language. Word borrowing takes place when a foreign word comes to be used so often by speakers of another language that it becomes a part of their native language.

Many words now part of the English language have been borrowed from Latin. Latin has contributed more words to the English vocabulary than any other foreign language. Greek has also contributed a number. The different elements making up words borrowed from Latin are often quite clear at once to students of Latin, but students who have not studied Latin can, with a little study, learn some of these important word elements, for the same Latin word elements occur again and again in a multitude of English words. Once learned, they provide a key to the meaning of many unfamiliar words.

Short elements that come before the main part of a word are called *prefixes; circum–* and *trans–* are common prefixes. The main part of the word is called the *root; –port–* and *–fer–* are roots. The part which is added at the end of the main part of the word is the *suffix; –ion* and *–ence* are suffixes. *Transportation* and *circumference* are words formed from these elements.

26e. Learn some of the common Latin and Greek prefixes.

EXERCISE 8. Using your dictionary, give the meaning

of the prefix printed in bold-faced type. Then, again by referring to the dictionary, give the meaning of the root that
follows and show how the combination gives the meaning
of the word.

EXAMPLE   *advent* = *ad* (*to*) + *vent* (*come*) = *arrive*

1. aberration	4. circumvent
2. adhere	5. compile
3. biannual	

Latin Prefixes

Learn the meaning of the following prefixes.

LATIN PREFIX	MEANING
contra–	against
de–	from
dis–	away, from, not
ex–	out of
in–	in, into, not
inter–	between, among
intra–	within
non–	not

EXERCISE 9. Show the word meanings as you did in Exercise 8, above.

1. contraband	4. incarnate
2. disintegrate	5. interpose
3. excavate	6. intramural

LATIN PREFIX	MEANING
per–	through
post–	after
pre–	before
pro–	before
re–	back, again
retro–	back
semi–	half
sub–	under
super–	above
trans–	across

EXERCISE 10. Using the dictionary, write the meaning of each word in the following list. Be prepared to give the meaning of each prefix and to explain how it is related to the meaning of the word.

1. perennial
2. posthumous
3. preempt
4. profane
5. revoke

6. retroactive
7. semiannual
8. subjugate
9. superhuman
10. translucent

Greek Prefixes

The following Greek prefixes are found in many words in English as well as in other languages. Learn them for the exercise that follows.

GREEK PREFIX	MEANING
anti–	against
em–, en–	in
hemi–	half
hyper–	over, above

EXERCISE 11. In a numbered list on your paper, write each prefix and, on the line below, each word. After each prefix, write its meaning. By referring to the dictionary, give a definition of each word.

1. antibiotic
2. hypercritical
3. embellish

4. encroach
5. hemisphere

EXERCISE 12. By referring to the dictionary, define the following words by showing the relationship of the Greek prefix to the meaning.

1. hypo–   (under) + tension =
2. para–   (beside) + phrase =
3. peri–   (around) + meter =
4. pro–   (before) + logue =
5. syn–   (together) + thesis =

Changed Prefixes

Sometimes, as the exercises have shown, English words use the original forms of Latin and Greek prefixes. But sometimes the original forms have undergone change. The word *abbreviate*, despite its present form, does not illustrate an original *ab-* prefix but instead an original *ad-* prefix. The *d* of this prefix changed to *b* because it was much easier to say *abbreviate* than *adbreviate*. With the change in pronunciation came a change in spelling. The word now has two *b*'s in it. This kind of change is called *assimilation* and can be seen in many other prefixes besides *ad*.

ad

ad + cumulate = accumulate
ad + cord = accord
ad + peal = appeal
ad + tain = attain

com

com + lect = collect
com + cord = concord
com + rupt = corrupt
com + exist = coexist

dis

dis + fer = differ
dis + ficult = difficult
dis + gest = digest
dis + lute = dilute

ex

ex + fect = effect
ex + fort = effort
ex + lect = elect
ex + rode = erode

sub

sub + ceed = succeed
sub + fix = suffix
sub + port = support
sub + pend = suspend

in

in + legal = illegal
in + mortal = immortal
in + regular = irregular
in + reparable = irreparable

As you can see, assimilation often disguises the original prefix. Despite this change, you can easily analyze words into their original components with the aid of any dictionary. It is a great aid to vocabulary building to do so.

EXERCISE 13. Number your paper 1–10. Write opposite each number the following words in order. Then, in the second column, write the original form of the prefix. Use your dictionary to find this. In the third column write the root or base part of the word; this will be the remaining part of it.

EXAMPLE 1. divert
            1. *divert*   *dis–*   *vert*

1. access	6. collapse
2. allude	7. collide
3. annex	8. confuse
4. appose	9. corrode
5. arraign	10. efficient

EXERCISE 14. Follow directions for Exercise 13.

1. efface	6. succumb
2. egress	7. suppose
3. elude	8. sustain
4. immerse	9. symbol
5. impart	10. sympathy

EXERCISE 15. Number your paper 1–10. After each number, copy the words that use the italicized syllable as a *prefix*. Do not copy the other words, in which the syllable is not a prefix. You may use a dictionary.

1.	*ad–*	adamant, adder (snake), adjust, admire, advise
2.	*bi–*	Biblical, bibliography, bilateral, bilingual, biplane
3.	*com–*	coma, comedy, comet, commute, compose
4.	*de–*	deacon, debtor, decimal, defect, decline
5.	*dis–*	disappoint, discard, disciple, disease, dislocate
6.	*para–*	parachute, parade, paradise, paragraph, parasol
7.	*per–*	perceive, percussion, perky, permeate, permit
8.	*pre–*	preach, precious, precise, preface, pretzel
9.	*re–*	rebound, recent, recite, reduce, regal
10.	*sub–*	subconscious, subject, subjugate, submerge, subscribe

Latin and Greek Roots

It isn't hard to tell what beginning elements of words are prefixes. The *un–* of *unclear,* the *mis–* of *mistreat,* and the *re–* of *return* are obviously prefixes. It is somewhat more difficult, however, to identify a root.

Some roots are called *free forms.* Free forms can appear

with prefixes (*untrue, distrust, misspell*), but they can also appear by themselves (*true, trust, spell*).

Bound forms, on the other hand, can appear only with prefixes or suffixes. They cannot exist alone. We can have, for example, *conclude, transgress,* and *receive,* but we cannot have *clude, gress,* and *ceive.*

Free or bound, however, roots are easy to learn and, once learned, they allow us to understand the meanings of many different words.

26f. Learn some of the common Latin and Greek roots.

Learn the meaning of the following Latin roots in preparation for the exercise that follows.

LATIN ROOTS	MEANING
–dic–, –dict–	say, speak
–fac–, –fact–	do, make
–junct–	join
–pon–, –pos–	place, put
–scrib–, –script–	write
–spec–, –spic–	look, see
–tract–	draw, pull
–vert–, –vers–	turn
–voc–	call
–volv–	roll, turn

EXERCISE 16. Copy the words in bold-faced type onto your paper. Referring to the dictionary, underline the root of each word, write the meaning of each root, and give the meaning of the word as it is used in the paragraph.

The governor read the letter which the secretary handed her and began to dictate an answer in faultless **diction.** Her **facile** delivery was not marked by any hesitation for thought as she explained her **position.** "At this critical **juncture** in the affairs of our state," she said, "we place confidence in the integrity of our legislators. We do not all **subscribe** to the same party policies, but we rely on one another's **perspicuity** to see the issues clearly. These **distractions,** designed to **subvert** the public welfare, are bound to fail, and in the face of the public outrage which has been **provoked,** we will do the duty that **devolves** upon us."

EXERCISE 17. Learn the following Greek roots and their meanings. While studying these words, refer to a dictionary to see how the meanings of the words in the third column are found in the meanings of their roots.

GREEK ROOT	GENERAL MEANING	WORD
1. –anthrop–	man	anthropology
2. –chron–	time	chronometer
3. –gen–	birth	genealogy
4. –geo–	earth	geology
5. –hetero–	different	heterogeneous

Study the meaning of these Greek roots.

GREEK ROOT	MEANING
–bio–	life
–homo–	same
–hydr–	water
–log–	word, science
–mon–, –mono–	one
–morph–	form

EXERCISE 18. Using the Greek roots above, define the following words by dividing each word into its proper parts. Refer to a dictionary.

EXAMPLE 1. monogamy
1. *mono (one)* + *gamy (marriage)* = *one marriage*

1. homogeneous
2. anthropomorphic
3. biology
4. monologue
5. metamorphosis

GREEK ROOT	MEANING
–neo–	new
–ortho–	straight
–pan–	all
–phon–	sound
–psych–	mind
–scop–	seeing
–tech–	skill
–tele–	far

EXERCISE 19. Using the preceding lists of Greek roots, copy the elements in bold-faced type, and write their meanings in relation to the words below. Then, by referring to the dictionary, write the meaning of the entire word.

EXAMPLE   1. live in a **demo**cracy
1. *demo — people; democracy — rule of the people*

1. **anthropo**id ape
2. **psycho**somatic ailment
3. a **hydra**ulic jack
4. an **amorphous** substance
5. writing a **mono**graph
6. a **pan**demic disease
7. the science of **eu**genics
8. **phon**etic symbols
9. a famous **geo**physicist
10. the **ortho**pedist operated
11. mental **tele**pathy
12. the **chron**ology of history
13. of wide **scope**
14. the words are **homo**nyms
15. a **neo**phyte in a convent

EXERCISE 20. Number your paper 1–10. Looking up the following words in the dictionary, select the appropriate word for each blank in the sentences below, and write it after the proper number. Be prepared in class to identify and explain the prefixes and roots or bases.

anagram
epilogue
epitome
hypodermic
lithograph
metabolism
neolithic
orthodontist
philanthropist
protozoan

1. A concluding section added to a literary work is called an ——.
2. The later Stone Age is referred to as the —— age.
3. A dentist who specializes in straightening and adjusting teeth is called an ——.
4. Many adults dislike the sight of a —— needle.
5. A microscopic, one-celled animal is called a ——.
6. A word formed from another by transposing the letters is called an ——.
7. A person who loves and does good for humanity is called a ——.
8. A picture made from a stone or a plate is called a ——.

9. The chemical process by which cells derive energy from food and get rid of wastes is called ——.

10. A condensed account or summary is called an ——.

EXERCISE 21. Copy column A onto your paper. Referring to your dictionary, write next to each word the letter of the best meaning from column B. Be prepared in class to identify prefixes and roots or bases in these words.

A	B
1. anarchy	a. the slaying of a king
2. anathema	b. a speech of praise
3. epitaph	c. a device for measuring
4. eulogy	d. a box for storing things
5. euthanasia	e. stopping and starting again
6. indictment	f. an implied comparison
7. intermittent	g. absence of a system of government
8. metaphor	h. a mass of stone
9. regicide	i. legal accusation by the grand jury
10. repository	j. painless death
	k. a person or a thing accursed
	l. a short statement on a tombstone

REVIEW EXERCISE. Divide each of the following words into prefixes and roots, and explain how these parts make up the meaning of the word.

EXAMPLE 1. predict
    1. *pre (before)* + *dict (say)* = *to say beforehand*

1. circumspect	11. transport
2. retrospect	12. interpose
3. repose	13. symbiosis
4. aspect	14. permeate
5. subordinate	15. induce
6. adjacent	16. recede
7. controversial	17. posthumous
8. conspicuous	18. parasite
9. bipartisan	19. homonym
10. diverge	20. periscope

WORD ORIGINS

26g. Learn the origins of words as an aid to remembering meaning.

Often, learning the origin and history of a new word will help you remember it and use it well. The study of word origins may also provide some surprising information about words you have known for a long time.

Words with Interesting Histories

Many words have very interesting histories. Often our modern English words conceal within themselves references to romantic persons and places or to old, well-known stories. We all know the word *jersey* for instance, for a pullover upper garment, but few of us know that this word comes from the name of the Island of Jersey in the channel between England and France. We all know the word *tantalize*, but few of us know that this word goes back to the Greek name *Tantalos*. Tantalos was a mythical figure who repeated the secrets told him by Zeus. He was punished by being placed in water that he could never drink because it always receded away from him and by having above him branches laden with fruit that always eluded his hungry grasp. Your dictionary is likely to give you short summaries of these histories.

EXERCISE 22. Each of the following words in italics is derived from the name of a mythological or actual person. Number 1–10 on your paper. Referring to your dictionary, give the meaning and origin of the words in italics below.

EXAMPLE   1. The outraged citizens resolved to *boycott* the store of the quarrelsome merchant.
1. *boycott — refuse to do business with — from Captain Boycott, the first person so treated*

1. The *chauvinistic* politician made a warlike speech.
2. The winner said her *mentor* deserved more credit than she did.

3. The comedian kept us laughing by coming out with one *spoonerism* after another.
4. His *jovial* manner deserted him as he grew weary.
5. Rip Van Winkle's wife was a *termagant*.
6. The quiz contestant met her *nemesis*.
7. Only *herculean* strength could have accomplished the task which lay ahead.
8. It is sometimes difficult for a steady person to get along with one of *mercurial* disposition.
9. Faced by a *titanic* task, the man had the inclination to give up.
10. The quick thinking of the police officer prevented *panic*.

Recently Borrowed Words

English is filled with borrowed words. In fact, in the English language there are many more words borrowed from French, Latin, and Greek than there are from the original Anglo-Saxon or Old English phase of the language (the fifth to the eleventh centuries). Words given to illustrate Latin and Greek prefixes, bases, and roots in the preceding pages illustrate this. Many of these originally borrowed words are now so familiar to us that it comes as a surprise to think that they ever were foreign. But we have continued to borrow foreign words ever since early times, and we are still borrowing them. Sometimes we run across words borrowed rather recently, words that have been in the English language for so short a time that we still feel that they are foreign rather than English. These words may give us problems in determining their meanings (as well as their forms, spellings, and pronunciations).

EXERCISE 23. Refer to the dictionary to find the meaning of each foreign word or phrase in column A. Copy column A on your paper. After each item write the name of the language it comes from; then write the letter of the matching item in column B.

A	B
1. nom de plume	a. a dabbler in the arts
2. junta	b. a stroke of good luck
3. dilettante	c. noninterfering
4. bonanza	d. pen name
5. laissez-faire	e. a secret council

EXERCISE 24. Consult your dictionary; write the meaning of the following words on your paper, and use them in a sentence.

EXAMPLE   1. à la carte
   1. *à la carte* — *with a stated price for each dish. Because he wanted a special combination of food, he ordered his meal à la carte.*

1. à la mode	3. fait accompli
2. entre nous	4. tour de force

EXERCISE 25. Consult your dictionary; write the meaning of the following words and use them in a sentence.

1. bona fide	3. gratis
2. ex officio	4. ad hoc

EXERCISE 26. Look up each word in column A in your dictionary. Write after each number the letter of the item in Column B that expresses the meaning of the word.

A	B
1. alma mater	a. sudden and decisive move
2. con amore	b. principal woman singer in opera
3. blitzkrieg	c. slip in manners
4. denouement	d. till we meet again
5. hoi polloi	e. one's school or college
6. smörgåsbord	f. outcome of a play or story
7. coup d'état	g. the masses
8. prima donna	h. a variety of side dishes
9. auf Wiedersehen	i. with tenderness
10. faux pas	j. violent offensive in war

Word List

As a result of your study of this chapter, you will recognize many of the words in the following list. You will find that a great many contain familiar prefixes and roots. Make it a regular practice to learn new words from the list. Add them to the list in your notebook, giving the pronunciation, meaning, and derivation as you find them in the dictionary. Ten words a week will be as many as you can handle efficiently. After learning the words, use them as often as you can in your writing and speaking.

aberration	artifice	circumspect
abound	ascertain	clangor
abstemious	assiduous	cliché
abut		coffer
accredit	atrocious	colloquial
accrue	augury	comely
acumen	axiom	commute
affable	balmy	
affidavit	bandy	compatible
affiliate	bauble	concession
	bedlam	condolence
affluent	beneficent	conducive
alacrity	bestride	conifer
alienate	botch	consign
allege		consolidate
alleviate	boycott	contemporary
ambiguous	brigand	contingency
amnesty	brunt	copious
anagram	brusque	
analogy	buffoon	cursory
anneal	cajole	dearth
	candor	debase
anthropology	cant	decimate
antipathy	caprice	decorum
apprehensive	carnage	defile
apprise		defunct
arbiter	carp	delectable
archaic	charisma	demagogue
aroma	chastise	disrupt

dissipate
distraction
diversion
dogmatic
dross
edify
effrontery
electorate
elite
emaciate

encompass
encumber
engender
enjoin
epicure
epitome
equilibrium
erratic
espouse
exacting

exhilaration
expedient
explicit
extricate
fabricate
facetious
farcical
fastidious
fiasco
figurative

flagrant
fraudulent
furbish
galvanize
garb
garrulous
genealogy
gird
glib
gregarious

hackneyed
harbinger
heresy
hoax
holocaust
humanitarian
hypercritical
idyll
illicit
imbue

impassive
impeccable
imperceptible
impetuous
imposition
inadvertent
inalienable
inarticulate
inclement
incognito

incoherent
incongruous
indigent
indomitable
inertia
infallible
innate
innovation
inscrutable
instigate

interloper
intrepid
intrinsic
introvert
irksome
itinerary
jargon
lampoon
lassitude
latitude

lexicon
loathe
longitude
loquacious
ludicrous
luxuriant
magnanimous
maladroit
mandatory
maudlin

mendicant
mentor
mettle
mien
militant
misanthrope
miscreant
mollify
mosque
mull

mutable
mystic
negligible
nondescript
notoriety
obese
oblivious
odious
omniscient
ornate

orthography
ossify
ostracize
painstaking
palatable
pallor
panacea
paradox
paraphrase
parsimonious

patent
pecuniary
peremptory
periphery
personification
perspective
phalanx
phlegmatic
pillory
plaintiff

plait
polemic
posthumous
postulate
potency
precept
preclude
precursor
predispose
prelude

prepossess
pretension
pretext
prevalent
prevaricate
probation
proboscis
prolific
promontory
propriety

prosaic
protract
protuberant
provision

provocation
proximity
puerile
pulverize
purge
purloin

qualm
quibble
rampant
rankle
raucous
recant
recipient
recourse
recrimination
rejuvenate

remiss
remonstrate
reprehend
repress
requiem
resourceful
respiration
retainer
retribution
rift

rivulet
ruminate
sadistic
sagacious
satiate
scenario
scintillate
scruples

sedulous
senile

simulate
skeptical
sojourn
soliloquy
sordid
sporadic
steppe
stratagem
stringent
subjugate

subsidize
succulent
superfluous
supersede
symposium
synopsis
tacit
tentative
throes
transitory

translucent
ulterior
unremitting
usury
vacillate
venerate
vociferous
voluble
wreak
zephyr

Chapter 27

Spelling

Improving Your Spelling

You must have heard the words "I never could spell" in the course of your high school career, and you probably realize that this is just another excuse for poor spelling. Naturally good spellers are rare people. If you belong to this group, you are indeed fortunate. If you do not and know you have difficulty, now is the time to do something about it. You can improve your spelling if you want to and if you are willing to make the effort. No one else can be of much help to you. *Learning to spell is your responsibility.*

GOOD SPELLING HABITS

There is no one way to learn to spell. What works for one person may not work for you, but careful observation and good visual memory will help no matter what method you adopt. By using a combination of several methods, you can in time become a good speller. Some of the ways that have helped others to spell are listed below. Read them over; put them into practice.

1. In your notebook, keep a list of the words you misspell. Set aside a few pages in your notebook and jot down all the words you misspell in your written work for all subjects. At first, this job of entering word after word will seem wearisome and never-ending; the list itself, as it daily grows longer, may threaten to preempt your whole notebook and leave room for nothing else. Nevertheless, you can take heart, for as the therapy takes effect, fewer and fewer words will need to be added to the list, and the day will come eventually when weeks will pass before another mistake forces you to check your notebook.

A three-column spelling sheet is best. In the first column, correctly spell the word you have missed and circle the troublesome part. In the second column, divide the word into syllables. This insures against misspelling the word by first mispronouncing it. In the third column, jot down any little counsel to yourself, warning, or trick of association that may help you to spell the word.

1. Feb(ru)ary   Feb-ru-ar-y   Pronounce correctly.
2. di(s)approval   dis-ap-prov-al   Study Rule 27c.
3. can(di)date   can-di-date   Word has three small words in it: *can, did, ate.*

2. Get the dictionary habit. Don't guess at the spelling of a word. There is no consistency in guessing. You may guess right today and wrong tomorrow and be no better off. Actually the simple operation itself of opening the dictionary, leafing through it, and searching down the page until you come upon your word fortifies your memory with its correct spelling and reduces the chances of misspelling it again. In addition, you can hardly fail to come across some of the cognate forms of the word you are looking for, and by making the acquaintances of these "cousins" to the word in question, you deepen your knowledge of the word itself. It is much harder to misspell *denomination* after you know its kinship with such words as *nominate, nominal, denominator,* etc.

3. Learn to spell words by syllables. If you divide a word into small parts which can be pronounced by themselves, you divide a word into syllables. Even the hardest words look easy when they are broken down into syllables. For example, the word *pul'sate* has two syllables; the word *bul'le tin* has three syllables; the word *en vi'ron ment* has four syllables.

4. Avoid mispronunciations that lead to spelling errors.
Careful pronunciation will help you to spell many words.
The person who says *sup rise* for *surprise* will probably
spell the word incorrectly, leaving out the first *r*. The
person who says *mod ren* for *modern* will also probably
misspell the word. You need to learn the correct pronunciation of a word in order to spell it right.

Study the pronunciation of the words in the following
list. Notice how incorrect pronunciation leads to incorrect
spelling.

e*s*cape	(*not* e*x*cape)
r*i*diculous	(*not* r*e*diculous)
en*t*rance	(*not* ent*e*rance)
temper*a*ment	(*not* temp*e*rment)
equi*p*ment	(*not* equi*pt*ment)
a*th*letic	(*not* ath*a*letic)
main*t*enance	(*not* main*tain*ance)
rec*o*gnize	(*not* rec*o*nize)
heigh*t*	(*not* heigh*th*)
*per*spiration	(*not* pr*e*spiration)

5. Proofread your papers before handing them in. *Proof-*
reading is the process of rereading carefully for errors
whatever you have written. Proofreading is the best cure
for carelessness in punctuation, capitalization, spelling, and
grammar. It takes only a few minutes, yet it makes a great
difference in the correctness of your work.

SPELLING RULES

Our English language owes its richness to the vast number
of words it has borrowed from foreign sources. The cost
of this richness, however, is very wide variety in spelling.
Words that sound alike are, all too often, not spelled alike.
Nevertheless, there are strong family likenesses among
many words, and the simple rules describing them are easy
to learn. Learn these rules and you will be saved many
trips to the dictionary.

ie and *ei*

27a. Write *ie* when the sound is long *e,* except after *c.*

EXAMPLES piece, belief, niece, deceive, receive, conceive
EXCEPTIONS either, seize, neither, weird, leisure

Write *ei* when the sound is not long *e,* especially when the sound is long *a.*

EXAMPLES neighbor, weigh, veil, freight, forfeit, height
EXCEPTIONS friend, mischief

EXERCISE 1. Write the following words, supplying the missing letters (*e* and *i*) in the correct order. Be able to explain how the rule applies to each.

1. ach . . . ve
2. rec . . . pt
3. p . . . rce
4. bes . . . ge
5. rel . . . f
6. w . . . ld
7. y . . . ld
8. gr . . . f
9. c . . . ling
10. dec . . . t
11. rec . . . ve
12. dec . . . ve
13. conc . . . ve
14. sl . . . gh
15. v . . . l
16. th . . . r
17. h . . . ght
18. f . . . rce

–cede, –ceed, and *–sede*

27b. Only one English word ends in *–sede—supersede;* only three words end in *–ceed—exceed, proceed,* and *succeed;* all other words of similar sound end in *–cede.*

EXAMPLES recede, concede, precede

Adding Prefixes

A prefix is one or more than one letter or syllable added to the beginning of a word to change its meaning.

27c. When a prefix is added to a word, the spelling of the word itself remains the same.

il + legible = **il**legible
in + sensitive = **in**sensitive
im + partial = **im**partial
un + usual = **un**usual
un + necessary = **un**necessary
re + capture = **re**capture
dis + advantage = **dis**advantage
dis + similar = **dis**similar
mis + lead = **mis**lead
mis + spell = **mis**spell
over + run = **over**run
over + look = **over**look

Adding Suffixes

A suffix is one or more than one letter or syllable added to the end of a word to change its meaning.

27d. When the suffixes _–ness_ and _–ly_ are added to a word, the spelling of the word itself is not changed.

EXAMPLES   usual + ly = usually   mean + ness = meanness
EXCEPTIONS   Words ending in _y_ change the _y_ to _i_ before _–ness_
and _–ly:_ steady — steadily, sloppy — sloppiness. One-syllable
adjectives ending in _y_, however, generally follow Rule 27d:
shy — shyness, dry — dryly.

EXERCISE 2.   Spell correctly the words indicated.

1. _accidental_ with the suffix _ly_
2. _heavy_ with the suffix _ness_
3. _satisfied_ with the prefix _dis_
4. _mean_ with the suffix _ness_
5. _legal_ with the prefix _il_
6. _spell_ with the prefix _mis_
7. _understand_ with the prefix _mis_
8. _sincere_ with the suffix _ly_
9. _nerve_ with the prefix _un_
10. _complete_ with the suffix _ly_
11. _qualified_ with the prefix _un_
12. _kind_ with the suffix _ness_
13. _literate_ with the prefix _il_
14. _ordinary_ with the suffix _ly_
15. _ability_ with the prefix _in_
16. _mature_ with the prefix _im_
17. _consider_ with the prefix _re_
18. _adequate_ with the prefix _in_
19. _appoint_ with the prefix _dis_
20. _sudden_ with the suffix _ness_
21. _use_ with the prefix _mis_
22. _stated_ with the prefix _mis_
23. _noticed_ with the prefix _un_
24. _special_ with the suffix _ly_
25. _rate_ with the prefix _over_

27e. Drop the final _e_ before a suffix beginning with a vowel.

EXAMPLES   dine + ing = dining
           sense + ible = sensible
           use + able = usable

EXCEPTIONS   Keep the final _e_ before a suffix beginning with _a_ or
_o_ if necessary to retain the soft sound of _c_ or _g_ preceding the _e_.

   serviceable, advantageous, manageable
   dye + ing = dyeing   [to prevent confusion with dying]

27f. Keep the final _e_ before a suffix beginning with a consonant.

EXAMPLES   use + ful = useful
             advertise + ment = advertisement
             care + ful = careful
EXCEPTIONS   true + ly = truly
             argue + ment = argument

EXERCISE 3. Write correctly the words formed as indicated.

1. guide + ance
2. scare + ing
3. courage + ous
4. approve + al
5. desire + able
6. separate + ing
7. nine + ty
8. taste + less
9. retire + ing
10. advance + ing
11. pronounce + able
12. compare + able
13. defense + less
14. hope + ful
15. whole + ly
16. true + ly
17. achieve + ment
18. use + ing
19. severe + ly
20. continue + ous

27g. With words ending in *y* preceded by a consonant, change the *y* to *i* before any suffix not beginning with an *i*.

EXAMPLES   lively + ness = liveliness
             bury + ing = burying
             bury + al = burial

EXERCISE 4. Write correctly the words formed as indicated.

1. happy + est
2. friendly + est
3. merry + est
4. marry + ing
5. marry + ed
6. prophesy + ing
7. prophesy + ed
8. carry + er
9. beauty + ful
10. spy + ing
11. pity + ful
12. pity + ing
13. mercy + ful
14. satisfy + ed
15. try + ed
16. pretty + ness
17. busy + ly
18. busy + ing
19. gory + ness
20. glory + fied

27h. Double the final consonant before a suffix that begins with a vowel if both of the following conditions exist:

(1) the word has only one syllable or is accented on the last syllable.

(2) the word ends in a single consonant preceded by a single vowel.

EXAMPLES   win + ing = winning   [one-syllable word]
              omit + ed = omitted   [accent on the last syllable]
              begin + er = beginner   [accent on the last syllable]
              differ + ence = difference   [accent on the first syllable]
              droop + ed = drooped   [single consonant ending preceded by a *double* vowel]

EXERCISE 5. Write correctly the words formed as indicated.

1. hit + er
2. propel + er
3. shovel + ing
4. beg + ing
5. refer + ed
6. refer + al
7. repel + ent
8. confer + ed
9. suffer + ance
10. deter + ent
11. develop + ed
12. pin + ing
13. hop + ing
14. shop + ed
15. remit + ance
16. deep + en
17. big + est
18. rebel + ion

The Plural of Nouns

27i. Observe the rules for spelling the plural of nouns.

(1) The regular way to form the plural of a noun is to add an *s*.

EXAMPLES   dog, dogs   pencil, pencils

(2) The plural of some nouns is formed by adding *es*. Words ending in *s*, *x*, *z*, *sh*, and *ch* form the plural by adding *es*.

The *e* is necessary to make the plural form pronounceable.

EXAMPLES   waltz, waltzes   trench, trenches
bush, bushes   glass, glasses

(3) The plural of nouns ending in *y* following a consonant is formed by changing the *y* to *i* and adding *es*.

EXAMPLES   city, cities   spy, spies
enemy, enemies   penny, pennies

(4) The plural of nouns ending in *y* following a vowel is formed by adding an *s*.

EXAMPLES   turkey, turkeys   essay, essays

(5) The plural of most nouns ending in *f* or *fe* is formed by adding *s*. The plural of some nouns ending in *f* or *fe* is formed by changing the *f* or *fe* to *v* and adding *es*.

EXAMPLES   Add *s:*

        belief, beliefs   chief, chiefs
        roof, roofs   cliff, cliffs

       Change *f* or *fe* to *v* and add *es:*

        wife, wives   wolf, wolves
        knife, knives   thief, thieves
                    leaf, leaves

(6) The plural of nouns ending in *o* preceded by a vowel is formed by adding *s*. The plural of most nouns ending in *o* preceded by a consonant is formed by adding *es*.

EXAMPLES   *o* preceded by a vowel:

        patio, patios   radio, radios

       o preceded by a consonant:

        tomato, tomatoes   hero, heroes

EXCEPTIONS   Words ending in *o* that refer to music form the plural by adding *s:*

        alto, altos   piano, pianos
        soprano, sopranos   solo, solos

(7) The plural of a few nouns is formed in irregular ways.

EXAMPLES   child, children   woman, women   mouse, mice
ox, oxen   tooth, teeth

(8) The plural of compound nouns consisting of a noun plus a modifier is formed by making the noun plural.

In the following examples, the phrases *in chief* and *in-law,* and the words *on* and *up,* are all modifiers. It is the nouns modified by them that are made plural.

EXAMPLES   editor in chief, editors in chief
son-in-law, sons-in-law
looker-on, lookers-on
runner-up, runners-up

(9) The plural of a few compound nouns is formed in irregular ways.

EXAMPLES   drive-in, drive-ins
lean-to, lean-tos
two-year-old, two-year-olds

(10) Some nouns are the same in the singular and the plural.

EXAMPLES   Chinese, Chinese   trout, trout   sheep, sheep
deer, deer   salmon, salmon

(11) The plural of foreign words is sometimes formed as in the original language.

EXAMPLES   alumnus [man], alumni [men]
alumna [woman], alumnae [women]
vertebra, vertebrae
parenthesis, parentheses
datum, data
monsieur, messieurs

► NOTE   The plural of other foreign words may be formed either as in the foreign language or in the regular way in English by adding *s* or *es.* Sometimes the English plural is preferred. For such words, consult the dictionary.

EXAMPLES   formula, formulae or formulas [preferred]
index, indices or indexes [preferred]
concerto, concerti or concertos [preferred]

(12) The plural of numbers, letters, signs, and words considered as words is formed by adding an apostrophe and *s*.

EXAMPLES In the equation are two *t*'s.
There are three 7's in my address.
Please don't use so many *and*'s.

EXERCISE 6. Write the plural form of each of the following nouns and the number of the rule that applies.

1. dish
2. girl
3. valley
4. oasis
5. calf
6. porch
7. sky
8. goose
9. π
10. monkey
11. Japanese
12. ox
13. father-in-law
14. deer
15. solo
16. self
17. board of education
18. alumnus
19. loaf
20. hero

EXERCISE 7. Write the plural form of each of the following nouns and the number of the rule that applies.

1. alley
2. old-timer
3. lieutenant governor
4. half
5. donkey
6. theory
7. handkerchief
8. bacillus
9. gallery
10. echo
11. justice of the peace
12. stitch
13. radio
14. plateful
15. roof
16. burglary
17. mouthful
18. *b* (the letter)
19. man
20. gas

EXERCISE 8. By referring to the rules you have learned, explain orally the spelling of each of the following:

1. crises
2. deceive
3. writing (*e* dropped)
4. believe
5. sopranos
6. misstep
7. meanness
8. noticeable
9. relief
10. cities

11. unhonored
12. data
13. beautifully
14. weird
15. typing (*e* dropped)

16. overrun
17. overflows
18. neighbor
19. wives
20. dissimilar

Words Frequently Confused

affect	[verb] *Affect* is usually a verb meaning *to influence.* Did that tearful movie *affect* you?
effect	[noun or verb] As a verb, *effect* means *to accomplish.* New glasses *effected* a remarkable change in his vision. As a noun, *effect* means the *result of some action.* What *effect* did the rain have on the garden?
all right	[This is the only acceptable spelling. The spelling *alright* is not acceptable.]
already	*previously* We have *already* painted the sets.
all ready	*all are ready* We were *all ready* to leave.
all together	*everyone in the same place* The teammates were *all together* in the gym.
altogether	*entirely* I am not *altogether* convinced.
brake	[noun or verb] *to slow yourself down* or the device you use to do so At the curve, Georgia *braked* the speeding car.
break	[noun or verb] *to fracture* or the fracture itself Don't *break* the speed limit.
capital	[Correct spelling for all uses except when the word means a *government building.*]

What is the *capital* of Colorado?
You need *capital* to start a business.
Begin all sentences with *capital* letters.
Do you believe in *capital* punishment?

capitol　*government building* [frequently capitalized]
We could see the *capitol* from our hotel.

---

choose　[verb, present tense]
Alicia and Katherine, *choose* partners now.

chose　[verb, past tense]
When the signal was given, the girls *chose* two seniors.

---

coarse　*rough, crude*
When he spilled the *coarse* salt, he used *coarse* language.

course　*path of action;* also used with *of* to mean *as was to be expected*
Of course, you are always right.
She skipped the first *course* at dinner.
The *course* in speech helped my diction.
A new golf *course* opened last week.

---

complement　[noun or verb] *to make whole or complete* or *that which makes whole or complete*
The *complement*, or full crew, is six hundred people.
The *complement* of 60° is 30°.

compliment　[noun or verb] *respect, affection,* or *esteem*
Convey my *compliments* to the captain.
I *complimented* her on her success.

---

consul　[noun] *a diplomat appointed by a government to reside in a foreign country and look after the interests of fellow citizens traveling or doing business there*
The American *consul* in Rangoon arranged for my trip to the interior.

council, councilor　[noun] *a group meeting to discuss and take action on official matters; a member of such a group*

The *councilors* on the Security *Council* voted for the Canadian resolution.

counsel,   [noun or verb] *advice* or *to advise; an adviser*
   counselor   Sue's aunt *counseled* her to take judo lessons.
Ask your guidance *counselor.*

---

des'ert   *a dry region*
The car crossed the *desert* at night.

desert'   *to leave*
The rats *deserted* the unlucky ship.

dessert   *the last part of a meal*
For *dessert* we had custard.

EXERCISE 9. Number your paper 1–15. Write after the proper number the correct one of the words given in parentheses in the sentences below.

1. The illness had a strange (affect, effect) on Margie.
2. During lunch, the soccer team was (all together, altogether) at one huge table.
3. My small cousin knows the (capitol, capital) city of every state in our country.
4. The (coarse, course) material made her skin itch.
5. Of (course, coarse), you burned the (desert, dessert) again.
6. The British (council, consul) removed his pince-nez and (counciled, counseled) Marlowe to leave Stanleyville before the rains came.
7. It seemed as if we had walked miles before we reached the main door of the (capital, capitol).
8. Your answer isn't (all together, altogether) correct, but you're on the right track.
9. After all his worry, everything turned out (all right, alright).
10. Our two fast guards are (complimented, complemented) perfectly by an exceedingly tall center.
11. A typing (coarse, course) is recommended for anyone planning to go to college.
12. We traveled for three days across the (desert, dessert).
13. The actors were (all ready, already) to audition for the play.

14. If you don't have your car's (brakes, breaks) inspected every year, you will be (braking, breaking) a state law.
15. Did you (choose, chose) a topic for your essay yet?

EXERCISE 10. Write sentences in which you use correctly each of the words just studied.

---

formally   *in a formal manner*
             For funerals, weddings, and christenings, one should dress *formally*.

formerly   *previously*
             The high ridges of the Blue Ridge Mountains were *formerly* the bed of an ancient sea.

---

hear   *using your ears*
             You will have to speak louder; I can't *hear* you.

here   *this place*
             You can't sit *here;* this section is only for juniors.

---

its   possessive of *it*
             The town hasn't raised *its* tax rate in three years.

it's   *it is*
             It's not time to get up.

---

lead   [present tense] *to go first*
             You *lead* because you know the way.

led   [past tense of *lead*]
             He *led* us five miles out of the way.

lead   [pronounced led] *a heavy metal;* also *graphite in a pencil*
             These books are as heavy as *lead*.

---

loose   *free, not close together*
             Put all the *loose* papers in the folder.
             His little brother has two *loose* teeth.

lose   [pronounced looz] *to suffer loss*
             Do not *lose* your tickets.

---

miner   [noun] *a collier* or *worker in a mine*

| | *Miners'* canaries told them when the air grew bad in the deep shafts. |
| **minor** | *lesser* or *under legal age*
In some states *minors* may not operate a vehicle after dark. |

moral	*good;* also *a lesson of conduct* We admire a *moral* person. The *moral* of the story is to look before you leap.
morale	*mental condition, spirit* After three defeats, the team's *morale* was low.

passed	[verb, past tense of *pass*] We *passed* the papers to the front.
past	[noun or adjective or preposition] To understand the present, you must study the *past*. Adele read the minutes of the *past* meeting. The dog walked right *past* the cat and never noticed it.

EXERCISE 11. Number your paper 1–15. Write after the proper number the correct one of the words given in parentheses in the sentences below.

1. Where did you (here, hear) that story?
2. You can (lead, led) a horse to water, but you can't make it drink.
3. If you (lose, loose) the directions, we'll never get there.
4. For the (passed, past) week she has done nothing but work on her term paper.
5. The general spoke to the troops to improve their (moral, morale).
6. While the heir was still a (minor, miner), the estate was held in trust.
7. Our horse (lead, led) all the others around the track.
8. In only a few minutes the guest speaker will be (hear, here).
9. If (it's, its) not too much trouble, would you mail this package for me?

10. After she went on a diet, her clothes were too (lose, loose).

11. (Formerly, Formally), California was part of New Spain.

12. After the house had been painted, (it's, its) appearance was vastly improved.

13. In 1848, gold (minors, miners) flocked to California, hoping to strike it rich.

14. (Its, It's) not every day that her parents let her use the car.

15. After two years of struggling with French I, Barney finally (passed, past) the course.

EXERCISE 12. Write sentences in which you use correctly each of the words just studied.

personal	*individual* The manager gave the customer his *personal* attention.
personnel	*a group of people employed in the same place* The management added four new employees to the *personnel*.
principal	*head of a school;* also an adjective, *main* or *most important* The *principal* of our school is Mr. Grebinar. The *principal* export of Brazil is coffee.
principle	*a rule of conduct;* also *a main fact* or *law* Her *principles* are very high. On what *principle* did you base your argument?
quiet	*silent, still* To study properly, one should make sure there is complete *quiet*.
quite	*wholly* or *rather* or *very* Are you *quite* sure the studio is soundproof?
shone	[past tense of *shine*] The star *shone* in the sky.
shown	*revealed* or *demonstrated* The slides were *shown* after dinner.

stationary	*in a fixed position* One of the desks is movable; the other is *stationary*.
stationery	*writing paper* That purple and perfumed *stationery* is in bad taste.
than	[a conjunction, used for comparisons] She is smarter *than* I.
then	[an adverb or conjunction] *at that time* or *next* We swam for an hour; *then* we went home. They didn't know me *then*.
their	[possessive of *they*] *Their* new apartment has a view of the river.
there	*a place;* also an expletive I haven't been *there* in ages. *There* is too much pepper in my soup.
they're	*they are* *They're* singing off key.

EXERCISE 13. Number your paper 1–15. Write after the proper number the correct one of the words given in parentheses in the sentences below.

1. He doesn't understand any of the (principals, principles) of physics.
2. The sun (shone, shown) all day.
3. The rabbit suddenly stopped and remained (stationery, stationary) for a few minutes.
4. He acts much older (than, then) he really is.
5. She spoke in a (quite, quiet) voice, (quite, quiet) out of keeping with her usually raucous manner.
6. You ask too many (personnel, personal) questions.
7. A collection of his paintings was (shone, shown) to the public last week.
8. You should never bother the animals when (their, they're, there) eating.
9. In school we study the (principals, principles) on which our country was founded.

10. (Quite, Quiet) soon after the strange uproar, all became (quite, quiet) again.

11. The bookstore is having a big sale on (stationery, stationary).

12. We are going to (there, their, they're) house.

13. All the (personal, personnel) in the store received a bonus at Christmas.

14. If you see the (principle, principal) in the hall, tell him he is wanted in the main office.

15. I don't care what (their, they're, there) parents let them do; you still aren't going to come in so late at night.

EXERCISE 14. Write sentences in which you use correctly each of the words just studied.

to	[preposition; also part of the infinitive form of the verb] You must return the books *to* the library. He began *to* whistle.
too	[adverb] *also, too much* Vito plays the trumpet, and Carrie plays it *too*. You are *too* young to drive.
two	*One plus one* I will graduate in *two* years.
waist	*the midsection* She wore a sash around her *waist*.
waste	[noun or verb] *to spend foolishly* or *a needless expense* *Waste* not; want not.
weather	*conditions outdoors* The *weather* has been perfect all week.
whether	[as in *whether or not*] They didn't know *whether* or not their parents would let them go canoeing.
who's	*who is, who has* *Who's* been using my socks? *Who's* there?

whose   [possessive of *who*]
                   Whose book is that?

your   [possessive of *you*]
                   Your coat is in the closet.

you're   *you are*
                   You're never on time.

EXERCISE 15. Number your paper 1–15. Write after the proper number the correct one of the words given in parentheses in the sentences below.

1. Around his (waste, waist) he wore a handmade leather belt.
2. (You're, Your) guidance counselor wants to see you today.
3. (Weather, Whether) or not you can take six subjects next term depends upon your grades this term.
4. Because there was (too, to, two) much traffic on the road, we didn't enjoy the ride.
5. (Whose, Who's) going to use her ticket now?
6. (Your, You're) going to have to work harder if you want to be a junior next year.
7. It really doesn't matter (whose, who's) fault it is.
8. You (to, two, too) can be a good speller if you really have the desire.
9. "(Whose, Who's) been leaving the lights on unnecessarily?" shouted Dad.
10. (Weather, Whether) or not it rains or snows, we will be there.
11. This is fine (whether, weather) for a softball game.
12. (Your, You're) sure that Miss Thompson wanted to see me?
13. I don't know (whose, who's) taller, Brad or you.
14. We never can have (two, too, to) many people working on the charity drive.
15. The list on the bulletin board will tell you (whose, who's) on the honor roll.

EXERCISE 16. Write sentences in which you use correctly each of the words just studied.

REVIEW EXERCISE. Number your paper 1–33. Select the correct one of the words in parentheses in each sentence, and write it after the proper number.

1. The dome of the (Capitol, Capital) could be seen from every part of the city.
2. If you want to win the election, you will have to plan your (coarse, course) of action now.
3. The paint has (all ready, already) begun to peel.
4. If you don't learn to (break, brake) gently, your passengers may hurt themselves.
5. If you think (its, it's) too warm, turn the heat down.
6. My (morale, moral) sank to a new low when I failed the Latin test.
7. Since I've got you (all together, altogether), I want to tell you some good news.
8. Do you remember (whether, weather) or not Mr. Allen gave us a homework assignment?
9. You must start proper nouns with a (capitol, capital) letter.
10. I had (already, all ready) finished ten problems in algebra when I realized we had to do only five.
11. Bonnie addressed us (formerly, formally): "Ladies and gentlemen of the sophomore class."
12. Whenever you (lead, led) the way, we always get lost.
13. (Their, There) hasn't been a drop of rain in months.
14. He keeps his (loose, lose) change in a cup in the china closet.
15. (Their, They're, There) are two *m*'s in *recommend*.
16. The spotlight (shone, shown) on the actress as she walked to the center of the stage.
17. Can't you write better (than, then) that, Pamela?
18. Where do you think (your, you're) going?
19. Because Chris is on a diet, he always skips (desert, dessert).
20. He has a (principal, principle) part in the play.
21. After two days at sea, he knew he wouldn't feel (alright, all right) until the boat docked.
22. The lion broke (loose, lose).
23. Slung about her (waste, waist) was a sweater.
24. (Whose, Who's) responsible for this mess?

25. If you haven't (all ready, already) bought your tickets, you should do so now.
26. Whenever (you're, your) in doubt about the spelling of a word, consult the dictionary.
27. Don't you (dessert, desert) me in my hour of need.
28. The navy was testing (it's, its) newest submarine.
29. Her coat was made from a very (course, coarse) tweed.
30. Crossing the (desert, dessert) at night, we avoided the hot rays of the sun.
31. The Town (Counsel, Council) ordered the contractor to repair the roads at once.
32. Every morning at 8:40, the (principle, principal) reads the announcements of the day.
33. She had a (personal, personnel) invitation from the mayor.

One Hundred Spelling Demons

ache	doctor	know
again	does	laid
always	done	loose
among	don't	lose
answer	early	making
any	easy	many
been	enough	meant
beginning	every	minute
believe	existence	much
blue	February	none
break	forty	often
built	friend	once
business	grammar	piece
busy	guess	raise
buy	half	read
can't	having	ready
choose	hear	said
color	here	says
coming	hoarse	seems
cough	hour	separate
could	instead	shoes
country	just	similar
dear	knew	since

some	tonight	whether
straight	too	which
sugar	trouble	whole
sure	truly	women
tear	Tuesday	won't
their	two	would
there	very	write
they	wear	writing
though	Wednesday	wrote
through	week	
tired	where	

Three Hundred Spelling Words

absence	angel	changeable
absorption	annual	characteristic
abundant	answered	chemistry
acceptable	apparatus	chief
accidentally	appearance	circumstance
accommodation	appropriate	civilization
accompaniment	approximately	cocoon
accurate	arousing	commencement
accustomed	arrangement	
achievement		commissioner
	ascend	committed
acquaintance	association	comparative
actuality	athlete	comparison
adequately	bankruptcy	competition
administration	basically	conceivable
adolescent	beneficial	confidential
aggressive	benefited	confirmation
agriculture	bicycle	conscientious
amateur	breathe	consciousness
ambassador	brilliant	
analysis		consequently
	calendar	considerable
analyze	category	consistency

continuous
controlled
controversial
cordially
corps
correspondence
criticize

curiosity
curriculum
definition
delegate
denied
develop
difference
disastrous
disciple
dissatisfied

distinction
distinguished
dividend
dominant
dormitory
earnest
easily
ecstasy
eighth
eliminate

embroidery
endeavor
enemy
enormous
equipment
especially
essential
estimation
etiquette
exaggeration

examination
exceedingly

exceptional
excitable
executive
exercise
exhaustion
exhibition
expense
extension

extraordinary
fallacy
fantasies
favorably
fiery
financial
foreigner
forfeit
fragile
fulfill

fundamentally
gasoline
grammatically
grateful
guidance
gymnasium
handkerchief
happiness
heroic
hindrance

humorist
hygiene
hypocrisy
illustrate
imitation
immense
inability
incidentally
indispensable
influential

innocence

inquiry
institute
intellect
interference
interpretation
interruption
interval
irrelevant
irresistible

island
jealousy
journal
laborious
liability
lightning
likelihood
liveliest
locally
luxury

magnificence
maintenance
maneuver
mansion
martyr
maturity
medical
merchandise
merit
miniature

mischievous
missile
misspelled
monotony
mortgage
municipal
narrative
naturally
neighbor
noticeable

nuisance
obstacle
occasionally
occupy
odor
offensive
omitted
opinion
opposition
optimism

ordinary
organization
ornament
pageant
pamphlet
parachute
parallel
pastime
peaceable
peasant

peril
permanent
persistent
perspiration
pertain
phase
picnic
pigeon
playwright
pleasant

poison
politician
positively
possibility
practically

practice
precede
precisely
predominant
preferred

prejudice
preliminary
preparation
primitive
priority
prisoner
procedure
proceedings
procession
prominent

proposition
prosperous
prove
psychology
publicity
purposes
qualities
quantities
questionnaire
readily

reference
referring
regard
register
rehearsal
religious
remembrance
representative
requirement
resistance

resolution
responsibility
restaurant
ridiculous
satisfactorily
security
senator
sensibility
sheer
sheriff

significance
simile
situated
solution
sophomore
souvenir
specific
specimen
spiritual
strenuous

stretch
studying
substantial
subtle
succession
summarize
superintendent
suppress
surgeon
suspense

syllable
symbol
symphony
technique
temperature

tendency
tournament
traffic
twelfth
tying

tyranny
unanimous
undoubtedly
unforgettable
unpleasant

unusually
vacancies
varies
vengeance
villain

Speaking
and
Listening

PART SEVEN

Chapter **28**

Public Speaking

Giving a Talk and Listening

In high school you will often have to speak to groups of your fellow students. You will present your ideas in class, at club meetings, and at assemblies. You may be called upon to relate a personal experience, explain how to make or do something, or argue for or against a proposed plan. If you can speak clearly, easily, and forcefully, you will gain a skill that can help you in any career.

The ability to speak before groups is a valuable asset, but an equally important talent is the ability to listen. By *listening* to what is said and not just *hearing* it, you can grasp the gist of a speaker's remarks without the need for repetition. You can also distinguish fact from opinion and good sense from nonsense.

PREPARING A TALK

28a. Choose an appropriate topic.

Choose a topic that you know a great deal about. Doing so restricts your choice to your own background and encourages you to talk about things you have had experience with—your hobbies, special talents, jobs, and unusual experiences. It also ensures that you will speak with enthusiasm since the subject is close to you. If what you say engages your own interest powerfully, it will interest your audience as well. Enthusiasm is contagious.

Choose your topic far in advance. Think about it daily —
mulling over both what you will say and the way you will
say it. The longer this sifting process goes on, the better
the result.

EXERCISE 1. List five possible subjects you feel able to
speak about. Submit the list to your teacher for comments
and suggestions. When it is returned, put it in your notebook for future use.

28b. Limit your topic.

In the few minutes allotted to you, you may not be able
to tell everything you know about your topic. You must
therefore narrow your topic so that you can cover it in the
time allowed. For example:

TOO GENERAL   Modern aircraft
SUITABLE SUBJECT   What makes an airplane fly?
                   Vertical-takeoff aircraft
                   Helicopters can help solve traffic congestion.

EXERCISE 2. Choose one of the topics you listed for
Exercise 1 and limit it to a narrower topic. Submit the new
topic to your teacher for comments and suggestions.

28c. Have a purpose for your talk.

A speaker should have a definite aim. If you have a purpose and keep it in mind, you can *calculate* the effect upon
your audience of the remarks or gestures you are thinking
of using. You can then eliminate every feature that does not
seem to advance your purpose.

Almost every subject can be developed for a specific
purpose. The purpose may be *to inform, to entertain,* or
to persuade.

Suppose, for example, that the subject of your talk is
Western movies. If your purpose is to *inform,* you may decide to discuss the first Westerns or the rise of the tradition
from the dime novel.

If your purpose is to *entertain,* you might tell the class about famous Hollywood stars and how they began their careers in the movies.

And if your purpose is to *persuade,* you might urge the class to join in composing a letter to the moviemakers, accusing them of distorting the real traditions of the old West.

As soon as you have determined your purpose, write it out in an explicit statement, or thesis.

TOPIC   Recycling bottles and cans

PURPOSE   To inform. I shall explain clearly what types of bottles and cans are best for recycling. I will give examples of successful neighborhood recycling projects.

EXERCISE 3. Choose three subjects from the list approved by your teacher in Exercise 1. For each, compose an explicit statement of purpose and submit it to your teacher for suggestions and comments.

28d. Gather material for your talk.

Where will you find material for a talk? Start with yourself. Consider the vast number of facts and opinions you already have in your head. These will give your talk a fresh, original viewpoint, and you will discover which phases of the topic you will need to study further.

If you cannot find enough material for a talk from your own experience, go to outside sources such as your friends and acquaintances, newspaper and magazine articles, radio and television programs, and books.

Once your interest has settled upon some general subject, talk to your friends about it to deepen your understanding of it. Listen to radio and television for information. Consult your school and neighborhood libraries.

28e. Outline your talk.

Avoid the temptation to write out and memorize your speech. Instead, outline the structure of your speech. You may, if you wish, write out and memorize the opening and concluding sentences, but no more than that.

The outline of an anecdote is just a reminder of the sequence of events you intend to tell. An outline of an argument or explanation is more detailed. Head the outline with the topic, and then write out the statement of purpose. After this comes the outline itself. Here is a typical outline for a persuasive talk.

Sample Outline

Topic: Water pollution must be stopped!

Purpose: To persuade listeners to protect our water supply

  I. Current supply of fresh water
    A. Increasing demand—100 billion liters used every day
    B. Decreasing supply—as a result of water pollution

 II. Causes of water pollution
    A. Garbage dumped by cities and towns
    B. Chemicals dumped by industries
    C. Detergents containing phosphates
    D. Oil spills
    E. Pesticides

III. What the average citizen can do
    A. Use laundry detergents without phosphates
    B. Conserve water whenever possible
    C. Write letters to state and federal legislators
    D. Watch for sources of water pollution; report offenders to environmental authorities

EXERCISE 4. Make outlines for the three subjects worked on in Exercise 3.

28f. Make sure that your talk has a good introduction and conclusion.

In your introduction, try to arouse interest. Often you can do this with an arresting sentence or question.

EXAMPLE   Pollution never seemed important to me until the day I took a canoe trip down Bushmill Creek.

There are two disappointing ways for a talk to end: (1) to sputter to a stop like a motor out of gas and (2) to be checked in full course by the teacher's admonition, "Time's up." Do not allow your speech to end so. Conclude strongly by summing up what you have said or by leaving in the mind of your audience a dominant impression of your talk.

EXAMPLE   Rusty cans, discarded tires, and other garbage may destroy our water in years to come. Let's join together and stop this pollution!

EXERCISE 5. Write an attention-getting introduction and an emphatic conclusion for one of the subjects worked on in the previous exercises.

GIVING THE TALK

So far we have been discussing the *content* of a good speech. This section will discuss the *technique*.

Good public speakers are in close touch with their audiences. They look at the audience as they talk. They have friendly manners, speak distinctly, and pitch their voices so that they are easily heard. Although they are slightly more formal when addressing large groups, they always speak as naturally as if they were conversing with friends.

If you look on public speaking as conversation with a large group and take every opportunity you can to speak in public, you will notice yourself growing in self-confidence and skill.

28g. Conquer nervousness.

Do not reproach yourself if you are somewhat tense. Even veteran performers are tense before they go on. Tension is merely the body's signal that it is ready for whatever demands the next few minutes will make on it. Once you are on the "stage," excess tension will usually disappear.

The best antidotes for nervousness are these three:

1. Know your subject. Know your subject so thoroughly that it tells itself.

2. Practice. Practice imprints on your memory the sequence of your talk and makes it very hard to get "stuck."

3. Relax. Deep breathing helps. One well-known trick of professional orators is to "sigh" deeply before inhaling. By forcing all the air out of your lungs, you will also relax your muscles.

28h. Develop a good speaking manner.

1. Rehearse your presentation. Using your outline as a guide, practice your speech aloud at home. Do not write out or memorize what you are going to say. Each rehearsal will be different, and when you finally deliver your speech, it will differ from all your rehearsals.

2. Use descriptive language. As you practice, search for images and accurate words and expressions that will make your talk more vivid. Look for words that have life and sparkle.

EXAMPLES My little brother squirmed onto the chair and let his legs dangle.

She toppled track records like rows of dominoes.

3. Enunciate clearly and accurately. While practicing, be sure to speak distinctly. Slovenly speech is caused by laziness of the lips and tongue. Be overprecise in practice, but when you speak before your classmates, concentrate on *what* you are saying rather than on *how* you are saying it. There will be some carry-over from the practice to the presentation.

28i. Use nonverbal communication.

Your audience will certainly be watching you as you speak. How you stand, how you move about, and how you gesture can communicate unspoken, or nonverbal, signals to them. Think of these unspoken signals as part of your speech.

Limit, or control, your movements for effective nonverbal communication.

1. Watch your posture. If you are standing, keep your weight evenly distributed on both feet. If you are sitting, place your feet squarely on the floor. Do not cross your legs. Careful posture will help you to avoid slouching, which is a distracting nonverbal signal.

2. Establish eye contact with your listeners. A speaker who looks at the floor or who stares at note cards will easily lose an audience's attention. Good speakers move their glance around the room, focusing on the faces of listeners. This eye contact with the audience makes the talk more personal and easier to follow. It also enables you to notice how well your talk is being understood.

3. Choose gestures with care. Self-conscious speakers often gesture wildly, calling more attention to their hands and arms than to their words. Effective gestures are visual clues to meaning. Hands, for example, can indicate size, shape, or direction. As you rehearse your speech, think also of the gestures you will use.

THREE SPEAKING SITUATIONS

Although all speeches have certain things in common, you can use different techniques depending on the kind of speech you are giving. The most common speeches you will be called upon to deliver will probably be the narrative talk, the explanatory talk, and the persuasive talk.

The Narrative Talk

In the narrative talk, you tell about a personal experience or relate an anecdote. It is not difficult to find a subject for such a talk if you keep in mind that it is the *manner* and not just the subject matter that makes such talks interesting. A quarrel with your brother or a funny experience on the bus can be just as fascinating as the description of a Caribbean cruise.

28j. Make your narrative talk vivid.

1. Begin with action. After you have decided upon your purpose, plunge right into your story without any preamble.

EXAMPLE   How many of you have been in a completely strange place and yet were unmistakably certain *that you had seen it all before* — perhaps in a dream? Eerie, isn't it? Well, it happened to me!

2. Maintain suspense. Lead your listeners up to the climax, giving them no inkling until the last moment of how the story will end. Then end it and take your seat. To linger after the end of the story, explaining away small, unimportant details, weakens the dramatic effect you are aiming at.

EXERCISE 6. Relate an unusual personal experience to the class. If you can, select an incident that illustrates a point. Arouse and maintain suspense. Use descriptive language. Pay attention to your posture and your enunciation. Practice at home before delivering your talk. Limit your talk to three minutes.

EXERCISE 7. Relate an experience or anecdote to illustrate a proverb. The following list contains suggestions.

1. A stitch in time saves nine.
2. Waste not, want not.
3. An empty barrel makes the most noise.
4. A fool and his money are soon parted.
5. A watched pot never boils.
6. Easy come, easy go.
7. Pride goeth before a fall.
8. Spare the rod and spoil the child.
9. A cat may look at a king.

EXERCISE 8. Relate an unusual incident in the life of a famous man or woman. A list of suggested persons follows.

1. John F. Kennedy
2. Maria Tallchief
3. Susan B. Anthony
4. Bessie Smith

5. Martin Luther King, Jr.   8. Abraham Lincoln
6. Roberto Clemente   9. Ynes Mexia
7. I. M. Pei   10. Babe Zaharias

The Explanatory Talk

From time to time you will be called upon to explain how to make or to do something. To explain so that your listeners will understand easily, you must plan carefully and observe certain principles of organization and delivery.

28k. Make your explanatory talk clear.

1. Limit your topic. Restrict your choice to a topic you know (or can get to know) thoroughly. The narrower the topic, the more completely you can treat it in the time allowed.

INTEREST   Auto mechanics
CHOOSE   Reboring the cylinder head
INTEREST   Archery
CHOOSE   How to fletch your own arrows

2. Organize your explanation. Your outline is all-important in a talk of this kind. In it you determine the arrangement of ideas in a step-by-step progression from the simple to the complex, the familiar to the unfamiliar, or in whatever order best suits your subject.

3. Master all technical terms. If you choose a subject that ordinarily uses technical terms, master this vocabulary so that you can explain technical terms as you go along. It would be absurd for a student to speak of a tennis racket as a "tennis bat," a distributor as "that little pot with all the wires going in," or then a chihuahua as "a skinny little dog."

4. Use visual aids. If you can bring to class the object, tool, or device you are going to explain and then demonstrate how it works, it will make your explanation clearer. If you cannot bring an object or device, illustrate your talk by drawing a diagram on the chalkboard.

While you talk, hold the object you are going to demonstrate in front of you so that everyone can see it. If you use a diagram, stand to one side and refer to it with a pointer.

EXERCISE 9. Give an explanatory talk to the class. Your talk should last about five minutes. Use one of the topics from the list below or choose your own.

1. A science experiment that you can do at home
2. Balanced meals
3. How our local government is organized
4. Training a dog
5. How to drive safely

The Persuasive Talk

Speakers must plan carefully, arrange arguments thoughtfully, and speak forcefully if they want to persuade others or get them to act.

28l. Make your persuasive talk effective.

1. Choose a controversial question. Simple questions of fact are not arguable, but questions of policy are.

FACT Presidents are elected by vote of the Electoral College.
POLICY Should we abolish the Electoral College?

2. Arrange your arguments carefully. Rework your outline until the speech it represents is logical, well supported, and hard-hitting. When you cite an authoritative opinion in support of your own, you must jot down the name, publication, and page number just as you would in a footnote for a composition.

3. Rehearse your talk. Rehearsing your talk in front of your parents or friends gives them the opportunity to raise questions and objections that you have overlooked. Once you are aware of these flaws in your argument, you can make changes to correct them.

EXERCISE 10. Give a persuasive talk to the class on some subject you think important. Choose one of the topics listed below or select one of your own.

1. More money should go into the space program.
2. A free college education ought to be the right of all.
3. Networks should stop showing violence on television.
4. Students are given too much homework.
5. Put a woman in the White House!

LISTENING WITH A PURPOSE

This section will help you to become a more skillful listener. As such, you will be able to apply your full attention to any matter that warrants it — to understand what is said; to sift fact from opinion, the weighty from the trivial; and to evaluate what you hear.

28m. Listen courteously.

Good listening manners require that you listen and do nothing else. Do not let yourself be distracted. Be patient and quiet if a speaker experiences difficulty. You will be grateful for such treatment when your turn comes.

28n. Listen accurately.

The greatest enemy to accurate listening is a wandering mind. You can often force your attention to stick to its job by giving it the following tasks:

1. Listen to understand and recall what was said. Of course we cannot recall everything, but memory can be trained, and by constant practice we can remember a lot more than we might suppose. Pay close attention to what is said and review it immediately afterward in your mind, rehearsing the main points and repeating them to yourself in the order given.

EXERCISE 11. Compose five questions similar to those that follow. Read them aloud, pausing about five seconds between each question to allow your classmates time to jot down their answers. When you have finished, your classmates will check their answers to determine how accurately they have listened.

1. In the series of numbers $8 - 9 - 4 - 3 - 1$, the third number is ———?

2. In the list of words $on - off - at - or - in$, the fourth word is ———?

3. In the list of words $but - can - stop - then - until$, the word beginning with c is ———?

4. In the announcement "Send your replies to Box 665, Los Angeles, California 90047, before March 31, together with a box top from our product," the post office box number is ———?

5. In the statement "Fran will keep the score, Lucy will be captain of one team, and Rose of the other, and Lena and Pam will pitch," what is Fran's assignment?

EXERCISE 12. Compose an announcement in which essential information is omitted. Read it aloud and test your classmates' attentiveness by asking them to point out the details you have forgotten.

EXAMPLE Tomorrow our basketball team will play one of the strongest teams in our county league. The game will be played at 4 P.M. Admission is free to all members of our Student Organization. Nonmembers can purchase tickets for fifty cents. This promises to be one of the most exciting games of the season. Everyone should attend. [Note that the announcement omits the name of the opposing team and where the game will be played.]

2. Listen to understand the underlying structure of a talk or a lecture. This exercise trains your powers of analysis so that you can understand and recall the gist of a complicated talk by knowing what its main arguments will probably be. It can be done from the signals a speaker gives in the opening remarks indicating what the main ideas are going to be.

For instance, of the following two sets of opening remarks, the listener might ask, "What is the speaker's topic?" and then "How will the argument proceed?" The listener might then jot down the notes that follow each set of remarks.

> There are two reasons, among others, for finishing high school: first, to get a better job; second, to extend your interests and thus get more enjoyment out of life.

NOTES   Finish high school
1. Better job
2. Better person

> This morning we pay tribute to Theodore Roosevelt as a conservationist, President, and advocate of the outdoor life.

NOTES   Theodore Roosevelt
1. As conservationist
2. As President
3. As outdoor enthusiast

EXERCISE 13. Cut out the introductory paragraph of a short magazine article. Read it to the class, asking them what they think the main points of the article will be. Then compare these versions with the real one.

3. Listen to grasp the main ideas. As the speaker finishes the introductory remarks and develops the subject, the listener, pencil in hand, asks, "What arguments support the speaker's main points?" and "What facts are offered as proof?"

A speaker's main points frequently stand out because of the emphasis given them. Forceful speakers punctuate each main idea by tone, gesture, and expression. They restate the arguments frequently, illustrating them, citing statistics in their support, and bringing in authoritative opinion in their behalf.

The transitions from one point to the next are signaled by words like *therefore, consequently, on the other hand,* and *however* and should be carefully noted by the listener. Other clues to the development of an argument are words like *for example* and *for instance,* which usually indicate that the ideas that follow illustrate a point. Still others show that the speaker is about to summarize: *in conclusion, finally, to sum up.*

EXERCISE 14. Your teacher will read to you a brief magazine article for about five or ten minutes. As you listen, write an outline of the lecture or article; then compare it with the outline your teacher puts on the board.

28o. Listen critically.

The critical listener insists upon evaluating what is said. Critical listening is the art of making distinctions.

1. Weigh the evidence. To do this, you must distinguish fact from opinion.

FACT   Abraham Lincoln was born on February 12, 1809.
OPINION   Abraham Lincoln was the greatest President this country ever had.

FACT   At sea level water freezes at 0°C.
OPINION   Warm water is better for swimming.

Distinguish between reliable and unreliable authority.

RELIABLE   The U.S. Department of Commerce reports that the rate of inflation increased last month.
UNRELIABLE   Wednesday Jones, the popular star, says that inflation statistics are never accurate.

Distinguish between generalizations from sufficient evidence and those from insufficient evidence.

SUFFICIENT   Decatur High's team won every game in our league; our team lost every game. Therefore, Decatur's team is better than ours this season.
INSUFFICIENT   I know three students from Decatur High School. Each has red hair. Therefore, most Decatur students have red hair.

Distinguish between proper and improper comparison or analogy.

PROPER   Esme, whom I can usually beat at bowling, beats

Ruth regularly. Therefore, I probably can beat Ruth
too.

IMPROPER   John, who lives next door, read *Sounder* and didn't
like it. Therefore, I probably won't like it either.

2. Recognize and avoid unfair argument. Because it is
always easy to let emotion rather than reason control our
judgments, the critical listener must be on guard against
propaganda devices that may deceive or misguide. The
following are some of these propaganda devices:

Prejudice. Opinions based on prejudice are really not
opinions at all, for in most cases they simply ignore the
truth.

EXAMPLES   Country resident: City dwellers are stuck-up, devious,
and untrustworthy.
City resident: Country folks are lazy, unimaginative,
and suspicious.

Bandwagon appeals. These play on the fear of being
"different."

EXAMPLE   All over the country people are switching to Warwick
soup. It's the thing to do.

Name-calling. By labeling problems with simple and
emotionally charged names and slogans, the propagandist
avoids rational argument. Name-calling can also damage
someone's reputation by repeating false charges.

EXAMPLE   Of Federal safety guidelines: "This is just more government red tape."

Slogans. A favorite device of propagandists, catchy
slogans are easily remembered, quickly shouted, and impossible to refute. Like name-calling, slogans are designed
to take the place of sober reasoning.

EXAMPLES   Our country right or wrong!
Be the first to own one!

Snob appeal. Most people like to think of themselves
as successful and deserving. Advertisers play on these feelings by trying to make their products status symbols —
visible signs of success.

EXAMPLE   Move up to the Champion class in ten-speed bicycles!

The unproved assertion. Advertisers and speakers often make statements without proof. Unless a statement is supported by reasons, figures, examples, or the opinions of competent and unbiased authorities, it should be questioned. The following statements seem to prove a point but actually do not because no evidence is offered.

EXAMPLES   Cigarette smoking causes cancer. It injures body tissue. It irritates the lungs, poisons the blood, and affects digestion.

Cigarette smoking does not cause cancer. Smokers are not physically impaired. There is no danger to the throat, lungs, heart, or arteries. Smoking is harmless.

EXERCISE 15. In the following statements you will find examples of invalid and unfair argument. Identify each type of unfair argument and explain briefly how each violates the standards of good reasoning.

1. The wise merchant will never employ a teen-ager. As any newspaper shows, teen-agers are undependable, dangerous, and larcenous.

2. My opponent is a demagogue whose philosophy is "soak the rich." This kind of policy will surely kill the goose that lays the golden eggs.

3. Olaf, Niels, and Karen are all excellent skiers. They are Swedish. All Swedes are excellent skiers.

4. Oneonta High won all of their games right after adopting a new cheer. For Heaven's sake, let's end our losing streak by adopting a new cheer, too!

5. The math test was terribly unfair! I spent three days reviewing for it and only got a *C*.

6. The Representative was against space travel for this reason: "If humans were meant to fly, they would have been given wings."

7. General Smith is certain to make a fine governor. After all, she had a brilliant military career and was decorated many times for her heroism in battle.

8. Let's end foreign aid at once. Foreigners don't deserve our help. They don't believe in the American way and are so slick in diplomatic dealings that we, who have been taught always to live up to our end of a deal, are certain to lose our shirts.

9. Never vote for a Democratic candidate, for it is well known that Democrats are determined to soak the rich.

10. Senator Jones failed to vote for the nuclear arms treaty. That action shows that he is a hawk on defense issues.

EXERCISE 16. From your reading or television viewing, collect two examples each of the following items.

1. A statement by a reliable authority
2. A statement by an unreliable authority
3. A generalization from sufficient evidence
4. A generalization from insufficient evidence
5. A bandwagon appeal
6. A slogan
7. An unproved assertion
8. A proved assertion

EXERCISE 17. Compose a brief, one-paragraph argument for or against some idea, in which you deliberately trespass against the rules for fair and honest thinking. Try to make your argument somewhat subtle so that your classmates must exercise their ingenuity to discover the abuse. If you cannot compose one yourself, look through a magazine, and cut out an advertisement making obvious use of some propaganda device. Bring it to class for discussion.

SUMMARY OF LISTENING TECHNIQUES

1. Give the speaker your full attention.
2. Be patient and do not interrupt the speaker.

3. Review the speaker's main points in your mind immediately after the speaker has finished speaking.
4. Pay attention to signals which the speaker may give during a talk to indicate the main points presented.
5. Weigh the evidence the speaker presents. Distinguish fact from opinion, reliable and unreliable authority, sufficient and insufficient generalization, and proper and improper comparision or analogy.
6. Recognize and avoid unfair argument, such as name-calling, snob appeal, and unproved assertion.

Chapter 29

Group Discussion

**Group Discussion,
Parliamentary Procedure,
The Interview**

Group discussion skills will help you participate effectively in college and in a career. Through discussion you will learn the meaning of freedom of speech
and the responsibilities that go with it. You will discover
that persons with differing views can disagree in an atmosphere of mutual respect and can work together for the
common good without abandoning their beliefs.

Even when discussion does not result in a solution, the
time spent is seldom wasted because the participants may
perceive the extent of a problem more clearly by ex-
changing opinions and may become more willing to compromise.

TYPES OF GROUP DISCUSSION

There are four kinds of group discussion:

Social conversation is private, unplanned, and touches
lightly on many topics. It requires no leader, although a
host or hostess may occasionally steer it. Its aim is enjoyment, persuasion, or instruction.

Informal group discussion resembles social conversation except that it is usually more purposeful and deals with
a single topic or a limited number of topics decided beforehand by the participants. An informal group, such as a small
committee, may or may not be guided by a discussion
leader.

Formal group discussion is public and planned. It
considers many aspects of a single topic. It is directed and

summarized by a discussion leader. Its aim is to reach an agreement, solve a problem, or start action.

A *debate* is public and planned, like formal group discussion, but considers only two sides of a question. The supporters of one side attempt to defeat their opponents by arguments. The victor is determined by a judge or group of judges.

A debate may grow out of a group discussion. The numerous solutions developed in a discussion may be narrowed to one, which is then offered to a wider public for acceptance or rejection.

29a. Learn the characteristics of the various forms of group discussion.

The *round table* is a group discussion in which the participants exchange views around a table (not necessarily round) under the guidance of a discussion leader. The number of people usually does not exceed a dozen. The discussion is informal. There is no audience.

The most common example of a round-table discussion is the committee meeting. Most organizations conduct a large part of their business through committees. A committee considers matters referred to it and reports its findings and recommendations to the entire organization.

A *forum* is any type of speaking program that is followed by audience participation. For example, a lecture followed by questions from the audience is a forum. A forum is most successful when the audience is small; otherwise, people are reluctant to stand up and speak their minds.

A *symposium* consists of prepared talks by several speakers on different aspects of a single topic. When all the speakers have finished their presentations, the discussion leader invites the audience to ask questions, contribute additional information, or express agreement or disagreement with the speakers' views.

A *panel discussion* is like an overheard conversation. It consists of a leader and from four to eight participants seated, usually in a semicircle, before an audience. The participants remain seated during the discussion. They speak in conversational style, generally not longer than one or two minutes at a time. They express opinions, disagree with and question one another. The leader acts as a moderator, stimulating, directing, and summarizing the discussion. After a while the audience joins in the conversation. The leader summarizes the discussion before bringing it to an end.

PREPARATION FOR GROUP DISCUSSION

29b. Select a topic that lends itself to profitable group discussion.

Before selecting a topic for discussion, ask:
1. Is it worthwhile?
2. Is it timely?
3. Is it related to the needs, experience, and interests of listeners and speakers?
4. Is it stimulating?
5. Is it many-sided?

What are good sources of topics for group discussion? Your own experience may suggest some; for example, "Teen-age problems," "Trends in popular music," or "Choosing a career." Your school courses may suggest others; for instance, "Why study mathematics and science?" or "The most valuable subject in the curriculum." Books, newspapers, magazine articles, movies, and television programs can often stimulate discussion. Current events, especially controversial matters, can also capture and hold an audience's attention.

A discussion topic should be a question of policy rather than a question of fact. "Do we have a supply of gasoline?" is a question of fact, and the only appropriate reply is a direct, factual answer. "Should we stop using gasoline to power cars?" is a question of policy that stirs discussion.

Topics that are trivial or timeworn, have no audience appeal, do not evoke strong differences of opinion, or can be answered by *yes* or *no* are not suitable. Select an up-to-date controversial topic.

EXAMPLES   What's wrong with today's economy?
How can we prevent food shortages?
Who should pay for college?

29c. Prepare for a group discussion by thinking, talking, and reading about the topic.

Many discussions fail because of insufficient preparation by the participants.

To prepare for a discussion, everyone must think, talk, and read about the topic before the discussion takes place. When the topic is announced:

1. Think about it. What is your opinion? On what evidence is it based?

2. Talk to others about it. Discuss it with your friends and parents. Discuss it with someone who is an authority on the subject. Be ready to modify your previous opinion in the light of your new knowledge.

3. Consult reference books, recent publications, magazine articles, and editorials. Inform yourself as thoroughly as you can about the topic. Keep an open mind while you are learning.

29d. Learn the duties of the discussion leader.

In addition to thinking and learning about the topic before the discussion, a discussion leader is responsible for knowing the backgrounds and special interests of each speaker. If possible, a preliminary meeting of all the speakers should be arranged to go over the topic and procedure of the discussion.

When the discussion begins, the leader should make a brief introductory statement focusing on the purpose of the discussion. The discussion leader both introduces each speaker to the audience and mentions something about each speaker's background or interests.

While the discussion continues, the leader should ask questions of the speakers. The leader should also try to prevent fruitless digressions and ensure that everyone has a chance to speak.

At the close of the discussion, the leader should summarize the major points and thank the audience and speakers.

29e. Learn the duties of speakers in a round table, forum, symposium, or panel discussion.

Speakers invited to a discussion should be able to listen carefully and courteously to others, speak so that everyone can hear, and be sure that the comments they give are directly related to the topic.

29f. Learn the duties of members of the audience.

A member of the audience should listen to the speakers with an alert mind, take notes if necessary, and join in the discussion when the leader invites questions from the spectators. Questions should, of course, relate directly to the topic under discussion and be spoken with a clear voice that everyone can hear.

EXERCISE 1. List five topics suitable for group discussion. Test them against the criteria listed in the preceding sections. The topics may be related to school, community, state, national, or international affairs.

TAKING PART IN GROUP DISCUSSION

You can be more successful in communicating your ideas to others if you learn something about speaking and listening effectively in group discussions.

You and the Group

A group is made up of individuals who are attempting to achieve a common goal. A basketball team, for example, is a group of players who are trying to win a game. A photography club is a group of photographers who might want to organize an exhibition.

Within every group, each individual must accept and work for the group's common goal. An individual, however, might have private goals not shared by the group. Psychologists call these private goals a *hidden agenda*. As you enter a group discussion, you should be aware of the difference between the goal of the discussion and the private goals of individual members. Avoid the impulse of imposing your private intentions on the whole group. Participating in a group discussion depends chiefly upon individual cooperation.

29g. Learn how to speak effectively in group discussion.

1. Think before you speak. Know what you are going to say before you begin. Take a few seconds to organize your ideas before you start talking; clear thinking precedes clear speaking.

2. Keep the other person in mind. Try to understand the other person's point of view. Avoid sarcasm and ridicule; they hurt unnecessarily and are a sign that your own arguments are weak. In the midst of heated discussion, remain calm. Your calmness will show up in your tone of voice, facial expression, and rate of speaking.

3. Be brief. Omit long and unnecessary explanations. Know the point you want to make and go directly to it. Speak simply but naturally and enthusiastically. Listeners like an enthusiastic speaker.

29h. Learn how to listen accurately and critically while taking part in group discussion.

In group discussion the interplay of personalities is often so interesting that your attention may wander or you may fail to recognize that a speaker's comments are not relevant to the topic.

You can focus your attention by taking notes. Jotting down the arguments will enable you to see the merits of each point. Follow these principles:

1. Recognize and guard against your own prejudices. Don't let emotions color your thinking. For example, your reactions to a speaker's appearance, accent, or gestures may affect your acceptance or rejection of what you hear. Think fairly and test ideas on rational, not emotional, grounds.

2. Recognize a speaker's bias and take it into account. When a speaker has an ax to grind, a listener must be careful. The arguments may be valid, but they may also be one-sided and rooted in prejudice.

3. Watch for words, phrases, and attitudes that are emotionally loaded. Some words report a fact objectively. They have few emotional overtones, if any. Others are loaded with emotion.

Compare the following pairs of words. Notice how one member of each pair is relatively colorless, while the other arouses feelings.

house	shack	dwelling	mansion
reply	rebuke	defeat	rout
verse	doggerel	recline	sprawl
farmer	peasant	failure	fiasco
work	drudgery	dog	mongrel

Loaded words carry positive or negative charges. A positively charged word creates a favorable reaction; a negatively charged word, an unfavorable one. Propagandists make use of loaded words to influence listeners. They employ positively charged words to sway you to their way of thinking and negatively charged words to make you reject what they oppose.

EXERCISE 2. Number your paper 1–10. Indicate by plus or minus signs which of the following words affect you positively or negatively.

1. adorable
2. skinny
3. generous
4. crude

5. glamorous   8. rebellious
6. fabulous   9. sympathy
7. miserly   10. screech

4. Don't be misled by catchy slogans and generalized introductory statements. Advertisers and political organizations often employ slogans to popularize ideas, candidates, or products. A complex argument cannot be summarized fairly in a capsule expression.

EXAMPLES   See America first. [slogan promoting travel in the United States, as opposed to foreign travel]
Put yourself in our shoes. [advertising slogan]

Generalized introductory statements often have no basis in fact, but they imply that disagreement is impossible.

EXAMPLES   It is common knowledge that . . .
Everybody knows that . . .

5. Look for and weigh evidence for every important statement. If a speaker offers no evidence, ask for it. If the evidence is insufficient, ask for more.

EXERCISE 3.   Conduct a round-table discussion on a topic that concerns all the participants. Appoint a discussion leader who will end the discussion after twenty minutes, summarize, and invite class discussion. Suggested topics:

1. The school yearbook
2. Improving the student organization
3. Building school spirit
4. Improving the school cafeteria
5. Assembly programs

EXERCISE 4.   Conduct a symposium on discipline. The speakers should represent the viewpoints of a student, a parent, a law enforcement officer, an educator, and a community leader.

EXERCISE 5.   Select a discussion leader and present a panel discussion on any one of the following topics or your own topic. Each panel should meet beforehand to settle matters of procedure and scope.

1. Radio and television advertising
2. Comic books
3. Youthful crime
4. Violence on the screen
5. Prejudice — and how to overcome it
6. The impact of the young voter
7. The ideal school
8. Professional vs. amateur sports
9. Our foreign policy
10. Ways of preventing war

EXERCISE 6. Why should you be particularly careful in listening to each of the following speakers?

1. The president of a college fraternity speaking about the advantages of fraternity life

2. A movie actress advertising a cold cream

3. A candidate of a political party speaking about the party's platform

4. A disc jockey delivering a commercial

5. A parent of a failing student criticizing a school

EVALUATION OF GROUP DISCUSSION

29i. Evaluate a group discussion by asking key questions about it.

By considering the merits and faults of a group discussion after it is over, you can learn to improve future discussions. These questions will help you evaluate a group discussion.

1. Was the discussion purposeful? Were the causes of the problem considered? Were various solutions proposed and analyzed? Did the discussion ramble, or did it proceed in an orderly fashion?

2. Were the outcomes worthwhile? A group discussion need not reach a solution or agreement. It may be successful if it brings areas of disagreement into the open.

3. Were the participants thoroughly familiar with the problem? Did they present facts, instances, statements of

competent and unbiased authorities, and statistics to support their opinions?

 4. Was the discussion lively and general? Was there a give-and-take of opinion in an atmosphere of mutual respect? Did all participate? Did anyone monopolize the meeting, or did everyone speak briefly and to the point?

 5. Did the participants reach a solution justified by the evidence? Do you agree with the solution? Why?

 6. Were the audience's questions thought-provoking? Did the speakers answer them directly and fully?

 7. Was the discussion courteous? Did each speaker exercise self-control by refraining from interrupting when another was speaking? Were statements and objections phrased courteously?

 8. Did the discussion leader's introductory remarks arouse interest? Did the discussion avoid valueless digressions? Was everyone encouraged to join in? Was there a summary?

EXERCISE 7. Criticize a radio or television discussion you have heard. Consider such matters as choice of topic, the speakers' familiarity with the topic, the quality of the discussion, and audience participation. In what ways could the discussion have been improved?

PARLIAMENTARY PROCEDURE

Many organizations conduct their meetings according to a code known as *rules of order* or *parliamentary procedure.*

 Parliamentary procedure protects the rights of all and enables individuals to work together efficiently. It is a means of determining the will of the majority and at the same time safeguarding the rights of the minority.

Elections

When a club is organized, the founding members draw up a constitution with its bylaws. This document sets forth the name and purpose of the club and the rules by which it will op‿rate. Among these rules is one regulating the election of officers.

29j. Officers are elected and perform duties according to a constitution.

Officers may be nominated by a nominating committee or individual members may make nominations from the floor. Elections are usually held immediately after nominations are closed.

A majority vote is usually required for election unless a bylaw states otherwise. If no one receives a majority, a new vote must be taken, limited to the two candidates who received the highest number of votes on the first ballot. Depending upon the constitution of the organization, officers may be elected by either an open or a secret ballot.

Duties of Officers

The president presides over meetings, appoints committees, calls special meetings if necessary, and sees that the organization's constitution and bylaws are observed.

The vice-president acts in place of the president if the latter is absent. The vice-president may have other duties specified in the constitution.

The secretary notifies members of meetings, takes the minutes, keeps a record of attendance, and answers letters as the president directs.

The treasurer receives dues and other income, pays the club's bills, and keeps a record of all receipts and disbursements. At every meeting the treasurer gives a report on the organization's current financial status.

Club Business

29k. The regular procedure at meetings is called the order of business.

The following is a typical order of business:

EXAMPLE   1. Call to order
             2. Roll call
             3. Reading of minutes of previous meeting
             4. Treasurer's report
             5. Committee reports
             6. Unfinished business
             7. New business
             8. Adjournment

29l. A motion is a proposal for discussion and action.

EXAMPLES I move that we purchase new uniforms for the basketball team.
I move that we publish a monthly bulletin.
I move that this question be referred to a committee of three appointed by the chair.
I move we adjourn.

An organization transacts all its business at meetings through motions.

Steps in Making a Motion

1. A member requests and receives recognition by the chair. If two or more members rise at the same time, the chair recognizes the one who addressed the chair first.

MEMBER   "Mr. (Madam) Chairman."
  CHAIR   "Mr. Jones."

2. The member states his motion.

MEMBER   "I move that our club hold a skating party."

3. Another member seconds the motion. This means the member agrees with the motion. All motions must be seconded before they can be considered.

ANOTHER MEMBER   "I second the motion."

4. The chair repeats the motion, using the original words.

CHAIR "It is moved and seconded that our club hold a skating party. Is there any discussion?"

5. The members discuss the motion.
6. When the discussion is finished, the chair repeats the motion.
7. The chair puts the motion to a vote.

CHAIR "All those in favor, say 'aye.' Those opposed, 'nay.'"

8. The chair announces the result.

CHAIR "The motion is carried."

If the vote is taken by a show of hands or by ballot, the chair may announce the exact count.

CHAIR "By a vote of 25 to 8, the motion is carried."

Except for special motions, only one motion may be considered at a time.

EXERCISE 8. Practice the steps in making a motion. With one class member acting as chair, the others will offer various motions. Suggested subjects for motions:

1. Abolition of homework
2. Class picnic
3. Purchase of books
4. Petition to principal
5. Field trip
6. Publication of class newspaper

Amending a Motion

To amend a motion means to change the wording of the motion. Not more than one amendment can be considered at a time. Another amendment may be proposed when the first has been voted on.

29m. A motion may be amended by adding, striking out, or substituting words.

EXAMPLES I move to amend the original motion by adding the word "monthly" before "dance."

> I move to amend the original motion by striking out the word "new."
>
> I move to amend the original motion by substituting the word "semiannual" in place of "annual."

EXERCISE 9. Practice making and amending motions using the topics listed in Exercise 8 or others of your own devising.

Special Motions

Certain motions affect how a meeting is run and how decisions are made.

Motion to adjourn. The purpose of this motion is to bring the meeting to an end. It cannot be debated or amended and must be put to a vote as soon as it is seconded.

EXAMPLE   I move that this meeting adjourn.

Motion to table. This action can postpone debate or a vote on a particular motion. If passed, the motion being considered is set aside until members agree to "take from the table." A motion to table cannot be debated or amended.

EXAMPLE   I move to table this motion.

Motion to close debate. This motion cuts off discussion and brings a question to a vote.

The motion to close debate may not be debated or amended. It requires a *two-thirds* vote for adoption. (Notice that any motion restricting freedom of speech requires a two-thirds vote in order to protect minority rights.)

EXAMPLE   I move to close debate and vote on this question at
           once.

Motion to refer to committee. This motion assigns a question to a committee for study and report. This motion can be debated and amended.

MOTION   I move that this question be referred to committee.
AMENDMENT   I move that the motion be amended by adding the
              words "and that the committee report its findings at
              our next meeting."

Point of Order

A point of order is not a motion. It requires no second and no vote. Points of order require members to follow the rules of order. Typical points of order are: absence of a quorum, irrelevant remarks by a speaker, motion that violates a club's constitution.

MEMBER "Mr. (Madam) Chairman, I rise to a point of order."

CHAIR "State your point of order."

MEMBER "I make the point of order that the meeting is so noisy the speaker cannot be heard."

CHAIR "The point is well taken and the meeting will come to order."

EXERCISE 10. Practice the following procedures in class.

1. Proposing, discussing, and voting on a main motion
2. Rising to a point of order
3. Adjourning a meeting
4. Nominating and electing officers
5. Proposing a special motion

EXERCISE 11. With one class member acting as chair, other members of the class will propose, discuss, and vote upon motions. For example:

1. That the members purchase a birthday gift for the custodian-engineer
2. That students be allowed to use the cafeteria for cooking lessons
3. That the admission price for school dances be increased
4. That one member should attend parent-teacher meetings
5. That future meetings be held each week

EXERCISE 12. Attend a meeting of a club, council, or association, and report orally on the way the meeting was conducted. What did you learn about parliamentary procedure that you did not previously know?

EXERCISE 13. Read one of the following references and report on it. Explain a topic not taken up in this chapter so clearly that everyone understands. (Some suggested topics: duties and rights of members, reading and approving minutes, the motion to postpone, the motion to reconsider.)

1. Cushing's *Manual of Parliamentary Procedure*
2. Eliot's *Basic Rules of Order*
3. Robert's *Rules of Order*
4. Sturgis' *Standard Code of Parliamentary Procedure*

EXERCISE 14. Two features of parliamentary procedure are freedom of discussion and majority rule. Of the two, which is the more important? Why?

SUMMARY OF PARLIAMENTARY PROCEDURE

1. Parliamentary procedure protects the rights of all and enables individuals to work together efficiently.
2. A club's bylaws set forth the rules regarding the election of officers.
3. Meetings are conducted according to the order of business.
4. A motion is a proposal offered to the membership for discussion and action.
5. An organization conducts all of its business at meetings through motions.
6. Motions, except for certain special motions, can be amended.
7. Points of order require members to follow the rules of order.

THE INTERVIEW

The interview is purposeful. It is concerned with one matter only. While it is conducted in a friendly spirit, it avoids the variety of topics and the digressions which are the charm of informal conversation. In some forms of interview there is a give-and-take of opinion between the participants, and in other forms one person necessarily monopolizes the conversation; but always there is a dominating purpose which the interview tries to achieve. One common type of interview which you should be familiar with is the interview for gathering information.

The Interview for Gathering Information

While preparing a composition, you may wish to obtain information from someone who is knowledgeable in your particular topic.

Be sure to make arrangements for this interview well in advance. You may request the interview in a letter, by a telephone call, or through a personal visit. State who you are and the reason for your request. Mention in general terms what days and times are most acceptable to you for a meeting, but allow the other person to specify the exact time and place.

Preparing for the Interview

Your questions should be planned carefully in advance. Write each question on a separate card or page so that you will have enough room to jot down the replies. If you are using a tape recorder, of course, you need not follow this procedure.

Give plenty of thought to each question you ask. Your interview will be much more successful if you can focus on important issues and avoid minor details. Therefore, ask questions that will elicit useful responses. Newspaper reporters, who conduct interviews daily, often prepare only a few, broad questions. The answers they receive suggest follow-up questions.

Ask questions that require extended replies. For example, rather than asking "Do you think students should be required to study a foreign language?" ask instead,

"Why should students be required to study a foreign language?" The first question can be answered with a simple *yes* or *no*. The second question requires a much more detailed answer.

Be sure that the questions you ask are clear and straight-forward. If the other person seems confused by your question, be prepared to restate it.

Conducting the Interview

Arrive on time. Allow for traffic delays in setting out for your appointment. It is better to be early than late. Lateness for an appointment is discourteous, and it may create a bad impression.

Try not to rush through the interview, asking questions in rapid-fire order. Allow yourself and the other person enough time to consider and respond thoughtfully to each question. During the interview, remain tactful and courteous. Do not try to provoke argument although you may disagree with some of the points being made.

Using a Tape Recorder

Before recording the interview, be sure to ask permission of the person whom you are interviewing. At the end of the interview, agree to play back the recording if you are asked to do so. Permit the person to modify any statements you have recorded.

Concluding the Interview

Before concluding the interview, ask whether there is any aspect of the topic not touched on which the other person would like to discuss. When the interview has run its course, express appreciation for the privilege extended to you and take your leave.

Whatever the purpose of the interview, it is usually a good policy to send a thank-you note.

EXERCISE 15. Conduct an interview to gather information for a composition. Get your teacher's approval of the subject of your interview, and be prepared to report on it in class.

Index and
Tab Key Index

Index

A

Abbreviations
  in dictionaries, 488, 489
  in *Readers' Guide,* 470
  of states, in letters, 360, 365,
    371–72
  punctuation after, 397
  rules for using, 453–54
Accent marks, in dictionaries,
  498–99
Accept, except, 196
Action verb, 11, 153
Active voice, 166–68
Address, direct, commas with,
  413
Addresses, commas with, 412–
  13
Adjective clause
  defined, 84
  diagramed, 87
  relative pronouns in, 85–86
  used in combining sentences,
    239
Adjective phrase
  defined, 60
  diagramed, 63
Adjectives
  after linking verb, 180
  articles as, 8
  comparison of, 184–88
  defined, 7
  diagramed, 49
  distinguished from pronouns,
    9–10
  ending in *-ly,* 180
  function of, 7–8
  introductory, for sentence
    variety, 245
  nouns used as, 11
  position of, in sentences,
    179–80
  predicate, 41

  proper, capitalization of, 378–
    79
  separated from word it modi-
    fies, 8
  telling *which one, what kind,*
    how many, 7–8
  used in combining sentences,
    232
Adverb clause
  commas with, 406–07
  defined, 88
  diagramed, 89
  subordinating conjunction in,
    88–89
  used in combining sentences,
    240–41
Adverb phrase
  defined, 61
  diagramed, 62–63
Adverbs
  comparison of, 184–88
  defined, 16
  diagramed, 49
  distinguished from *-ly* adjec-
    tive, 19, 180
  distinguished from preposi-
    tions, 22
  form of, 180
  introductory, for sentence
    variety, 245
  modifying an adjective, 17–18
  modifying an adverb, 18–19
  modifying a verb, 17
  telling *when, where, how, to*
    what extent, 17
  used in combining sentences,
    232
Affect, effect, 197, 537
Agreement of pronoun and
  antecedent, 124–26
  antecedents joined by *and,*
    126

Agreement of pronoun, *cont'd*
  antecedents joined by *or, nor,*
    126
  gender, 125–26
Agreement of subject and verb
  after *here is, there is,* 119
  collective nouns, 117–18
  doesn't don't, 121–22
  each, everyone, etc., 111
  every, many a, 121
  intervening phrases, 109–10
  predicate nominative, mis-
    taken agreement with, 119
  several, few, both, many, 112
  some, any, none, all, most,
    112–13
  subjects joined by *and,* 115
  subjects joined by *or, nor,*
    115–16
  title of a work of art, 121
  words stating amount, 120–21
All, number of, 112
All ready, already, 537
All right, 537
All the farther, all the faster,
    197
All together, altogether, 537
Allusion, illusion, 197
Almanacs, 476–77
American Authors 1600–1900,
    476
Among, between, 198
And etc., 197
Antecedent, 124
Antonyms, 491
Any, number of, 112
Anybody, number of, 111
Anyone, number of, 111
Anywheres, 197
Apostrophe
  in contractions, 439–40
  it's, its, 436
  misuse of, with possessive
    pronouns, 436
  to form plural letters, num-
    bers, etc., 441–42

to form plural possessives,
    435–36
to form possessive of com-
    pound words, words show-
    ing individual or joint pos-
    session, etc., 437
to form singular possessives,
    435, 436
Appendix, 468
Application, letter of, 369–71
Appositive
  as sentence fragment, 223
  commas with, 410
  defined, 77
  diagramed, 78
Appositive phrase, 77, 247
  used in combining sentences,
    235
Article
  capitalization in titles, 388
  defined, 8
Articles, magazine (*Readers'
    Guide*), 469–70
As, case of pronoun after, 150
As, like, 204
As if, 204
At, 197
Atlases, 476
Author card, 464–65
Authors, reference books about,
    475–76
Auxiliary verb = Helping verb

B

Bad, badly, 180–81
Bad, comparison of, 186
Bartlett's *Familiar Quotations,*
    477
Base of sentence, 38–39
Be, list of forms of, 13, 136
Begin, principal parts of, 155
Being as, being that, 198
Beside, besides, 198

Better, best, 186
Between, among, 198
Bibliography, 468
Biographical reference books, 474–75
Blow, principal parts of, 155
Body
  of a business letter, 362
  of a composition, 303–04
Both, number of, 112
Brake, break, 537
Break, principal parts of, 155
Breve, 497
Bring, principal parts of, 155
Bring, take, 198–99
British Authors of the Nineteenth Century, 475
Burst, principal parts of, 155
Business letter
  appearance, 357–64
  application, letter of, 369–71
  body, 362
  closing, 362–63
  envelope, 363–65
  folding, 364
  form, 357–64
  heading, 360
  inside address, 360–61
  order letter, 368–69
  parts of, 360–63
  punctuation in, 360, 362
  request letter, 365–66
  salutation, 361–62
  signature, 363
  stationery, 358
Bust, busted, 199
But, in double negative, 212

C

Call number, 463–64, 465
Can't hardly, can't scarcely, 200, 212
Capital, capitol, 537–38

Capitalization
  diagnostic test, 376–77
  dictionary as guide to, 486
  of business firms and products, 382–83, 384
  of calendar items, 383
  of course names with numbers, 384
  of first word in direct quotation, 428–29
  of first word in line of poetry, 378
  of first word in sentence, 377
  of geographical names, 379–80
  of government bodies, 382–83
  of *I* and *O*, 378
  of institutions, 382–83
  of languages, 384
  of names of particular places, things, and events, 383, 384
  of names of persons, 379
  of nationalities, 383–84
  of proper adjectives, 378–79
  of proper nouns, 378–79
  of races and religions, 383–84
  of school subjects, 384
  of seasons, 383
  of special events, 383
  of titles of persons, 387
  of titles of publications, works of art, etc., 388
  of words referring to Deity, 389
  of words showing family relationship, 387–88
  summary style sheet, 391–92
Card catalogue, 464–66
Case, 131–41
Character description, writing of, 323–27
Choose, chose, 538
Choose, principal parts of, 155
Chronological order, 280–81

Clarity, in letter writing, 357
Clause
  adjective, 84–87
  adverb, 88–89
  defined, 81
  diagramed, 87, 89, 92, 94–95
  distinguished from phrase, 81
  essential, 403–05
  independent, 81–82
  introductory, for sentence variety, 248
  main = independent
  nonessential, 403–05
  nonrestrictive = nonessential
  noun, 90–92
  restrictive = essential
  subordinate, 82–92
Clincher = Concluding sentence
Closing, business letter, 362–63
Coarse, course, 538
Coherence
  in the composition (linking expressions), 304–06
  in the paragraph (order of details, connectives), 271, 280–87
Collective nouns
  list of, 118
  number of, 117–18
College dictionaries, 483–84
Collier's Encyclopedia, 474
Colon
  after salutation of a business letter, 424
  before a list, 423–24
  before a long statement, 424
  in writing Biblical chapters and verses, 424
  in writing the time, 424
  position of, outside closing quotation marks, 430
Combining sentences
  by inserting adjectives, adverbs, or prepositional phrases, 232
  by using an adjective clause, 239
  by using an adverb clause, 240–41
  by using appositive phrases, 235
  by using compound subjects and verbs, 236–37
  by using a noun clause, 241
  by using participial phrases, 233
  by writing a complex sentence, 238–42
  by writing a compound sentence, 237
Come, principal parts of, 155
Comma
  after closing in letters, 362–63, 413
  after introductory elements, 406–07
  after salutation in friendly letters, 413
  between parts of a compound sentence, 400–01
  in a series, 397–99
  in direct address, 413
  in letters, 413
  summary of uses, 416
  to set off nonessential phrases and clauses, 403–05
  with appositive, 410–11
  with coordinate adjectives, 398–99
  with dates and addresses, 412–13
  with interrupters, 410–11
  with parenthetical expressions, 411
  with quotation marks, 429, 430
Comma splice = Run-on sentence
Common noun, 4–5
Comparative degree, 184–88
Comparison of modifiers

Comparison of modifiers,
continued
double, 187
illogical, 187
irregular, 186
regular, 185
Complement
after linking verb, 41
compound, 45
defined, 39
diagramed, 53
direct object, 43–44
indirect object, 43–45
never an adverb, 40
never in a phrase, 40
subject, 41–42
Complement, compliment, 538
Complete predicate, defined,
29–31
Complete subject, defined, 31
Complex sentence, 94–95
combining sentences by writing, 238–42
Complimentary close = Closing
Composition
arranging ideas in order, 299
checklist for, 306–07
choosing a subject for, 290–
91
coherence in, 305–06
determining the purpose, 294
division into paragraphs,
303–04
grouping related ideas, 298
introduction, body, conclusion, 303–04
limiting the subject, 292–93
linking expressions in, 305–
06
listing ideas for, 296–98
materials for, 290
outlining, 299–302
purpose, 294
revision, 306–10
titles for, 295
topics for, 310–14

transitions in, 304–06
Compound direct object, 45
Compound indirect object, 45
Compound noun, 5
Compound predicate, 35–36
Compound predicate nominative, 45
Compound sentence, 93–94
combining sentences by writing, 237
comma in, 400–01
Compound subject, 35
used in combining sentences,
236–37
Compound verb, 35–36
used in combining sentences,
236
Compound-complex sentence,
95
Conclusion, of a composition,
304
of a talk, 558–59
Conjugation of verbs, 159–64
Conjunctions
coordinating, 23
correlative, 23
defined, 22
subordinating, 23, 88
Connectives
between paragraphs, 304–06
within a paragraph, 271, 285–
87
Consistency of tense, 165
Consonants
defined, 495–96
dictionary markings for, 495–
96
Consul, council, counsel, 538–
39
Contemporary Authors, 476
*Contemporary Authors, First
Revision,* 476
Context, as clue to word meaning, 503–08
Contractions, use of apostrophe
in, 439–41

Coordinating conjunctions, 23
Copulative verb = Linking verb
Copyright page, 467
Correction symbols, 455–58
Correlative conjunctions, 23
Could of, 200
Course, coarse, 538
Creative writing, 341–56
Critical review, 327–31
Current Biography, 475

D

Dangling modifiers, 189–90
Dashes, 445–46
Dates, commas with, 412–13
Declarative sentence, defined, 46
Definitions, writing of, 336–39
Demonstrative pronoun, 6
Dependent clause = Subordinate clause
Derivation of words, 489–90
Descriptive paragraph, 279–82
Desert, dessert, 539
Details, in paragraph development, 265–66, 272–81, 284–85
vivid, 324–26, 350–51
Dewey decimal system, 462–64
Diacritical marks
accent, 498–99
breve, 497
macron, 496
vowel sounds, 496–98
Diagnostic test for capitalization, 376–77
Diagnostic test for vocabulary, 501–02
Diagraming
compound-complex sentences, 95
compound sentences, 94

compound subjects, 49–50
compound verbs, 49–50
conjunctions, 49–50, 94–95
direct and indirect objects, 54
modifying words, 49–51
predicate adjective, 53–54
predicate nominative, 53–54
prepositional phrases, 62–63
subject and verb, 48–49
there beginning a sentence, 50–51
understood subject, 48–49
Dialogue, paragraphing of, 431
Dictionaries
abbreviations in, 488, 489
accent marks in, 498–99
arrangement of information in, 482
as guide to capitalization, 486
as guide to pronunciation, 486–88, 494–99
as guide to spelling, 485–86, 528
biographical entries in, 491–92
college, 483–84
derivations in, 489–90
diacritical marks in, 495–99
geographical entries in, 492–93
guide words in, 482
illustrations in, 491
information in, 485–93
kinds of, 482–84
labels, 490
meanings in, 488–89, 508–09
miscellaneous information in, 493
parts of speech in, 488
syllable division in, 486
synonyms and antonyms in, 491
unabridged, 483
use of schwa in, 497–98
Direct address, commas with, 413

Direct object
  compound, 45
  defined, 43–44
  diagramed, 54
Direct quotations, punctuation
  of, 428–32
Discover, invent, 200–01
Discussion
  evaluating, 581–82
  participating in, 577–80
  preparation for, 575–77
  types of, 573–75
Dividing words, 442–45, 454–
  55
Do, principal parts of, 155
Doesn't, agreement with subject, 121–22, 201
Don't, agreement with subject,
  121–22, 201
Double comparison of modifiers, 187
Double negative, 212
Double subject, 202
Drink, principal parts of, 156
Drive, principal parts of, 156

E

Each, number of, 111
Effect, affect, 197, 537
ei, ie, spelling rule for, 530
Either, number of, 111
Emigrate, immigrate, 201
Encyclopaedia Britannica, 473,
  474
Encyclopedia Americana, 473,
  474
Encyclopedias, 473–74
End marks, 394–97, 430
End papers, 468
Envelope, of business letter,
  363–65
Essay of opinion, 331–35

Essay test, writing answers to,
  319–22
Essential clause, punctuation
  of, 403–05
European Authors 1000–1900,
  476
Everybody, number of, 111
Everyone, number of, 111
Everywheres, 197
Except, accept, 196
Exclamation mark, 47, 394–95
  with quotation marks, 429,
  430
Exclamatory sentence, defined,
  47
Explanatory talk, 563–64
Explanatory writing, 315–18
Expletive, 51
Exposition, 290–314
Expository paragraph, 272–77
Extended definition, writing of,
  337–39

F

Fall, principal parts of, 156
Familiar Quotations, Bartlett's,
  477
Famous people, dictionary in-
  formation about, 491–92
Few, number of, 112
Fewer, less, 201
Fiction, library arrangement of,
  461–62
Folding a business letter, 364
Foreign words, underlining for,
  427
Formal English, 103–04
Formally, formerly, 540
Fractions, hyphens with, 444
Fragment = Sentence fragment
Freeze, principal parts of, 156
Frontispiece, 467

Future perfect tense, 163–64
Future tense, 160–63

G

Gender, 125–26
Geographical names, capitalization of, 379–80
Gerund
    defined, 70
    diagramed, 75
Gerund phrase
    defined, 71–72
    diagramed, 75
Give, principal parts of, 156
Glossary, 468
Go, principal parts of, 156
Good, comparison of, 186
Good, well, 181–82, 201–02
Good usage, special problems in
    accept, except, 196
    affect, effect, 197
    all the farther, all the faster, 197
    beside, besides, 198
    between, among, 198
    bring, take, 198–99
    double negative, 212
    double subject, 202
    less, fewer, 201
    of, with *inside, off*, etc., 204–05
    them, used incorrectly for *those, these*, 207
    this here, that there, 207
    ways, used incorrectly for *way*, 207
    when, where, used incorrectly in definitions, 208
    who, whom, 143–46
Goode's World Atlas, 476

H

Had of, 202
Had ought, 202
Hammond's Contemporary World Atlas, 476
Haven't but, haven't only, 212
He, she, etc., as double subject, 202
Heading, in business letters, 360
Hear, here, 540
Helping verbs, 14
Here, beginning a sentence, diagramed, 50–51
Here is, number of subject after, 119
Hisself, theirselves, 7
Historical atlases, 476
Home Book of Modern Verse, Stevenson's, 478–79
Home Book of Quotations, Stevenson's, 478
Home Book of Verse, Stevenson's, 478–79
Hyphen, uses of, 442–45

I

ie, ei, spelling rule for, 530
Illusion, allusion, 197
Illustrations, in dictionaries, 491
Immigrate, emigrate, 201
Imperative sentence, defined, 47

Greek prefixes and roots, 512–17

Imply, infer, 202
Indefinite pronouns, list of, 6
Independent clause, 81–82
Index, 468
Indirect object
compound, 45
defined, 44
diagramed, 54
Indirect quotation, 428
Infer, imply, 202
Infinitive
defined, 72
diagramed, 76–77
distinguished from preposi-
tional phrase, 73
with *to* omitted, 74
Infinitive clause, 73
Infinitive phrase
defined, 73
diagramed, 76–77
Informal English, 103, 104–05,
490
Inside address of business let-
ter, 360–61
Interjection, defined, 24
Interrogative pronoun, 6
Interrogative sentence, defined,
47
Interrupters, commas with,
410–11
Interviews, 588–91
Introduction, of a composition,
303
of a talk, 558–59
Introductory elements, punc-
tuation of, 406–07
Invent, discover, 200–01
Irregular comparison, 186
Irregular verbs, 155–56
Italics (underlining)
compared with quotation
marks for titles, 432
for foreign words, etc., 427
for titles, 426–27
Its, it's, 540
It's me, 136

J
Joint possession, use of apostrophe in, 437

K
Kind of, sort of, 203–04
Know, principal parts of, 155

L
Latin prefixes and roots, 512–17
Lay, lie, 169
Lead, led, lead, 540
Learn, teach, 204
Least, in comparisons, 185
Leave, let, 204
Less, fewer, 201
Less, in comparisons, 185
Levels of usage, 102–05. (*See
also* Standard English and
Nonstandard English.)
Library
arrangement of, 461–64
call number, 462–63, 465
card catalogue, 464–66
Dewey decimal system, 462–
64
fiction, 461–62
finding magazine articles
(*Readers' Guide*), 469–70
nonfiction, 462–64
organization of, 461–64
reference books, 471–79
vertical file, 471
Lie, lay, 169
Like, as, 204
Like, as if, 204

Limited definition, writing of, 336–37
Limiting the subject for composition, 292–93
Linking expressions
  between paragraphs, 304–06
  lists of, 287, 305
  within paragraphs, 285–87
Linking verb, 13–14, 153
Listening
  accuracy in, 565
  during group discussion, 578–80
  manners, 565
  recognizing unfair argument, 569–71
  weighing evidence, 568
Literature, reference books on, 477–79
Loose, lose, 540

M

Macron, 496
Magazine articles listed in *Readers' Guide,* 469–70
Main clause = Independent clause
Manuscript form, 452–58
Many
  comparison of, 186
  number of, 112
Metaphor, 352–53
Miner, minor, 540–41
.Misplaced modifiers, 191–94
Models for letter writing
  application, 370
  envelope for business, 364
  forms, 359
  order, 369
  request, 366
Modifiers
  comparison of, 184–88
  dangling, 189–90

defined, 179
  misplaced, 191–94
Moral, morale, 541
Most, number of, 112
Much, comparison of, 186

N

Narrative, 355–56
Narrative paragraph, 282–83
Narrative talk, 561–63
Negative, double, 212
Neither, number of, 111
New Century Cyclopedia of Names, 474–75
No, in double negative, 212
No one, number of, 111
Nobody, number of, 111
Nominative case
  for predicate nominative, 136
  for subject of verb, 133–34
  in incomplete constructions, 150
None
  in double negative, 212
  number of, 112
Nonessential clause, 403–05
Nonfiction, library arrangement of, 462–64
Nonrestrictive clause = Nonessential clause
Nonstandard English, 102
Noun
  common, 4–5
  compound, 5
  defined, 3
  plurals, formation of, 533–36
  proper, 4–5, 378–80
  used as adjectives, 11
Noun clause
  defined, 90–91
  diagramed, 92
  used in combining sentences, 241–42

Nowheres, 197
Number, defined, 107–08
Numbers, hyphens with, 444
  rules for writing of, 454

O

Object
  direct, defined, 43–44
  indirect, defined, 44
  of verb, case of, 138
Object of preposition
  case of, 141
  defined, 59
Objective case, 137–38, 141
  object of preposition in, 141
  object of verb in, 138
Observation, 341–42
Of, with *inside, off,* etc., 204–05
Official Associated Press Almanac, The, 476
One, number of, 111
Order letter, 368–69
Ought, 205
Outlining a composition, 299–301
  a talk, 557–58

P

Paragraph
  checklist for revision, 288–89
  coherence in, 271
  concluding sentence, 262–63
  connectives in, 285–87
  defined, 260
  descriptive, 279–82
  developed by contrast or comparison, 277
  developed by details or examples, 265–66, 272–81, 284–85

developed by reasons, 283–85
  expository, 272–77
  linking expressions in, 285–87
  narrative, 282–83
  order of ideas in, 274–77
  persuasive, 283–87
  plan for, 266
  specific details in, 265–66
  structure of, 260–63
  topic sentence, 260–62
  unity in, 267–68
  unrelated ideas in, 268
Parentheses, 446–47
Parenthetical expressions, commas with, 411
Parliamentary procedure
  amending motions, 585–86
  club business, 583–84
  duties of officers, 583
  elections, 582–83
  point of order, 587
  special motions, 586
Part of speech, dictionary labels for, 488
Participial phrase
  as dangling modifier, 189–90
  as sentence fragment, 221
  commas with, 406
  defined, 68
  diagramed, 77
  introductory, for sentence variety, 246
  nonessential, 403–05
  used in combining sentences, 233
Participle
  defined, 64
  diagramed, 74–77
  introductory, for sentence variety, 245
Parts of speech
  adjective, defined, 7
  adverb, defined, 16
  conjunction, defined, 22

Parts of speech, *continued*
  determined by use, 24–25
  interjection, defined, 24
  noun, defined, 3
  preposition, defined, 21
  pronoun, defined, 5
  summary of, 27
  verb, defined, 11
Passed, past, 541
Passive voice, 166–68
Past participle, defined, 65
Past perfect tense, 163
Past tense, 159–63
People, dictionary information
    about, 491–92
Period
  after abbreviation, 397
  as end mark, 394–95, 397
  position of, inside quotation
    marks, 430
Personal, personnel, 542
Personal pronouns, 5–7, 125,
    131–32
Persuasive paragraph, 283–87
Persuasive talk, 564
Phrase
  adjective, 60
  adverb, 61
  appositive, 77–78
  defined, 58
  distinguished from clause, 81
  gerund, defined, 71
  infinitive, defined, 73
  nonessential, 403–05
  participial, defined, 68
  prepositional, 59–63
  verb, 14–15
  verbal, 64–77
Places, dictionary information
    about, 492–93
Plural number, defined, 107–08
Plurals, formation of, 533–36
Positive degree of comparison,
    184–88
Possessive case, 434–37

Predicate
  complete, 29–30
  compound, 35–36
  defined, 29
  simple, 29–30
Predicate adjective
  compound, 45
  defined, 41
  diagramed, 53–54
Predicate nominative
  case of, 136
  compound, 45
  defined, 41
  diagramed, 53–54
  mistaken agreement with, 119
Preface, foreword, or introduc-
    tion, 467
Prefixes
  changed, 515
  defined, 512
  Greek and Latin, 512–15
  hyphen with, 444
  spelling of words with, 530
Prefixes and roots, as aids to
    word meaning, 512–17
Prepositional phrases
  as sentence fragment, 222
  defined, 59
  diagramed, 62–63
  examples of, 59
  introductory, for sentence
    variety, 246
  used as adjective, 60
  used as adverb, 61
  used in combining sentences,
    232
Prepositions
  compound, list of, 22
  defined, 21
  distinguished from adverbs,
    22
  list of, 21
  object of, 21
Present participle, 65, 154
Present perfect tense, 163

Present tense, 149, 161, 162
Principal, principle, 542
Principal parts of verbs, 154–56
  defined, 154
  irregular, 155–56
  regular, 154–55
Progressive tense, 163
Pronoun
  after *than, as,* 150
  agreement with antecedent,
    124–26
  case of, 131–41
  defined, 5
  demonstrative, 6
  distinguished from adjective,
    9–10
  in double subject, 212
  in incomplete constructions,
    150
  indefinite, 6, 111
  interrogative, 6
  personal, 5–7
  possessive, 7, 9
  reflexive, 6–7
  relative, 6, 85
  unacceptable forms of, 7
  who, which, that, distin-
    guished, 208
  who and *whom,* 143–46
Pronunciation
  as an aid to spelling, 511
  dictionary indications of,
    486–88, 494–99
  reading diacritical marks, 495
Proper adjective, capitalization
  of, 378–79
Proper noun, capitalization of,
  378–80
  defined, 4–5
Public speaking
  conclusion, 558–59
  explanatory talk, 563–64
  giving a talk, 559–60
  introduction, 558–59
  narrative talk, 561–62

  outlining, 557–58
  persuasive talk, 564
  preparing a talk, 555–56
Punctuation
  after an abbreviation, 397
  apostrophe, 434–37, 439–42
  colon, 423–24, 430
  comma, 362–63, 397–416,
    429, 430
  dash, 445–46
  end marks, 394–97, 430
  exclamation point, 394–95,
    429, 430
  hyphen, 442–45
  italics, 426–27
  parentheses, 446–47
  period, 394–95, 397, 430
  question mark, 394, 429, 430
  quotation marks, 428–33
  semicolon, 420–21, 430

Q

Question mark, 394, 429, 430
Quiet, quite, 542
Quotation marks
  compared with italics for
    titles, 432
  dialogue, paragraphing of,
    431
  for direct quotations, 428–32
  single, for quotations within
    quotation, 432
  to enclose titles of stories,
    articles, etc., 432–33
  with other marks of punctua-
    tion, 429–30

R

Raise, rise, 174
Rand McNally's *New Cosmo-
  politan World Atlas,* 476
*Random House Dictionary of
  of English Language,* 483

Readers' Guide to Periodical Literature, 469–70
Reference books
about authors, 475–76
about literature, 477–79
almanacs, 476–77
atlases, 476
biographical, 474–75
dictionaries, 472, 482–84
encyclopedias, 473–74
for finding quotations, 477–79
yearbooks, 476–77
Reflexive pronouns, 6–7
Regular comparison, 185
Regular verb, 154–55
Relative pronouns
case of, 144–45
defined, 85
list of, 6, 85
number of, 126
who, which, that, distinguished, 208
who and *whom,* 143–46
Request letter, 365–66
Respectfully, respectively, 205
Restrictive clause = Essential clause
Ride, principal parts of, 156
Ring, principal parts of, 156
Rise, raise, 174
Roget's Thesaurus of English Words and Phrases, 472
Roots and prefixes, in word analysis, 512–17
Run, principal parts of, 156
Run-on sentence, 227–28

S

Salutation, in business letter, 361–62
Same, 206
Schwa, 497-98
See, principal parts of, 156
"See" card, 465

Semicolon
between independent clauses containing commas, 421
between independent clauses not joined by *and, but,* etc., 420–21
position of, outside closing quotation marks, 430
Sentence
base of, 38–39
classified by purpose, 46–47
classified by structure, 93–95
combining, 231–42
complements, 39, 41–45
complex, 94–95
compound, 93–94
compound-complex, 95
declarative, 46
defined, 28–29
diagraming, 48–54, 94–95
distinguished from fragment, 37, 219–20
exclamatory, 47
imperative, 47
interrogative, 47
kinds of, 93–95
parts of a, 28–29
run-on, 227–28
simple, 93
subject and predicate, 28–29, 31–32
variety in, 244–52
Sentence combining, *see* Combining sentences
Sentence fragment
common types of, 221–25
defined, 219
distinguished from sentence, 37, 219–20
Series, commas in, 397–99
Set, sit, 172
Several, number of, 112
Shall, will, 206
Shone, shown, 542
Shrink, principal parts of, 156
Signature, of business letter, 363

Simile, 352–53
Simple predicate, 29–30
Simple sentence, 93
Simple subject, 31–32
Single quotation marks, use of, 432
Singular number, defined, 107–08
Sit, set, 172
Slang words, dictionary labels for, 490
with quotation marks, 432–33
Slow, slowly, 182
So, for *so that,* therefore, 206–07
Some, number of, 112
Some, somewhat, 207
Somebody, number of, 111
Someone, number of, 111
Sort of, kind of, 203–04
Spatial order, 281
Speaking, *see* Public Speaking; Discussion; Parliamentary Procedure
Speak, principal parts of, 156
Spelling
-*cede,* -*ceed,* -*sede,* 530
demons, 547–48
dictionary as guide to, 485–86, 528
doubling final consonant, 533
final *e* before suffix, 531–32
good habits in, 527–29
ie, ei, 530
plurals, 533–36
pronunciation and, 529
rules, 529–36
words commonly misspelled, 548–50
words often confused, 537–45
words with prefixes, 530
words with suffixes, 531–33
Spelling lists
demons, 547–48
words commonly misspelled, 548–50

words often confused, 537–45
Standard English, 102–05
formal, 103–05
informal, 103, 104–05
State-of-being verb = Linking verb
States, abbreviations of, in letters, 360, 375, 371–72
Statesman's Yearbook, 477
Stationary, stationery, 543
Stationery, for business letter, 358
Steal, principal parts of, 156
Stevenson's *Home Book of Modern Verse,* 478–79
Style, 230
Subject (of sentence)
after *there* or *here,* 34
agreement with verb, 107–22
case of, 134–35
complete, 31–32
compound, 35, 115
defined, 28–29
double, 202
how to find, 32
in questions, 34
in unusual position, 34
never in a phrase, 36
simple, 31–32
understood, 35, 48
Subject card, 464–65
Subject complements, 41–43
(*See also* Predicate adjective, Predicate nominative.)
Subordinate clause
as a sentence fragment, 224–25
defined, 82
in diagraming, 87, 89, 91, 94–95
relationship to independent clauses, 82–83
relative pronouns in, 85–86
uses of, 84–92
Subordinating conjunctions, list of, 88, 241

Suffixes
  defined, 531
  final *e* before (spelling), 531–32
  spelling words with, 531–33
Superlative degree of comparison, 184–88
Swim, principal parts of, 156
Syllables
  as an aid in spelling, 528
  dictionary marking of, 486–87, 498–99
Synonyms, 491

T

Table of contents, 467
Take, bring, 198–99
Take, principal parts of, 156
Teach, learn, 204
Tense, consistency of, 165
Than, pronoun after, 150
Than, then, 207, 543
That, which, who, distinguished, 208
That there, this here, 207
Their, there, they're, 543
Theirselves, hisself, 7
Them, for *these* or *those,* 207
Then, than, 207, 543
There, beginning a sentence, diagramed, 50–51
There, their, they're, 543
There is, number of subject after, 119
Thesaurus of English Words and Phrases, Roget's, 472
This here, that there, 207
Throw, principal parts of, 156
Title card, 464–65
Title page, 467

Titles
  of persons, capitalizations of, 387
  of publications, capitalizations of, 388
  of works of art, number of, 121
  use of italics and quotation marks with, 432
To, too, two, 544
Tone, in letter writing, 357
Topic outline, for composition, 299–301
Topic sentence, 260–62
Topics for composition, list of, 310–14
Transitional devices
  in compositions, 304–06
  in paragraphs, 285–87
Try and, 207

U

Unabridged dictionary, 483
Underlining (italics), 426–27
Understood subject, 35, 48
Unity, in the paragraph, 267–68
Usage, levels of, 102–05
Usage, special problems in, *see* Good usage
Usage labels, in dictionaries, 490

V

Variety in sentences
  beginning with a phrase, 246

Variety in sentences, *continued*
  beginning with a subordinate
    clause, 248
  beginning with single-word
    modifiers, 245
  varying length of sentences,
    231–42
  varying sentence beginnings,
    244–48
  varying the kinds of sen-
    tences, 250–52
Verb phrase
  as simple predicate, 30–31
  defined, 14–15
Verbal phrases, 64–77
Verbals
  gerund, defined, 70
  infinitive, defined, 73
  participle, defined, 64
Verbs
  action, 11–12
  active and passive voices,
    166–68
  agreement with subject, 107–
    22
  as simple predicate, 29–30
  be, forms of, 13
  compound, 35–36
  conjugation of, 159–64
  consistency of tense, 165
  defined, 11
  helping, list of, 15
  intransitive, 12
  irregular, 155–56
  linking, 13–14, 153
  principal parts, 154–56
  regular, 154–55
  tenses of, 159–65
  transitive, 12
  voice of, 166–68
  with predicate nominative,
    119
Vertical file, use of, 471
Vivid diction, 325–26
Vocabulary

diagnostic test, 501–02
finding the right word, 510
meanings in context, 503–08
notebook, 503
prefixes and roots, 512–17
ways to learn new words,
  502–11
word list, 524–26
Voice, active and passive, 166–
  68
Vowel sounds, diacritical markings for, 496–98

W

Waist, waste, 544
Ways, for *way,* 207
Weather, whether, 544
*Webster's Biographical Dic-
  tionary,* 474
*Webster's Dictionary of Syn-
  onyms,* 472
*Webster's New Collegiate Dic-
  tionary,* 484, 489
*Webster's Third New Interna-
  tional Dictionary,* 483
Well, comparison of, 186
Well, good, 181–82, 201–02
When, misused in writing a def-
  inition, 208
Where, beginning a sentence,
  diagramed, 50–51
Where, misused in writing a
  definition, 208
Whether, weather, 544
Who, which, that, distinguished,
  208
Who, whom, 143–46
Who's, whose, 544–45
Who's Who, 475
Who's Who in America, 475

Will, shall, 206
Word origins, 521–22
Words appealing to the senses, 345–49
Words often confused, 537–45
World Almanac and Book of Facts, The, 476
World Book Encyclopedia, 474
Worse, worst, 186
Write, principal parts of, 156
Writers Directory, The, 476

Y

Yearbooks, 476–77
Your, you're, 545

Z

Zip code, 365, 371–72

Tab Key Index

GRAMMAR

1   The Parts of Speech

1a   noun, 3
1b   pronoun, 5
1c   adjective, 7
1d   verb, 11
1e   adverb, 16
1f   preposition, 21
1g   conjunction, 22
1h   interjection, 24
1i   determining part of speech, 24

2   The Sentence

2a   sentence defined, 28
2b   subject & predicate, 28
2c   simple predicate, or verb, 30
2d   simple subject, 31
2e   compound subject, 35
2f   compound verb, 35
2g   subject never in prepositional phrase, 36
2h   complement defined, 39
2i   subject complement, 41
2j   direct object, 43
2k   indirect object, 44
2l   sentences classified by purpose, 46

3   The Phrase

3a   phrases defined, 58
3b   prepositional phrase, 59
3c   object of preposition, 59
3d   adjective phrase, 60
3e   adverb phrase, 61
3f   participle defined, 64–65
3g   participle phrase, 68
3h   gerund defined, 70
3i   gerund phrase, 71
3j   infinitive defined, 72
3k   infinitive phrase, 73
3l   appositive defined, 77
3m   appositive phrase, 77

4   The Clause

4a   clause defined, 81
4b   independent clause, 81
4c   subordinate clause, 82
4d   adjective clause, 84
4e   adverb clause, 88
4f   noun clause, 90
4g   sentences classified by structure, 93–95

USAGE

5   Kinds of Usage

6   Correct Agreement

6a   singular & plural defined, 107
6b   agreement in number, 108
6c   phrase between subject & verb, 109
6d   singular pronouns, 111
6e   plural pronouns, 112
6f   other indefinite pronouns, 112
6g-i   compound subject, 115–16

6j	collective nouns, 117
6k	predicate nominative, 119
6l	verb before subject, 119
6m	words stating amount, 120
6n	*every* & *many a,* 121
6o	titles, 121
6p	*don't* & *doesn't,* 121
6q	pronoun & antecedent agreement, 125–26

7   **Using Pronouns Correctly**

7a-b	nominative case, 133, 136
7c-d	objective case, 138, 141
7e	who & whom, 143
7f	incomplete constructions, 150

8   **Using Verbs Correctly**

8a	principal parts, 154
8b	regular verbs, 154
8c	irregular verbs, 155
8d-e	tenses, 159, 162–64
8f	unnecessary change in tense, 165

9   **Using Modifiers Correctly**

9a	modifiers following verbs, 179
9b	comparison, 184–85
9c	comparative & superlative degrees, 186
9d	comparison within group, 187
9e	double comparisons, 187
9f	clear comparisons, 188
9g	dangling modifiers, 189
9h	placement of modifiers, 191–93

10   **Glossary of Usage**

COMPOSITION: SENTENCE STRUCTURE

11   **Writing Complete Sentences**

11a	sentence fragments, 219
11b	run-on sentences, 227

12   **Sentence Combining and Revising**

12a-f	combining short, related sentences, 232–38
12g	varied beginnings, 244–48
12h	varied structure, 250

COMPOSITION

13   **The Paragraph**

13a	paragraph defined, 260
13b	topic sentence, 260
13c	paragraph development, 265
13d	paragraph unity, 267
13e	coherence, 271
13f	four types of paragraphs, 271
13g	developing expository paragraph, 272
13h	coherence in expository paragraph, 274–77
13i	developing descriptive paragraph, 279
13j	coherence in descriptive paragraph, 280–81
13k	developing narrative paragraph, 282

13l developing persuasive paragraph, 283

13m using connectives, 285–86

14 Exposition

14a choosing a subject, 290

14b limiting a subject, 292–95

14c planning the composition, 295–99

14d outlining, 300–01

14e the first draft, 302

14f revising, 306

14g the final draft, 307

15 Specific Writing Assignments

16 Creative Writing

17 The Business Letter

17a standard practice, 358

MECHANICS

18 Capitalization

18a first word in sentence, 377

18b *O & I*, 378

18c proper nouns & adjectives, 378–84

18d school subjects, 384

18e titles, 387–89

19 Punctuation

19a periods, 394

19b question marks, 394

19c exclamation points, 394

19d imperatives, 395

19e abbreviations, 397

19f-g commas in series, 397–98

19h comma between clauses, 400

19i commas to set off non-essential parts, 403

19j comma after introductory elements, 406

19k commas to set off interrupters, 410–11

19l conventional uses of commas, 412–13

19m unnecessary commas, 413

20 Punctuation

20a-c semicolon between clauses, 420–21

20d semicolons in series, 421

20e colon before list, 423

20f colon before statement, 424

20g conventional uses of colon, 424

21 Punctuation

21a underlining titles, 426

21b words, letters, & figures, 427

21c quotation marks for direct quotation, 428

21d quotation marks & capital letter, 428

21e divided quotations, 428

21f setting off quotations, 29

21g quotation marks & other punctuation, 430

21h-i quotation marks & paragraphs, 431

21j single quotation marks, 432

21k quotation marks for titles, 432

21l quotation marks with unusual terms, 432

22	**Punctuation**
22a-d	apostrophe to form possessive, 435–37
22e	possessive of compound words, 437
22f	multiple possession, 437
22g	apostrophe to form contractions, 440
22h	apostrophe to form plurals, 441
22i-l	hyphens, 442–45
22m-n	dashes, 445
22o	parentheses, 446

23	**Manuscript Form**
23a	accepted standards, 452
23b	using abbreviations, 453
23c	writing numbers, 454
23d	dividing words, 454
23e	correction symbols, 455

AIDS TO GOOD ENGLISH

24	**The Library**
24a	arrangement of books, 461
24b	card catalogue, 464
24c	parts of a book, 466
24d	*Readers' Guide,* 469
24e	vertical file, 471
24f	reference books, 471

25	**The Dictionary**
25a	kinds of dictionaries, 482
25b	kinds of information, 485
25c	pronunciation, 494

26	**Vocabulary**
26a	vocabulary notebook, 501
26b	learning from context, 501
26c	use of dictionary, 508
26d	using exact word, 510
26e	learning prefixes, 512
26f	learning roots, 517
26g	learning word origins, 521

27	**Spelling**
27a	*ie & ei,* 530
27b	*-sede, -ceed,* & *-cede,* 530
27c	adding prefixes, 530
27d-h	adding suffixes, 531–33
27i	plurals of nouns, 533–36

SPEAKING AND LISTENING

28	**Public Speaking**
28a-b	choosing a topic, 555–56
28c-f	organizing a talk, 556–58
28g-i	delivering a talk, 559–60
28j	narrative talk, 562
28k	explanatory talk, 563
28l	persuasive talk, 564
28m-o	listening to speakers, 565–68

29	**Group Discussion**
29a	types of group discussions, 574
29b	selecting a topic, 575
29c-f	duties of participants, 576–77
29g	speaking effectively, 578
29h	listening accurately, 578
29i	evaluating, 581
29j-m	parliamentary procedure, 583–85

Key to
English Workshop Drill

To supplement the lessons in *English Grammar and Composition, Fourth Course,* there is additional practice in grammar, usage, punctuation, capitalization, composition, vocabulary, and spelling in *English Workshop, Fourth Course.* This chart correlates the textbook rules with the lessons in *English Workshop.*

Text Rule	Workshop Lesson	Text Rule	Workshop Lesson	Text Rule	Workshop Lesson
1a	1	4e	31	12f	116,117,118
1b	1	4f	35		
1c	1	4g	36	13a	120
1d	2			13b	121
1e	3	6a	71	13c	123,124
1f	4	6b	71	13d	122
1g	5	6c	73	13f	125,126
1h	5	6d	74	13g	127,128,
1i	6	6g-i	74		129,130
		6k	73		
2a	58	6l	75	14a	131
2b	16	6n	74		
2c	16	6p	72	17a	142
2d	16	6q	77		
2e	16			18c	9,10
2f	16	7a-b	83,84	18d	12
2g	73	7c-d	83,84	18e	11
2h	18–19	7e	33		
2i	18	7f	85	19f-g	44
2j	18			19h	50
2k	19	8a	92	19i	57
2l	17	8b	92	19j	51
		8c	92,93,94,	19k	46,48
3b	4		96,97	19l	47
3c	4				
3d	4	9a	102	20a-c	63
3e	4	9f	108	20g	142
3f	37	9g	108		
3g	37	9h	108	21c	68
3h	39			21d	68
3j	39	11a	58	21e	69
3l	45	11b	60	21f-g	68
3m	77				
		12a	112	22a-d	24,25
4a	31	12b	115	22g	27
4b	31	12c	114	22h	27,22
4c	31	12d	113		
4d	33	12e	113	27i	14,22

Correction Symbols

ms	error in manuscript form or neatness
cap	error in use of capital letters
p	error in punctuation
sp	error in spelling
frag	sentence fragment
ss	error in sentence structure
k	awkward sentence
nc	not clear
rs	run-on sentence
gr	error in grammar
w	error in word choice
¶	You should have begun a new paragraph here.
t	error in tense
∧	You have omitted something.